CANADIAN
CURRICULUM
STUDIES

EDITED BY
Susan E. Gibson

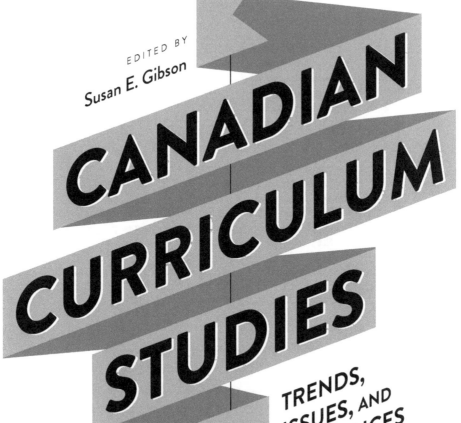

CANADIAN CURRICULUM STUDIES

TRENDS, ISSUES, AND INFLUENCES

PACIFIC EDUCATIONAL PRESS

VANCOUVER

17 16 15 14 13 12 — 1 2 3 4 5

Published by Pacific Educational Press
Faculty of Education
University of British Columbia
411 – 2389 Health Sciences Mall
Vancouver, BC V6T 1Z3
Telephone: 604-822-5385
Fax: 604-822-6603
Email: pep.sales@ubc.ca
Website: http://pacificedpress.ca

LIBRARY AND ARCHIVES CANADA CATALOGUING IN PUBLICATION

Canadian curriculum studies : trends, issues, and influences / editor,
    Susan Elaine Gibson.

Includes bibliographical references and index.
ISBN 978-1-926966-14-4

1. Education—Curricula. 2. Education—Curricula—Canada.
3. Curriculum planning—Canada. 4. Education—Canada—Forecasting.
I. Gibson, Susan Elaine, 1953–

LB1564.C3C35 2012   375.000971   C2012-902239-X

Course Instructors: Teaching suggestions for classroom use of this
book can be found on the publisher's website.

Editorial Note: The articles in this collection were edited for
consistency of style and to correct spelling or grammatical errors.
Reflective questions were added to each article.

Design and layout: Five Seventeen
Cover background adapted from: "Hasselblad Acu Matt Screen"
    by Duncan Allan © 2009
Cover background colour: Sharlene Eugenio
Editing: Nadine Pedersen, Nancy Wilson
Proofreading: Patricia Wolfe
Indexing: Elph Text Services

Printed in Canada

MIX
Paper from
responsible sources
FSC® C004071

Contents

Part III

Contemporary Issues and Trends in Canadian Curriculum   233

Foreword

A powerful aspect of language is how effectively a single word can end up framing one's thinking about a phenomenon. One may think of *curriculum* as a relatively ordinary and innocent word. A curriculum can amount to the day-to-day flow of classes in a school, year in and year out. It can reflect many influences, from the mandates of the province to the events of a single day. It can be influenced by the architecture of the school building and the culture of the community that surrounds it. In this way, what is called curriculum can seem to take in the whole of the school experience and thus, being the sum of everything, it may risk amounting to nothing in its ability to draw one's attention to anything of real importance about education.

Yet that is not entirely the case with this term. For what gives curriculum its power of framing and focusing one's attention within education is, in part, how little it comes up when people talk about teaching. As educators, we generally prefer to talk about school in terms of teaching subjects, whether mathematics or language arts, rather than a curriculum. In teacher education programs, we generally prepare teachers to work within those subject lines, and we watch the media jump on the test-score results for each of the subjects. We also observe provincial Ministries of Education issuing guidelines for the teaching of the subject areas. Questions of curriculum, then—that is, questions concerned with general ways in which the broader goals of learning are identified and organized in schools—tend to be left aside. This places curriculum beyond the general horizon of what gets talked about in education. It is as if we have to look up from the day-to-day demands of the classroom to catch a glimpse of what is at stake in thinking about the shape and form of education as a curriculum.

This is not to say that *curriculum* is an impractical way of thinking about what is taught and why. This collection of articles, skilfully selected and assembled by Susan E. Gibson, is full of the practical matters of teaching and learning as the Canadian scholars gathered here address a remarkable range of concerns within curriculum studies. Yet these articles also demonstrate how curriculum has a way of elevating the questions at issue. Far more is at stake here than improving the efficiency with which mathematics is taught or raising test scores in the language arts. Rather, the focus is on what is worth teaching and knowing. Here, the span of work in curriculum studies, from across the country and over the last few decades, is extremely well represented. This collection makes it clear that to think of education in terms of the curriculum is to get at the purpose and value of this massive public and private enterprise. It is to reflect on our sense of learning, as something we owe to the world and as a way of affecting the world.

The study of curriculum, in this sense, is concerned with how the classic *big question* in education of *what knowledge is most worth knowing* has been asked and how it has been answered. The articles in this collection demonstrate ways of approaching such a question, without presuming that a singular or definitive answer lies at the end of the rainbow. If anything, curriculum studies has made its own critical and thoughtful contribution to complicating the question of what is to be taught. This book demonstrates that curriculum studies facilitates and encourages a way of thinking *through* education, whether one is looking at how this concept of *curriculum* is defined and used, or what forms the curriculum has taken over the course of Canada's educational history, or why certain exclusions and shortfalls have marred the curriculum. Thinking through the curriculum is one of the best ways we have for thinking about who and what we are, with all of the urgency and pressing sense of having to bring the results of this inquiry before a classroom of rowdy children on the first day of school on a still-warm September day.

Such questions may lead, in the first instance, to asking how the world of knowledge has come to be divided in such neat and tidy ways into the subject areas of mathematics, language arts, and all the rest. For a much longer period in Western history, from the medieval era and into the early modern period, the curriculum consisted of the *trivium* of grammar, logic, and rhetoric, followed by the *quadrivium* of arithmetic, geometry, music, and astronomy. And for just as long a period, across the Canadian landscape, indigenous peoples engaged in forms of learning without such subject divisions, as they saw to the passing down of knowledge through the generations.

What is it, then, to begin to consider the issues and trends of curriculum studies in this way? It is to be led to questions of how learning and knowledge have been given the shape that we now take as natural and unquestionable. These questions have to do with what it has meant to teach another, what it is that we imagine that we have learned ourselves. It is to seek out the value of that learning for ourselves, but more importantly, I think, to explore the value of our own learning for others.

This collection is a way of coming to terms with such questions. In that sense, it exemplifies what I have long thought of as one of the many things that we do owe to our students, as much as to ourselves, on this matter of curriculum. For if I was pressed, I would identify one thing, above all, that this way of thinking about curriculum can be said to encourage. It fosters a need for each of us to become students of our own education, and to find ways of helping others do the same. This is obviously not to be the whole of any curriculum. Rather, it is intended as a way of critically reflecting on the course and curriculum of our lives and what we value. This seems like an entirely sound starting point before presuming, for example, to prescribe a curriculum for others. This well-assembled compilation of curriculum studies provides an excellent foundation for thinking about how we have come to this point in our own education and in our efforts to advance the education of others.

John Willinsky

Acknowledgements

For their unfailing encouragement and support, I would like to thank my family and especially my daughter, Amber, who assisted with some of the preparation work for this book.

This book would not have been possible without the contributions of all of the authors of the articles that have been reprinted here. I am grateful for the work of the late Ted Aoki, Cynthia Chambers, Paul Clarke, Kurt Clausen, Karyn Cooper, Rebecca Coulter, Kieran Egan, Michael Firmin, Mark Glor, Julie Johnston, Yatta Kanu, Anna Kirova, Lynn Lemisko, Brenda MacKay, Lorna McLean, Anne Murray Orr, Margaret Olson, David Pratt, Lynette Shultz, Julia Temple, Louis Volante, Kelly Young, and Jon Young. For biographical information about these authors, refer to the "Contributors" section of this book.

I would like to acknowledge the graduate students in my Fall 2011 curriculum class. Their invaluable assistance helped me to decide which articles to include in this anthology.

I would also like to thank the diligent editors at Pacific Educational Press, Nadine Pedersen and Nancy Wilson, for their sage advice and dedication to this project, as well as the design and production staff who were involved with this publication.

Finally, I am indebted to John Willinsky for his profound and insightful comments in the foreword to this book.

Susan E. Gibson

Introduction

Curriculum is a point of departure rather than a destination.

—Cynthia Chambers

Curriculum is an ongoing, if complicated conversation.

—William Pinar

Quotes such as these ones by Cynthia Chambers (2003, p. 239) and William Pinar (2004, p. 188) capture what it is that makes the study of school curriculum such an interesting undertaking. You are about to embark on an inquiry into the conflicted world of curriculum. As you read the articles in this book, you will see that Canadian curriculum development has never followed an easy path. Many educators have ventured into the curriculum wilderness confident that they knew what was best for their students, only to discover that the tools they thought would guide them were sometimes flawed, that their assumptions about how their students would receive their ideas were faulty, and that they had to change directions many times to accommodate shifting terrain.

The articles in this collection are intended to engage you in curriculum's "ongoing, complicated conversation." Throughout this book many opinions are shared and many questions are asked to guide your inquiry. These will help expand your understanding of what curriculum entails and how it got to be the way it is. They will lead you to explore the factors that currently influence curricular decision-making in Canada, and look at what *should be* influencing it.

While there is no definitive "destination" for this inquiry, it is my hope that this anthology will help readers develop a clearer sense of what the term "curriculum" encompasses; clarify assumptions about curriculum; better understand some of the social, cultural, political, geographical, and historical influences on curriculum; and recognize the key ideas, factors, issues, and trends in contemporary curriculum deliberations. Ultimately, I hope that as a reader, you will build upon the ideas in this book to envision possible curricular futures for educators and students.

I have been teaching curriculum-related courses at both the graduate and undergraduate levels since 1986. The collection of articles in this book came about due to my frustration with the lack of readily available Canadian material for these courses, necessitating the use of American-focused textbooks. This was problematic for me given that Canada has its own unique and interesting history in the area of curriculum development. Consequently, to supplement the American texts, I began searching for articles written by Canadians about Canadian curriculum. In particular, I was interested in finding articles that: dealt with the struggle to define the content of curriculum given Canada's cultural, linguistic, and geographical diversity; illustrated the profound influences of having an education system that is a provincial responsibility rather than a federal one; and highlighted the multiplicity of influences that have shaped, and will no doubt continue to shape, our curriculum. Eventually my collection became substantial enough that the idea of putting the various pieces together as an anthology came to be.

While I am grateful to the authors whose articles have been reprinted in this volume, I would like to acknowledge that this book is in no way a comprehensive collection of all of the valuable work that has been done by Canadian curriculum theorists and writers over the history of the formal education system in Canada. Rather this collection is offered as a starting point for discussion and reflection, with the hope that it will lead to deeper understanding about how the curriculum in Canadian schools has developed.

While some of the articles in this anthology would seem dated if taken out of context, they were selected because they provide information needed to understand curriculum development in both a historical and contemporary context. Many things have evolved since some of the articles were originally published (for example, territorial boundaries, population size, approved terms such as "First Nations" versus "Indian," and technological advancements), yet many of the core issues remain relevant today. For example, a common theme throughout the articles is one of how to best represent what it means to be Canadian in our curriculum.

This book is divided into three parts, each containing a collection of articles on a related theme. The first part, "Defining Curriculum," grapples with the meaning of the term "curriculum"—a rather nebulous educational concept. Numerous Canadian scholars have written in this area, particularly about the challenges facing curriculum developers and educators when it comes to agreeing on what should be included as curriculum. The readings in this section are just a sample of some of the writing about the challenges of, and possibilities for, defining curriculum.

The second part of this book, "Historical Influences on the Curriculum in Canada," examines some of the historical trends and the social, political, and economic factors that have influenced Canadian curriculum since the start of formal schooling in the late 1800s. This section is not intended as an inclusive chronological overview of all of the key curriculum events over that history but rather as a series of snapshots of a few important time periods—for example, the post-Depression and post-*Sputnik* eras—when significant socio-economic and political events impacted curriculum decision-making. The articles examine the beginnings of some enduring debates that continue to influence Canadian curriculum development. These include the definition of Canadian identity, the role of philosophical beliefs about teaching and learning, cultural diversity and multiculturalism, religious education, anglophone versus francophone instruction, and the influences of geographical contexts—for example, coastal versus prairie or north versus south—on curricular content. If a more comprehensive, chronological overview of the history of curriculum development in Canada would be helpful, you may wish to refer to some websites in the "Further Reading" section of this book.

The final part of the book, "Contemporary Issues and Trends in Canadian Curriculum," covers some of the latest directions and the challenges that curriculum developers and educators are facing. The articles examine ethnic diversity, Aboriginal education, gender, sexuality, assessment, global education, religious education, and environmental stewardship. This is by no means an exhaustive list of all of the possible topics that are currently under debate, nor do the articles cover all aspects of each of the issues presented, rather they are offered here as a good place to begin curriculum conversations about contemporary issues. The "Further Reading" section of this book lists additional readings, along with articles on the topic of technology and digital literacy as an example of another contemporary issue that you may wish to investigate.

The objective of this anthology is to increase your awareness of Canada's unique history of curriculum development, of how educational thinking is influenced by circumstances far beyond the classroom, and of some of the important issues and trends in curriculum evolution now and into the future. Just as Chambers notes that curriculum is not a destination, but a point of departure, I hope that this book will serve as a guide for a thought-provoking journey.

Susan E. Gibson
University of Alberta

REFERENCES

Chambers, C. (2003). "As Canadian as possible under the circumstances": A view of contemporary curriculum discourses in Canada. In W. Pinar (Ed.), *International handbook of curriculum research* (pp. 221–252). Mahwah, N.J.: Lawrence Erlbaum.

Pinar, W. (2004). *What is curriculum theory?* Mahwah, NJ: Lawrence Erlbaum.

Part I

Defining Curriculum

Defining Curriculum

Curriculum is a very complex and contentious term. Curriculum is often equated with the content that is to be taught or the "program of studies." One of my students captured how many educators feel about curriculum when she related:

> ...I have always blindly and uncritically accepted it [curriculum] to be the documents that prescribe the program of studies with learner expectations and outcomes laid out in a linear fashion. I had faithfully tried to follow all the "rules" set out in these documents within the prescribed timeline so that I would know for certain that my students were learning what they needed to know.

Before undertaking an examination of curriculum events in Canada's past and present, ask yourself the following key question:

- What do I think the term "curriculum" means and why do I think that way?

The readings in this section were collected to help you to rethink and expand ideas about what should be considered when defining curriculum. As educators we all hold a particular set of beliefs about how students learn, about how they should be taught, and about what they should be taught. Those who develop the curriculum also have their own beliefs, which are reflected in curriculum documents.

As implementers of the official curriculum in the classroom, teachers need to be aware of both their own beliefs and those reflected in these curriculum documents, as, consciously or unconsciously, these beliefs shape learning and teaching experiences—a phenomenon that is often referred to as the "hidden curriculum" (Jackson, 1968).

John Dewey, in his seminal article "My Pedagogic Creed" (1897), outlined a number of important questions that can assist in these deliberations about what curriculum entails. These questions include:

- What is education?
- What is the subject matter of education?
- What is the school?
- What is the relationship between the school and society?
- And what is the nature of teaching method?

All of these questions address important aspects of curriculum that need to be considered, especially as your beliefs about how to answer each of these questions shape your view of curriculum.

Likewise Joseph Schwab's "The Practical 3: Translation into Curriculum" (1973) identified four "commonplaces" of curriculum:

- the teacher (what teachers bring to the educational experience);
- the subject matter (what should be learned);
- the learner (what students bring to the educational experience); and
- the milieu (how external factors influence the nature of instruction and the milieu in which the learning takes place).

These commonplaces also provide a helpful framework for thinking about what constitutes curriculum. As you read the articles presented in this section of the book, you may wish to reflect on the goals of schooling, the knowledge considered to be of most worth, the forms of knowing that are valued, who contributes to curriculum development, and what the roles are of both teachers and learners in learning.

The article "'Currere' to the Rescue? Teachers as 'Amateur Intellectuals' in a Knowledge Society" by Yatta Kanu and Mark Glor supports the argument that any exploration of what curriculum means should first begin with self-exploration into questions such as the ones posed by Dewey. The authors propose the use of an autobiographical method of "currere" as a way to encourage personal reflection in order for educators to better understand their own histories, to expose and challenge their beliefs, to understand who they are as teachers and who is controlling their work, and to envision other possible futures.

The remainder of the chapters in this section are intended to facilitate further exploration of the concept of "curriculum." These range from determining what needs to be considered when deliberating on the curriculum; to thinking about how the curriculum as experienced in the classroom can be different from the "official" curriculum; to reflecting on who the stakeholders are who influence curriculum, and how their beliefs shape their ideas about what needs to be included in the official curriculum; to the roles played by the students and the teacher in living the curriculum in the classroom.

In "What is curriculum?", Kieran Egan explores the historical roots of the word "curriculum" and identifies a number of challenges in trying to define curriculum, one being the debate over whether it should be focused on the "what" (the content and objectives), on the "how" (instruction), or both.

In his article "Teaching as In-dwelling Between Two Curriculum Worlds," Ted Aoki expands on the notion of moving away from viewing curriculum solely as a set of objectives to thinking about how the curriculum plays out in the classroom. Aoki describes what he calls the "two curriculum worlds" that all teachers encounter—curriculum-as-plan and curriculum-as-lived-experiences. This reading introduces the real-life tensions experienced by one teacher, Miss O, as she struggles with a constant juggling act between who she knows her students are and what she is mandated to teach.

Of course, the tension between curriculum-as-plan and curriculum-as-lived-experiences results partly from who is shaping the curriculum, who is delivering the curriculum, and who is receiving the curriculum. In "Competing Voices for the Curriculum," Egan shows how differing beliefs about the purpose of schools and the important knowledge to be taught in schools can cause curriculum confusion and tension. He identifies a number of the "stakeholders" of education (e.g., parents, government, corporations) and describes how their beliefs based on three overarching ideas—schools as socializing agents, schools as transmitters of common core knowledge, and schools as developers of individual potential—are the root causes of often hidden conflicts in education.

Karyn Cooper in "When Curriculum Becomes a Stranger" adds to Aoki's story of Miss O by providing another example of the tensions caused when teachers encounter curriculum-as-plan in the classroom in the form of prepackaged curriculum materials. Cooper talks about the "estrangement" that children and teachers often feel when they experience the official curriculum in this form.

In "Transforming Narrative Encounters," Anne Murray Orr and Margaret Olson build upon Aoki's ideas about "two worlds" even further as they share their stories of encounters with learners whose experiences with the curriculum did not match that of their teachers. The authors argue that educators need to always consider the place of their students in curricular decision-making. To do this, they recommend working alongside students in order to see the curriculum in the classroom as "multistoried."

These are just a few articles of many that explore different ideas of what curriculum is, how it is shaped, and how teachers can work with and beyond the "official" curriculum to provide relevant experiences for their students. As you complete this section of the book, your investigation should lead you to new insights about the influence of individual beliefs on curriculum decision-making; about the constant evolving state of change in the curriculum, especially regarding what is taught and how it is taught; and about the need to consider the place of the learner, the teacher, and their lived experience in the classroom, in all curriculum deliberations.

REFERENCES

Dewey, J. (1897). My pedagogic creed. *School Journal, 54,* 77–80. Accessed at http://dewey.pragmatism.org/creed.htm

Jackson, P. (1968). *Life in classrooms.* New York: Holt, Rinehart and Winston.

Schwab, J. (1973). The practical 3: Translation into curriculum. *The School Review, 81*(4), 501–522.

1

"Currere" to the Rescue?

Teachers as "Amateur Intellectuals" in a Knowledge Society

YATTA KANU
MARK GLOR

INTRODUCTION

Teaching today is increasingly complex work where teachers find themselves caught in a triangle of interests and imperatives. This triangle requires teachers to be: (a) catalysts of the promises of opportunity and prosperity of the knowledge society; (b) counterpoints to the threats posed by the knowledge society to community, security, and the public good; and (c) casualties of the standardization imposed by the imperatives of the knowledge society (Hargreaves, 2003). How must teachers proceed with their work as educators within the professional paradox and conditions of fragmentation created by the knowledge society? We argue in this paper that functioning in less fragmentary ways within this paradox would require teachers to transform themselves into what Edward Said (1996) calls "amateur intellectuals" who are skeptical of mainstream political and social trends and who raise moral issues at the heart of even the most technical and professional activity. We posit Pinar's (1974, 1976) autobiographical method of *currere* as a beginning point for the transformation of teachers into amateur intellectuals.

THE PARADOX OF TEACHING IN A KNOWLEDGE SOCIETY

"We are living in a defining moment of educational history when the world in which teachers do their work is changing profoundly. . . . " So writes Andy

Hargreaves (2003) in *Teaching in the Knowledge Society*, his most cogent critique, to date, of the current wave of over-regulation and standardization in education, which neoliberal discourses defend as increasing equity and fairness while holding all students to the same high standards. As Hargreaves notes, we (post-industrial societies in the West) are living in knowledge economies that are driven by ingenuity, creativity, inventiveness, and the capacity to cope with rapid change. Schools in knowledge societies have to cultivate these qualities in young people for their nations to survive and stay competitive. But Hargreaves also observes that while knowledge economies stimulate growth and prosperity they primarily serve the private good, and, in their relentless competitiveness and pursuit of profit and self-interest, they fragment the social order and widen the wealth gap. Particularly disconcerting for public education, knowledge economies impose "soul-less standardization" that leaves some students behind by eroding curricula and pedagogies that build on the experience, language, and cultural identity of these students, decreasing teachers' autonomy of judgment, undermining moral vision and social commitment in schools, and derailing the very creativity, ingenuity, and flexibility that schools are supposed to cultivate. The paradox of teaching in a knowledge society is that while schools and teachers are expected to create the human skills and capacities that enable knowledge economies to survive and succeed, they are also expected to teach the compassion, sense of community, and emotional sympathy that mitigate and counteract the immense problems that knowledge economies create (Hargreaves, 2003). The predominantly market-oriented forms of life and practice at the heart of knowledge economies have, therefore, fragmented the work of teachers as never before.

How must teachers proceed with their responsibility as educators within this professional paradox and conditions of fragmentation? In this paper, we argue that functioning in less fragmentary ways within this paradox would require teachers to become what Edward Said (1996), in *Representations of the Intellectual*, calls "amateur" intellectuals. By this Said means intellectuals who remain skeptical of mainstream political and social trends, who are critical of the institutions which employ them, and who cultivate a position of exile that maintains an intellectual skepticism towards their own work, especially their apparent successes. Said (1996) writes:

> The intellectual today ought to be an amateur who considers that to be a thinking and concerned member of society one is entitled to raise moral issues at the heart of even the most technical and professional activity . . . The intellectual's spirit as an amateur can enter and transform the merely professional

routine most of us go through into something more lively and radical; instead of doing what one is supposed to do, one can ask why one does it, who benefits from it, and how can it reconnect with a personal project and original thought. (pp. 82–83)

Said's representation of the intellectual as "amateur" suggests that teachers, as private and public intellectuals in a complex and fast-changing knowledge society, must learn to teach in ways they were not taught, commit to continuous learning and reflection, and work and learn both alone and in professional teams where they can raise moral questions about practice and access knowledge from the collective intelligence of the team. Teaching in the larger sense would have to be considered in terms of *phronesis* which Paul Ricoeur (1992), in reference to a vocation or profession, describes as living and acting ethically or, as Hans Smits (in Lund, Panayotidis, Smits, & Towers, 2006, p. 2) recently put it, "acting well in terms of some sense of overall good." Such an orientation to professional practice requires skepticism toward all of one's educational experience which, as Elliot Eisner (1995) reminds us, is a product of both the features of the world and the biography of the individual: "Our experience is influenced by our past as it interacts with our present"(p. 26). Slavoj Zizek (2005) has recently noted that, in the specific social conditions of commodity exchange and the global market economy, "the modern notion of the profession implies that I experience myself as an individual who is not directly 'born into' his social role. What I will become depends on the interplay between contingent social circumstances and my free choice . . . " (pp. 129–130).

Thus teachers have the free choice to begin the analysis and the reflection required to reverse the neoliberal imperatives at the heart of knowledge economies and transform themselves into amateur intellectuals capable of developing conceptions of education that run counter to the emphasis on utilitarian aims which would have us evaluate schools and nations in terms of the quality of the nation's future workforce (McDonough & Feinberg, 2003).

We posit William Pinar's (1974, 1976) autobiographical/biographical method of *currere* as a beginning point for the transformation of teachers into amateur intellectuals. The method of *currere* foregrounds the relationship between narrative (life history) and practice and provides opportunities to theorize particular moments in one's educational history, to dialogue with these moments, and examine possibilities for change.

THE METHOD OF CURRERE

Currere is a reflexive cycle in which thought bends back upon itself and thus recovers its volition.
(Madeleine R. Grumet, 1976, pp. 130–131)

Life can only be understood backwards, but it must be lived forwards.
(Soren Kierkegaard, cited in Habermas, 2003, p. 4)

Formulated in the 1970s by William Pinar and other curriculum scholars as the Latin infinitive of "curriculum"—meaning "to run the course"—the concept of *currere* refers to an existential experience of institutional structures (Pinar, 1974). The method of *currere* is devised to disclose and examine such experience "so that we may see more of it and see more clearly. With such seeing can come deepened understanding of the running and with this can come deepened agency" (Pinar & Grumet, 1976, p. vii). Pinar describes the method of *currere* as autobiographical/ biographical, consisting of four steps or moments depicting both temporal and reflective movements in the study of educational experience: the regressive, the progressive, the analytical, and the synthetical (Pinar, Reynolds, Slattery, & Taubman, 1995, p. 520).

In the regressive moment one's lived experience becomes the data source. To generate data, one utilizes the psychoanalytic technique of free-association "to recall the past, and enlarge, and thereby transform one's memory." Regression requires one to return to the past, "to recapture it as it was and as it hovers over the present" (Pinar et al., 1995, p. 520). In the progressive moment one looks toward what is not yet present, what is not yet the case, and imagines possible futures. The analytical moment involves a kind of phenomenological bracketing where one distances oneself from the past and asks: "How is the future present in the past, the past in the future, and the present in both?" (p. 520). The synthetical moment brings it all together as one re-enters the lived present and interrogates its meaning.

Grumet (1981) describes *currere* as an attempt "to reveal the ways that histories (both collective and individual) and hope suffuse our moments, and to study them through telling our stories of educational experience" (p. 118). *Currere* returns educational experience to the person who lived it, so that the experience can be examined for latent and manifest meaning and the political implications of such reflection and interpretation. "In doing so, *currere* discloses new structures in the process of naming old ones" (Pinar et al., 1995, p. 521).

As this paper will show, narrative (Bruner, 1992; Connelly & Clandinin, 1990), voice (Miller, 1990; Britzman, 1986), collaborative dialogue (Gitlin, 1990;

Belenky, Clinchy, Goldberger, & Tarule, 1986), connectivity of public and private (Grumet, 1988), collaborative autobiography (Butt, 1990), and personal practical knowledge (Clandinin, 1987) have all emerged as important concepts in the effort to understand *currere* as autobiographical and biographical text. This groundbreaking work allows educators and students of curriculum "to sketch the relations among school knowledge, life history, and intellectual development in ways that might function self-transformatively" (Pinar et al., 1995, p. 515). Understanding and acting upon the past to influence the future affords growth and transformation for the intellectual.

THE TRANSFORMATIVE POTENTIAL OF AUTOBIOGRAPHY/BIOGRAPHY

In writing on the meaning of meaning, Jerome Bruner (1992) makes a distinction between two ways of knowing: narrative knowing and paradigmatic knowing. Narrative knowing occurs through reflection on personal experience through storytelling while paradigmatic knowledge is created through scientific inquiry. Narratives (e.g., life histories) have become important sources teachers might use to improve their own teaching (Eisner, 1995). The freedom from traditional scientific methods and the return to narrative knowing allows an examination of the past but also the opportunity to influence the future. Jean-Paul Sartre (1963) comments, "the most rudimentary behavior must be determined both in relation to the real and present factors which condition it and in relation to a certain object, still to come" (p. 91). This examination of events in self-causes is what Alfred Schütz (1967), in his writings on social theory, has described as strangeness and familiarity. Schütz expands further and writes, "Strangeness and familiarity are not limited to the social field but are general categories of our interpretation of the world." Once we encounter something in experience that we did not know before, we begin a process of inquiry. Trying to integrate our inquiry with the meanings we have created over time, we transform our experience into an additional element of what we know. Doing so, "we have enlarged and adjusted our stock of experience" (Schütz, 1967, p. 105).

Some theorists have suggested that individuals do not have the capacity to understand their life experiences critically. Mills (1981) disagrees and argues that the individual has the capacity to understand critically his/her life experiences and present dilemmas by situating herself/himself within history. By creating these dilemmas the individual is able to create situations in the past and in the future. These situations can then be contemplated with a critical understanding. Following Mills' thoughts, Deborah Britzman (1986) contends that individuals do have the capacity to participate in shaping and responding to the social forces that have directly influenced and continue to influence their lives. By uncovering biographies there can be an empowerment and a movement away from cultural authority and cultural reproduction. However, just uncovering biographies and examining them with critical understanding is not enough unless they prove to be unsatisfactory. The only way to prove the beliefs inherent in biographies to be unsatisfactory is if "they are challenged and one is unable to assimilate them into existing conceptions" (Bullough, 1997, p. 78; see also Pajares, 1992). This challenging of beliefs is what John Dewey (1938) discussed in *Experience and Education*. In that work, Dewey wrote about experience and its relationship to learning and teaching: "Every experience affects for better or worse the attitudes which help decide the quality of further experiences" (p. 38). Dewey believed that teachers must be aware of the "possibilities inherent in ordinary experience" (p. 89), that the "business of the educator is to see in what direction an experience is heading" (p. 38). It is impossible to see the direction of experience without reflecting on what the teacher brings to the experience from his/her past. To be able to see the direction an experience is heading the educator must understand his/her own history.

To understand the past is only one part. What the challenging of the past can also create is what Aronowitz and Giroux (1985) have called a transformative intellectual who envisions what is possible rather than merely accepting what is probable. When teachers examine their own histories and those "connections to the past which in part define who they are and how they mediate and function in the world"(p. 160) they can unravel existing arrangements in public education and reconceptualize public education as more than the soulless standardization that has alienated students, killed creativity and inspiration, and provoked tidal waves of resignation and early retirement among educators. But the examination of one's history can become an exercise in what many have called self-psychoanalysis where transformation of self and world does not take place. Educators, therefore, need to do more than just examine their own pasts. Reminiscent of Said (1996), they need to cultivate a position of exile from those pasts and the practices they have engendered and imagine a possible and different future. In this sense, Kierkegaard's statement (cited in Habermas, 2003) that individuals need to "detach from environment, become aware of individuality, become aware of actions and become responsible for them, then enter into a commitment with others" (p. 6) warrants thought. This detachment from environment is only possible if one understands the environment one is in. Much like a fish only comprehends water when it is removed from it, a person can only understand their environment when they are detached as well. However, unlike the fish which is physically removed from its environment by another species, a human being is unlikely to be removed from their environment unless they choose to be removed. Furthermore, in the knowledge society in which educators function today, there are elements that are attempting to keep consciousness closed for economic gain. Capitalist imperatives suggest that the knowledge society depends on requiring individuals not to think about consequences, alternative futures, or the public good.

When an individual goes through the process of detachment, a realization occurs of the impact of one's actions on others' lives. This realization has the effect of awaking one from a dream/nightmare where one gains insight into the harm caused to others, self, the immediate environment, and the world. This awaking allows possible growth to occur, but it is costly to the individual. Kegan writes that growth "involves the leaving behind of an old way of being in the world. Often it involves, at least for a time, leaving behind others who have been identified with that being" (cited in Bullough, 1997, p. 75) and, often, a misunderstanding by those others of why the individual is detaching. This growth often brings forward what Kegan describes as "disequilibrium" which challenges the self and forces the individual to regain equilibrium by reconciling the part of the self that has been made exposed. Kegan contends that not growing is costlier still, as a temporary balance may become a permanent one as current institutions sustain and support a comfortable historical relationship. This leaves talent undeveloped, as it is too simplistic to challenge abilities.

A possible method to bring about and resolve the disequilibrium that Kierkegaard and Kegan discuss is collaborative dialogue. Belenky, Clinchy, Goldberger, and Tarule (1986) link the notions of experience, collaborative dialogue, and reflection:

> In order for reflection to occur, the oral and written forms of language must pass back and forth between persons who both speak and listen or read and write—sharing, expanding, and reflecting on each other's experiences. Such interchanges lead to ways of knowing that enable individuals to enter into the social and intellectual life of their community. Without them, individuals remain isolated from others; and without the tools for representing their experiences, people also remain isolated from self. (Belenky et al., p. 26)

In essence, one cannot remain detached from the environment in which one examines oneself without entering into collaborative dialogue with others. This collaborative dialogue is predicated on what Noddings (1991) has described as "stories." Her statement that "Stories have the power to direct and change our lives" (p. 157) becomes powerful once one comes to an understanding that our stories need to be understood. The way that our stories begin to be understood is through conversation with others. In reality then, one must enter in and out of one's environment, gathering data and reflecting. As educators we need to understand that stories (narratives) are in essence what our art is about.

Connelly and Clandinin (1990) argue that, from the perspective of schooling, a teaching act is a "narrative in action," that is, an "expression of biography and history . . . in a particular situation" (p. 184). In actuality our knowledge as educators comes from the reality in which we exist, sharing our narratives with students and receiving theirs back. Educators must have the ability to enter into narratives and reflection to transform the future. However, this collaborative dialogue, to be effective, must be equal between the individuals entering it and must be seen as relevant. Gitlin (1990) argues that a precondition for dialogue is that "all participants see the discourse as important and have a say in determining its course" (p. 447). Gitlin maintains that dialogue should "make prejudgments apparent" so that their critical testing can empower the participants to "challenge taken-for-granted notions that influence the way they see the world and judge their practice" (p. 448).

It is evident from the foregoing discussion that becoming a transformative, amateur intellectual is not an easy task to understand much less implement. One must be able to move out of oneself, become conscious of reality and a possible future, move back into reality and share narrative, and move back out once more to examine and reflect on self and narrative. As Kegan (cited in Bullough, 1997) noted, this is extremely costly to the self, to the point where one begins to question if one has the ability or desire to understand, much less take on this task of becoming an amateur, transformative intellectual. However, as educators we have a responsibility to take on this challenge in order to be able to embrace and practise teaching as *phronesis* within the professional paradox that knowledge economies have created for us. In the next part of this paper we examine more specifically the role of *currere* in the transformation of teachers into amateur intellectuals.

ON BECOMING AMATEUR TRANSFORMATIVE INTELLECTUALS: CURRERE TO THE RESCUE?

Maxine Greene (2001) argues that when teachers are given the opportunity to articulate, or to give some "kind of shape to their lived experience, all kinds of questions may arise. Gaps appear in the narrative; awarenesses of lacks and deficiencies become visible; bright moments and epiphanies highlight the dark times, the fears, the felt failures" (p. 83). The key phrase in the above statement is "given the opportunity." Opportunity in this context is not just provided to educators. Educators need to seek out those opportunities to expand their narrative, to seek those epiphanies, and to ultimately transform themselves into phronetic professionals serving the interest of the public good. At core, teachers need to become learners of themselves and start to ask questions of themselves—"questions that demand answers if restlessness or hunger or unhappiness is to be allayed" (Greene, 2001, p. 83). This seeking out of questions will only occur when teachers move out of the conception of teaching only as rules, processes, and procedures to be employed toward the achievement of utilitarian goals. Important as these might be, such an instrumental and technical conception of teaching fragments the unity of practice as an overarching orientation to *phronesis*. Many teachers, as casualties of the knowledge society, have come to see teaching as a sink-or-swim world where only the immediate moments are of concern. Reaction, not pro-action, has become the norm and the accepted way of doing things in the school. Teachers scramble to acquire standardized "scientifically proven" instructional strategies that can be applied to classroom situations that have already been preordained by others, without contemplating the effects upon the students as distinctive cultural and emotional beings. The "ignoring of the reasons for and consequences of what appears to work" (Britzman, 1986, p. 225) leads to a closing of the dialogue of the mind for the self, and a closing of dialogue with and about others. Eisner argues that even more is lost through this lack of questioning. He writes, "getting in touch is itself an act of discrimination, a finely-grained, sensitively nuanced selective process in which the mind is fully engaged" (cited in Cole and Knowles, 2000, p. 28). By not fully engaging the mind and seeking out the questions that need to be answered we fail to understand who we are as individuals and as teachers; we fail to understand what is controlling what we do and to what effect; we remain fragmented, shadows of what we could be.

Given the hope of a new existence, a chance to be whole once again, how do educators begin the transformation into amateur intellectuals? As explicated above, educators need to be willing to begin self-examination through the process of "telling and living, re-telling and reliving the meanings and significances of our lives to begin to help us understand ourselves, how we came to be who we are, and where we are going" (Clandinin & Connelly, cited in Cole & Knowles, p. 28). Educators need to attend to more than the immediate present, but must engage in what Britzman (1986) calls the "hidden work" of negotiating the past and future demands (p. 221). Such negotiation will lead to disequilibrium which will cause discomfort but "disequilibrium is a necessary condition for transformation" (p. 230). The opening up of ourselves and our professional practice to examination will proverbially shine light into many of the spaces that perhaps educators are uncomfortable to acknowledge need inspection. But this process need not be threatening, as has been culturally generated through our pasts. This fear must be examined for what it is—a method to stop transformation from occurring. Instead of being trapped by the old metaphors that generate fear and solitude there is the possibility that we can envision new metaphors that allow us to "think of old situations in new ways" (McWilliams, 1995, p. 40). The results may be new lines of action and new teaching behaviours coming from new ways of thinking about problems. This can become a liberation that can bring about solidarity and transformation instead of solitude and rut.

When teachers are willing to begin the process of transformation that *currere* allows, many positives can occur. First the method of *currere* allows educators to develop a collaborative autobiography. Richard Butt, in his research, strives to understand biography and autobiography as "educational praxis" (cited in Pinar et al., 1995, p. 556). Educational praxis ties into the idea of a transformative intellectual in that there is a movement towards not only writing autobiographical, reflexive narratives but also sharing such narratives with others. The idea is to create narratives from which one can learn about teaching but not in the sense of definitive lessons. As Stenberg (2005) writes, reflexive narratives are not intended to offer final or complete renderings of the self as a subject. Instead, "they provide opportunities to theorize a particular moment, dialogue with it, and examine possibilities for change" (p. 76). Collaborative autobiography allows teachers to understand their lives via a community that values self-understanding, but acts towards a future that is collective. Butt's notion of praxis fulfills Pinar's idea of "the regressive" (data collected about the past through reflection and free association) and "the progressive" (looking forward to what may be a possible future). With collective autobiography, however, it must be understood that the individual involved in the collective must be able to step away and examine the situation and its meaning (Pinar's "analytical" and "synthetical" moments). This is also in fulfillment of the ideas put forward by Kierkegaard and Kegan that educators need to detach to be able to examine, but must then enter into the collective to begin the process of acting on their environment with an idea of a possible future. Some theorists have criticized the idea of collective biography as entailing the possibility for risk to the individuals involved in the process (for example, the risk of self-exposure). However, as educators we need to remember Kegan's warning that not growing is costlier still.

Second, beyond the collective, *currere* provides teachers with the capacity to gain voice, as individuals, within or even against the system. Voice, according to Britzman, "is meaning that resides within the individual and enables that individual to participate in a community. . . . The struggle for voice begins when a person attempts to communicate meaning to someone else. Finding the words, speaking for oneself, and feeling heard by others are all a part of this process" (cited in Connelly & Clandinin, 1990, p. 4). By examining why/how they are not individuals in the system, but are assumed to be broad categories of technicians meant to implement others' prescribed changes, teachers can find their voice. This voice can then be used to implement transformative change in response to individual student needs. When educators understand their own voice, they can help students find their voice. It cannot be assumed that teachers will be just granted voice. The process of self-examination that generates voice is a time-consuming task that may not be easily supported or facilitated by the current system of bureaucratization and standardization. Often educators, in moving to gain voice, will encounter others who may attempt to limit their voice. This act of limiting voice may not even be done consciously by those who are conducting the action. They may only be involved in replicating, subconsciously, the system of which they have been a part. However, an educator who has been awakened through an examination of their own narrative has a profound opportunity to make a difference. Even if they are the one lone voice crying out in the wilderness, they are still a voice.

Third, *currere* has the potential to bring educators to the understanding that they possess personal practical knowledge which guides their everyday work as educators. This personal practical knowledge is conceived of as "that combination of theoretical and practical knowledge born of lived experience" (Pinar et al., 1995, p. 557). Through critical examination and understanding of that knowledge, which has guiding power in teachers' lives and work, teachers can feel empowered to make transformative change. In a knowledge society, teachers' experiential knowledge, along with research evidence that informs practice, can contribute significantly to improve schools. No longer will teachers be at the bottom of the education hierarchy with university researchers, government departments of curriculum writers, and social and economic trend-setters all sending down edicts to be digested and implemented by teachers. Teachers become more than the tools of others, and now are able to understand the effect of their actions in relation to the world around them. They begin to understand that they have power within the system to transform rather than simply adjusting. To gain this power, however, there needs to be an awareness of how the system has shaped their lives and their consciousness. The only way to gain this understanding is through an examination of the narratives that are influencing their actions consciously and subconsciously.

Lastly, *currere* provides a connection of the public and private spaces of teachers that Madeleine Grumet (1988) discusses in her highly regarded book, *Bitter Milk: Women and Teaching*. According to Grumet, educators experience a separation between their public spaces and private spaces through the current educative models that create a dichotomy in their consciousness. In the *currere/ autobiographical* method, public and private, institution and individual, abstract and concrete are all interconnected. The examination of personal narrative creates a connection between private and public that is missing within the current fragmented education system. The rejoining of the two selves within a model of autobiography leads to a deeper sense of understanding through connectivity. Understanding of an educator's holistic identity allows for the possibility that movement can occur towards the fuller examination of self.

The transformative possibilities of *currere* are substantial once teachers accept that teaching in a knowledge society means profound changes to how they see and do their work as educators. This acceptance, however, is based upon a desire for change. For instance, there is the difficulty that even when educators are presented with the opportunity for transformation that *currere* offers, many may not accept such opportunity because to accept would mean disequilibrium which they may wish to avoid. Hence achieving real change where amateur and transformative intellectuals become the norm requires a type of revolution that is difficult to bring about within the teaching profession. Hope, however, resides in pre-service teacher education where prospective teachers can be exposed to the transformative potential of *currere* before they reach the schools and become part of the system. We project this hope with the full realization that prospective teachers are not *tabula rasa* but rather have already been part of the system through their own education. However, the chance to enter into self-discovery through *currere* may be greater in pre-service teacher education before prospective teachers enter the profession. In the next section, therefore, we explore the potential of *currere* for pre-service teacher preparation.

CURRERE FOR PRE-SERVICE TEACHER EDUCATION

It is a well-known truism that prospective teachers enter teacher education programs with the taken-for-granted notion that they know what a teacher is and does. They have been part of the school system for well over a decade and have a conception in their mind of what a teacher is. As Britzman (1986) writes, prospective teachers "bring their implicit institutional biographies—the cumulative experience of their school lives—which in turn, inform their knowledge of the student's world, of school structure, and of curriculum" (p. 221). As the prospective teacher brings this knowledge into the institution, the teacher education program often brings forward ideas that then are filtered through the lenses that the prospective teacher has gained from their past. The lessons of experience that prospective teachers learn through the education faculty and later their practicum will be "strongly influenced by the assumptions, conceptions, beliefs, dispositions, and capabilities they bring to the program" (Zeichner, 1996, p. 216). To facilitate their development into amateur transformative intellectuals, prospective teachers need to be given the opportunity to examine these experiences for those lenses that they are wearing.

Zeichner writes that we need to follow Shulman's thinking concerning transformation of one's own personal knowledge so that sense can be made. Transformation of knowledge through an examination of the prospective teacher's past allows for a critical consciousness to be developed early in the process—a consciousness that allows one to interrogate what one does, who benefits from it, and how it can be reconnected to a personal project through agentive action. Most if not all teacher education programs acknowledge that the past has a strong influence on how prospective teachers see their roles as future teachers. Sue Johnston (1993), however, observes that "there have been few suggestions about what can be done about these past experiences within teacher education programs" (p. 79). She contends that the influence of past experience is ignored,

> in the hope that new learning will replace them—that is, a process of unconscious displacement is envisaged. At other times, conscious efforts are made to change these views of teaching which arise from the teacher's own experiences as a student. Rarely are they fully acknowledged and efforts made to help student teachers understand the influence of their thinking and negotiate new ways of thinking about teaching as a result of this understanding. (p. 79)

A system, therefore, needs to be developed where prospective teachers have an opportunity to disengage from their environment and search out those experiences in their consciousness and sub-consciousness in order for the amateur transformative intellectual to develop. Often, even where knowledge accumulated from past experiences is examined, it is done so as a potential resource. This knowledge is portrayed as an asset, but rarely is it acknowledged as a liability for those beginning teachers who have not sufficiently examined their own school experiences in light of current theory, social and economic trends, and alternative futures. Thus autobiography is left as an examination of the past but with little acknowledgement of its role in the future. *Currere*, as autobiographical inquiry, engages prospective teachers with their past and present environments and a look towards the future. It does so by inviting them to reflect on three basic questions that are intended to help them challenge deeply entrenched conceptions of teaching: What do I understand teaching to be? How, through my experience and personal history, did I come to understand teaching this way? How do I wish to become in my professional future? Autobiographical inquiry conveys how teachers' knowledge is formed, held, and how it can be studied and understood transformatively.

In transforming teachers' knowledge, *currere* offers more than what has worked in other institutions or what has been successful and celebrated in the literature. As Zeichner (1996) warns, "the answer to problems of the practicum is not to be found in merely having student teachers write journals, construct cases, tell teaching stories, or conduct action research" (p. 224). All of these are good practices, but they can easily become unstudied tools utilized by prospective teachers without an understanding of why they are being implemented. Without linkage with critical understandings of personal stories, these methods become little more than techniques to be implemented because they are mandated to occur. As a side note, Zeichner's (1996) warning must also extend to administrators who try to implement such practices in their schools. While educators should be encouraged to seek out their narratives, bringing in "systems" where teachers are mandated to conduct journal writing, tell stories, or conduct action research will not create amateur transformative intellectuals. That process needs to occur through a seeking of the self because one wants to seek out the self.

Transformation may also occur during pre-service teacher education through the very nature of *currere*, that is, the educational experience or curriculum provided to those who will become teachers. As Pinar writes, citing Grumet,

> [I]t is the curriculum which provides new experience for the student, which stands out against the ground of ordinary experience, both revealing and transforming it. . . . The curriculum becomes, in this scheme, the middle passage, that passage in which movement is possible from the familiar to the unfamiliar, to estrangement, then to a transformed situation. (Pinar et al., 1995, p. 548)

At the heart of many current teacher education programs, however, is an apprenticeship type model that immerses prospective teachers into a submissive role, and cloaks and sustains the very structures that prevent them from becoming more than what others prescribe. In such programs prospective teachers are faced with the knowledge that they have to be able to survive the situation in which they are placed. They are in a subservient role under the supervising teachers with whom they are placed and the faculty advisors who hold the power of pass/fail over them. What tends to be implied during the practicum is an orderly existence that continues what the supervising teacher has started in their classroom. What needs to be understood, however, is that professional teaching knowledge is constructed and deconstructed through observant, reflective, decision-making teachers in response to unpredictable and rapidly changing circumstances. Prospective teachers need the opportunity to examine what it means to be a teacher in contexts of constant change and unpredictability. They need to be helped to develop capacities for taking risks and undertaking inquiries when confronted by new demands. More importantly, they need the opportunity to enter into dialogue about such risks and inquiries with a teacher supervisor/faculty advisor who is willing to abandon the "power over" approach in favour of "power with" student teachers.

As mentioned previously, dialogue needs to be a place where both sides feel respected, equal, and empowered. However, the apprenticeship nature of many teacher preparation programs stymies equality and empowerment due to "assumptions about the benefits of . . . granting authority to the perceptions of the supervisor over the experiences of the student teacher/learner" (Paris & Gespass, 2001, p. 398). The argument can be made that true equality between student teachers and their supervisors can never be attained due to the inherently unequal nature of the relationship. Steps, however, can be taken to change the system into one where the prospective teacher can feel empowered to raise technical and moral questions pertaining to practice, and take risks to introduce change. Others before us have suggested that empowerment would entail such steps as moving toward a mentorship model where student teachers are renamed as "teacher candidates," sending out letters that welcome prospective teachers to their school placements, or providing them a space at the school that they can call their own. We, however, propose much larger steps, such as creating spaces within teacher education for student teachers to examine their own educational experiences, how these experiences shape their conceptions and practices of teaching, and how they can be transformed so that, as teachers, they can act well in terms of some sense of an overall good for all students. Such spaces must be created both in the university courses and in the practicum because paying lip-service to the process at the university without a strategy for implementation in the practicum will lead to prospective teachers becoming actors that play a role in one part of their program but not in the other. They will self-examine because they are told to do so at the university but then they will move to the schools where they are told that "this is the real world now, where real work is done." When the survival mode begins to take hold in the schools, self-analysis, growth, and the potential for transformation cease.

CONCLUSION

Teaching today is increasingly complex work where teachers find themselves caught in what Hargreaves (2003) calls "a triangle of interests and imperatives." This triangle requires teachers to be (a) catalysts of the knowledge society and all its promises of opportunity and prosperity; (b) counterpoints to the threats posed by the knowledge society to community, security, and the public good; and (c) casualties of the standardization imposed by the imperatives of the knowledge society (p. 10). The effects of these three interacting forces are shaping the nature of teaching and what it means to be a teacher in a knowledge society. We have argued in this paper that functioning holistically and meaningfully within these forces would require teachers to transform themselves into "amateur intellectuals" who raise ethical/moral issues at the heart of even the most standardized, technical professional activity. Believing that a teacher is an individual who is "not born directly into his or her social role" but is rather a product of the features of the world and his or her biography, we have posited and explored the potential that the autobiographical method of *currere* offers for the transformation of teachers into amateur intellectuals.

Through *currere*, the chains can be examined and a weak spot can be found to break the constraints on the engagement of teaching as *phronesis* in a knowledge society. Some say that any act of remembering is a fictional re-creation. Grumet, for example, asserts that text revealed through the autobiographical method never completely coincides with the experience it signifies. Interpretation is a "revelatory enterprise . . . Imitations, half-truths, contradictions, and distractions hover around every tale we tell" (Grumet, cited in Cole & Knowles, 2000, p. 44). In light of this assertion, we posit that one should not be concerned about remembering correctly, or having more questions than answers. The key is the path or journey one takes and what is discovered. To look at the world and marvel at one's place in it, we must be encouraged to use our imaginations, but not only so that our imaginations of the future seek to find some sort of satisfaction for ourselves. According to Maxine Greene (2001), "What we need to be warned against is the use of imagination as a means of withdrawal from uncongenial surroundings instead of as a means of stimulating transformative thinking"(p. 86). There is hope in transformative thinking. We have the opportunity to learn from our past experiences that have shaped our utilitarian understandings of curriculum and pedagogy and to take on what Hannah Arendt has called "an enlarged way of thinking" (cited in Greene, 2001, p. 85). Our identities can be more than just what others have given to us to make sense of their realities. We (the authors) are both history teachers but we can become more than history teachers. Through *currere,* the possibility exists for us to become amateur transformative history makers, as it does for all educators.

REFLECTIVE QUESTIONS

1. What is currently driving the curriculum according to Kanu and Glor?
2. What do the authors see as the power of stories (narratives)?
3. What does "currere" mean to you?
4. Is self-reflection only valuable if the teacher doing it is open to change? Defend your position.
5. Have you ever undergone the process of becoming an "amateur intellectual"? What were some of the challenges and some of your "ah-ha" moments?

REFERENCES

Aronowitz, S., & Giroux, H. A. (1985). *Education under siege: The conservative, liberal, and radical debate over schooling.* South Hadley, MA: Bergin & Garvey.

Belenky M., Clinchy, B., Goldberger, N., & Tarule, J. (1986). *Women's ways of knowing: The development of self, voice, and mind.* New York: Basic Books.

Britzman, D. (1986). Myths in the making of a teacher. *Harvard Educational Review, 56,* 442–472.

Bruner, J. (1992). *Acts of meaning.* Cambridge, MA: Harvard University Press.

Bullough, R. V. (1997). *First year teacher: Eight years later.* New York: Teachers College Press.

Butt, R. (1990). Autobiographic praxis and self education. In J. Willinsky (Ed.), *The educational legacy of romanticism* (pp. 257–286). Waterloo, Ontario: Wilfrid Laurier Press.

Clandinin, J. (1987). Teachers' personal practical knowledge: What counts as "personal" is studies of the personal. *Journal of Curriculum Studies, 19*(6), 487–500.

Cole, D., & Knowles, G. (2000). *Researching teaching.* Needlan Heights, MA: Allyn and Bacon.

Connelly, M., & Clandinin, J. (1990). Stories of experience and narrative inquiry. *Educational Researcher, 19,* 174–198.

Dewey, J. (1938). *Experience and education.* New York: Macmillan.

Eisner, E. (1985). Aesthetic modes of knowing. In E. Eisner (Ed.), *Learning and teaching the ways of knowing. Eighty-fourth Yearbook of the National Society for the Study of Education* (pp. 23–36). Chicago: University of Chicago Press.

Eisner, E. (1995). Preparing teachers for schools of the 21st century. *Peabody Journal of Education, 70*(3), Spring 1995.

Gitlin, A. (1990). Educative research, voice, and school change. *Harvard Educational Review, 60,* pp. 443–466.

Greene, M. (Ed.). (2001). *Handbook of research on teaching.* Washington, DC: American Educational Research Association.

Grumet, M. (1976). Psychoanalytic foundations. In W. Pinar & M. Grumet, *Toward a poor curriculum* (pp. 31–50). Dubuque, IA: Kendall/Hunt.

Grumet, M. (1981). Restitution and reconstruction of educational experience: An autobiographical method for curriculum theory. In M. Lawn & R. Barton (Eds.), *Rethinking curriculum studies.* London: Croom Helm.

Grumet, M. (1988). *Bitter milk: Women and teaching.* Amherst, MA: University of Massachusetts Press.

Habermas, J. (2003). *The future of human nature.* London: Polity.

Hargreaves, A. (2003). *Teaching in the knowledge society: Education in the age of insecurity.* New York: Teachers College Press.

Johnston, S. (1993). Conversations with student teachers. *Teaching & Teacher Education, 10,* 215–234.

Lund, D., Panayotidis, L., Smits, H., & Towers, J. (2006). Fragmenting narratives: The ethics of narrating difference. *Journal of Canadian Association for Curriculum Studies, 4*(1), 1–23.

McDonough, K., & Feinberg, W. (2003). *Citizenship education in liberal democratic societies: Teaching for cosmopolitan values and collective identities.* Oxford, England: Oxford University Press.

McWilliams, J. (1995). Is it finding or following the path? *English Journal, 84*(2), 33–37.

Miller, J. L. (1990). *Creating spaces and finding voices: Teachers collaborating for empowerment.* Albany, NY: Teachers College Press.

Mills, C. W. (1981). *The sociological imagination.* New York: Oxford University Press.

Noddings, N. (1991). Stories in dialogue: Caring and interpersonal reasoning. In C. Witherell & N. Noddings (Eds.), *Stories lives tell: Narrative and dialogue in education.* New York: Teachers College Press.

Pajares, F. (1992). Teacher beliefs and educational research: Clearing up a messy concept. *Review of Educational Research, 62*(3), 307–332.

Paris, C., & Gespass, S. (2001). Examining the mismatch between learner-centered teaching and teacher-centered supervision. *Journal of Teacher Education, 52*(5), 398–412.

Pinar, W. (1974). Currere: Toward reconceptualization. In J. Jelinek (Ed.). *Basic problems in modern education* (pp. 147–171). Tempe, AZ: Arizona State University, College of Education.

Pinar, W., & Grumet, M. (1976). *Toward a poor curriculum.* Dubuque, IA: Kendall/Hunt.

Pinar, W. F., Reynolds, W. M., Slattery, P., & Taubman, P. M. (1995). *Understanding curriculum: An introduction to the study of historical and contemporary curriculum discourses.* New York: Peter Lang.

Ricoeur, P. (1992). *Oneself as another* (K. Blamey, Trans.). Chicago: University of Chicago Press.

Said, E. (1996). *Representations of the intellectual. The 1993 Reith Lectures.* New York: Vintage.

Sartre, J. P. (1963). *Search for a method.* New York: Knopf.

Schütz, A. (1967). *Studies in social theory: Collected papers,* Vol. 2. The Hague: Martinus Nijhoff.

Stenberg, S. (2005). *Professing and pedagogy: Learning the teaching of English.* Urbana, Ill: National Council of Teachers of English.

Zeichner, K. (1996). Designing educative practicum experiences for prospective teachers. In *Currents of reform in pre-service teacher education* (pp. 215–234). New York: Teachers College Press.

Zizek, S. (2005). Against human rights. *Newleft Review, 34*(115), 115–131.

2

What is curriculum?

KIERAN EGAN

In all human societies, children are initiated into particular modes of making sense of their experience and the world about them, and also into a set of norms, knowledge, and skills which the society requires for its continuance. In most societies most of the time, this "curriculum" of initiation is not questioned; frequently it is enshrined in myths, rituals, and immemorial practices, which have absolute authority. One symptom—or perhaps condition—of pluralism is the conflict and argument about what this curriculum of initiation should contain. Today, however, the conflicts and arguments are even more profound and undermine rational discussion of what the curriculum should contain. Much discussion in the professional field of curriculum, at present, focuses on the basic question of what curriculum is, and this suggests severe disorientation.

At a superficial level, confusion about what curriculum is, and thus what people concerned with it should do, involves argument about whether curriculum subsumes instruction—and thus whether a student of curriculum should also be a student of instructional methods—or whether curriculum involves all learning experiences, or refers simply to a blueprint for achieving restricted objectives in a school setting, or includes the statement of objectives as well, or also the evaluation of their achievement, and so on. The field seems to have no clear logical boundaries. Most accounts that try to make sense of the current state of the professional field of curriculum study describe a set of more or less distinct activities carried on in its name and then argue for a preference, or suggest a compromise or further alternative. Those who try to make sense of the present confusion by reference to the past, rarely go back beyond the emergence of the curriculum field as a profession in North America in this century.

In this brief essay, I want to take a somewhat longer perspective to see whether even a very general sketch of some relevant influences might not provide a clear picture of the present situation and offer some guidance for the future. It will be useful to begin with a brief look at the history of the word "curriculum," touching down almost randomly through the centuries to see what changes there have been in its meaning.

It is, of course, a Latin word carried directly over into English. Its first Latin meaning was "a running," "a race," "a course," with secondary meanings of a "race-course," "a career." By picking out just two of Cicero's uses of the word, we can get a sense of the direction in which it has developed. Defending Rabirius, he tossed off the neat epigram: "*Exiguum nobis vitae curriculum natura circumscripsit, immensum gloriae*" [Nature has confined our lives within a short space, but that for our glory is infinite] (*Pro Rabirio*, 10. 30). "Curriculum" is used here to refer to the temporal space in which we live; to the confines within which things may happen; to the container, as opposed to the contents. Later in his life, Cicero described his current work—he is on the seventh volume of his *Antiquities*, is collecting further historical data, revising speeches for publication, and studying law and Greek literature—"*Hae sunt exercitationes ingenii, haec curricula mentis*" [These are the spurs of my intellect, the course of my mind runs on] (*De Senectute*, 11. 38). "Curriculum" here refers, however slightly, to the things he is studying, the content. This metaphorical extension, firstly from the race-course and running to intellectual pursuits, and then from reference to the temporal constraints within which things happen to reference to the things that happen within the constraints, prefigures the general movement of the term through the ancient and modern world. The kind of questions one might ask about a race-course—How long is it? What obstacles are there?—extend easily to the kind of questions one might ask about an intellectual curriculum—How long is it? What kinds of things does it contain?

These remained the important curriculum questions throughout the medieval world. The questions for the designers of curricula may be formulated as "What should the curriculum contain?" and, following the answers to that question, "What is the best way to organize these contents?" Questions of method and instruction were taken largely as given. Lacking our ready supply of printed sources of knowledge, the most obvious source about a subject was a person who was already a master of it. The master told the novices about the subject, in lecture and argument.

Through the early modern period in England, we see little change in the use of the word. It apparently did not find its way into the vernacular until the nineteenth century. In 1643 the Munimenta of Glasgow University refer to the "*curriculum quinquae annorum*" [curriculum of five years], maintaining the ancient Latin ambiguity, in our terms, between container and contained; that is, reference is made to the contents of the curriculum in terms of its temporal constraints. The questions curriculum designers asked changed little during this period, even though the old questions gave rise to violent and polemical debates. Though the common seventeenth century opinion assumed that "all the Faculties of the Mind, both active and passive, are mightily heightened and improved by exercise" (Rymer, 1965), there were profound disagreements about *what* content should be used to exercise the Mind.

Even during this period of violent debate, questions of method were largely ignored, and questions about the organization of content were still considered unimportant. There was little change in this state of affairs over the next century. Boswell, searching around for a topic of discussion one Tuesday morning, asked Dr. Johnson what was the best thing to teach children first. Johnson replied: "There is no matter what you teach them first, any more than what leg you shall put in your breeches first. Sir, you may stand disputing which is best to put in first, but in the meantime your backside is bare. Sir, while you stand considering which of two things you should teach your child first, another boy has learnt 'em both" (Pottle, 1950, p. 323).

When brought into the English vernacular, apparently following the German lead, "curriculum" had still some way to go along the metaphorical extension from indicating the container—the period of study—to indicating the contained—the course content. In 1828, John Russell noted after his travels: "When the [German] student finishes his curriculum, [he] leaves the university" (p. 134). In a similar sense, item 39 of Glasgow University's calender for 1829 states: "The Curriculum of students who mean to take a degree in surgery [is] to be three years." By the end of the nineteenth century the word has changed very rapidly, and typical uses have lost any lingering sense of the "container," or temporal constraints, and mean simply the content. Thus, Matthew Arnold might write in *Friendship's Garland* of "the grand, old, fortifying classical curriculum."

The gradual, and relatively small, metaphorical shift in the meaning of "curriculum" over two millennia suggests stability and clarity. To deal with curriculum issues was to address the question of *what* should be taught. What has happened to disrupt this stability? Why the sudden confusion? I think we can best trace its source to the development in influence over the last two centuries of a second curriculum question: *How* should things be taught?

I will indicate briefly two examples of the early appearance of methodology questions becoming important in curriculum. The first is practical and the second more general and theoretical.

During the middle and latter part of the eighteenth century, France—like Russia a century later—combined the most advanced intellectual and social activity with a rigid and primitive political structure. One practical expression of advanced intellectual and social ideas was the school for deaf-mutes founded in Paris under the influence of Pinel. Pinel believed that deaf-mutes could be trained to communicate and become functioning members of society. He believed, too, that the insane could be cured and should be treated as patients, not kept as more or less entertaining inmates of a human zoo. Because of the nature of his subjects and task, the most important curriculum question for Pinel was not what should be taught, but how could he teach—what methods and procedures were best for educating his charges? The question of content was more or less taken as given.

The physician appointed to the new institute for deaf-mutes was the young Jean-Marc-Gaspard Itard. Shortly after he began work at the institute, Itard read about the capture of a wild boy in the woods of Aveyron. The child had apparently survived alone in the woods from his early years, could neither speak nor understand language, and seemed entirely savage. Itard arranged for the boy to be brought to the institute, and later to his own home, where he worked to civilize and educate him. The results of Itard's first six or seven years' work with the boy are contained in two reports which he wrote for the Minister of the Interior.[1] The reports attest to Itard's ingenuity in devising methods to teach the boy basic perceptions and skills. Again, his first curriculum question was *how*—*what* was taken as more or less given.

One of Itard's pupils was Edward Seguin, who formalized many of Itard's methods in developing a program for the education of the mentally handicapped. Seguin's more general success than that of either Pinel or Itard earned him the title, "Apostle of the Idiot." Seguin in turn had a profound influence on Maria Montessori, whose early work was with mentally handicapped children. The story of Montessori's adaptation of these methods for use in educating children of normal intelligence and the enormous influence of her work is familiar enough so as not to need recapitulating here.

The point of this brief overview is to indicate how concern with methodology in education moved, slowly at first and then with accumulating speed, from an interest confined to those dealing with extreme cases to the mainstream of normal schooling. One expression of the second broad influence that stimulated and supported this move may be found in the writings of Rousseau.

The first chapter of *Du Contrat Social* opens with the words: "L'homme est né libre, et partout il est dans les fers" [Man is born free, but is everywhere in chains]. Earlier than Itard, and no doubt profoundly influencing him, Rousseau expressed a new kind of optimistic view of man and man's potential. He claimed that people are basically good, and if they do not seem so most of the time, it is because of the inequities society's institutions impose on them. It is hard now to appreciate the amazing power of this idea and the romantic flood that gave it impetus through the nineteenth century.

To simplify dramatically: the belief that children are naturally good, and will naturally incline to the good if not prevented by social and institutional constraints, leads one to believe that educational methods which allow the freedom to attain this goodness will by definition be beneficial. Thus, methods and procedures became important focuses of attention for educators. Furthermore, if children will naturally choose the good given freedom of choice, then children's own interests should be allowed to decide at least some part of *what* their curriculum should contain. That is, the question of *what* became less crucial for the curriculum designer. These implications, of course, were not felt in practice overnight, but we may trace their accumulating force through the nineteenth and early twentieth century. One of their apostles in America, of course, was John Dewey. His criticisms of Montessori in *Democracy and Education* are about her rigidness in specifying activities for children and not trusting the children's ability to learn from their own "experience." The story of Dewey's caveats and qualifications being ignored in the romantic onsweep of his "progressive" followers is, again, too familiar to need retelling here.

One strand of this development needs picking up and emphasizing. The emphasis on the question *how*, as distinct from *what*, led to focusing on the individual learner as an important variable. Thus individual differences, in styles of learning, ability to learn, developmental stages, interests, socioeconomic background, and so on, had to be taken into account before one could begin to specify *what* the curriculum should contain. That is, curriculum decisions in the traditional sense required dealing initially with the range of data provided by psychological and sociological inquiries.

During this century, then, we may see the confluence of trends that have created considerable difficulties in dealing with curriculum. (Needless to say, the trends whose development are crudely sketched above have won ground only against persisting opposition from traditionalists who support the primacy of the question, *what*.)

One difficulty has developed as a result of the unusual concurrence of the professionalizing of the field of curriculum study and the remarkably rapid spread of that field across almost the full range of educational concerns. Typically, a field becomes professionalized as it becomes distinct and restricted. The traditional curriculum question about *what* should be taught can no longer stand as a distinct question in the face of discoveries about individual differences. Questions of method are unquestionably relevant to curriculum decisions. The difficulty in admitting the question, *how*, into curriculum matters is that there becomes little of educational relevance that can be excluded from the curriculum field. This means that one can do almost anything in education and claim plausibly to be working in "curriculum."

While the significance of methodological questions increased, a further influence was helping to undermine the centrality of questions about content. We have seen during this century the stumbling, (at least), and in many quarters the destruction of bourgeois confidence and optimism that was embodied in the nineteenth century revolutions—technological, aesthetic, intellectual, and political—that have affected the way people nearly everywhere on earth now live and think. We have seen what may be called a general failure of nerve, of vision, and of direction. To know what the curriculum should contain requires a sense of what the contents are for. If one lacks a clear sense of the purpose of education, then one is deprived of an essential means of specifying what the curriculum should contain. More commonly now, this problem is stated in terms of the accumulating pace of change, making decisions about a content-based curriculum meaningless. Who can specify what skills will be needed in the future? This manner of stating the problem *exemplifies* the failure of nerve: it suggests we have no control over the future; we cannot make of it what seems best to us. A typical Victorian would have had contempt for this abnegation of responsibility and opportunity.

The accumulation of the trends indicated above—a romantic view of man, the perception of the educational significance of individual differences, the failure of nerve, and the consequent desire to avoid responsibility for specifying curriculum content—is best exemplified in movements like those that fit under the umbrella title of Open Education. Children's needs or interests are held largely responsible for the selection of curriculum content. (The popular term "needs" is, of course, systematically ambiguous; it serves, however, to permit people to decide covertly what these needs are without having to take responsibility for their decisions.) Teachers are not seen as responsible for transmitting any particular knowledge; rather they are "facilitators" who may organize learning activities. Students are not to learn specific things so much as *how* to learn. At all points where the question of *what* the curriculum should contain arises, a procedural answer is given.

I mention Open Education because it seems to exemplify the completed transition from questions of content to questions of method. Someone can spend time researching and promoting Open Education and be considered to be engaged in curriculum work. That is, curriculum professionals may reject any concern with the question of *what* the curriculum should contain, except in so far as their primary concern with *how* the educational process should be organized leads to implications for content.

The problem for curriculum as a distinctive field of inquiry within education that is suggested by this rapid gallop through the centuries is that once opened up to the *how* questions it loses any comprehensible boundaries. That is, curriculum does not exist as a distinctive field of inquiry within education. Curriculum inquiry is educational inquiry; both properly address the *what* and *how* questions together and deal with all the ramifications of trying to answer, "What should children learn, in what sequence, and by what methods?"

If one considers the writings that characterize the field of curriculum, they can be read either as fitting readily under at least one of the other currently available labels within education—educational psychology, philosophy, sociology, administration, policy studies, etc.—or they are about curriculum as a field of inquiry. There is no literature that exclusively belongs to the field of curriculum except that which offers meta-level comments on the crises of, the possibility of, the appropriate activities of, the curriculum field.

This may appear a damning conclusion—that distinctively "curriculum" literature is not about the curriculum, but is navel-gazing rumination on the status of the field of curriculum. But there is another way of interpreting this conclusion, one which may help explain why curriculum as a field of inquiry seems to have been in crisis since its professionalization. There is a common view in which education is seen as an area divided among overlapping but generally distinctive sub-areas of inquiry, such as educational psychology, sociology, philosophy, curriculum, policy studies, and so on. This view is reflected in the divisions within typical schools and colleges of education.

But if "Curriculum" is coterminous with "Education," this model is wholly inappropriate, and any attempt to locate the proper area for curriculum inquiry within education is bound to produce confusion. Rather, one may characterize curriculum as a field populated by those who profess not to draw their expertise about education from some noneducational discipline.

The stronger claim may be to see "curriculum" as the field which implicitly rejects the appropriateness of importing into education methodological tools devised to inquire into different phenomena—whether psychological, philosophical, sociological, etc. These tools might provide their users with a greater sense of security and methodological rigour, but these are bought at the cost of any *educational* value of their use of the tools within education.

To use, for economy's sake, the popular sense of Kuhn's terms, we may say that working with a paradigm drawn from a particular field of inquiry can only produce knowledge of interest to that field. Educational psychology, for example, has produced much knowledge of psychological interest but little of value for education. Education, and so curriculum, may be characterized as "pre-paradigmatic." Of necessity, inquiry in these fields will lack the methodological security and rigour of inquiry in such relatively secure fields as psychology or sociology. Common sense can offer much more to education and curriculum than any rigorous methodology.[2]

What is curriculum? Curriculum is the study of any and all educational phenomena. It may draw on any external discipline for methodological help but does not allow the methodology to determine inquiry. Of necessity, it will be methodologically looser and less secure than disciplines with developed "paradigms," but this is a condition of studying education at this stage and producing knowledge that may have educational value.

A further conclusion for the practice of curriculum inquiry is that focus on either *how* or *what* at the expense of the other is improper. The present fashion that elevates *how* questions leads to disproportion and undermines good sense in talking about education. While we ponder *how* questions, another child has learned two things where our children have learned none, and our educational backside remains bare. Proportion and good sense demand that we turn our attention increasingly to *what* questions and present strong arguments for or against specific curriculum content. We have to summon the nerve to believe that we can make the future what we want and better prepare children to deal with it.

REFLECTIVE QUESTIONS

1. Does the notion of schools providing a curriculum of initiation into society ring true for you? How so?
2. In 1978, Egan suggested a "severe disorientation" regarding what curriculum is. Would you say this disorientation still exists over thirty years later?
3. What are some of the challenges that Egan sees in defining curriculum? How do you think curricular content should be determined?
4. Explain how Egan's definition of curriculum as "the study of any and all educational phenomena" has influenced/changed your thinking about how to define curriculum.
5. What kind of knowledge should be valued? How can we adequately predict what future citizens are going to need to know and be able to do?

NOTES

1. Available now as Itard (1962). The reports have been used faithfully in the making of Truffaut's moving film *The Wild Child*. See also Malson and Itard (1972) and Lane (1977).
2. For an elaboration of this argument see my book *Educational Development*.

REFERENCES

Cicero. *Oratio pro Rabirio Perduellonis Reo*, 10. 30.

Cicero. *De Senectute*, 11. 38.

Egan, K. (1979). *Educational development*. New York: Oxford University Press.

Itard, J. (1962). *The wild boy of Aveyron*. G. & M. Humphrey (Trans.). New York: Appleton-Century-Crofts.

Lane, H. (1977). *The wild boy of Aveyron*. London: Allen and Unwin.

Malson, L., & Itard, J. (1972). *Wolf-children and the problem of human nature*. New York: Monthly Review Press.

Pottle, F. (Ed.). (1950). *Boswell's London Journal 1762–1763*. New York: McGraw Hill.

Russell, J. *Tour of Germany*, i. 3. 134.

Rymer, T. (1965). *An essay concerning critical and curious learning*. Augustan Reprint Society Publication, 113. Los Angeles: University of California. (First published 1698).

3

Teaching as In-dwelling Between Two Curriculum Worlds

TED T. AOKI

Even before Day 1 of the term, our teacher, Miss O, walks into her assigned grade 5 classroom. Because Miss O is already a teacher, by her mere presence in the classroom as teacher, she initiates a transformation of a sociocultural and physical environment into something different. Even before a pupil walks in, she silently asks: "Can I establish myself here as a teacher?" and the classroom's desks, walls, chalkboards, floor, books, and resources jointly reply, albeit wordlessly, by what they are. They respond to Miss O's intention and presence. And when the pupils arrive, things and pupils arrange themselves, as it were, around Miss O's intention. They become "suitable," "teachable," "harmful," "difficult," "hopeful," "damaging." The environment ceases to be environment, and in its place comes into being a pedagogic situation, a lived situation pregnantly alive in the presence of people.

Within this situation, Miss O soon finds that her pedagogic situation is a living in tensionality—a tensionality that emerges, in part, from in-dwelling in a zone between two curriculum worlds: the worlds of curriculum-as-plan and curriculum-as-lived-experiences.

CURRICULUM-AS-PLAN

The first of these, the curriculum-as-plan, usually has its origin outside the classroom, such as the Ministry of Education or the school district office. But whatever the source, it is penetratingly and insistently present in Miss O's classroom.

This curriculum-as-plan is the curriculum which Miss O is asked to teach the grade 5 pupils who are entrusted to her care.

In curriculum-as-plan are the works of curriculum planners, usually selected teachers from the field, under the direction of some ministry official often designated as the curriculum director of a subject or a group of subjects. As works of people, inevitably, they are imbued with the planners' orientations to the world, which inevitably include their own interests and assumptions about ways of knowing and about how teachers and students are to be understood. These interests, assumptions, and approaches, usually implicit in the text of the curriculum-as-plan, frame a set of curriculum statements: statements of *intent* and *interest* (given in the language of "goals," "aims," and "objectives"), statements of what teachers and students should do (usually given in the language of *activities*), statements of official and recommended *resources* for teachers and students, and usually implicitly, statements of *evaluation* (given, if at all, in the language of ends and means).

If the planners regard teachers as essentially installers of the curriculum, implementing assumes an instrumental flavour. It becomes a process, making of teacher installers, in the fashion of plumbers who install their wares. Within this scheme of things, teachers are asked to be doers, and often they are asked to participate in implementation workshops on "how to do this and that." Teachers are "trained," and in becoming trained, they become effective in trained ways of "doing." At times, at such workshops, ignored are the teachers' own skills that emerge from the reflection upon their experiences of teaching, and more seriously, there is forgetfulness that what matters deeply in the situated world of the classroom is how the teachers' "doings" flow from who they are, their beings. That is, there is a forgetfulness that teaching is fundamentally a mode of being.

CURRICULUM-AS-LIVED-EXPERIENCES

The other curriculum world is the situated world of curriculum-as-lived that Miss O and her pupils experience. For Miss O it is a world of face-to-face living with Andrew, with his mop of red hair, who struggles hard to learn to read; with Sara, whom Miss O can count on to tackle her language assignment with aplomb; with popular Margaret, who bubbles and who is quick to offer help to others and to welcome others' help; with Tom, a frequent daydreamer, who loves to allow his thoughts to roam beyond the windows of the classroom; and some twenty others in class, each living out a story of what it is to live school life as grade 5s. Miss O's pedagogic situation is a world of students with proper names—like Andrew, Sara, Margaret, and Tom—who are, for Miss O, very human, unique beings. Miss O knows their uniqueness from having lived daily with them. And she knows that their uniqueness disappears into the shadow when they are spoken of in the prosaically abstract language of the external curriculum planners who are, in a sense, condemned to plan for faceless people, students shorn of their uniqueness or for all teachers, who become generalized entities often defined in terms of performance roles.

On one side of Miss O's desk are marked class assignments ready to be returned with some appropriate remarks of approval or disapproval—some directed to the whole class, others directed to selected pupils. And on her desk, too, sits a half written memo eventually to be delivered to the office to make sure that a film ordered three months ago will be available for the first class in the afternoon.

Living within this swirl of busyness where her personal life and her life as teacher shade into each other, Miss O struggles with mundane curriculum questions: What shall I teach tomorrow? How shall I teach? These are quotidian questions of a teacher who knows, from having experienced life with her pupils, that there are immediate concerns she must address to keep the class alive and moving.

DWELLING IN THE ZONE OF BETWEEN

In asking these questions our teacher, Miss O, knows that an abstraction that has distanced but "accountable" relevance for her exists, a formalized curriculum which has instituted legitimacy. She knows that, as an institutionalized teacher, she is accountable for what and how she teaches, but she also knows that the ministry's curriculum-as-plan assumes a fiction of sameness throughout the whole province, and that this fiction is possible only by wresting out the unique. This kind of curriculum knowing she understands, for she knows that generalized knowing is likely disembodied knowing that disavows the living presence of people, a knowing that appeals primarily to the intellectual. So she knows that this generalized knowing views a teacher like her as one of the thousands of certificated teachers in the province, and children like Andrew, Sara, Margaret, and Tom merely as grade 5 pupils, children without unique names, without freckles, without missing teeth, without their private hopes and dreams.

But she knows deeply from her caring for Tom, Andrew, Margaret, Sara, and others that they are counting on her as their teacher, that they trust her to do what she must do as their teacher to lead them out into new possibilities, that is, to educate them. She knows that whenever and wherever she can, between her markings and the lesson plannings, she must listen and be attuned to the care that calls from the very living with her own grade 5 pupils.

So in this way Miss O in-dwells between two horizons—the horizon of the curriculum-as-plan as she understands it and the horizon of the curriculum-as-lived-experiences with her pupils. Both of these call upon Miss O and make their claims on her. She is asked to give a hearing to both simultaneously. This is the tensionality within which Miss O inevitably dwells as teacher. And she knows that inevitably the quality of life lived within the tensionality depends much on the quality of the pedagogic being that she is.

Miss O knows that it is possible to regard all tensions as being negative and that so regarded, tensions are "to be got rid of." But such a regard, Miss O feels, rests on a misunderstanding that comes from forgetting that to be alive is to live in tension; that, in fact, it is the tensionality that allows good thoughts and actions to arise when properly tensioned chords are struck, and that tensionless strings are not only unable to give voice to songs, but also unable to allow a song to be sung. Miss O understands that this tensionality in her pedagogical situation is a mode of being a teacher, a mode that could be oppressive and depressive, marked by despair and hopelessness, and at other times, challenging and stimulating, evoking hopefulness for venturing forth.

At times Miss O experiences discouragement by the little concern the public seems to display for teachers' well-being—zero salary increases, colleagues' layoffs and problems of too few teachers resolved simply by increasing class size with little regard for the quality of the curriculum-as-lived-experiences. Yet even in such greyness, her blood quickens when she encounters Andrew's look, Sara's rare call for help, Margaret's smile, Tom's exuberant forgetfulness, when light that comes from contacts with children glows anew.

And Miss O knows that some people understand teaching for the second year a grade 5 class, as she is doing, is teaching the same class as last year, in the same room as last year, in the same school as last year, with the same number of pupils as last year. But Miss O knows that although technically people may talk that way, in teaching this year's grade 5 class, the seemingly same lessons are not the same, nor are the grade 5 pupils though they sit in the same desks, nor is Miss O herself for she knows she has changed from having reflected upon her teaching experiences last year with her grade 5s. She no longer is the same teacher. Miss O knows that "implementing" the curriculum-as-plan in this year's lived situation calls for a fresh interpretive work constituted in the presence of very alive, new students.

Our Miss O knows that some of her colleagues who faithfully try to reproduce the curriculum-as-plan are not mindful of the lived situation, and that in so doing, they are unaware that they are making themselves into mere technical doers. In so making, they embrace merely a technical sense of excellence matched by a sense of compliance to the curriculum-as-plan, which exists outside of themselves. They tend to forget that gaining such fidelity may be at the expense of the attunement to the aliveness of the situation.

She knows, too, that some of her colleagues who are tuned in to the pragmatics of what works in everyday school busyness—the curriculum grounded in the pragmatics of life as experienced in everyday life—may become skilful in managing the classes and resources from period to period—and survive well—keeping the students preoccupied and busy. But our teacher, Miss O, wonders whether a concern for total fidelity to an external curriculum-as-plan and a lack of simultaneous concern for the aliveness of the situation does not extinguish the understanding of teaching as "a leading out to new possibilities," to the "not yet." She wonders, too, if an over-concern for mere survival in the lived world of experiences may not cause a teacher to forget to ask the question, Survive? What for? the fundamental question of the meaning of what it is to live life, including school life. Miss O realizes the challenges and difficulties that living within a Zone of Between entails, but she learns, too, that living as a teacher in tensionality is indeed living teaching as a mode of being that with all its ever-present risks, beckons the teacher to struggle to be true to what teaching essentially is. Miss O, our teacher, knows that in-dwelling in the zone between curriculum-as-plan and curriculum-as-lived-experiences is not so much a matter of overcoming the tensionality but more a matter of dwelling aright within it.

COMMENTS

In our effort to understand the world of curriculum, we joined our teacher, Miss O, in her in-dwelling between two curriculum worlds: the world of curriculum-as-plan and the world of curriculum-as-lived-experiences. We have seen a glimmer of what it is like for a teacher to be situated in the Zone of Between. The calling into presence of two curriculum forms, even though often singularly understood—like the reading curriculum, the social studies curriculum, the music curriculum, etc.—allows us to understand more fully teachers' curriculum life. Some features of this life are sketched below.

1. We can see in Miss O's story, how truncated our understanding becomes when we see only a single curriculum-as-plan awaiting implementation. In this truncation, teachers are often technicized and transformed into mere technical implementers, and good teaching is reduced to mere technical effectiveness. The portrayal of Miss O's in-dwelling in the Zone of Between calls upon us to surmount such reductionism to seek out a more fully human understanding of who a teacher is and what teaching truly is.

2. The portrayal of Miss O's in-dwelling shows us, too, how the appeal of commonplace logic can, at times, give credibility to simplistic and mechanical understandings of pedagogic life which sees a linear movement *from* curriculum-as-plan *to* curriculum-as-lived-experiences. The story of

her in-dwelling in the Zone of Between, by revealing the naïveté of the linear understanding with its linear logic, calls upon us to take heed of understanding in-dwelling as a dialectic between complementaries with a logic of its own. For many of us, grounded in linear logic, such an understanding may seem to be a totally new way of understanding. Hence, many of us may need to open ourselves to this fundamental way in which we all experience life.

3. We also can see in Miss O's story how in-dwelling dialectically is a living in tensionality, a mode of being that knows not only that living school life means living simultaneously with limitations and with openness, but also that this openness harbours within risks and possibilities as we quest for a change from the "is" to the "not yet." This tensionality calls upon us as pedagogues to make time for meaningful striving and struggling, time for letting things be, time for question, time for singing, time for crying, time for anger, time for praying and hoping. Within this tensionality, guided by a sense of the pedagogic good, we are called upon as teachers to be alert to the possibilities of our pedagogic touch, pedagogic tact, pedagogic attunement—those subtle features about being teachers that we know, but not yet in our lexicon for we have tended to be seduced by the seemingly lofty and prosaic talk in the language of conceptual abstractions. We must recognize the flight from the meaningful and turn back again to an understanding of our own being as teachers. It is here, I feel, that teachers can contribute to fresh curriculum understandings.

4. In Miss O's in-dwelling in the Zone of Between we see the teacher's dwelling place as a sanctified clearing where the teacher and students gather—somewhat like the place before the hearth at home—an extraordinarily unique and precious place, a hopeful place, a trustful place, a careful place—essentially a human place dedicated to ventures devoted to a leading out, an authentic "e(out)/ducere(lead)," from the "is" to new possibilities yet unknown.

5. We are beginning to hear that in Canada, some architects—developers of lived space who have claimed disciplined understanding of human space, guided by their zeal for high technology—have constructed buildings (places-to-experience-life) that now are called sick buildings. We hear that the architects of these buildings were not attuned to the fundamental meaning of space-as-lived-experiences. What does this say to curriculum architects?

For curriculum planners who understand the nuances of the in-dwelling of teachers in the Zone of Between, the challenge seems clear. If, as many of us believe, the quality of curriculum-as-lived-experiences is the heart and core as to why we exist as teachers, principals, superintendents, curriculum developers, curriculum consultants, and teacher educators, curriculum planning should have as its central interest a way of contributing to the aliveness of school life as lived by teachers and students. Hence, what authorizes curriculum developers to be curriculum developers is not only their expertness in doing tasks of curriculum development, but more so a deeply conscious sensitivity to what it means to have a developer's touch, a developer's tact, a developer's attunement that acknowledges in some deep sense the uniqueness of every teaching situation. Such a sensitivity calls for humility without which they will not be able to minister to the calling of teachers who are themselves dedicated to searching out a deep sense of what it means to educate and to be educated. To raise curriculum planning from being mired in a technical view is a major challenge to curriculum developers of this day.

REFLECTIVE QUESTIONS

1. To what extent do Aoki's curriculum-as-plan versus curriculum-as-lived-experiences play out in your educational practice?
2. Is the tensionality he describes a positive notion? Provide justification for your thinking.
3. What are some of the other tensions that you and other educators encounter?
4. What kinds of things would you see in a classroom that espouses a curriculum-as-lived-experiences pedagogy?
5. "Teaching is fundamentally a mode of being." What does this mean to you? Do you agree with Aoki's statement?

4

Competing Voices for the Curriculum

KIERAN EGAN

The competing voices the title refers to are those of parents, governments, press, professional educators, the corporate world, "the public" as an entity somehow supposed to be distinct from each of the above, and others that emerge from time to time making claims on the school curriculum. These are often referred to as the "stakeholders" who, as stakeholders, are assumed to have a right of influence on the school curriculum. The state, corporate sector, and the educational community are supposed to have interests in common but also somewhat different, such that the ideal curriculum of each group would vary somewhat, though perhaps with a more or less common core. Analyses of the "rights," the claims, and the influences of the different stakeholders tend to focus on their political clout, the means they have of influencing the curriculum, their demographic make-up, the particular curriculum revisions their interests dictate, and so on.

I want to suggest that a lot of this focus is misplaced, and that it is probably not very useful if considered without analysis of the ideas held by these stakeholders. If we know about the ideas they have to think with, we can make a much more economical and effective analysis of their influence on the curriculum. Dealing with general theoretical issues may seem remote from the activities in that school down the road to practical people, and may seem remote from the pragmatic issues of power over the curriculum. I will try to show that unless we get these theoretical issues front and centre, much of our common-sense, pragmatic discussion of the struggles for the curriculum will likely be a waste of time.

I will take as my starting point J. M. Keynes' famous, or infamous, conclusion to his *General Theory of Employment, Interest and Money* (1936)—(I will change the words slightly to fit an educational rather than an economic context):

> The ideas of educational theorists, both when they are right and when they are wrong, are more powerful than is commonly understood. Indeed education is ruled by little else. Practical people, who believe themselves to be quite exempt from any intellectual influences, are usually the slaves of some defunct educational theorist. Mad people in authority, who hear voices in the air, are distilling their frenzy from some academic scribbler of a few years back. I am sure that the power of educational stakeholders is vastly exaggerated compared with the gradual encroachment of ideas. Not, indeed, immediately, but after a certain interval; for in the field of education there are not many who are influenced by new theories after they are twenty-five or thirty years of age, so the ideas which administrators and politicians and even teachers apply to current schooling are not likely to be the newest. But, soon or late, it is ideas, not "stakeholders," which are dangerous for good or ill.

To understand the struggle for the curriculum, then, one needs to have a clear idea of what ideas govern the actions of those engaged in the struggle, what the stakeholders think they are doing. And so one needs to get clear what they have to think with about issues of the curriculum, what ideas determine their actions. What follows, then, is a brief and very general attempt to get some handle on the prime determiner of the behaviour of the various educational stakeholders, the dominant ideas of education that they use. I will argue that there are only three significant educational ideas, and that we can better understand the moves of the various stakeholders by seeing that they tend to hold these three different ideas in different proportions. I will discuss these ideas briefly, putting them in the context of their initial appearances—so that we might also have some sense of whose ideas shape current struggles, of which academic scribblers are the real combatants, the real proponents in the stakeholders' mimic battles.

The three ideas are that we must shape the young to the current norms and conventions of adult society, that we must teach them the knowledge that will ensure that their thinking conforms with what is real and true about the world, and that we must encourage the development of each student's individual potential. These three ideas have rolled together over the centuries into what is our currently dominant conception of education.

I will try to show, furthermore, that not only does this analysis of ideas give us a better grasp on what is at stake in battles for the curriculum, but it also can give us a better understanding of why we have such practical problems in making schools more educationally effective institutions. Commonly, each group of stakeholders tends not only to have a particular interest in the curriculum, but also tends to blame some other stakeholder or stakeholders for the ineffectiveness of schools. (Among the various stakeholders, only professional educators will sometimes claim that schools are doing a good educational job. The various reports, task forces, commissions that have pronounced on public education in the Western world for the last half-century have been almost unanimous in their condemnations of schools.) We are told that inadequately educated teachers are to blame, or the absence of market incentives, or the inequities of capitalist societies, or the lack of local control over schools, or the genetic intellectual incapacity of 85 per cent of the population to benefit from instruction in more than basic literacy and skills, or drugs, or the breakdown of the nuclear family and family values, or an irrelevant academic curriculum, or a trivial curriculum filled only with the immediately relevant, or short-sighted politicians demanding hopelessly crude achievement tests while grossly underfunding the education system, or a lack of commitment to excellence, or vacuous schools of education, or mindless TV and other mass media, or failure to attend to some specific research results, and so on.

Along with the cacophony of blame comes a panoply of prescriptions: introduce market incentives, make the curriculum more "relevant"/academic, reform teacher-training, ensure students' active involvement in their learning, and so on. I will try to show that none of the above, nor any of the other suspects who are usually rounded up, is the cause of schools' ineffectiveness, and consequently, none of the related prescriptions is likely to make things better. Rather, our problem can be better identified by focusing on the ideas that are in conflict, and, in our current case, we may see that our problem derives from schools trying to implement a fundamentally incoherent conception of education. I will try to indicate the incoherence of the general conception of education that governs most people's ideas of what schools ought to be doing. So, I will outline the three general ideas that determine people's thinking about education today, and I will then try to show in what ways these three great ideas are mutually incompatible, and I will conclude by trying to show how this abstract theoretical discussion can help us better understand our current educational disputes and our practical educational problems.

EDUCATION'S THREE IDEAS
The First Idea: Socialization

Central to any educational scheme is initiation of the young into the knowledge, skills, values, and commitments common to the adult members of the society. Oral cultures long ago invented techniques to ensure that the young would efficiently learn and remember the social group's store of knowledge and skills and would also take on the values and emotional commitments that sustain the structure of each particular society and establish the sense of identity of its individual members.

Prominent among the techniques developed in oral cultures for socializing the young were the use of rhyme, rhythm, metre, and vivid images to help fix important lore in the minds of the young. Perhaps the most powerful technique invented, and perhaps the greatest of all social inventions, was the coding of lore into stories. This had the dual effect of making the contents more easily remembered (crucial in cultures where all knowledge had to be preserved in living memories) and also of shaping the hearers' emotional commitment to those contents at the same time. So once one could code the lore that was vital to one's society into stories, lore concerned with such things as proper kinship relations and appropriate behaviour, economic activities, property rights, class status, medical knowledge and its application, and so on, one could ensure greater cohesiveness within the social group.

Human beings have an enormous plasticity early in life to adapt to a kaleidoscopically indeterminate range of cultural forms, beliefs, and patterns of behaviour. The central task of socialization is to inculcate a restricted set of norms and beliefs—that set which constitutes the adult society the child will grow into. Societies can survive and maintain their sense of identity only if a certain degree of homogeneity is achieved in shaping its new members; and "education perpetuates and reinforces this homogeneity by fixing in the child, from the beginning, the essential similarities that collective life demands" (Durkheim, 1956, p. 70).

Whoever governs the initiation process—the storytellers or the ministry of education and the school board—acts on behalf of the norms and values that are dominant in the society at large. Their job is to perform the homogenizing task Durkheim refers to; it is a process of convergence towards particular norms and values. To put it at its simplest, socializing aims to make people more alike. If a school today in Cuba or Iran routinely graduated liberal, capitalist entrepreneurs, it would be considered a disaster. In Winnipeg, Wigan, Wabash, or Wollongong, this would not be considered so bad. Indeed, what would be considered outrageous in Iran is a deliberate aim of Wollongong schools.

The process of socialization is central to the mandate of schools today. Our schools have the duty to ensure that students graduate with an understanding of their society and of their place and possibilities within it, that they have the skills required for its perpetuation, and that they hold the values and commitments that are common to the society at large. While we might not feel comfortable with the term, we accept that a prominent aim of schools is this homogenization of children.

The spokespersons of governments, taxpayers, and businesses that require the schools to produce a skilled workforce of good citizens, echo those who learned long ago the techniques for reproducing in the young the values and beliefs, the skills and lore, that best contribute to the untroubled perpetuation of the tribe. The public voices that primarily associate education with jobs, the economy, and the production of good citizens reflect a predominantly socializing emphasis.

The very structure of modern schools in the West, with their age cohorts, class groupings, team sports, and so on, encourage conformity to modern Western social norms. Such structures can accommodate only a limited range of nonconformity. Students learn, more or less, to fit in for their own good. We need not see this process of socialization and homogenization as the dehumanizing, right wing conspiracy it was "exposed" to be by 1960s romantic radical writers on education (e.g., Goodman, 1962; Kozol, 1967; Roszak, 1969; Young, 1971). Of course, pushed to extremes—which is where the sixties and modern radicals consider the regular public school to be—the socially necessary homogenizing process can become totalitarian in its demands for conformity. But most pluralistic Western societies build defences against those who are most eager to censor children's reading or restrict their behaviour and shape their beliefs excessively.

So, the currently dominant conception of education includes as one of its main constituent ideas the socialization of the young. This constituent is evident in those voices that support curriculum time being given over to such subjects as consumer education, programs combating drug use, programs in auto maintenance, and other areas that promote useful knowledge and skills. Sometimes they may argue that schools should graduate students only when they are equipped to do a job. I have kept an old letter from an Ann Landers' column from someone who signed, sadly, as "Too Soon Old—Too Late Smart." The letter expresses frustration with schools in which "our children are subjected to 12 years of 'education' without learning how to conduct themselves in real-life situations" and suggests as a remedy that schools introduce a course on the hazards and consequences of shoplifting in the fifth or sixth grade, that several days a week be devoted to the subject of cigarette smoke, that there be instruction in the dangers of alcoholism, that sex education be a "must" in every school not later than the seventh grade, that there be courses on "life"—how to settle arguments, how to express anger and hostility, how to deal with competitive feelings involving brothers and sisters, how to live with alcoholic parents, what to do about "funny uncles" and passes made by homosexual peers. The writer concludes that of course algebra and geometry are important, but that information on how to handle one's life should take precedence.

Too Soon Old—Too Late Smart expresses very clearly how the curriculum would be changed if socializing were made more prominent in the schools'

mandate. Those who share this view see the school as primarily a social agency which should be ever-sensitive to society's changing needs, and flexible in
changing its programs to respond to those needs. Recently their voices have been
prominent in demands that schools ensure that students become familiar with
computers and their range of applications. They support counselling programs
and like to see school counsellors, working along with parents, helping students
adjust to the strains and challenges of modern society. Sports, travel, exchanges,
visits to monuments and courts and government buildings, social studies activities that help students understand their local environment, tend all to be supported as helping to socialize the young. The teacher, from the perspective of
this idea, is an important social worker, primarily valuable as a role model who
exemplifies the values, beliefs, and norms of the dominant society; knowledge
of subject matter cannot substitute for "character," wholesomeness, and easy and
open communication with students.

The Second Idea: Plato and the Truth about Reality

Plato (c. 428–347 BCE) had a new idea about how people should be educated.
He wrote *The Republic* as a kind of elaborate prospectus for his Academy. Not
conforming with the best modern advertising practice, he laid out his ideas in a
manner that involved constantly arguing the inadequacy of the forms of education offered by his competitors. Plato wanted to show that the worldly wise, the
well-socialized, practical person equipped with all the skills of a good and effective citizen was not just educationally inadequate, but actually contemptible.
The assertive and confident Thrasymachus of *The Republic* and the worldly wise
Calicles of the *Georgias* are shown to be other than the masters of affairs they
seem; they are shown to be slaves of conventional ideas because they cannot
reflect self-critically on those ideas. That ability to reflect on ideas, to pull them
this way and that until some bedrock of truth and certainty is established, was
the promised result of the curriculum described in *The Republic* and offered in
Plato's Academy. Plato certainly wanted the graduates of his school to be politically active and to change the world, but first they had to be philosophers and
understand it.

Plato's revolutionary idea was that education should not be primarily concerned with equipping students to develop the knowledge and skills best suited
to ensuring their success as citizens, sharing the norms and values of their peers.
Rather, education was to be a process of learning those forms of knowledge that
would give students a privileged, rational view of reality. Only by disciplined
study of increasingly abstract forms of knowledge could the mind transcend
the conventional beliefs, prejudices, and stereotypes of the time, and finally see

reality clearly. He proposes that the everyday world disclosed by our perceptions and conventional beliefs can somehow be better understood by a rational grasp of some transcendent world of abstract theoretic ideas, which are accessible only after decades of refined scholarly activity guided by a kind of spiritual commitment. Now this hasn't been everyone's cup of tea by any means.

But Plato succeeded in expressing his central idea with such clarity, force, vividness, and imaginative wit that everyone who has written about education in the West since has been profoundly influenced by it. It has also been a disturbing idea. Who, after all, wants to live and die a prisoner to conventional prejudices and stereotypes, frightened of reality, never seeing the world as it really is? And how can one know that one is dealing with reality rather than with illusions and stereotypes? Plato's claim that his "academic" curriculum alone can carry the mind to rationality and a secure access to reality has been so influential that we can hardly imagine a conception of education without it.

And, indeed, nearly everyone today takes it for granted that schools should attend to the intellectual cultivation of the young in ways that are not justified simply in terms of social utility. We include in the curriculum a range of subject matter that we assume will do something valuable for students' minds and give them a more realistic grasp of the world. So, we consider it important to teach them that Saturn is a planet that orbits the Sun, rather than have them believe that it is a wandering star erratically orbiting the Earth and influencing their daily fortune by its association with other stars. We teach division of fractions, algebra, drama, ancient history, and much else for which most students will never have a practical need. The place of such topics in the curriculum is usually justified in rather vague terms, variously argued by those who claim that they are of "educational value" and benefit the minds of students. In Plato's idea, the mind is what it learns, and so selecting the content of the curriculum is vital. Consequently, too, he seems reluctant to have concluded that women should be educated equally with men.

So, how is the Platonic idea of education represented today? One prominent conception can be introduced via an image suggested by the work of the astronomer, Carl Sagan. Sagan has been energetic in organizing a search for signs of extraterrestrial intelligence by means of radio telescopes. He presents a vividly romantic picture of a conversation among intelligent beings in our galaxy, which we are just now developing the technology to enter. By plugging in, we might suddenly have access to a conversation of unimaginable richness and wonder. In a more immediately possible sense, modern proponents of the Platonic idea of education suggest that accessing a transcendent conversation is precisely what education does for the individual. Michael Oakeshott (1991), for example, represents education as entry into a conversation that began long ago in the jungles and plains of Africa, gathered further voices, perspectives, and varied experience in the ancient kingdoms of the East, then additional distinctive voices and experience in ancient Greece and Rome, and so on. The conversation is now one of immense richness, wonder, and diversity. An individual can live and die happily, be socialized harmoniously in her or his special milieu, but remain almost entirely ignorant of this great cultural conversation, as we will likely do with regard to Sagan's imagined galactic interchange. But if it were really there in radio waves across the galaxy and we had the means to join it, would we not be foolish to ignore it? Would we not be culpably impoverishing our experience? The task of education, in this view, is to connect children with the great cultural conversation which very definitely is there, and which transcends any particular political society or special milieu or any particular form of local experience or conventional sets of norms and values. To pass up the chance to engage in this conversation is culpably to impoverish our experience; it is to live like Proust's dog in the library—possibly content, but ignorant of the potential riches around one.

Those who want the schools to connect children to this great cultural conversation, and to serve as bastions of civilization against the cretinizing mindlessness of pop culture (these are the kind of terms they like), who want students to be engaged by the disinterested pursuit of truth through the hard academic disciplines that will make them knowledgeable, discriminating, and skeptical, give new voice to the idea Plato bequeathed to us. These are people who value Plato's idea higher than the other two. For them, school is properly a place apart from society: a place dedicated to knowledge, skills, and activities that are of "persisting value," transcending the requirements of current social life. Indeed, what students learn is to establish the grounds from which they can judge the appropriateness of the values, norms, beliefs, and practices of society. Schools dominated by this idea consequently tend to be called elitist.

This idea leads its proponents to infer that the institutions that should give direction to the school curriculum are not those of society at large but those of higher education, particularly the university. Knowledge is valued less for its social utility and more for its presumed benefit to the mind of the student—so Latin will have a higher status than auto maintenance in such a view. "Excellence" has recently been a prominent slogan for modern neo-conservative promoters of this Platonic idea. Their outrage is directed particularly at students' ignorance of their cultural heritage (cf. the British Black Papers on Education during the 1960s and 1970s; Hirsch, 1987; Ravitch & Finn, 1987). They would like to refocus schooling on teaching an academic program and remove or downplay programs that do not serve that central purpose of the school. The curriculum would be constructed primarily on grounds of intellectual and cultural, rather than more generally social, value, and so literature and history, the sciences and mathematics will receive most curriculum time, and subjects like Latin, Greek, and art history will stake a claim to a presence in the curriculum denied them when the other ideas have been predominant. In schools dominated by this idea, the teacher will tend to occupy a more distant, authoritative and even authoritarian role because teachers properly embody the authority that comes from being an expert in the relevant subject matter.

The Third Idea: Rousseau and Nature's Guidance

Jean-Jacques Rousseau (1712–1778) thought that most of the educational practice he saw around him was disastrous. He was happy to acknowledge that Plato's *The Republic* "is the finest treatise on education ever written," but he concluded that it lacked something, and that lack was undermining its implementation. What happened when dull pedagogues took hold of Plato's idea at sixth or seventh hand was that they focused on the forms of knowledge that made up the curriculum, organized those into what seemed the best logical order, then beat them into the students. The typical result was misery, violence, and frustration, a syndrome not unknown today, though we may mark some success, influenced by Rousseau, at reducing the physical violence inflicted on children in the name of education.

Pedagogues, Rousseau (1911) observed, "are always looking for the man in the child, without considering what he is before he becomes a man" (p. 1). In *Émile*, he focused attention instead on the nature of the developing child, concentrating less on what ought to be learned and more on what children at different ages are capable of learning and on how learning might proceed most effectively. He saw his book, *Émile*, as a kind of supplement to *The Republic*, rectifying its major omission and updating the master's work. But, as we'll see, *Émile* was built on assumptions profoundly at odds with Plato's.

Rousseau's central and continuous theme was that if you want students to understand what you teach, then you must make your methods of teaching conform with the nature of students' learning: "The internal development of our faculties and organs is the education of nature. The use we learn to make of this development is the education of men" (p. 11). So, to be able to educate, we must first understand that internal development process. The most important area of educational study, then, is the nature of students' development, learning, motivation, and so on. The more we know about these, the more efficient and humane we can make the educational process. The key is the underlying natural development: "Fix your eye on nature, follow the path traced by her" (p. 14).

As nature was to be our guide, and Rousseau clearly believed the nature of males and females to be significantly different, "nature" thus dictated a quite different education for Sophie from that of Émile—an education that encouraged the "domination and violation of women" (Darling & Van de Pijpekamp, 1994, p. 115).

Émile was published in 1762, and promptly ordered to be burned in Paris and Geneva. This no doubt helped sales considerably, as it went from printing to printing. No doubt the sentimental image of the child helped the book's popularity too (Warner, 1940), even while Rousseau himself was dispatching his own unwanted children to foundling hospitals. But the rhetorical force with which *Émile* conveys its conception of the benefits that follow from attending to the nature of the student carried his ideas across Europe. In more recent times, John Dewey and Jean Piaget have been profoundly influenced by Rousseau, and the degree to which their ideas have affected practice is one index of his continuing influence.

Careful observation and study of students, recognition of the distinctive forms of learning and sense-making that characterize different ages, construction of methods of teaching that engage students' distinctive forms of learning, emphasis on individual differences among learners, observation that students learn much better when they are themselves active, and insistence that the student's own discovery is vastly more effective than the tutor's "words, words, words," are all features of Rousseau's educational scheme. While it would be false to claim him as the originator of all these ideas, he did bring them together into a powerful and coherent conception of education. These are ideas that have become a part of the "common-sense" or the taken-for-granted folklore of so many educationalists today. It would now be considered strange not to recognize the importance of students' varying learning styles, or not to recognize the value of methods of teaching that encourage students' active inquiry, or not to accommodate to the significant differences among students at different ages. Rousseau's central idea, that is to say, provides another of the main constituents of the dominant conception of education that schools today try to implement.

The modern voices that encourage schools to focus on fulfilling the individual potential of each student, that emphasize that students should "learn how to learn" as a higher priority than amassing academic knowledge, that support programs in "critical thinking," that evaluate educational success not in terms of what knowledge students have acquired so much as in terms of what they can do with what they know, reflect this third educational idea. Active, inquiring students who are enjoying learning are the ideal of schools dominated by this idea. The focus of education, in this view, is the experience of the child. The construction of a common core curriculum for all children is not simply undesirable to promoters of this idea, but impossible. Each child's experience, even of the same curriculum content, is necessarily different. We should recognize this, and let the unique experience and needs of each child be the determiner of the curriculum, even to the radical point of making the curriculum a response to the questions students raise (Postman & Weingartner, 1969). The educator's attention should be focused on the individual development of each child and on the provision of the experiences that can optimally further this development. The commonest expression of this idea today combines the variously interpreted progressivism of John Dewey (Kleibard, 1986) with Piaget's developmentalism and the psychologizing of the study of children—the modern form of discovering their "nature" that Rousseau recommended. In the classroom, and outside it, "discovery learning" is valued, manipulables and museums are recommended for students' exploration, discussion is encouraged, project work by individuals or groups is provided for. Careful attention is given to the results of empirical studies of children's learning, development, motivation, and so on, and teaching and curricula are adjusted to conform with such "research findings." The teacher, in such a school, is not an authority so much as a facilitator, a provider of the best resources, a shaper of the environment from the responses of their actions on which the students will learn.

INCOMPATIBILITIES

Are these three ideas really incompatible? Surely we can find a way of addressing these somewhat distinct aims for education without having them undermine each other? Why can we not socialize students to prevailing norms and values, while also ensuring that they accumulate the kind of knowledge that will give a truer view of the world, and also help them to fulfill the potential of each stage of development? A rigorous academic program surely does not conflict with society's needs, and facts about learning, development, and motivation surely can only help us better implement both the academic program and socialization? At least, Plato's concern with the *what* of education is surely not at war with Rousseau's concern with the *how*? Don't they properly complement each other? Looked at in sufficiently general and vague a manner, it may indeed seem that the distinctive ideas that constitute our conception of education are not as incompatible as I have been suggesting. Certainly the everyday business of schooling in Western societies has been going ahead on the assumption that evident problems are due to improper management, or poor teaching, or genetic constraints on students' abilities to learn, or flawed curriculum organization, and not to some profound theoretical incompatibility among constituents of our concept of education. But I think the incompatibility is there, and it is at the root of our practical problems. Let us consider the incompatibilities of each constituent idea with the others.

Plato and Socializing

The homogenizing aim of socialization, which is to reproduce in each student a particular set of beliefs, conventions, commitments, norms of behaviour, and values is necessarily at odds with a process that aims to show the hollowness and inadequacy of those beliefs, conventions, commitments, and so on. They are, after all, the glue that holds society's foundations in place. If Socrates was Plato's ideal example of the educated person, it is evident why the democratic citizens of Athens condemned him to death. The radical skepticism that his kind of education engendered threatened the foundations of society. He was condemned for corrupting the youth. What he was corrupting, or corroding, was their acceptance of the conventions, beliefs, values that were fundamental to the life of their society. His fellow citizens saw his behaviour as a kind of treason.

No one now believes that Plato's ideal aim of direct knowledge of the real, the true, the good, and the beautiful is attainable. What is attainable, though, is the skeptical, philosophical, informed mind that energetically inquires into the nature and meaning of things, that is unsatisfied by conventional answers, that repudiates belief in whatever cannot be adequately supported by good arguments or evidence, and that embodies the good-humoured corrosive of Socratic irony. This kind of consciousness has not often been greatly valued by those who govern societies; it is a disruptive force. Everyday social life, particularly in complex modern economic systems, proceeds more smoothly and blandly without the irritant created by following Plato's educational prescription too closely. If people are busy asking "but is this really the best way to live?" all the time, they simply can't get on with everyday business with single-minded efficiency.

Of course we want the promised benefits of both educational ideas. We want the social harmony and the psychological stability that successful socialization encourages, but we also want the cultivation of the mind, the skepticism, and dedication to rationality that Plato's program encourages. Designing schools to achieve either one is difficult. Our schools today are supposed to encourage conformity to specific norms and values while encouraging skepticisms of them at the same time.

Rousseau and Plato

But if we see Plato as dealing with the *what* of education and Rousseau with the *how*, then we need not consider them incompatible. This common resolution of apparent conflicts would be fine were it not the case that it falsely represents both ideas. The above compromise, leaving Plato's descendants with the content and aims of education and Rousseau's with the methods, appeals to many as a neat division of labour. So the educational philosophers can deal with content and aims, drawing on the knowledge generated by the educational psychologists about learning and development. It seems so obvious that facts about students' development can blend with philosophers' research into the nature and structure of knowledge to yield a more easily understood math or history curriculum. It seems so obvious that such collaboration should be so common that one would expect the absence of it to compel reassessment of what looks, but clearly isn't, obvious.

One problem for the neat compromise is that, in the Rousseauian and Deweyan view, the means and ends of education are tied together. They argue that distinct means cannot be employed in education to achieve distinct ends. The means used in Rousseauian and Deweyan instruction are *parts* of their educational ends. They favour discovery procedures, for example, not because they are more efficient means to some distinct educational ends, but because they are a component of their educational ends. Discovery procedures, in Rousseau's terms, disclose nature and in so doing stimulate the development of a pure, uninfected reason. In Dewey's terms, discovery procedures mirror the scientific method whose acquisition by students is a crucial component of their education. We have incorporated this idea into our currently dominant conception of education. Put crudely, we recognize the inappropriateness of beating children who have failed to memorize the text on compassion; we feel a bit uncomfortable about compelling attendance at institutions that try to teach the values of liberty and democracy; and it is increasingly clear that choice of method of teaching is not a simple strategic matter disconnected from our educational ends. In our educational means are our ends; in our educational ends are our means.

A further problem may be seen by observing that Plato and his descendants have their own conception of educational development. Students progress, in Plato's scheme, from the stages of *eikasia*, to *pistis*, to *dianoia*, to *noesis*. But these stages are interestingly different from Rousseau's and from Piaget's. Plato's stages represent greater clarity in understanding. Education, in Plato's view and in that of modern proponents of the academic idea, is marked by students' progress through stages of mastery of increasingly sophisticated knowledge—regardless of how they may be progressing through some putative psychological developmental stages. For Rousseau, and Piaget, it is precisely the psychological developmental stages that mark education, and that must determine what kind of knowledge the student needs; as the development of the body proceeds almost regardless of the particular food it eats, so the mind will develop almost regardless of the particular knowledge it learns. For the Platonists, the only development of educational interest is the accumulation of the particular knowledge learned; the mind is nothing much else.

So Rousseau and his modern followers are not simply making methodological or procedural recommendations, which might allow us to do the Platonic academic job more efficiently. They are actually recommending a different job. Rousseau's idea is not one that yields us an easy accommodation with Plato's. These ideas conflict—most profoundly in identifying the cause and dynamic of the educational process. In the Platonic idea, learning particular forms of knowledge carries the educational process forward; in the Rousseauian idea, education results from an internal, developmental process unfolding within a supportive environment. In the Platonic view, knowledge drives development; in the Rousseauian view, development drives knowledge; it determines what knowledge is learnable, meaningful, and relevant. In the Platonic view, education is a time-related, epistemological process; in the Rousseauian view, it is an age-related, psychological process.

We could design schools to implement either of these conceptions of education, but we require our schools to implement both together. Our practical difficulties arise from our acceptance that both the Platonic and the Rousseauian ideas are necessary for education, but the more we try to implement one, the more we undermine the other.

The conflict between these two ideas has been the basis of the continuing struggles between "traditionalists" and "progressivists" during this century. One sees them at odds in almost every media account of educational issues, where the Platonic forces argue for "basics" and a solid academic curriculum, and the Rousseauians argue for "relevance" and space for students' exploration and discovery. A key battleground as I write this is the elementary social studies curriculum in North America; the "traditionalist" forces are pressuring for a revision that will reintroduce history and geography in place of the "progressivists'" preferred "relevant" focus on families, neighbourhoods, communities, interactions among communities, and so on; the "progressivist" forces argue that history and geography require abstract concepts and are not "developmentally appropriate" for young children and the "traditionalists" argue that any content can be made comprehensible if presented sensibly.

Socializing and Rousseau

When socializing, we derive our educational aim from society's norms and values; in the Rousseauian view, we should keep the child from contact with society's norms and values as long as possible, because they are "one mass of folly and contradiction" (Rousseau, 1911, p. 46). If we want to let the nature of the child develop and flower as fully as possible, we will constantly defend her or him against the shaping pressures of society. An aspect of this conflict is apparent today in many educators' attitudes to the general influence of TV on children. TV provides a powerful shaping to a set of prominent social norms and values, but educators resist much of this shaping in favour of activities that seem to them less likely to distort proper or "natural" development. "Natural" is not, of course, the term much used today, but it lurks around the various ways the Rousseauian position is restated, as in a number of books that appeal to a conception of a more natural kind of childhood which is being distorted or suppressed by current forms of socialization (e.g., Elkind, 1981; Postman, 1982). Some of the 1960s radicals were even plainer—Paul Goodman put it this way:

> The purpose of elementary pedagogy, through age twelve, should be to delay socialization, to protect children's free growth. . . . We must drastically cut back formal schooling because the present extended tutelage is against nature and arrests growth. (1970, p. 86)

No one, of course, is simply on the side of Rousseau against socialization, or vice versa. We all recognize that any developmental process has to take place within, and be influenced by, a particular society. Our problem comes about because of the attraction of Rousseau's ideas about a kind of development that honours something within, something uninfected by the compromises, by the corruptions and constrictions, that social life so commonly brings with it. We do not have to share Rousseau's own disgust with society (which returned him high regard and money) to recognize the attraction of his ideas. This Rousseauian idea of development entails the belief that the most important shaping of the individual must come from a natural, spontaneous, internal process, and proper education requires that all influences from society either conform with that process or be held at bay.

There doesn't seem room for much compromise here. We can't sensibly aim to shape a child's development half from nature and half from society. That creates the same problems as half punishing and half rehabilitating a prisoner. Such treatments interfere with one another. The more we do one, the more we undermine the other. By trying to compromise, we ensure only that neither is effective.

The incompatibility seems to me inevitable so long as people conceive of children as going through some regular, spontaneous process of intellectual development which can be optimized by shaping their learning environment to suit it. One cannot derive one's educational principles both from some conception of an ideal developmental process and also from some current norms and values of adult society; they are bound to be incompatible unless one lives in a perfect society. They are incompatible because socializing has a distinct end in view and

is a shaping, homogenizing, narrowing process towards that end, whereas supporting the fullest development of students' potentials involves releasing them
to explore and discover their uniqueness; it is an individualizing process that
encourages distinctiveness even to the point of eccentricity if necessary, and is
expansive without predetermined ends.

We see this conflict constantly between those who want our schools to ensure
that students have particular skills and hold particular beliefs and live according
to particular values and those who resist such shaping in the name of encouraging each student to explore and discover their individual talents, and form
their own beliefs and values. Most people, of course, want both, in some degree,
and see no incompatibility in this. It is the failure to recognize the fundamental
incompatibility, I am arguing, that leads most people to support an educational
system dedicated to achieving the impossible.

CONCLUSION

As I noted above, nobody holds to one of these ideas exclusively. The different
positions of education's stakeholders can be seen in the different degrees with
which they hold the three ideas. Also the fact that they all hold the three mutually incompatible ideas in whatever degrees ensures that their related prescriptions for improving education are likely to be unsuccessful.

We could characterize the positions of the various stakeholders in terms of
the three ideas. So, in general, corporate stakeholders want lots of socialization,
basic Plato (but not enough for systematic skepticism), and cautious dribbles of
Rousseau. Professional educators today, tend to want lots of Rousseau and a fair bit
of Plato with judicious amounts of socialization. Parents want lots of everything.
Upper-class conservatives tend to support lots of Plato, lots of socialization, with
small amounts of Rousseau, whereas radicals want lots of Rousseau, a fair amount
of socialization, with a little Plato. Well, this is at one level silly, but could be elaborated in ways that would more clearly establish the ways in which the major positions we see in the press or in policy documents simply reflect different amounts
of these three ideas. Most familiar is the Plato/Rousseau battle which has been
prominent during this century in terms of traditional versus progressive stances.

So what is the point of this kind of exercise? We are left with the problems
we started with, only seeing them in more abstract, theoretical terms. Well, this
is the point of ivory towers, in which one can abstract oneself from the details of
the particular battles that are going on among, in this case, education's stakeholders and try to see in a more fundamental sense what they are about. If we leave
it like this, of course, the exercise is futile. The point about understanding the
world is that it better enables us to change it. The problem with not understanding it adequately is that one's suggested solutions to problems will themselves

be inadequate, and often cause even worse problems. This seems to me the case for the panoply of recommendations for educational change that are touched on in the Introduction above. Our problem is that we have three profound and important ideas, which are all indispensable, but which are also in significant ways incompatible. The solution will have to start from resolving this theoretical incompatibility. Proposals that fail to do this will be futile.

So, I am suggesting, the regular exercises in curriculum reform that keep busy most employees of ministries of education across the country are largely futile. As long as the reformers are governed by the set of ideas sketched above, they will only contribute to the confusion. The hard-nosed, practical activitists no less than the soft-nosed, impractical idealists, and those in between, are, as Keynes pointed out, simply captives of old or watered-down versions of the above ideas, and their positions and prescriptions are entirely predictable once one can see the degrees in which they hold the three ideas. The huge industry of educational research seems similarly futile to the degree that it fails to deal with the fundamental confusion at the heart of education. Nearly all educationalists turn away from the obvious confusion and its distressing practical implications, and spend their professional lives on what are basically avoidance activities. Sooner or later, whether we like it or not, it is these ideas which have to be dealt with. To ignore them, to shrug them off, to leave it to others, to avoid them in whatever manner, is to make a pact with futility.

REFLECTIVE QUESTIONS

1. Who are the "competing voices" or stakeholders that Egan identifies as "making claims on the school curriculum" and how does he see these stakeholders influencing curriculum?
2. Is Egan missing any important stakeholders, for example, should the students be considered as stakeholders?
3. In this reading, what are the factors that are blamed for problems in education? Are there others in your opinion?
4. What does Egan argue are the three dominant ideas that the stakeholders use to argue their case for curriculum change? Do you agree with Egan? Support your answer.
5. Do you agree that one of the primary purposes of schooling is to socialize "the young into the knowledge, skills, values, and commitments common to the adult members of society?" What might such a curriculum include?
6. How important to the education of our students are "learning those forms of knowledge that would give students a privileged, rational view of reality"? What aspects of the current curriculum in schools would address this goal?

REFERENCES

Darling, J., & Van de Pijpekamp, M. (1994). Rousseau on the education, domination and violation of women. *British Journal of Educational Studies*, XXXXII(2), 115–132.

Durkheim, E. (1956). *Education and sociology.* S. D. Fox (Trans.). New York: Free Press.

Elkind, D. (1981). *Child development and education: A Piagetian perspective.* New York: Oxford University Press.

Goodman, P. (1962). *Compulsory miseducation and the community of scholars.* New York: Vintage.

Goodman, P. (1970). *New reformation.* New York: Random House.

Hirsch, E. D. (1987). *Cultural literacy.* Boston: Houghton-Mifflin.

Keynes, J. M. (1936). *General theory of employment, interest and money.* London: Macmillan.

Kleibard, H. M. (1986). *The struggle for the American curriculum: 1893–1958.* Boston: Routledge and Kegan Paul.

Kozol, J. (1967). *Death at an early age.* Boston: Houghton-Mifflin.

Oakeshott, M. (1991). *The voice of liberal learning: Michael Oakeshott on education.* T. Fuller (Ed.). New Haven: Yale University Press.

Plato. (1941). *The republic.* F. M. Cornford (Ed. & Trans.). London: Oxford University Press.

Postman, N. (1982). *The disappearance of childhood.* New York: Delacorte Press.

Postman, N., & Weingartner, C. (1969). *Teaching as a subversive activity.* New York: Delacorte.

Ravitch, D., & Finn, C. E. (1987). *What do our 17-year-olds know?* New York: Harper and Row.

Roszak, T. (1969). *The making of a counter-culture.* New York: Doubleday.

Rousseau, J.-J. (1911). *Émile.* B. Foxley (Trans.). London: Dent. (First published 1762.).

Warner. (1940). The basis of J.-J. Rousseau's contemporaneous reputation in England. *Modern Language Notes*, LV, 270–278.

Young, M. (1971). *Knowledge and control: New directions for the sociology of education.* London: Collier-Macmillan.

5

When Curriculum Becomes a Stranger

KARYN COOPER

CHILDHOOD IN A KIT

I begin with a true story.

I was walking to campus for an early morning meeting. New flowers punctuated nearly every yard. Rich hues of yellow, orange, and red splattered playfully across the soft ground, replacing winter's seemingly impenetrable cover of snow. I felt the soft spring breeze sweep across my face, gently, like a mother's hand brushing sleep from her child's eyes.

The voice of a small child interrupted my thoughts. "What's a stranger?" She was so close to me that I had to wonder just how she got there. And indeed, how had I managed not to mow her down like some weed in the crack of the sidewalk? That look, her question, and the ease with which she slipped her hand in mine as she tried to get me to walk her to school linger still.

This little girl's question is an intriguing one. Perhaps this question resulted from a confusion about either her school experience or her lived experience, or a dissonance between the two. Through speaking further with her, I gathered she might have been confused by the way the concept "stranger" had been presented to her at school. Clearly, she was concerned about the concept of "stranger," not about the issue of her own personal safety. I wondered whether she had been introduced to the concept of "stranger" through a curriculum kit at school. If so, I could perhaps understand her confusion.

As a teacher, I was once obliged to attend a workshop on the use of such a kit. While the concept of "stranger" is a complex one, kits such as the one that was the focus of the workshop did little to address the complexity in any comprehensive way. Like many of my colleagues, I chose not to use it. Instead, I tried to integrate concepts such as the one of stranger into a curriculum built out of the children's experience of their everyday lives. This teacher practice is not always appreciated or endorsed by those who mandate school curricula. Many of us have grown up with the notion that we can reason our way out of the problems of life and devices such as kits offer us the assurance that this is so. Workshops on effective teaching and assertive discipline are examples of the "rational" approach to teaching.

"Kits" are simply prepackaged curriculum materials that are in common usage across the curriculum in many countries. These kits may deal with a wide variety of topics such as historical events, subject-related genres such as poetry or novel studies, or sensitive issues like sexual abuse or safety concerns regarding not talking to strangers. Every attempt is made to make these products "teacher proof" by providing step-by-step instructions and, in some cases, even teacher scripts. As such, these kits serve as a convenient method of teaching children efficiently, although not necessarily effectively because the voices of students are seldom present in these conveniently standardized units of instruction. Overworked teachers who may be bereft of new and creative ideas find these prepackaged curriculum aids a valuable resource. The use of kits is not necessarily a harmful practice. Indeed, often the intentions behind them are good. Kits may help children understand and label their experience. However, the little girl's question made me wonder if such technical and generalized approaches to issues thought to affect children really do help them and their teachers make sense of the complexity of the life world in which they are already embedded.

At best, kits are merely surface outlines of the complex reality we experience, much the way a water beetle appears on the surface of a pond, seemingly unaware of the watery realms beneath its legs. The use of kits may be symptomatic of a larger problem within the "traditional" curriculum of Western schooling, as well as schooling in other parts of the world. Devices such as kits and other "teacher-proof" curriculum materials exemplify the way curricula mandated by the state have been traditionally used to control what is taught, how it is taught, and to whom it is taught—that is, the oppressive reinforcement of the conceptualization of childhood—and to implement social policies. In this scheme, teachers often become the handmaidens of the state, sometimes though not always, unwittingly implementing social policies that may undermine the possibility for critical thinking in our schools and ultimately provide for the oppression of children in the

Western world and beyond. Other scholars in the field of curriculum studies, for example McLaren (1989), suggest that in schools and teacher education programs:

> . . . an undue emphasis is placed on training teachers to be managers and implementers of preordained content, and on methods courses that rarely provide students with opportunity to analyze the ideological assumptions and underlying interests that structure the way teaching is taught. (p. 2)

Other scholars such as Clandinin and Connelly (1995) have shown us, specifically through teacher stories, that many teachers feel repressed, and often oppressed, by policies which come down "the conduit." The work of Clandinin and Connelly focuses, although not exclusively, on oppressive social policies which affect teachers. However, social policies that affect children, specifically as they are implemented through specialized institutions such as schools, are still relatively in unchartered terrain. As Smith (1991) says:

> . . . how it is that in spite of enormous public expenditure on formal educational programs for children and good rhetoric speaking on children's behalf, in actuality children are the most frequently abused and neglected of all the world's citizens, in countries like the United States and Canada as well as in the Third World. (p. 188)

The ways in which the state implements constraining social policy through curricula is particularly important if one is interested in how children everywhere have been oppressed. In the case of the little girl who asked me about strangers, the oppression is covert, not overt. Lessons in fearing strangers subdue her previous inclination to trust everyone, which she shows by the way she slips her hand into mine. The kit, as a quick device, derogates the child's understanding of the world as a friendly place. Curricula are community designs for a social order which the state produces to shape its citizens. Designs are structures which unfortunately can utilize kits—prepackaged curriculum materials—to that end.

Facing the little girl on the sidewalk that morning, I found myself uncomfortably reliving the dilemma with which I had often struggled as a teacher, that is, the dilemma surrounding the transmission of cultural attitudes and values. While this dilemma is visited on a more or less continual basis the world over, I pondered how I should behave towards the little girl so that I might not undermine what her teacher and parents had already told her and, at the same time, not betray my own beliefs about the questionable practice of identifying strangers as givers of harm. I knew that it is not usually strangers who harm children but those who are often closest to them: their parents, their extended family, or their family's friends.

Superficially, a kit such as the one about strangers may appear beneficial for children in our schools. Yet what is being transmitted through the use of such a kit and to what purpose? Ostensibly, the purpose of the kit is to prevent harm delivered by strangers. It functions, however, to also deflect attention from the harm done by parents, family, and paid attendants. And it does so because, in mainstream Canadian society, parenthood and parenting are deemed sacrosanct. Honour thy father and mother, the Bible says. "This refusal to acknowledge the consequences of former harm and injury to the child permeates our society and is reinforced by religious teachings. For thousands of years, all religious institutions have exhorted the faithful to respect their parents" (Miller, 1990, p. 32).

Hendrick (1994) points out, "First, the history of children and childhood, is inescapably inseparable from the history of social policy" (p. xii). The general effect of social policies has been to create a perception of children as predominantly ignorant, dependent, vulnerable, untutored, and very often threatening (p. xii). A closer look at the work of Hendrick (1994) allows us to explore ideas about the social construction of childhood. His deeply caring and compassionate work on the history of children, child welfare, and the social construction of childhood in England has resonance in Canada because many of our ideas and our institutions have been imported from, and modelled on, the British system.

The concept of childhood as a separate state comes late in history. The Industrial Revolution in nineteenth-century England as Hendrick (1994) and Aries (1972) point out, indicates that childhood as a distinct stage in the human life cycle did not exist. With industrialization, the custom of informally educating the young at home and through the local community gave way to the formal education of schools. The state now became an active participant in the education of children. Childhood was socially constructed to meet the needs and demands of industrialization. Hendrick remarks:

> . . . the making of childhood into a very specific kind of age-graded and age-related condition went through several stages, involving several different processes. Each new construction, one often overlapping with the other, has been described here in the appropriate chronological order as: the natural child, the Romantic child, the evangelical child, the factory child, the delinquent child, the schooled child and the psycho-medical child . . . the introduction and gradual consolidation of compulsory schooling confirmed the trend towards the creation of the innocence. This understanding of the "nature" of childhood was then subjected to scientific scrutiny and elaborated upon through further description and explanation by the Child Study movement. (Hendrick, 1994, p. 37)

Like textbooks and readers that came before, contemporary curricular devices such as kits are developed with a certain view of "the child" and childhood. However, many kits go beyond mere literacy and the acquisition of special skills by implementing various social policies which focus on issues affecting children's well-being—child welfare, child abuse, and health practices. So what is the problem with this?

Nineteenth- and twentieth-century reformers have campaigned for policies which ensure that children are protected. But, as Hendrick (1994) reminds us, certain features of policies that purport to protect children have also been historically responsible for doing them harm. Hendrick gives examples such as the "Edwardian concern with 'national efficiency,' and the perennial interest in social discipline, the stability of the family, and an appropriately educated labour force" (p. xiii). The concern with social discipline, for example, has sometimes meant that children are censured, ridiculed, or otherwise punished because they are children. Schooling today may not always be so distant from such Edwardian objectives. Barbara, an undergraduate student in a pre-service language learning class I teach, recently wrote this story. Her story is reminiscent of the Victorian or Edwardian notions of childhood we read about in novels such as *David Copperfield*. Barbara entitled her story of schooling, "A Blue Bird."

Our classroom was a perfect square with one doorway and two windows.

Desks were arranged in straight lines, five desks across and six down. They were assigned to us on the first day of class. You did not change places! We had rules in our school.

We had dress codes. Girls wore dresses, boys slacks and long sleeved shirts. No T-shirts, shorts or runners were allowed.

The teachers followed code, too. They wore only dark colours—black, brown, navy blue—with no accent and no pretty jewellery.

We followed a schedule. At 8:45 the bell rang and we ran to line up to enter school. At 8:50 we were allowed in if our lines were straight, one for boys and one for girls. By 8:55 we would be seated. At nine o'clock sharp, our door closed.

Once settled, we were instructed to stand for morning prayer, then seated. At 9:10 the morning announcements, made by the principal, would be heard throughout the school on the PA system. Classes would soon begin, each one lasting 30 minutes. Subjects taught were Arithmetic, Language Arts, Spelling, Religion, Social Studies, Health, Science, French, and Physical Education. At 10:15 we had recess for 15 minutes that included lineup time to enter the school.

Expectations in class were easy. Sit up straight, keep your head facing front. Fold your hands together on top of your desk, visible. Feet held apart and square under your desk. If you had a question your arm was raised straight above your head, held high, then you waited, until you were acknowledged and spoken to. You were not to leave your desk for any reasons.

The teacher lectured in front of our class. Sometimes she would walk up and down the aisles to see how work was progressing. We always had lots of exercises to complete. If you were slow, you stayed after school to complete class work.

Any disruption to the class due to talking out of turn, not answering properly, or getting out of your desk would find you in trouble. Usually students were sent to the corners to face the wall. Some students became permanent fixtures with their desks moved up against the chalkboard. A student rarely dared to turn their head once seated there.

The occasion when I was bad in class still remains with me. My punishment was innovative. To kneel in a praying position on the heat register located at the back of the class. The register was about 36 inches high and about the same in length. Another boy shared in the punishment. We climbed up, not knowing. We positioned our knees on the grate and prayed. After a while, we squirmed. Noticing that I had moved slightly off the grill, the teacher made me redo the punishment over recess. I had difficulty not moving so I again tried over part of the lunch hour. I had ample time to reflect.

Of course, not everyone had these types of experiences in class. Red birds were too smart to get into trouble. Blue birds only occasionally. Yellow birds were the real bad ones.

Heywood (1988), another historian, supports Hendrick's view that policies for children were not necessarily made with the children's best interests at heart. For example, when industrialists in the middle of the nineteenth century began paying cash incentives for high production, children could not participate because they lacked the stamina to keep up with production by machines. Because of their lower output, child workers ceased to be considered economically useful. They became superfluous. Industry needed a place to "park" children until they were old enough to be workers. Public schools were the answer. In Heywood's analysis, the mandate of the schools was to keep the children off the streets in order to train them to be good workers, but not to think for themselves.

Peikoff and Brickey (1991) state that from the mid-nineteenth to the early twentieth century in Canada, it was a time in which social reformers, as in England, devoted more energy to caring for children than in any other period. However, they demonstrate that policy initiatives directed to child labour and compulsory education did not emerge because of enlightened attitudes towards children. Rather, the consequences of the emergence of industrial capitalism was largely responsible for the ideological change that transformed children from little adults into precious creatures in need of special attention and care. Heywood (1988) also argues that economic factors underlie the development of public schools as a better place for working class children. He says that "from the *instituteurs*, the industrial lobby hoped, they [children] would acquire a basic instruction in the three R's, and, most importantly, learn the discipline and values that would make them 'good workers' " (p. 322).

The study of the history of childhood is the story of how adults have viewed and treated children. De Mause, a psycho-historian, states that "the history of childhood is a nightmare from which we have just begun to awaken" (1975, p. 85). De Mause claims that the further we look back in history the worse the treatment of children becomes. Aries (1972) and Sommerville (1990) have painted varying pictures of how people in the past have treated children: from under-protection to over-protection; from being little adults to being virtually a different species; from being innately evil to being paragons of innocence.

In North America, as in other parts of the world, humanity seems to hold to a rather innocent, but perhaps erroneous, belief that going forward in time means going forward in social improvement, yet most historians agree that throughout history children have been abused and neglected. As long as we only deal superficially with the way children are treated in our society, the nightmare will continue. Perhaps as the little girl's question that began this chapter suggests, learning to be made strangers to ourselves and each other is the biggest part of the nightmare.

Reflecting on the little girl's question and curricular directions available through kits led me to consider what it is really like to be a child living in our Western culture, or in any culture. One is inevitably concerned over the messages children receive about being children and becoming adults, about the way messages presume differences between child and adult which make us forget that identity continuously unfolds throughout our lifetime. Orwell (1953) points out:

> ... the child lives in a sort of alien under-water world which we can only penetrate by memory or divination. Our chief clue is the fact that we were once children ourselves, and many people appear to forget the atmosphere of their own childhood almost entirely. (p. 59)

Becoming an adult in this culture may mean becoming estranged from one's own childhood, and the curriculum we learn at school often reinforces and perpetuates the estrangement. The little girl I met reveals the essence of this separation.

THE CHILD REMEMBERED

How wonderful and yet strange it is to be a child. To find oneself as a child in a marvellous world that is without history, a world ripe with potential. One's task as a child is to make sense of a pre-given world and to make sense of its established social patterns, culture, and traditions. The world gives one no status except as being an infant member of a social group. It gives no power except that which is given to the child by adults. As Schütz suggests:

> Any member born or reared within the group accepts the ready-made standardized scheme of the cultural pattern handed down to him by ancestors, teachers, and authorities as an unquestioned and unquestionable guide in all situations which normally occur within the social world. (Schütz, 1971, p. 95)

While I largely agree with Schütz, I wonder whether a new member of a group always accepts without question the pre-given cultural patterns.

A story of an experience from Cara, a graduate student, exemplifies both a child's lack of status and power, her acquiescence to cultural patterns, and her need to make sense of situations that unfold about her.

> My grandfather stood before me, his rail-like frame almost grazing the full height of the room. His cool clear eyes turning to ice, focused with laser-like sharpness, no longer on my mother, but on me. "Honestly, Emma, where are her manners!" His question seemed to hover above me, suspended in air on a fragile thread.
>
> My mother's eyes avoided my gaze. Instantly, I knew that she would not be defending me. And in that moment, she looked awkward, quiet, miniscule; her eyes veiled in a shroud of complacency. Only moments before, I had felt so invincible, so full of life itself, and this vitality had carried me forward as I burst into that room. I, the room-buster, child of five, had forgotten my manners. And with eyes much too wide, and tongue wagging tales to tell, had broken grandfather's golden rules:
>
> • Silence is golden.
> • Children should be seen and not heard.
> • Do not interrupt adults who are in conversation.
>
> In enthusiasm over the little creature I had just seen outside, I had forgotten the rules, as sometimes I was wont to do. My grandfather' s tongue was like a whip: Did I know I was a rude child? Rude to interrupt grown-ups when they are speaking? Rude to butt in without being announced? Rude because I should know better?

RUDE, RUDE, RUDE

Well, what did I have to say for myself, my grandfather bellowed? I stammered: "I"—"I"; in a short space of time I had lost my I. Then my anger seemed to reclaim it, and I felt myself becoming real again. With red face and defiant eyes and all the strength in me I returned that ice blue glare. My words tumbled out of me: "Maybe I was rude, but it's still not fair for you to yell at me," I retorted. "Little people have feelings too."

A long silence ensued. Those freshly spoken words sat on me like paste, following me like a snail' s trail as I slowly made my way out to the car. I glanced back, hoping, thinking, wishing, that someone would follow me.

I wondered what would happen next, for I knew I had broken yet another golden rule; I had lost my temper. I felt sad, yet somehow big—full of the truth I knew I had spoken only moments before. Finally my mother appeared. I pretended not to notice her as she hurried down the path towards the car. Perhaps she noted my indifference, perhaps not. She framed her words rather carefully, explaining that all would be fine again provided I apologized to my grandfather immediately. I looked at her briefly and then with my index finger I began to focus on creating different patterns with the little dots that suddenly became noticeable in the upholstered ceiling just above me. (A child remembers.)

This story calls into being what it feels like to be little, full of curiosity and wonder, but running amok of what seems to be the inexplicable rules adults have made to govern behaviour. What we learn about ourselves, others, and our proper place in the scheme of things is not evidently always good for us. As a small child, not only could Cara not interrupt her grandfather and her mother, but she could not question them in an overt way. And so in school, children learn not to question the teacher. Britzman (2000), Fine (1987), and Gardner (1991) are but three who remind us that school is often a place where serious conversation or questions are deemed inappropriate.

That chance meeting with the little girl on the sidewalk brought me back to the story of my own childhood, to its loneliness and pain, and then it made me think how our school curricula embody and promote oppressive developmental ideals (Lyle, 2000).

Children often wrestle with profundity. I remembered that as a young child I struggled with the meaning of, and significance in, Remembrance Day. There seemed to be so much sadness and quiet just before that day and on that day. I really did not know the reason for the veil of silence: it was a mystery. Now, as teacher, teacher-educator, and parent I think about how school reinforces this mystery.

At school we coloured poppies. I remember one of my classmates getting into trouble because he coloured his poppy yellow and not red. It really was not until much later that the symbolism of the red poppy was made clear to me, after I finally summoned up the courage to ask my father. He told me a beautiful story about a young man who was a soldier and a poet. Because he was a poet, he could put into words the sadness of war and the great human suffering that everyone feels no matter which country eventually wins the war. My father said that each poppy represents the blood of someone killed in the war, be they father, son, or brother in someone's family, somewhere around the world.

Suddenly I understood the reason for the great silence that blanketed the Legion Hall every year and I also understood why I had been called a disrespectful child because I had drawn a happy face on one of those felt poppies handed out at school. Looking back, I now realize that my father had a different perspective to the dominant sacred story of war. He saw its suffering, not its glory. He also had a different perspective on life, particularly the importance of story as embodied knowledge.

As a child, I often felt like a prop in a play someone else (the teacher) had written. A five-year-old whom I recently met had a similar experience of school. She was telling her younger sister what school is all about: "Well, you sit on the rug. You colour at your desk and then you sit on the rug and sometimes there are stories and you sit on the rug for stories." When her little sister asked, "Why do you sit on the rug?" the older child replied, "Silly, you just sit on the rug." The younger child, perhaps thinking this unusual, said: "Is it a magic rug?" "No," replied the other, "It is just a rug for kids to sit on. Big people like teachers and stuff sit on chairs."

The five-year-old girl had to engage in an activity—sitting on the rug—that she made sense of in the best way she could. Sometimes, however, school children are forced to engage in activities that are so beyond their experience that they can make no sense of them at all. The little girl whom I met, in the incident described at the beginning of this paper, had her problems making sense of those in our midst who are our strangers.

When I was teaching grade 2, a citizenship ceremony took place in the gymnasium at our school. The whole school was asked to attend on rather short notice. My class did not understand the concept of citizenship. There was not adequate time to discuss such a concept with them or to try to build the concept of citizenship through their experience. Neither was there time for a discussion among staff about whether it would be appropriate for children of this age to attend. Many of the grade 2, grade 1, and kindergarten pupils had difficulty sitting still through the ceremony. It occurred to me that my role may have been one of simply keeping the children quiet so that our school could announce that such a prestigious ceremony took place at our school. As far as I could tell this incident did little except give the children the message that their role is "to be seen and not heard," a cultural tradition, which, many would argue, is no longer operating in contemporary child-rearing practices. While teachers cannot be expected to explain the reasons for everything they do, it seems to me that this five-year-old girl had difficulty making sense of her world for the same reasons my grade 2 students did: children are sometimes given little say apart from what adults grant them. Yet it would have been helpful to this five-year-old's cognitive development to know—or to be able to ask—the teacher why children sat on the rug and to that of my grade 2 children to have a discussion about citizenship. If we are open to listening to children's questions and struggling with their tangles and confusions, we acknowledge them as being reasonable beings and beings capable of reason. Indeed we may even learn from them!

Perhaps, as I suggested earlier, in looking into the face of the little girl whom I met on the sidewalk, I also remembered how I felt when, as teacher, I was expected to carry on traditions, or enforce rules that made no sense to me; or, worse, that made me feel as though I had somehow abandoned the child I once was. To become an adult and a teacher, I was trained, and had trained myself, to forget the atmosphere of my own childhood. Learning to be and being an adult in this culture may mean becoming estranged from one's own childhood. It may mean turning from our past as experienced towards a present that is outside our felt experience. We become an adult when we disconnect from the child we were; we arrive at what is named adulthood when we forget the journey we have been on. Perhaps being an adult means no longer asking oneself where one came from, where one is going, or who one is going to be. The "not-yet-adult" and "adult" categories of stage development theories may contribute to a polarized and oppositional relationship between adult and child (Sloan Cannella, 1997). After all, once adulthood is reached we know who we are; was not our childhood the preparation for that goal?

"What Will You Be?"

They never stop asking me,
"What will you be?—
A doctor, a dancer,
A diver at sea?"

They never stop bugging me:
"What will you be?"
As if they expect me to
Stop being me.

When I grow up I'm going to be a Sneeze,
And sprinkle Germs on all my Enemies.

When I grow up I'm going to be a Toad,
And dump on Silly Questions in the road.

When I grow up, I'm going to be a Child.
I'll Play the whole darn day and drive them Wild.

(Dennis Lee, 1977, p. 41)[1]

Not so very long ago, I was involved in a situation that brought me closer to understanding the little girl's questions. A close friend of mine was overcome with sadness in hearing the following news bulletin in the dead of winter. A dog had been hit by a car and was left to die at the side of the road. A passerby stopped to throw a blanket on the dog but many people passed by both on foot and in automobiles without stopping. Finally, someone stopped to attend to the dog but by that time the dog's paws were frozen to the ground. It is likely that the dog died not because it sustained fatal injuries by being hit by a car, but because it had been left to freeze to death.

My friend relayed this news report to me through tears. I immediately became angry, spouting off about the great inhumanity in our society, about how we treat helpless creatures and children, about the action that must be taken, about the hopelessness of the situation. My friend interrupted my tirade, saying: "Just let me cry for the dog."

I have thought about this incident many times because other ugly moments remind me of it and because my reaction of over-analysis of life situations appears to be a typical one. Possibly my friend has the right idea: first be aware of one's own immediate feelings (those which speak to us in the moment). It seems to me, based on my own experience as both a student and teacher, that traditional school curricula favours abstract thought, analytic reasoning, and linguistic ability over the affective and perceptual domain. I have learned well to do this as I analyzed the solution rather than responded to the immediate feelings of sadness. Turnbull (1983) suggests that, in other cultures such as in the Mbuti tribe, the affective domain is much more widely understood, and given much more prominence in every stage of the life cycle and in the educational system than it is in our own (p. 18). As a result, the actions of the members of the Mbuti tribe are separate from their life experience. In their culture childhood is not regarded as a separate state. Unlike in the West, there is no abstract or oppositional relationship between child and adult because each individual life is part of the endless cycle of life.

Along with teaching children to favour their emotional responses less and to be made accepting of analytic responses, in Western education, and systems of schooling around the world, we teach children to be passive, not to question authority, and, perhaps, eventually not to question much at all. Lindfors (1987) focuses on the mismatch between the curious nature of children and the tendency of traditional classrooms not to sanction curiosity and questions of a more personal nature. She cites examples from both informal exercises and classroom observations regarding the kinds of questions asked by preschool-kindergarten children, primary children, and intermediate-level children. The questions at each level were categorized into the following three groups:

1. Curiosity: Does not focus on satisfying any outside source.
2. Procedural: Focuses on satisfying an external source; helps one do what one is "supposed" to do.
3. Social-interactional: A question form functioning mainly to initiate or maintain or clarify a relationship. (Lindfors, 1987, p. 288)

The results are rather disturbing:

Of the 159 preschool-kindergarten questions analyzed, approximately 45 per cent (almost half) were social in nature, approximately 33 per cent (one third) were curiosity questions, and approximately 23 per cent (less than one fourth) were procedural. The situation changed dramatically at primary level. Here, of a total of 253 questions analyzed, the curiosity questions comprised only 19 per cent and social only 14 per cent, while procedural questions soared to 66 per cent (almost two thirds) of the total. The situation was similar at intermediate level, with 16 per cent of the total (116) being curiosity questions, another 16 per cent being social, and a staggering 68 per cent being procedural. (Lindfors, 1987, p. 288)

The numbers in Lindfor's study figure importantly in a teacher's life.

My feelings of being a stranger on much of the educational terrain I have travelled may be largely attributed to the fact that, on the one hand, I have been educated to forget, as Lindfor shows, "the atmosphere of my own childhood" and that, on the other hand, childhood is a difficult time to know. As Orwell puts it: "In studying childhood—or teaching children—one is up against the very great difficulty of knowing what a child really feels and thinks" (p. 59). But is it not difficult to really know how anyone feels? After all, are we not all, in one way or another, strangers to ourselves and to each other? I wonder if we do not often think that children's feelings are so different than our own because our cultural history has told us that this is so. Perhaps this is why, in our modern world culture, nothing is less explored and less valued than the child's point of view.

TOWARDS A CURRICULUM OF CHILDHOOD

The disjuncture between curricular materials as represented by the curriculum kit and the child's question about "What is a stranger?" perhaps reveals the connection between teacher disempowerment and child suppression. The child viewed the lesson on school safety from a child's perspective, specifically from the reality of her own lived experience. In this view, standardized prepackaged curriculum materials point to a sanitation of experience to the extent that reality is reduced to outlines and scripts which may serve to disempower both teacher and learner. Thus, both children and teachers are part of an oppressive system, where teachers in this process are neither oppressors not the oppressed, but, along with the children they teach, are confounded by being pulled between external views of societal constructs and their own lived experiences which often run counter to the external reality of school and society. To honour the experiences of childhood is to become aware of the voice of the child, in order to be able to understand and to critically engage such questions as "What is a stranger?"

REFLECTIVE QUESTIONS

1. What problems does Cooper see with "pre-packaged curriculum materials"?
2. Describe an experience that you have had with this type of "teacher-proof" curriculum. How do you recall feeling about it?
3. What curricular directions is Cooper advocating for?
4. How can children's stories inform "a curriculum of childhood"? What might such a curriculum look like?

NOTE

1. From *Garbage Delight* (Macmillan of Canada, 1977). Copyright © 1977 Dennis Lee. With permission of the author.

REFERENCES

Aries, P. (1972). *Centuries of childhood*. (R. Baldick, Trans.). New York: Vintage.

Britzman, D. (2000). On the future of awful thoughts in teacher education. *Teaching Education, 11*(1), 33–37.

Clandinin, D. J., & Connelly, F. M. (1995). *Teachers' professional knowledge landscapes*. New York: Teachers College Press.

De Mause, L. (1975). Our forebears made childhood a nightmare. *Psychology Today, 8*(11), 85–89.

Fine, M. (1987). Silencing in public schools. *Language Arts, 64*(2), 157–174.

Gardner, H. (1991). *The unschooled mind*. New York: Basic Books.

Hendrick, H. (1994). *Child welfare: England 1872–1989*. New York: Routledge.

Heywood, C. (1988). *Childhood in nineteenth-century France.* Cambridge, England: Cambridge University.

Lee, D. (1977). *Garbage delight.* Toronto: Macmillan of Canada.

Lindfors, J. (1987). *Children's language and learning.* New Jersey: Prentice-Hall.

Lyle, S. (2000). Narrative understanding: Developing a theoretical context for understanding how children make meaning in classroom settings. *Journal of Curriculum Studies, 32*(1), 45–63.

McLaren, P. (1989). *Life in schools: An introduction to critical pedagogy in the foundations of education.* Toronto: Irwin.

Miller, A. (1990). The search for the true self. In J. Abrams (Ed.), *Reclaiming the inner child* (pp. 126–138). Los Angeles: Jeremy P. Tarcher.

Orwell, G. (1953). *Such, such were the joys.* New York: Harcourt, Brace and Company.

Peikoff, T., & Brickey, S. (1991). Creating precious children and glorified mothers: A theoretical assessment of the transformation of childhood. In R. Smandych, G. Dodds, & A. Esau (Eds.), *Dimensions of childhood; Essays on the history of children and youth in Canada* (pp. 29–62). Manitoba, Canada: Legal Research Institute of the University of Manitoba.

Schütz, A. (1971). *Collected papers* II. The Hague: Martinus Nijhoff.

Sloan Cannella, G. (1997). *Deconstructing early childhood education.* New York: Peter Lang Publishing.

Smith, D. (1991). Hermeneutic inquiry: The hermeneutic imagination and the pedagogic text. In E. Short (Ed.), *Forms of curriculum inquiry* (pp. 188–209). New York: Suny.

Sommerville, C. (1990). *The rise and fall of childhood.* New York: Vintage.

Suransky, V. (1982). *The erosion of childhood.* Chicago: The University of Chicago.

Turnbull, C. (1983). *The human cycle.* New York: Simon & Schuster.

6

Transforming Narrative Encounters

ANNE MURRAY ORR
MARGARET OLSON

As I walked among the desks, I saw most children working away. Bob[1] was sitting looking at his page, and I glanced at it too. For the "what have you learned" question, he had written in upper case letters, NOTHING. I mentioned that this might not be the answer Miss Green was looking for, and that he might want to change it. (Murray Orr, 2005, p. 129)

The field note above is an example of a curriculum moment that we unpack and analyze in this article to illustrate the transformative possibilities for educators and students through attending to narrative in curriculum. By recognizing the curriculum making (Clandinin & Connelly, 1992) in which students, pre-service teachers, teachers, and teacher educators are engaged, we, the authors, find possibilities for shifts in our own understandings. As we tell and retell such stories, and come to a deeper awareness of how we shape and are shaped by these moments and our multiple understandings of them, we realize the transformative possibilities they provoke. Further, we gain insight into our identities and those of students by noticing and reflecting upon the mirrors and windows (Galda, 1998) provided by others' stories.

We have taken the curriculum moments in this article from two larger research projects. Murray Orr draws upon a research project in a grade 1–2 classroom site where she studied the experiences of children and their teachers as they worked together in school. She observed children's identity making in the classroom and in lunchtime book clubs. Olson draws from a research project in which she followed six pre-service teachers through their Bachelor of Education program, seeking to understand how they found moments of possibility for examining their own taken-for-granted assumptions about teaching and learning. The professional knowledge landscape metaphor developed by Clandinin and Connelly (1995) suggests the professional knowledge of teachers is "composed of a wide variety of components and [is] influenced by a wide variety of people, places, and things" (p. 5). Although our examples of curriculum moments come from very different places on the professional knowledge landscape, they were similarly provocative in terms of transformative possibilities for us and for our students. Greene (1995) writes of the importance of such transformation:

> I think that if I and other teachers truly want to provoke our students to break through the limits of the conventional and the taken for granted, we ourselves have to experience breaks with what has been established in our own lives; we have to keep arousing ourselves to begin again. (p. 109)

As narrative inquirers, we use a research framework developed by Clandinin and Connelly (2000) in which they describe a *"three-dimensional narrative inquiry space"* (p. 49, italics in the original) that "allows our inquiries to travel— *inward, outward, backward, forward,* and *situated within place"* (p. 49, italics in the original). Looking back at our field texts enables us to begin by looking outwardly to students' responses. These responses lead us inward to examine our pedagogical practices and forward to transformations in our practices that we hope will lead to better transformative possibilities for students situated in teacher education and school classrooms.

The three-dimensional narrative inquiry space provides a scaffold for analysis and interpretation in the form of the three dimensions: the temporal, the personal/social (a continuum between the two), and place. Using this structure allowed us to understand our curriculum moments from varied perspectives, as we "move[d] to the retelling and reliving of stories, that is, to inquiry into stories" (Clandinin, Pushor, & Murray Orr, 2007, p. 33). The exploration of these three dimensions and the retelling in which we engaged led to possibilities for seeing differently.

We use Clandinin and Connelly's (2000) terms, *field texts* and *research texts,* in this article. Research texts are the final published papers we write. Field texts are field notes, transcripts, work samples, and other materials gathered in the field. Clandinin and Connelly state, "because data tend to carry with them the idea of objective representation of research experience, it is important to note how imbued field texts are with interpretation" (p. 93). As we began to explain our methods in the narrative inquiries that are the source of curriculum moments in this article, we found it helpful to recognize that interpretation and analysis had already begun prior to the writing of research texts.

INQUIRING INTO TRANSFORMATIVE POSSIBILITIES OF CURRICULUM MAKING

In this discussion of our methods and conceptual framework, we consider curriculum to be understood as a multistoried (Olson, 2000a) course of life (Connelly & Clandinin, 1988), shaped by one's experiences. In this definition we draw upon Connelly and Clandinin's notion of teachers as curriculum planners and consider how students make curriculum alongside teachers in classrooms. We understand curriculum in narrative terms (Carr, 1986; Carter, 1993; Clandinin & Connelly, 2000) knowing that continuity and situation (Dewey, 1938) shape our lives. Sfard and Prusak (2005) highlight the relationship between narrative and identity: "Lengthy deliberations led us to the decision to *equate identities with stories about persons*. No, no mistake here: We did not say that identities were *finding their expression* in stories—we said they *were* stories" (p. 14, italics in original). Recognizing that each student and teacher is engaged in the act of composing a life (Bateson, 1990) and learning along the way (Bateson, 1994) is central to understanding curriculum in these ways.

As we explore two curriculum moments, the echoes of a student's actions or words, as well as those of the teacher, reverberating in their minds and bodies, can be seen as shaping not only the future events of the classroom but also how students and teachers compose and recompose their lives on the professional knowledge landscape. In this way, we view curriculum making and identity making as intertwined.

For us, following Dewey (1938), Schwab (1970), and Clandinin and Connelly (2000), the transformative possibilities for students, teachers, and researchers lie in the creation of spaces in which we may have experiences that encourage us to slow down and consider our multiple and shifting identities (Cooper & Olson, 1996; Santoro & Allard, 2005). A second aspect of these spaces is time to reimagine ourselves and our worlds (Olson, 2005), to reconsider our stories to live by (Connelly & Clandinin, 1999), following such experiences.

Although narrative writing and research have flourished and grown over the years (Carr, 1986; Egan & McEwan, 1995; Pinar, Reynolds, Slatterly, & Taubman, 1996; Turner, 1996; Kearney, 2002; Lewis, 2007), Clandinin and Connelly (1994) brought to our attention the idea that "the more difficult but important task in narrative is the retelling of stories that allow for growth and change" (p. 418). Shields (2005) describes narrative inquiry as a method that "can provide a theoretical and practical framework for (re)interpreting our lived experience" (p. 179). Careful examination and exploration of stories is essential in narrative inquiry. It is tempting to focus on the word *narrative* but skip lightly over the word *inquiry*. Yet it is the inquiry into the stories that may create an educative experience as individuals find new and more expansive ways to interpret their own and others' experiences. The retelling "can lead to seeing experience from different perspectives and can lead to a new spiral of retellings" (Olson, 2000b, p. 350). In this article, we inquire into narratives of two curriculum moments to help us imagine curriculum afresh. In the retelling of these moments we uncover multiple tensions that cause us to pause and see ourselves from slightly differ-ent perspectives and to glimpse transformative possibilities for ourselves and for students. Attending to tensions is an important means to understand the complex ways we negotiate curriculum in schools (Clandinin, Huber, Murphy, Murray Orr, Pearce, & Steeves, 2006; Craig, 2006; Hinchman & Oyler, 2000; Olson & Craig, 2005).

We view the relationships between teachers and students as central in creat-ing spaces for transformative curriculum encounters. The layers of knowledge that characterize this relationship are multiple, complex, and intimately tied to our selves. Lyons (1990) discusses the ethical and epistemological dimensions and dilemmas embedded in these layered relationships.

> Implied in the interactions between teachers and students . . . is the relation-ship between a teacher's views of knowing and his or her assessment of stu-dents as knowers, on the one hand, and students' own perspectives, on the other. It can be illustrated by the concept of nested epistemologies, or nested knowing. (p. 173)

We use the metaphor of windows and mirrors to interpret the nested episte-mologies of the people in the curriculum moments we describe. In reconsider-ing these curriculum moments, we begin to explicate the nested knowing that we bring to our teaching, and by finding windows into the epistemologies of our students we also find mirrors that reflect on our own pedagogical practices. Opportunities to inquire into curriculum moments, both in the moment and in later reflection (Schon, 1983), can surface various dimensions or layers (Atwood, 1988) of knowledge that previously escaped awareness.

A CURRICULUM MOMENT IN A GRADE 1–2 CLASSROOM: *I LEARNED NOTHING* (ANNE MURRAY ORR)

As part of my doctoral research (Murray Orr, 2005), I spent three days a week in a grade 1–2 classroom in a multicultural urban school in Western Canada.

During this time, I also facilitated a lunchtime book group with students from this class. The following field note is about a moment during a spring morning in that classroom. Miss Green was the classroom teacher and Bob was one of the students; I came to know both in class and in the lunchtime book conversations. The class had just finished an experiment called Colour Fun, involving mixing three colours of Jell-O together in various combinations. There had been excitement as this activity was carried out; most children seemed to enjoy the sensation of squishing the Jell-O together in small clear plastic bags. Then it was time to write about the experiment and Miss Green gave each child a worksheet. In the following field text, Murray Orr describes what happened next.

> The children were to complete a sheet about the Jell-O experiment, which involved drawing a picture of what happened, and then writing about 1) what you did and 2) what you learned. There were about three lines for each answer. As I walked among the desks, I saw most children working away on this. Bob was sitting looking at his page, and I glanced at it too. For the "what have you learned" question, he had written in upper case letters, NOTHING. I mentioned that this might not be the answer Miss Green was looking for, and that he might want to change it. He looked at me seriously, and remained still. He wasn't laughing about this, or showing it to anyone else. I wondered what was going through his head. I'm sure he already did know what colors the Jello would turn when mixed, so he probably hadn't learned something new there . . . so why wasn't he allowed to say so . . . I am implicated in this, I realize. I am so much a part of this school story, the story that says that fulfilling the teacher's expectations is more important than saying what you really think. (Murray Orr, 2005, p. 129)

Windows and Mirrors: Transformative Possibilities for Bob and Murray Orr

My initial reaction to Bob's "NOTHING" response was caught up in concerns about how Bob might be seen as impudent or rude. As I reflected on this incident some time later, in moving from field text to research text, I was struck by Bob's honesty and courage. No one else was doing anything remotely like this, and he did not have support or encouragement from other children in the class. He was making a solitary stand. He may have been attempting to create a situation of tension with Miss Green, but it seemed to me that Bob was simply being open in writing that he had learned nothing. I was aware of my unease, my worry that he might be storied negatively. I wanted Bob to back down, to erase his response, to write something more acceptable. I recognized, in retelling that moment, how fraught with contradictions my own stance was as a researcher in that classroom as I struggled with wanting to help make Bob over into my version of a good student.

Using the three-dimensional narrative inquiry space (Clandinin & Connelly, 2000) as my framework, I considered this curriculum moment in relation to the dimensions of the temporal, the personal/social, and place. Moving first into the personal/social dimension, I was, on one hand, trying to create spaces for children to play and work with their stories to live by through the lunchtime book group and other times I spent with them in school. On the other hand, I found myself wanting to make Bob over, to position him differently in the classroom, to step in and not only interrupt the story of who Bob was, but also Bob's own story of who he was, his story to live by (Connelly & Clandinin, 1999). These were the conflicting stories I was personally living in this moment. Not until later, however, as I considered the moment within the framework of the three-dimensional narrative inquiry space, reflecting on the personal and the social implications of that moment, as well as into the dimensions of time and place, did I understand the importance of this moment for me as a researcher and a teacher. I knew I had bumped against something, but did not know what until later when I was away from the school in a different space as I moved from field text to research text. This realization highlights the temporal aspect of my inquiry into this moment.

Continuing to consider the personal/social dimension of narrative inquiry, it appeared to me that by answering "NOTHING" as a response to the question about what he had learned, Bob was bumping against a dominant social narrative of how a good student behaves. I learned this story of school (Connelly & Clandinin, 1999) as a student; I knew good students work to please their teachers rather than say what they really think. Good teachers, correspondingly, encourage students to be docile and please others. Although there are other possible narratives of what makes a good student, it is this version I seemed to embody in this moment. I imagined a potential tension was brewing between Bob and his teacher who I felt sure would not be pleased with his answer. My words to Bob revealed a place of tension in my relationship with Bob, one I had not seen before. Why did I want to help Bob come up with a more acceptable answer? I fell into the position of a good teacher in the story of school, trying to help Bob become a good student, at the very moment when Bob was providing a glimpse of an alternative way to live in school by saying what he really thought.

Place, the third dimension of narrative inquiry space, is relevant because it is within the four walls of the school where this moment occurred. Had Bob and I been in another setting, his authentic (Duke, Purcell-Gates, Hall, & Tower, 2007) response to the question about what he had learned would not have been noteworthy and I would not have reacted by asking him to change his response. On the "storied school landscape" (Clandinin et al., 2006, p. 36), however, we were living and responding to one another and to the colour change activity within a plot line already established, one that had clear expectations for how we might act and respond.

Returning to the notion of transformative possibilities in curriculum moments, I began to see how, in slowing down that moment, by walking around that moment and considering it through the framework of a three-dimensional narrative inquiry space as I wrote, I engaged in a transformative process. My understanding of who I am/was as a researcher and teacher shifted as I glimpsed myself in the mirror this moment provided for me, and saw that my story to live by was not as smooth as I might have liked to imagine.

The temporal dimension comes into play again as I direct my focus to the present day. I am now a beginning teacher educator, one who carries the faces and voices of Bob and his classmates with me into the university classrooms where I spend my days with pre-service and in-service teachers. How does the transformative process of retelling that curriculum moment with Bob shape me as a teacher educator? As I develop course outlines and assignments, Bob's words, "I learned nothing," help me try to develop course experiences that are engaging, educative, and replete with transformative possibilities. I struggle to respond to students who indicate, perhaps in ways more subtle than Bob's, that they feel they are learning nothing in my courses. I attempt to make spaces in both the in- and out-of-classroom places (Connelly & Clandinin, 1999) of my courses for conversation around such tensions, rather than shoving them beneath the surface. Is this enough? I will keep trying as new possibilities emerge. My story to live by as a teacher educator is continually being retold as I learn from experiences such as the moment with Bob I have considered here.

NARRATIVE ENCOUNTERS IN TEACHER EDUCATION: *WHOSE STORIES COUNT?* (MARGARET OLSON)

Students come to the Bachelor of Education program having a wealth of narrative knowledge of how schools work, knowledge constructed over at least sixteen years of experience in schools as students (Lortie, 1975; Ritchie & Wilson, 2000). Although this narrative knowledge of schools has been largely unexamined, it forms the lens through which each student makes sense of the professional knowledge presented to them (Craig & Olson, 2002; Olson, 1995; Ritchie & Wilson, 2000). As a beginning university teacher, I struggled with finding ways to bring the narrative perspective I knew was so important into the university setting that seemed so full of theoretical abstractions.

In my tenth year of working in university classrooms, I continue to be intrigued and baffled by the multi-layeredness of both the process and the curriculum of teacher education. I imagine pre-service teachers at a nexus as both students of teaching and teachers of students spending some of their time in university classrooms as students and some of their time in school classrooms as teachers. The relationships and tensions between the curriculum of teacher education and the curriculum of schools provide a myriad of encounter points to examine. I hope to enable them to integrate these two worlds as well as find links between theoretical abstractions and their individual narrative knowing of schools and classrooms.

One of the courses I teach is a Sociology of Education course for first-year Bachelor of Education students, a course developed collaboratively over several years with other teacher educators. Although some might refer to this process as creating and revising a course, this assertion implies that the course is not an integral part of an instructors' narrative authority (Olson, 1995; Olson, 2008). Instead, I see such collaborative course redevelopment as an example of teacher educators storying and restorying (Connelly & Clandinin, 1990) a course as each brings new ways of teaching and learning to their conversations and practice.

Although many changes in the course have occurred over the years, a main focus continues to be enabling students to uncover inequities in the present school system and examine ways to transform schools to better fulfill the equity premise for all students. As Santoro and Allard (2005) point out, "working from the personal to the more general appeared to help these student-teachers gain some insight into the centrality of class and ethnicity within education" (p. 872). Therefore, another closely aligned focus of this course is to enable pre-service teachers to examine their own taken-for-granted assumptions embedded in their narrative knowledge about schooling. Three main questions frame the work in this course: Who am I as a person and a learner? What is the socio-political context of schooling? and What kind of educator do I hope to be and what do I imagine my practice will be as I begin my journey into teaching? The nine-week course includes a variety of activities to enable students to examine their narrative knowing: base groups, narrative journal writing (see Craig & Olson, 2002), use of a critical literacy framework, participation in learning centres focused on poverty, and a cultural capital auction (see Olson, 2008).

I continually struggle in my teaching to find ways to help students articulate, examine, confirm and/or transform their narrative knowledge in more informed ways. An assignment that focuses on curricular justice invites students to examine their narrative knowledge using a paradigmatic framework developed by Connell (1993). In this assignment, students use the three-dimensional narrative inquiry space to look both inward and outward as they describe a curricular event or activity they have experienced. They then analyze this event or activity based on Connell's three principles of curricular justice, examining curriculum from three distinct points of view: the least advantaged, democratic decision making, and the historical production of equality. We then ask students to reconstruct or restory this event or activity in ways that are more curricularly just. Through this assignment, we ask students to "rethink what they thought they knew" (Carse, 1986, p. 125), to restory their experience in more equitable ways.

The following story is an excerpt from Pat's curricular justice assignment which was part of the field text from a larger research project I had carried out.

> I did my practicum in a grade 4 classroom. We were doing the unit *Nova Scotia: Our Heritage* in Social Studies. My co-operating teacher told me how much he enjoyed doing this unit with the students each year. He had a wealth of information and things that he had collected over many years that we would use to prepare the room. We worked hard to get the room ready. I was proud of how the room looked, and felt a real sense of accomplishment as students entered that morning, ready to start our new unit. I hoped they would be as excited as I was. As I looked around the room I saw many examples of our heritage. Various tartans from different clans were on display. Bagpipes and maps of Scotland added to the atmosphere. I stopped to admire a picture on the bulletin board. In it was a young girl with sparkling blue eyes and flowing reddish-tinged hair. It could have been me. I turned my head to look down at Maria, a small, black-haired, dark-eyed, dark-skinned girl standing beside me. She too looked at the picture, looked at the room, then looked at me with puzzled eyes. Suddenly it hit me. Everything in the room reflected my own and my co-operating teacher's Scottish heritage. Where was any representation of this little girl's story? Her heritage? How many other students' stories had we neglected? The unit was entitled *Nova Scotia: Our Heritage*. Yet we were only representing one culture, one heritage—our own.

Windows and Mirrors: Transformative Possibilities for Pat and Olson

I now look at this curriculum moment in relation to the three dimensions of narrative inquiry: the temporal, the personal/social, and place. Students (and teachers) are often unaware that there are many possible ways to tell their stories. Looking outwardly at what Pat had written, I realize that using a process of narrative inquiry, in this case shaped by Connell's three principles of curricular justice, enabled Pat to see that the story of grade 4 social studies she was learning from her co-operating teacher was only one possible way to create the social studies curriculum story in that classroom. At the same time, Pat's story alerts me to the importance of place. When Pat shifted from the university to the public school classroom context, she was thrilled by how much she was learning from her co-operating teacher as he shared with her his ways of teaching this unit. She was very pleased with the information she was gathering and saw this teacher as a very knowledgeable man with whom she was fortunate to be working. Looking outward to the larger context of teacher education, it seems to me that this apprenticeship version of teacher education in which knowledge is passed down from expert to novice is one pre-service teachers seem to expect and find comfort in. Looking inward to my own teaching in the university context, I can see that asking pre-service teachers to critically inquire into their experiences conflicts with the apprenticeship and transmission modes they expect to find in the public school system. Looking forward, I wonder how I can work with students in the university setting to help them see the relevance of an inquiry stance within public school classrooms.

Looking outwardly to Pat and her co-operating teacher, I observe that as they worked together, Pat seemed to feel a real sense of accomplishment as she learned from her co-operating teacher and made contributions herself. Temporally, I see that as Pat looked back at her past cultural and school experiences, she was confirmed in her own knowledge as well as informed by his as they both lived a familiar story of Scottish heritage. This story mirrors for me that I need to continually stay awake to how I might be perpetuating my own cultural and teacher education experiences. Although I believe that a sense of professional camaraderie and collaboration is crucial in the professional development of pre-service teachers, I worry when a sense of inquiry seems to be missing from the relationship. Although I know that I am looking at this story from a different place on the professional knowledge landscape, I worry that fitting into the school culture can also lead to non-critical enculturation if an inquiry stance is not encouraged in the schools. On the other hand, perhaps it is exactly this different context that provides pre-service teachers the distance to inquire into their practices.

Connell's three principles of curricular justice provided a framework for students like Pat to reposition themselves in relation to their students and begin to reimagine in more inclusive and socially just ways the curriculum stories they were living. A moment of transformative possibility did occur for Pat when she shifted from focusing inwardly on her own and her co-operating teacher's narrative knowing of Scottish heritage and, in encountering Maria's puzzled gaze, realized that this display did not reflect Maria's heritage story. I believe looking outward to Connell's theoretical principles provided an impetus for this transformation.

This assignment enabled Pat and others to slow down enough in the busy public school classroom to inquire into their taken-for-granted assumptions. My reflection on this moment has also allowed me to slow down and inquire into my own teaching. Although I believe this assignment provided a link across contexts, I also wonder if it might create more tension for some as they try to juggle being both a student and a teacher. I find being a student of teaching a very reflexive position, but pre-service teachers do not always feel the same sense of learning, especially when they think they are already supposed "to know."

As I look forward I now wonder how I, as a teacher educator, might better enable pre-service teachers (and perhaps by implication, their co-operating teachers as well) to value an inquiry stance as part of their teaching practice.

REIMAGINING CURRICULUM: WHERE MIGHT THESE STORIES LEAD?

What are some of the ways we might reimagine curriculum as we look back at the stories told by Murray Orr and Olson about themselves and their students/research participants? One aspect that is foregrounded for us concerns the layers of school stories in which we are immersed as we tell our own narratives. We have an embodied knowing of the ways curricula can inform us, sometimes urging us and our students to conform to a good student story. Murray Orr, living out her embodied knowing of the good student/good teacher story, found herself wishing that Bob would conform to such a story, while Olson, in retelling Pat's story, realized how the social justice curriculum may subtly have urged students to conform to the definition of social justice, a reflection of broader world views held by their professor. Yet these moments did hold transformative possibilities for Murray Orr and Olson, perhaps because they were able to slow the moments down enough to consider them from different perspectives. We wonder if creating spaces for slowing down even a few of the moments in our classrooms may provide opportunities for transformation.

For Murray Orr, returning to the school with her writing to share with Bob, several months after this encounter, seemed to be a way to attend to this curriculum moment with him. Although Bob did not comment directly on this part of Murray Orr's writing about him, he did begin to tell stories of himself as resisting the *good student* story of school. Perhaps sharing this story with Bob was a way to engage him in a process of retelling his story to live by (Connelly & Clandinin, 1999). Sharing with Bob the tensions this story uncovered, as Murray Orr returned to it over time in her own writing, and each time she returned to the school to share more of her writing with Bob, may have provided the kind of space in which transforming might begin, for both Murray Orr and Bob.

Reflecting on Murray Orr's story of Bob, who wrote "I learned nothing" on his worksheet, we imagine Murray Orr's deepening knowledge of herself as a researcher in Bob's classroom, as a parent of schoolaged children, and as a teacher who knew that Bob was going to get himself in trouble with that line. Bob too seemed to bring his own epistemology to bear on the situation, writing not what someone else might want to hear, but deciding to write what he really thought. Murray Orr found a window into Bob's epistemology in this moment, one that helped her learn more about her own story to live by. When we consider that curricular moment through the framework of the three dimensions of narrative inquiry space, we begin to uncover the multiplicity that moment contained. Murray Orr's nested knowing (Lyons, 1990) reminds researchers that there are multiple layers of knowledge in every classroom interaction.

Reflecting on Olson's story of Pat, we consider that to create moments and spaces of possibility within classrooms, teachers benefit from having experienced the process themselves in their pre-service teacher education programs and in their ongoing professional learning (Olson & Craig, 2001). Creating spaces in teacher education where living and telling our stories, retelling and reimagining our lives, can occur is complex because, as MacIntyre (1984) points out, a practice is "a mode of understanding which has been transmitted often through many generations" (p. 201). When one of the most dominant stories of school is that of transmission from those who know to those who do not, it becomes a difficult story to interrupt and re-imagine for teachers as well as for students. In her university classes, Olson attempts to enable pre-service teachers like Pat to value their narrative knowing by creating spaces for them to share their stories of school in ways that allow them to value their narrative knowledge and the narrative knowledge of each other similar to the processes described in the work of Jalongo and Isenberg (1995) and Lynn and Smith-Maddox (2007). However, as shown in Olson's curricular justice story, creating and valuing this space can be a difficult process. When narrative knowledge is accepted as transmitted, little inquiry takes place. Olson continually finds herself living in the tension between supporting pre-service teachers' stories and interrupting them with different possible versions to open inquiry spaces rather than only narrative spaces. We believe these inquiry spaces create potential for narrative transformations to begin for pre-service teachers. The curricular justice assignment can provide one way to do this only when we are successful in presenting it to pre-service teachers as an opportunity for transformation rather than conformation. Finding a balance within the nested relational knowing between pre-service teachers and herself continually shifts moment by moment as Olson's and the pre-service teachers' knowledge is simultaneously informed and transformed by each other in conversation. Other nested layers of knowing occur when pre-service teachers spend time with their co-operative teachers in school classrooms. As Olson remembers Pat's story, she now wonders how it might help her retell her own experience in ways that are more educative for future students.

Perhaps if we wish to imagine curriculum afresh, we must use the moments our relationships with students and one another provide as our starting points, to, as Greene (1995) suggests, continually "begin again." Inquiring into the layers of knowing we and students find in small moments in our classrooms, and into the tensions that occur in our teaching and learning, seems to us a path that holds promise, a path that helps us think about curriculum as something we create together with our students in those ongoing moments of possibility.

REFLECTIVE QUESTIONS

1. What do the authors mean by curriculum being "multistoried"?
2. What is your understanding of narrative inquiry?
3. How do the authors suggest going about transforming curriculum in the classroom?
4. What role do the students play in this transformation? What is the role of the teacher?
5. Have you ever had a similar experience to those recounted by Murray Orr and Olson in your work as a teacher or as a pre-service teacher? What has been your experience?

NOTE

1.   All names of research participants are pseudonyms.

REFERENCES

Atwood, M. (1988). *Cat's eye*. Toronto: McClelland-Bantam, Inc.

Bateson, M. C. (1990). *Composing a life*. New York: Grove Press.

Bateson, M. C. (1994). *Peripheral visions: Learning along the way*. New York: Harper Collins.

Carr, D. (1986). *Time, narrative, and history*. Bloomington, IN: Indiana University Press.

Carse, J. (1986). *Finite and infinite games: A vision of life as play and possibility*. Toronto: Random House.

Carter, K. (1993). The place of story in the study of teaching and teacher education. *Educational Researcher, 22*(1), 5–12, 18.

Clandinin, D. J., & Connelly, F. M. (1992). The teacher as curriculum maker. In P. W. Jackson (Ed.), *Handbook of research on curriculum: A project of the American Educational Research Association* (pp. 363–401). New York: Macmillan.

Clandinin, D. J., & Connelly, F. M. (1994). Personal experience methods. In N. Denzin & Y. Lincoln (Eds.), *Handbook of qualitative research* (pp. 413–427). Thousand Oaks, CA: Sage.

Clandinin, D. J., & Connelly, F. M. (1995). *Teachers' professional knowledge landscapes*. New York: Teachers College Press.

Clandinin, D. J., & Connelly, F. M. (2000). *Narrative inquiry: Experience and story in qualitative research*. San Francisco: Jossey-Bass.

Clandinin, D. J., Huber, J., Huber, M., Murphy, M. S., Murray Orr, A., Pearce, M., & Steeves, P. (2006). *Composing diverse identities: Narrative inquiries into the interwoven lives of children and teachers*. New York: Routledge.

Clandinin, D. J., Pushor, D., & Murray Orr, A. (2007). Navigating sites for narrative inquiry. *Journal of Teacher Education, 58*(1), 21–35.

Connell, R. W. (1993). *Schools and social justice*. Toronto: Our Schools/Ourselves Education Foundation.

Connelly, F. M., & Clandinin, D. J. (1988). *Teachers as curriculum planners: Narratives of experience*. Toronto: OISE Press.

Connelly, F. M., & Clandinin, D. J. (1990). Stories of experience and narrative inquiry. *Educational Researcher, 19*, 2–14.

Connelly, F. M., & Clandinin, D. J (1999). *Shaping a professional identity: Stories of educational practice*. New York: Teachers College Press.

Cooper, K., & Olson, M. (1996). The multiple "I's" of teacher identity. In M. Kompf, W. R. Bond, D. Dworet, & R. T. Boak (Eds.), *Changing research and practice: Teachers' professionalism, identities, and knowledge* (pp. 78–89). London, UK: Falmer Press.

Craig, C. (2006). Why is dissemination so difficult? The nature of teacher knowledge and the spread of curriculum reform. *American Educational Research Journal, 43*(2), 257–293.

Craig, C. J., & Olson, M. R. (2002). The development of narrative authority in knowledge communities: A narrative approach to teacher learning. In N. Lyons & V. LaBoskey (Eds.), *Narrative inquiry in practice: Advancing the knowledge of teaching* (pp. 115–129). New York: Teachers College Press.

Dewey, J. (1938). *Experience and education*. New York: Macmillan.

Duke, N., Purcell-Gates, V., Hall, L., & Tower, C. (2007). Authentic literacy activities for developing comprehension and writing. *The Reading Teacher, 60*(4), 344–355.

Egan, K., & McEwan H. (Eds.) (1995). *Narrative in teaching, learning and research*. New York: Teachers College Press.

Galda, L. (1998). Mirrors and windows: Reading as transformation. In T. E. Raphael & K. H. Au (Eds.), *Literature-based instruction: Reshaping the curriculum* (pp. 1–11). Norwood, MA: Christopher-Gordon Publishers.

Greene, M. (1995). *Releasing the imagination: Essays on education, the arts, and social change*. San Francisco: Jossey Bass.

Hinchman, K., & Oyler, C. (2000). Us and them: Finding irony in our teaching methods. *Journal of Curriculum Studies, 32*(4), 495–508.

Jalongo, M. R., & Isenberg, J. P. (1995). *Teachers' stories: From personal narrative to professional insight*. San Francisco: Jossey-Bass.

Kearney, R. (2002). *On stories: Thinking in action*. New York: Routledge.

Lewis, P. (2007). *How we think, but not in school: A storied approach to teaching*. Rotterdam, the Netherlands: Sense Publishers.

Lortie, D. C. (1975). *Schoolteacher: A sociological study*. Chicago: University of Chicago Press.

Lynn, M., & Smith-Maddox, R. (2007). Pre-service teacher inquiry: Creating a space to dialogue about becoming a social justice educator. *Teaching and Teacher Education, 23*, 94–105.

Lyons, N. (1990). Dilemmas of knowing: Ethical and epistemological dimensions of teachers' work and development. *Harvard Educational Review, 60*(2), 159–180.

MacIntyre, A. (1984). *After virtue* (2nd ed.). Notre Dame, IN: University of Notre Dame Press.

Murray Orr, A. (2005). *Stories to live by: Book conversations as spaces for attending to children's lives in school*. Unpublished doctoral dissertation, University of Alberta.

Olson, M. (1995). Conceptualizing narrative authority: Implications for teacher education. *Teaching and Teacher Education, 11*(2), 119–135.

Olson, M. (2000a). Curriculum as a multistoried process. *Canadian Journal of Education, 25*(3), 169–187.

Olson, M. (2000b). Where the story leads: A response to Cheryl Craig. *Canadian Journal of Education, 25*(4), 349–452.

Olson, M. (2005). It's about time: Issues of time in knowledge construction for preservice teachers and practicing teachers in school contexts. In D. Beijaard, P. C. Meijer, G. Morine-Dersheimer, & H. Tillema (Eds.), *New directions in teachers' working and learning environment* (pp. 181–195). Dordrecht, Boston, London: Klewer Academic Publishers.

Olson, M. (2008). Valuing narrative authority, collaboration, and diversity in revitalizing a teacher education program. In C. Craig & L. Deretchin (Eds.), *2008 Association of Teacher Educators XVI yearbook: Imagining a renaissance in teacher education* (pp. 377–394). Lanham, MD: Rowman and Littlefield.

Olson, M., & Craig, C. J. (2001). Opportunities and challenges in the development of teachers' knowledge: The development of narrative authority through knowledge communities. *Teaching and Teacher Education, 17*, 667–684.

Olson, M., & Craig, C. (2005). Uncovering cover stories: Tensions and entailments in the development of teacher knowledge. *Curriculum Inquiry, 35*(2), 161–182.

Pinar, W., Reynolds, W., Slatterly, P., & Taubman, P. (1996). *Understanding curriculum: An introduction to the study of historical and contemporary curriculum discourses.* New York: Peter Lang.

Ritchie, J. S., & Wilson, D. E. (2000). *Teacher narrative as critical inquiry: Rewriting the script.* New York: Teachers College Press.

Santoro, N., & Allard, A. (2005). (Re)Examining identities: Working with diversity in the pre-service teaching experience. *Teaching and Teacher Education, 21*, 863–873.

Schon, D. A. (1983). *The reflective practitioner: How professionals think in action.* New York: Basic Books.

Schwab, J. J. (1970). *The practical: A language for curriculum.* Washington DC: National Education Association, Center for the Study of Instruction. (Reprinted in I. Westbury & N. Wilkoff (Eds.), *Science, curriculum, and liberal education: Selected essays.* Chicago: University of Chicago Press, 1978).

Sfard, A., & Prusak, A. (2005). Telling identities: In search of an analytic tool for investigating learning as a culturally shaped activity. *Educational Researcher, 34*(4), 14–22.

Shields, C. (2005). Using narrative inquiry to inform and guide our (re)interpretations of lived experience. *McGill Journal of Education, 40*, 179–188.

Turner, M. (1996). *The literary mind.* New York: Oxford University Press.

Historical Influences on the Curriculum in Canada

Historical Influences on the Curriculum in Canada

There is truth to the old cliché that one cannot possibly know where one is going, if one does not know where one has been. This is true also of understanding how Canadian curriculum developed over many decades to become what it is now. In order to better understand the curricular future, you must pause on your journey and look at some of the people and forces that shaped Canada's curriculum in the past. This second part of the book explores how Canada's school curriculum got to where it is today and identifies some of the challenges that have been faced by educators and curriculum developers in their curriculum deliberations.

During this second leg of your curriculum journey, you will read about some of the educational issues that laid the foundation for the current education system. These include the challenges of a provincially driven education system and the role of politically motivated curriculum decision-making. Other issues are the social, cultural, economic, religious, philosophical, and geographic influences on education. Further core issues are the important role of teachers as curriculum implementers and the influence of public demand for accountability. Some key questions you may wish to use to guide your reading in this section are:

- What have been some of the big ideas that curriculum thinkers grappled with in the past?
- Are any of these ideas enduring legacies?

The readings in this part of the book primarily examine what was happening in the socio-economic and political arenas in Canada from the 1930s to the 1990s. Prior to this time period there was a lengthy period of relative stability in Canadian schools with an emphasis on teacher-centred learning, regimentation and discipline, factual learning, and the acquisition of "reading ability, arithmetical skill and good behaviour" (Johnson, 1968, p. 133). Increased immigration to Canada from the 1890s through the 1920s saw schools and the curriculum being used to promote Anglo-Canadian nationalism.

Following the First World War, the curriculum was influenced by the "efficiency movement" as espoused by American curricularists such as John Franklin Bobbitt and Ralph Tyler. This movement took hold from the early 1920s to late 1940s. These were difficult times for Canadians as they went from one world war to another, with a devastating economic depression in between. In "The Historical Development of Private Education in Canada," authors Brenda MacKay and Michael Firmin present a historical and geographical review and analysis of the development of private and public education in Canada during this time. In doing so, they provide a useful overview of the influences that settlement, multiculturalism, and religion had on the Canadian education system and curriculum development. They also identify what they saw as four stages in the development of public education in Canada. These were: church control of education, the provision of universal free education, the establishment of provincial departments of education, and, lastly, the appointment of Ministers of Education in each province.

The 1930s to 1950s was a time of significant change in Canadian education. During this time, Canada's education system was influenced by the progressive education movement as advocated mostly by American theorists like John Dewey and William H. Kilpatrick. The most effective education was believed to be one that engaged children in "doing" through real-life activities and through learning with others. The years since have seen schools and the curriculum waver between this progressive, learner-centred, inquiry approach and the earlier traditionalist, teacher-centred, rote-learning approach (Tomkins, 2008). In "Connections, Contrarieties, and Convolutions: Curriculum and Pedagogic Reform in Alberta and Ontario, 1930–1955," Lynn Lemisko and Kurt Clausen provide two case studies of curricular and pedagogic reform during the 1930s to 1950s and show the multitude of factors that contributed to the difficulties in instituting curricular reform. They describe how progressive education in the form of the Enterprise Method, an integrated, learner-centred curriculum, played out differently in Alberta and Ontario due mainly to differences in political climate. They also discuss the important role that teachers played in influencing curriculum implementation at the classroom level. In "Getting Things Done: Donalda J. Dickie and Leadership Through Practice," Rebecca Coulter introduces her readers to Donalda Dickie, a key figure in Canada's progressive education movement during this same time period. Dickie's story not only provides further background regarding both the move toward and away from progressivism, but also a heartfelt account of what it was like for women to work in the curriculum field during this time period in Canada.

During the late 1950s and 1960s, the Cold War had an effect on Canadian education. The launching of the *Sputnik* satellite in 1957 by the Soviet Union signalled the beginning of the Space Race between the United States and the USSR. This race for dominance in space exploration led to a shift back to a more subject-centred curriculum in order to strengthen schools' performance in sciences and mathematics. This was also a time of postwar affluence, a baby boom, and a population explosion due to expanded immigration. During this period, education was seen as a way to prepare the new workforce for life in Canada. In "There is no magic whereby such qualities will be acquired at the voting age: Teachers, Curriculum, Pedagogy and Citizenship," Lorna McLean examines what it meant to be a "good" citizen during this time period and raises questions about what role democratic citizenship education has had, and should have now, in Canadian education. She also looks at the impact of school culture and outside service organizations on the shaping of students' educational experiences.

Moving to the last part of the twentieth century, David Pratt's "Characteristics of Canadian Curricula" provides a review of curriculum documents from across Canada in the 1980s and 1990s looking for commonalities in both content and presentation. The findings clearly show the challenges of trying to provide common educational experiences across the country when education and curriculum are controlled and developed at the provincial level.

One of the enduring legacies of the 1990s in Canada's curriculum deliberations has been the struggle for Canadian identity. In "A Topography for Canadian Curriculum Theory," Cynthia Chambers examines how Canadians perceived themselves at the end of the twentieth century and how well our curriculum and resources represented that identity. Chambers recommends answering the question "Who are we?" from the perspective of geographical space by first asking the question, "Where are we?" The author also highlights both the importance, and the inherent difficulty given our geographical diversity, of trying to integrate Canadian content into our curriculum. She maintains, however, that this is an important challenge to undertake.

Yatta Kanu also examines Canadian identity, but from a cultural perspective, in "Curriculum as Cultural Practice: Postcolonial Imagination." In this article,

Kanu proposes that we reimagine curriculum as a "hybrid or multinational curriculum" that "weaves" our Canadian identity with that of our ancestors' cultures in order to create a new identity that ensures meaning and enrichment for all.

And finally in "Reflecting Today, Creating Tomorrow: The Dual Role of Public Education," Jon Young debates two long-standing and divergent views of the purpose of schooling and the effects of both on curriculum decision-making. Ultimately, Young's ideas on this take us back to where we began our curriculum journey in Part I, as he challenges us once again to think about what the purpose should be of education and schooling, and what and whose knowledge should be represented by the curriculum as we plan for the twenty-first century.

REFERENCES

Johnson, F. H. (1968). *A brief history of Canadian education.* Toronto: McGraw-Hill.

Tomkins, G. S. (2008). *A common countenance: Stability and change in Canadian curriculum* (2nd. ed.). Vancouver, BC: Pacific Educational Press.

7

The Historical Development of Private Education in Canada

BRENDA MACKAY
MICHAEL W. FIRMIN

GEOGRAPHICAL SETTING

Ten provinces (and two territories): the Yukon, Northwest Territories, British Columbia, Alberta, Saskatchewan, Manitoba, Ontario, Quebec, Newfoundland, Prince Edward Island, New Brunswick, and Nova Scotia, comprise the second-largest country in the world. Size, economic resources, and population all significantly influence Canada's educational system (White, 2003). O'Driscoll (1988) and Lloyd (2002) suggest that the country's size and population have resulted in the uneven distribution of natural resources, thereby influencing education policies. Quebec and Ontario, for example, are the most affluent of Canada's ten provinces and tend to provide relatively well for the citizen's educational needs (Davidson-Harden & Majhanovich, 2004). Zine (2001) notes that Toronto, in particular, is one of the most culturally diverse cities in the world. The prairies, from Manitoba through Alberta to the Rockies, and British Columbia have also developed comprehensive educational facilities. By contrast, educational provision in the Atlantic provinces and the northern territories is still relatively underdeveloped.

Despite its great size, Canada's population, a mere thirty-three million, is distributed very unevenly. Over half of the nation's population is concentrated in the two central provinces of Quebec and Ontario. The four Western provinces of Manitoba, Saskatchewan, Alberta, and British Columbia have a population of less than ten million, while between two and three million live in the four

Atlantic provinces of Newfoundland, Prince Edward Island, Nova Scotia, and New Brunswick. English is the national language but almost one-quarter of the population also speaks French (some two million exclusively). Obviously, such diverse demographics have had educational implications for educating the children of Canada (Hladki, 1995).

Mallea and Young (1984) indicate that diversity is a distinguishing feature of Canadian citizens. This includes diversity of culture, language, and traditions. Gayfer (1978) attributes the present value placed on diversity to the settlement of the country and the multiple cultural identities of the early settlers. Johnson (1968) contrasted the historical "melting pot" model traditionally associated with America with that of a "mosaic" motif wherein a variety of cultural groups are united in a sense of national unity but, at the same time, retain their subgroup diversity. Shapiro (1985) has claimed that Canadian educational institutions are affected significantly by these plural cultural identities, especially the English and French historical influences.

THE HISTORICAL SETTING

Early in the seventeenth century, two major settlements in Canada were established by the French, in Acadia (Nova Scotia) and the colony of Quebec sited on the St. Lawrence River (O'Driscoll, 1988). The first colonists traded in furs and the earliest settlement began in 1604 when Acadia, Prince Edward Island, and New Brunswick were established. The French colonists were slow to settle in these areas. Agriculture encouraged more settlers, but conflict with the Indians and the British, and an indifferent government in France, retarded growth both in Acadia and Quebec. England gained control of Acadia in 1713. Later the Seven Years War between England and France finally ended in 1763 with a British victory and the conquest of the Quebec Colony, which possessed an estimated population of around 60,000 (Phillips, 1957).

Education first became a matter of governmental concern after the Seven Years War because it was closely tied to religion and in Quebec served to strengthen the Roman Catholic faith. Dickinson and Dolmage (1996) consider the uniting of religion and education to be one of Canada's most historically unique cultural features while Donaldson (1998) argues that Canada's contemporary educational system has been continually shaped by its historical context.

THE EMERGENCE OF PUBLIC/PRIVATE EDUCATION

To early Canadians, education was mostly a family matter. Prior to any early organization among the settlers, the Native peoples of Canada (the Indians and Eskimos) were educated within the families and communities in which they lived (Katz, 1974). Basic early educational practices and beliefs were passed on to the young by an older generation in order to maintain the individual culture and social order of the cultural group.

To the early European settlers, education was not only a family matter, but an important concern of the Christian churches (Audet, 1970). Titley and Miller (1982) describe education as being central to the maintenance of church control over the moral life of the early settlers. The parish priest often was the most educated person in the community and widely recognized as a natural leader in society. Johnson (1968) noted that the early settlers were followed by various missionaries who provided religious training and established schools.

The Reformation and Counter Reformation of the mid-sixteenth century co-incided with the arrival in Canada of the first colonists from Europe. The Roman Catholic Church and Protestants alike sought to spread religious zeal and spirit to the new world. Titley and Miller (1982) noted that it was inconceivable for the churches to separate their religious and educational mandates and the colonists willingly provided land grants to aid the cause of religious education and other types of social welfare.

FRENCH INFLUENCE

Johnson (1968) describes the first missionary teachers to arrive in New France (Quebec) as four French Roman Catholic *Recollet* (Franciscan) priests. Later, Jesuit priests also joined this group. During the seventeenth and eighteenth centuries, French Roman Catholics moved westwards and by 1842, Quebec, Manitoba, and Alberta had formal schooling. The foremost aim of the Roman Catholic Church in the Quebec Colony was to maintain a spiritual emphasis on the conversion of Native children to the Roman Catholic faith, together with the preservation of French culture and language in the face of British Protestant cultural domination (Phillips, 1957).

Audet (1970) argues that the English in Quebec sought to ensure that both English and French culture was maintained within a peaceful setting. The English might have attempted to achieve this objective by absorbing the French into their own culture, however, Gossage (1977) notes that French Canadians made strenuous efforts to preserve their religion and clung tenaciously to their native language as a basis for the emergence of an educational system. Both Audet and Phillips credit the British with allowing French-Canadian institutions to maintain their Catholic religious faith and the use of the French language.

BRITISH INFLUENCES

In the late 1700s there was an influx of English-speaking colonists from the New England states. Early British influence in 1791 was evident in the four Atlantic provinces, Lower Canada (Quebec), and Upper Canada (Ontario). In the latter,

English attitudes and traditions prevailed with education regarded as the responsibility of parents and the Church of England (Phillips, 1957).

The Society for the Propagation of the Gospel in Foreign Parts (SPG), an Anglican organization, opened a school in 1744 in Newfoundland. This was soon followed by many more designed to promote the Church of England and maintain its superior status. In the same period, Roman Catholic priests also arrived to cater for the many Irish settlers in Newfoundland. They were joined, in turn, by Methodist missionaries so that by the end of the eighteenth century, three major religious denominations were actively promoting education (Johnson, 1968).

The Anglican Church provided the basis for the educational system in Upper Canada and most of the teachers were Anglican clergy. Many Anglican schools provided an elitist type of education, often classical in orientation, designed for the "sons of gentlemen." Long-standing political tensions came to a head in 1837 between the elite Loyalist families known as the "Family Compact" and immigrants from Britain and America, more commonly known as "Reformers" (Moir, 1959). The Family Compact provided the Crown-appointed members of the legislative and executive councils of government while the Reformers had their power base in the popularly elected general assembly. It was this governmental composition that contributed to Upper Canada's distinct educational system (Adams, 1968).

From the Family Compact there emerged Scottish-born John Strachan, an Anglican teacher and influential Church of England leader (Bredin, 2000). Strachan believed in educating only the potential leaders of society derived, as he believed, from the wealthy class represented by the Family Compact. By implication, he viewed the Anglican Church as an extension of the state, educating the children who would later perpetuate Anglican supremacy through their control of the legislature.

The Education Act of 1807 was the first legislation of its kind in Upper Canada. It made provision for government grants to encourage the founding of schools of Anglican character for the wealthy class. Attendance was restricted to the wealthy by locating the (grammar) schools in towns, thereby requiring students to board and pay high tuition fees. No provision was made for elementary education through common schools. Some existed, but there was no government funding for them.

The 1807 act subsequently generated a strong public outcry and determined opposition from non-Anglican members of the Legislature (Bredin, 2000). Strachan responded to the criticism by enlarging the grammar school system. Eventually the Common Schools Act was passed in 1816. It contained the first legislative provision for elementary education. Although the so-called Grammar

School Act of 1807 remained intact, the new public school act proposed common schools for all children (Wilson, 1970). The Reformers were triumphant and a compromise between the two rival political groups resulted with Strachan becoming Upper Canada's first Superintendent of Schools.

CANADA EAST (QUEBEC)

Before the Fabrique Act of 1824, formal education in Canada East (Quebec) was controlled by a British, Anglican organization known as the Royal Institution for the Advancement of Learning, created by an act of 1801. Adams (1968) indicates that it was an attempt by the English-speaking minority to introduce a free school system. Power was delegated to a board of commissioners in order to appoint teachers and control the curriculum. The commissioners were granted special favours by the colonial government and the Church of England (Adams, 1968). The commission was soon perceived as a threat to the supremacy of the Roman Catholic Church amongst the predominantly French-speaking Catholic population.

Audet (1970) notes the changing roles of government and the churches at this time. The government was attempting to replace the churches as the principal power in education, but the Anglicans continued to exert their leadership and influence. Adams (1968) noted that by 1820 there was a three-way tug-of-war in education in Lower Canada between the Royal Institution Board, Catholic priests, and legislators.

The French-speaking population viewed the rapid growth of Anglican schools as a deliberate attempt by the British to Anglicize them and thereby threatening their language, religion, and culture. Sensing the need to react, Roman Catholics finally gained a majority in the popularly elected Assembly and passed the Fabrique Act of 1824 (the *Fabriques* were a group of church members who managed temporal affairs in the parishes). The act provided for the establishment of schools under church control (Johnson, 1968). The *Fabriques* were given total control of the administration of schools, with one-quarter of the running costs derived wholly from church revenues. That is, the money that the churches collected in their congregants' tithes, offerings, as well as money from centralized diocese funded approximately one-fourth of the total cost of education in their respective parishes. This satisfied the Roman Catholic hierarchy because the power of the Church was preserved through its power to regulate and direct education. The act also paved the way for a denominational system of schools in Lower Canada or Canada East.

Adams (1968) indicates that a subsequent Education Act of 1841, designed to promote an inclusive school system, while simultaneously providing for separate schooling of Catholics and Protestants, was passed in acknowledgement of the Roman Catholic clergy's loyalty to the British colonial government during the rebellion of 1837. The uprisings in Upper and Lower Canada resulted from attempts to loosen England's colonial control over Canada. The rebellion by French-speaking settlers was not supported by the clergy, since the uprisings mostly were fuelled by a current economic recession, not religious ideation. Following the rebellions, however, unrest sharpened among Upper and Lower Canadian clergy, since Protestants and Catholics were in the respective majorities of the provinces. Moreover, the current majorities were in potential danger of control due to the continued influx of American settlers moving to Canadian territories. The clergy desired minority protections in the establishment of local schools—regardless of whether the majority in a given province was Protestant or Catholic. Consequently, the 1841 act, which formally established the dual system of schooling in Quebec (Bowman, 1991), enabled a Catholic or Protestant minority in a particular locale to dissent and legally establish its own school system including full control over the educational process (Hiemstra, 1994). This general principle continues to hold particular meaning to Canadians (Hayday, 2003).

A further act of 1846 placed the administration of public education largely under the control of the Roman Catholic Church. Formal standards and school inspectors were established for local schools. Since Catholic priests and nuns typically were the most educated individuals in their local respective communities who prospectively met the established requirements, they tended to dominate the local school districts. Predictably, this generated Protestant opposition, which resulted in the government establishing two separate education systems. Two school commissions also were set up to manage and organize the Catholic (mostly French) and the Protestant (mostly English) private schools (Adams, 1968; Vriend, 1994).

CANADA WEST (ONTARIO)

In the early nineteenth century settlers were moving westwards across Canada, founding towns and villages, and many American teachers often were employed in rural schools. In due course it was decided to formalize a set of rules, including a requirement that all teachers must either be Canadian citizens or swear allegiance to the Canadian government. The Common School Act of 1816 was significant because it formalized the possibility of establishing uniquely Canadian schools for all children in any locality where there were twenty or more potential pupils (Wilson, 1970). District, or grammar schools, whose origins stemmed from the 1807 legislation, were not affected by this act and continued in their original format. A Methodist minister, Egerton Ryerson, is credited with being the educator who gave Upper Canada its school system (Johnson, 1968). Influenced by the Ontario system, he shaped Canada's entire English-speaking public school system. As Assistant Superintendent of Education, Ryerson travelled throughout Europe and the United States to view various educational systems before issuing a report to the Canadian government in 1846.

Wilson (1970) described several components of this report. Education was to be Christian, meaning that Scriptural truth and Christian principles would be embraced in the classroom, and compulsory, to ensure a free education for all children, regardless of their social class background. Ryerson also promoted practical education, including a curriculum conducive to preparing students to live and work in society.

Two Common School Acts (1846 and 1850) resulted from Ryerson's report. As Superintendent of Schools for Canada West, Ryerson's proposed act of 1846 gave Upper Canada a provincial school system, normal schools, and a supervision and inspection program (Bredin, 2000). The system followed the Irish National Schools model, dividing the population into Catholic and Protestant entities, and giving both the freedom to instruct in their own principles of religion. The act of 1850 introduced a property tax to finance public schooling thereby accomplishing Ryerson's goal of universal, free education for all children.

While Ryerson's ideal was a unified school system, Johnson (1968) claims that he also upheld the principle of separate schools in Canada West. Ryerson recognized the need for separate Catholic education, but he did not seek to extend its privileges. Instead, Ryerson desired that separate schools continue to promote a Protestant philosophy of education as a forerunner to the creation of an "English" Canada.

After an unsuccessful attempt to unite the two provinces in 1841, Ontario and Quebec, joined by Nova Scotia and New Brunswick, formed a broader confederation. In 1867 Canada became known as the Dominion of Canada by virtue of the British North America Act. The other five provinces subsequently followed until Newfoundland completed the Dominion of Ten Provinces and Two Territories in 1949. The Canada Act of 1982 gave the country its first formal constitution, independent of the long-standing British affiliation, although Elizabeth II retained her honorary title as Queen of Canada as part of the act (Canada has full sovereignty over its realm).

After the passage of the act of 1850, individual provincial public education systems became more organized and began to develop their own specific educational laws (Phillips, 1957). Provincial departments of education, an organized curriculum, and better-trained teachers soon followed. In addition to local taxation, provincial grants were also made available to support education.

THE ATLANTIC COLONIES

The area known as Acadia, functioning under French rule, established its first schools before 1713 (Phillips, 1957). Within their own milieu, the Atlantic colonies struggled with emerging school systems, each independent of the other. That is, there was no unified educational system, curriculum, or means of funding the schools in the respective colonies. Newfoundland's first colony was established in 1610 and its first school was formally opened in 1726 by an Anglican, Henry Jones. Johnson (1968) reports that by 1763, half of Newfoundland's population were Irish fishermen, hence the arrival of Roman Catholic priests in 1770. Methodist missionaries followed soon after. Rowe (1964) noted that it was not until 1836 that the first Education Act was passed, providing financial assistance to schools. Further legislation in the 1840s increased denominational grants (Rowe, 1964). In 1850, the Church of England, in growing competition with the Methodists, tried to have grants subdivided between the two denominations. That is, the Church of England desired that any monies allocated for private education be shared between schools operated under Methodist and Church of England auspices. However, the Methodists stood firm and, in later years, the government established equal grants for Anglicans, Methodists, and Roman Catholics alike. An act of 1892 also recognized the Salvation Army as a denomination for the award of school grants. Many years later (1954) the Pentecostal Assemblies established an educational presence for the first time.

Nova Scotia, formally Acadia, came into existence in 1713. In the beginning, education was a private affair. The first School Act, passed in 1766, gave authority to the Church of England to establish schools. Thereafter, Nova Scotia became a haven for Loyalists who developed religion and education in the province (Hamilton, 1970). An act of 1780 established monetary provision for grammar schools, and in 1808 legislation was passed to establish common or elementary schools (Mathis & Pearl, 1999). Weeren (1993) indicates that for the most part Nova Scotia decided to allow local communities to decide for themselves how best to handle private education, although by the 1860s there was a general mandate that teachers were to respect the Christian religion and Christian morality.

Phillips (1957) suggested that education in New Brunswick was markedly inferior to that in Nova Scotia. Until 1783, the province was not extensively settled. Thereafter, the area experienced an influx of Loyalists and issues such as Confederation in the 1860s dominated provincial politics. However, in 1858 the Parish School Act was passed, allowing New Brunswick to use a property tax to fund its basic public school system. This act defined New Brunswick's non-sectarian school system but it was the cause of later political strife due to the desire of some people to provide separate school legislation. Final settlement of this issue was not realized until the Common School Act of 1871, which made the non-sectarian principle binding on all.

The colonial education system also existed on Prince Edward Island (Hamilton, 1970). The colony was started in 1769 as Ile St. Jean, but later renamed Prince Edward Island. In the early 1800s, some private and many "home" private schools existed as a result of Protestant/Catholic rivalry and whether or not the Bible should be authorized for use in public schools. The Public School Act of 1877 reformed existing legislation so that all schools became non-sectarian.

THE WEST

At the time of Confederation in 1867, that part of Canada still to be known as the Western provinces was basically an uninhabited region stretching from the Great Lakes west to the Pacific and north to the Atlantic. In Western Canada, the Hudson's Bay Company supported education and by 1808 provided teachers for the children of its labourers in the Red River Valley of Manitoba (Lupul, 1970). The company also encouraged all religious denominations to establish churches and schools in the west and provided financial assistance to both Anglicans and Roman Catholics alike.

The area between the Red River and the Rocky Mountains eventually became the provinces of Saskatchewan and Alberta. Phillips (1957) noted that denominational schools began in 1859. In 1875, the Northwest Territories Act provided for further school support. Lawr and Gidney (1973) noted that in most settlements where one faith was predominant, denominational schools were formed. The Free Land Homestead Act of 1872 encouraged migration to the west, and the first state control of schools was enacted by the passage of an ordinance in 1884. West of the Rockies, the first Vancouver Island colonial school was established in Victoria in 1852 (Lupul, 1970). By 1865 there were five such schools in the area. The Common School Act of 1865 gave Vancouver Island a free, but highly centralized and non-denominational school system, wholly financed by government.

Lawr and Gidney (1973) highlighted the fact that many new settlements often attracted more than one religious group and it therefore became very difficult for teachers to form a common school. Protestants often sent their children to non-denominational schools, but they were still schools, which reflected Scripture reading, hymns, and prayer. This practice became a compromise for the various Protestant groups but one that attracted the necessary funding for schools. The only denomination to remain independent of this practice was the Roman Catholic Church.

Between 1857 and 1862, the mainland colony of British Columbia saw several denominational schools established. In 1866 Vancouver Island and the colony of British Columbia united in order to form the province of British Columbia, and public education was introduced by way of the Common School Ordinance of 1869. Raptis (2002) notes that since British Columbia's inception, cultural diversity has been one of its hallmark characteristics.

TWENTIETH-CENTURY PRIVATE EDUCATION

The 1850s saw growing efforts to establish a national school system (Foster & Smith, 2001) as Canada moved towards Confederation. Egerton Ryerson, the former Head of Education for Upper Canada, lobbied to establish a national educational office (Hodgins, 1897) that would separate church and state, thereby negating any sectarian education. For both Upper and Lower Canada, this could potentially have unified culture and strengthened nationalism. Adams (1968) believed that this would have cancelled existing separate school legislation. At the same time, however, Catholic clergy continued to press for a wider range of inclusion for separate schools.

Adams (1968) suggested that a notable piece of legislation was enacted in 1863 just prior to Confederation. During this time frame, Canadian politics was embroiled in numerous controversies surrounding Canada's sovereignty. With the bloody Civil War raging in the United States, Canada became concerned about nationalistic issues, such as the maintenance of a sufficient militia and a unified educational system. Statesman Richard Scott took advantage of the nationalistic genre to focus on education's role in Canada's nationalism. His proposed bill to nationally support religious education failed in 1861 and 1862, but eventually was modified and passed in 1863. The Scott Bill, as it was popularly referred to, was drawn up under the direction of Roman Catholic clergy, in order to extend provisions to separate schools. Sissons (1959) indicated that through this bill, separate education became an integral aspect of Canadian education. By 1867, when Confederation was achieved, any hope of a Canadian national system of education was extinguished (Peszle, 1999). Section 93 of the British North American Act placed education in the hands of the ten provinces. Today, the national Canadian government only superintends directly military/defence education and education related to the status of Aboriginal peoples (Davidson-Harden & Majhanovich, 2004). The 1867 act also guaranteed the right of religious minorities to exist as part of the educational system (Foster & Smith, 2001). Stamp (1970) claimed that, at the time of Confederation, church, state, and educational leaders coexisted in a relatively harmonious working relationship.

Phillips (1957) described the development of public schooling in Canada as having progressed through four stages. The first was characterized by church-controlled education and lasted from the early 1700s through to the mid-1800s.

Stage two, which extended to the late 1800s, saw the introduction of more cen-tralized authority, universal free education, and taxation for schooling at the local level. Stage three, the early 1900s, saw the development of provincial de-partments of education, a more consistent curriculum, better trained teachers, and the start of provincial government financial support for schools. The fourth stage, since the Second World War, has been characterized by the appointment of Ministers of Education in each provincial government and a far greater in-volvement of government in all aspects of education

Contemporary Canadian provincial governments fund a diversity of schools including the public school systems, the separate school systems catering for Roman Catholic and specific Protestant denominations and, finally, a variety of private or independent groups (Easton, 1988). Most of the new Pentecostal Christian education operates within the general guidelines of the latter group.

There are relatively few non-religious, private schools in contemporary Canada and those that do exist tend to be small in size. However, O'Driscoll (1988) reported that private school enrolments had started to increase in the 1970s. By the late 1980s there numbered approximately a quarter of a million students and presently around a third of a million Canadian children are edu-cated annually in approximately 1,500 private schools. The Western provinces tended to have more elementary students than the Eastern provinces (Easton, 1988). O'Driscoll described private schools as generally operating "quietly in the background, with a minimum of government interest, regulation, or support" (p. 184). Private schools in Ontario, New Brunswick, Nova Scotia, Prince Edward Island, and Newfoundland receive no government funding. In Quebec and the four Western provinces, provision is made for public funding subject to various forms of government control.

All private schools in Canada operate under provincial or territorial acts, there being no general national act of education (Kroeker, 2004). Approximately 6 per cent of Canadian children participate in some form of private education (Davies, Aurini, & Quirke, 2002). Funding for private education varies from province to province. It is nonexistent in the Yukon, but as much as 75 per cent in Quebec (Axelrod, 2005; Canadian Education Association, 1984).

THE ROLE OF MULTICULTURALISM

Mallea and Young (1984) reported that the federal Canadian government for-mally adopted a multicultural policy in 1971, rather than the assimilation of diverse cultures into one. As such, individual Canadians are encouraged to con-tinue practising their own unique cultural identities, while simultaneously de-riving pride in being Canadian citizens (Davies, 1999). English-speaking people still constitute the majority of the population. The French-speaking minority remains relatively stable but there has been a marked increase in a variety of non Anglo-French ethnic groups—including Europeans, Asians, and Blacks—as well as new religious sects. Originally concentrated in the prairie provinces of Western Canada, new multicultural groups currently comprise over one-quarter of the Canadian population. Obviously, this has intensified the diversity of variables that now influence education. Hladki (1995) argues that diversity in education is a cornerstone for all contemporary Canadian education policy. Rufo-Lignos (2000) also claims that the public/private debate in education remains fluid and ongoing and will require continual reassessment. Knowledge of Canada's educational past is an essential foundation for future dialogue on a subject that affects all Canadians.

REFLECTIVE QUESTIONS

1. Briefly synthesize the history of education in Canada. What role did curriculum development play in this historical overview?
2. In the reading, the claim is made that Canadian educational institutions are significantly influenced by plural cultural identities. Do you agree? Why or why not?
3. What other influences have shaped the curriculum in Canada's history?
4. In what ways does this reading clarify why Canada does not have a centralized, national curriculum? Should it?
5. What do the authors mean by private education? How did it come about in Canada? Has it changed today?
6. What are your views on private education? What benefits can this type of education provide that public education cannot?

REFERENCES

Adams, H. (1968). *The education of Canadians 1800–1867*, Montreal: Harvest House.

Audet, L. (1970). The French heritage. In D. Wilson, R. Stamp, & L Audet (Eds.), *Canadian education: A history* (pp. 2–23). Scarborough, ON: Prentice-Hall of Canada.

Axelrod, P. (2005). Public money for private schools? Revisiting an old debate. *Education Canada, 45*, 17–19.

Bowman, L. (1991). Catholic religious education in Ontario, opportunities and challenges for the 1990s: Implications. . . . *Religious Education, 86*, 362–377.

Bredin, R. H. (2000, December). Struggling with diversity: The state education of the pluralistic, upper Canadian population, 1791–1841. Doctoral dissertation, University of Toronto, Canada, 2000. *Dissertation Abstracts International, 61*(06), 2218A (AAT NQ50010).

Canadian Education Association. (1984). *Public funding of private schools in Canada*. Research Rep. No. Nov.-84. Toronto: Canadian Education Association.

Davidson-Harden, A., & Majhanovich, S. (2004). Privatisation of education in Canada: A survey of trends. *International Review of Education, 50*, 263–287.

Davies, S. (1999). From moral duty to cultural rights: A case study of political framing in education. *Sociology of Education, 72*, 1–21.

Davies, S., Aurini, J., & Quirke, L. (2002). New markets for private education in Canada. *Education Canada, 42*, 36–39.

Dickinson, G. M., & Dolmage, W. R. (1996). Education, religion, and the courts in Ontario. *Canadian Journal of Education, 21*, 363–383.

Donaldson, E. (1998). Book review: The promise of schooling. *Canadian Journal of Education, 23*, 464–466.

Easton, S. (1988). *Education in Canada: An analysis of elementary, secondary and vocational schooling.* Singapore: The Fraser Institute.

Foster, W. F., & Smith, W. J. (2001). Religion and education in Canada: Part III—An analysis of provincial legislation. *Education Law Journal, 11*, 203–261.

Gayfer, M. (1978). *An overview of Canadian education.* Toronto: Canadian Education Association.

Gossage, C. (1977). *A question of privilege: Canada's independent schools.* Toronto: Peter Martin Associates.

Hamilton, W. (1970). Society and schools in Nova Scotia, New Brunswick and Prince Edward Island. In D. Wilson, R. Stamp, & L. Audet (Eds.), *Canadian education: A history* (pp. 86–125). Scarborough, ON: Prentice-Hall of Canada.

Hayday, M. (2003, November). Bilingual today, united tomorrow: Canadian federalism and the development of the Official Languages in Education Program, 1968–1984. Doctoral dissertation, University of Ottawa, Canada, 2003. *Dissertation Abstracts International, 64*(05), 1808A (AAT NQ79297).

Hiemstra, J. L. (1994). Religious schooling and prejudice in Canada: Implications for public funding of Christian schools. *Journal of Research on Christian Education, 3*, 199–215.

Hladki, J. (1995). Towards a politics of difference in education: A Canadian perspective. *International Studies in Sociology of Education, 5*, 41–56.

Hodgins, J. (1897). *The legislation and history of separate schools in Upper Canada.* Toronto: William Briggs, Wesley Building.

Johnson, H. (1968). *A brief history of Canadian education.* Toronto: McGraw-Hill Canada.

Katz, J. (1974). *Education in Canada.* Hamden, CT: Archon Books.

Kroeker, F. (2004). Overcoming a crucial objection to state support for religious schooling. *Philosophy of Education Yearbook*, 63–71.

Lawr, D., & Gidney, R. (1973). *Educating Canadians.* Toronto: Van Nostrand Reinhold.

Lloyd, D. B. (2002, October). The perceived effects of alternate funding on school division policy and practice for K–12 education in Canada. Doctoral dissertation, Walden University, 2002. *Dissertation Abstracts International, 63*(04), 1262A (AAT 3049900).

Lupul, M. (1970). Education in western Canada before 1873. In D. Wilson, R. Stamp, & L. Audet (Eds.), *Canadian education: A history* (pp. 241–164). Scarborough, ON: Prentice Hall of Canada.

Mallea, J., & Young, J. (1984). *Cultural diversity and Canadian education.* Ottawa, ON: Carleton University Press.

Mathis, W. J., & Pearl, M. L. (1999, April). *Public funding of religious schools: Legal and political implications of current court cases.* Paper presented at the annual meeting of the American Educational Research Association, Montreal, Canada.

Moir, J. (1959). *Church and state in Canada west.* Toronto: University of Toronto Press.

O'Driscoll, D. (1988). Canada. In G. Kurian (Ed.), *World education encyclopedia: Vol. 1.* New York: Facts on File Publications.

Peszle, T. L. (1999, February). Language rights in Quebec education: Sources of law. Master's thesis, McGill University, Canada, 1997. *Masters Abstracts International, 37*(01), 37 (AAT MQ29561).

Phillips, C. (1957). *The development of education in Canada*. Toronto: W. J. Gage & Company.

Raptis, H. S. (2002, April). Dealing with diversity: Multicultural education in British Columbia, 1872–1981. Doctoral dissertation, University of Victoria, Canada, 2001. *Dissertation Abstracts International, 62*(10), 3321A (AAT NQ62524).

Rowe, F. (1964). *The development of education in Newfoundland*. Toronto: The Ryerson Press.

Rufo-Lignos, P. M. (2000, January). Towards a new typology of public and private schools. Doctoral dissertation, Columbia University Teachers College, 1999. *Dissertation Abstracts International, 60*(07), 2316A (AAT 9939546).

Shapiro, B. (1985). *The report of the commission on private schools in Ontario*. Ontario: Ontario Government Printing Office.

Sissons, C. (1959). *Church and state in Canadian education*. Toronto: The Ryerson Press.

Stamp, R. (1970). Education and the economics and social milieu: The English-Canadian scene from the 1870's to 1914. In D. Wilson, R. Stamp, & L. Audet (Eds.), *Canadian education: A history* (pp. 290–313). Scarborough, ON: Prentice-Hall of Canada.

Titley, E., & Miller, P. (1982). *Education in Canada—An interpretation*. Calgary, AB: Detselig Enterprises.

Vriend, J. (1994). Eden despoiled: A questionable experiment in school choice. *Journal of Research on Christian Education, 3*, 217–232.

Weeren, D. (1993). Collaboration, containment and conflict regarding religious education: Three Canadian cases. *Religious Education, 88*, 136–149.

White, L. A. (2003). Liberalism, group rights and the boundaries of toleration: The case of minority religious schools in Ontario. *Canadian Journal of Political Science, 36*, 975–1003.

Wilson, D. (1970). The Ryerson years in Canada west. In D. Wilson, R. Stamp, & L. Audet (Eds.), *Canadian education: A history* (pp. 214–240). Scarborough, ON: Prentice-Hall of Canada.

Zine, J. (2001). Muslim youth in Canadian schools: Education and the politics of religious identity. *Anthropology & Education Quarterly, 32*, 399–423.

8

Connections, Contrarieties, and Convolutions:

Curriculum and Pedagogic Reform in Alberta and Ontario, 1930–1955

LYNN SPEER LEMISKO
KURT W. CLAUSEN

Alberta and Ontario experimented with a number of dramatic organizational, curricular, and pedagogic reforms between *c.* 1930 and the mid-1950s based on propositions put forward by the Progressive Education movement.[1] Informed by progressive ideology, the Departments of Education in both provinces re-organized the grade-level structure from two to four divisions and abolished most formal promotional examinations. Even more indicative of the influence of progressive philosophy, both jurisdictions introduced a child-centred, subject-integrated, activity-based approach known as the Enterprise Method. Equally significant, both Departments fused the content-centred courses history, geography, and civics into a new integrated course: social studies. Taught across all grade levels, this new subject emphasized development of co-operative, democratic behaviour and inquisitiveness through experiential learning.[2] In short, although variations between the two provinces existed, both jurisdictions put forward a concept in curriculum creation that emerged from the same root desire that characterized the Canadian progressive education movement in general: the development of social skills and the individual was more important than amassing knowledge.

By the mid-1950s the progressive spirit to integrate subjects of the curriculum seems to have foundered in both provinces. In Alberta, for instance, the 1953 Department of Education *Bulletin 2*, issued to guide teachers in developing enterprises, no longer insisted on the integration of health and science in enterprises.[3] The term *enterprise* did remain on the pages of curriculum documents for another generation, but interest in the deeply integrated approach waned during the 1950s and faded away in the early 1960s. The deepest division between the provinces can be found in their treatment of social studies. In Alberta, this integrated subject has continued to be part of the core curriculum at all grade levels, while in Ontario for the past fifty years it has been offered only to primary-junior students.

What were the similarities and differences between Alberta's and Ontario's experiences with these innovations? What helped and hindered these curricular and pedagogic reform efforts? And, why did they falter? To address these questions, we conducted a comparative historical study to demonstrate that appropriate teacher education, appropriate funding, and development of appropriate supporting resources were required to ensure that implementation of the reform remained coherent with its underlying theory; that teachers, resource developers, and curriculum developers needed to thoroughly understand the philosophical underpinnings of the reform to ensure a coherent epistemological, pedagogical, and evaluation approach; and that the general social, political, and intellectual environment had a significant impact on each province's ability to engage in and maintain the reform effort.

METHODOLOGY, DEFINITIONS, LIMITATIONS

Canadian educational historians have provided insights into educational policy by examining particular instances of curricular and pedagogic reform efforts as they unfolded within specific regional and provincial jurisdictions (e.g., Hallman, 1992; Thomson, 2000). They have also drawn broader generalizations by referring to Canadian policy as a whole (e.g., Barrow, 1979; Titley, 1990). Rarer in number are comparative studies that examine similarities and differences in programs and implementation among provinces. Such comparisons are necessary for the development of a more complex understanding of factors that have affected curriculum and pedagogic reform in Canada. Although George Tomkins (1986), for example, argued that a common set of ideas underpinned curriculum development in English Canada, one wonders if curriculum choices are or were ever guided by a shared set of assumptions, especially when considering the socio-political and regional diversity of the nation and the fact that education is under provincial jurisdiction.

Given the current trend toward the creation of common regional curricula, we feel it is important that Canadian educators develop not only an understanding of how unique educational circumstances have affected education in certain localities, but also an understanding of how similarities and differences appear between regions across Canada. By examining studies that compare and contrast provincial experiences in dealing with curricular and pedagogic reform, educators might come closer to comprehending whether Canadians have a shared conception of education and schooling. Based on this thinking, we designed this study to compare the development and implementation of integrated programs and pedagogy in Alberta and Ontario between 1930 and 1955.

We selected this period because it was a time of intense curricular and pedagogic experimentation across Canada influenced by the Canadian progressive education movement, which, according to Patterson (1970), "represented a revolt against existing formal and traditional schooling [advocating] . . . freedom for the pupil to develop naturally; interest to serve as the motive for all work; the teacher to be a guide, not a task-master" (p. 373; see also Tomkins, 1986, p. 190). Although variations in ideology among Canadian progressive educators occurred, many endeavoured to introduce child-centred, hands-on pedagogies and developed new programs of study to provide schooling to closely match the needs and interests of children. In the first wave of curricular reform, educators added non-traditional subjects: agriculture, health, and civics. Later, progressive curriculum reformers designed programs to integrate traditional and non-traditional subjects like history, geography, and civics into the blended subject called social studies. In addition, they designed the project approach or "Enterprise," to integrate social studies with science, health, and other subjects as necessary for a project. For our analysis, we use the effort that Canadian progressives made to integrate a variety of traditional subjects into a single subject or project as a marker of the flourishing or floundering of progressivism during this era.

We selected Ontario and Alberta because these two provinces were considered educational leaders during various time periods. Ontario was the first Anglo-Canadian province to develop and implement a centralized curriculum and pedagogy for publicly funded grade schools. We chose Alberta because, although other jurisdictions did experiment with progressive ideas and practices, "Alberta led all provinces in its enthusiastic acceptance of progressivism" (Tomkins, 1986, p. 194) and, according to Tomkins (1986) the curriculum revisions undertaken in this province between 1936 and 1940, were "the high water mark in the acceptance of progressive education" (p. 195).

In comparing the two provinces, we reconstructed historical conditions through the examination, interpretation, and corroboration of both primary and secondary source documents, including contemporary curricula, departmental annual reports, articles, letters, speech transcripts, minutes, as well as other historical studies. These data sources allowed us to recreate past events and circumstances in each province. In turn, we compared events in one province to the other to provide more complex insights into the factors that affected the development and implementation of the reformed programs.

EDUCATIONAL CIRCUMSTANCES AND ATTITUDES LEADING UP TO THE 1930S

Comparing Circumstances

In the first decade of the twentieth century, many outward aspects of the two provincial educational systems looked remarkably similar. In the programs of study, this resemblance was not surprising: the original curriculum instituted for Alberta schools, on establishment of the province in 1905, was closely modelled on the Ontario system of "standards" (Alberta, *Annual Report*, 1907, pp. 79–109; von Heyking, 1996, pp. 33–34). Like its eastern prototype, the purpose of the Alberta program was to provide a sound basic schooling in the fundamentals and to prepare the small number of students who went on to high school for further academic study. As well, both Ontario and Alberta had developed strongly centralized Departments of Education to deal with the quite scattered and, in places, secluded populations. Lastly, both had a small but vocal intellectual community that argued for progressive educational reform.

Despite these similarities, demographic differences existed between Ontario and Alberta that may have affected the way each jurisdiction perceived education. Ontario, for example, had undergone a lengthy period of land clearing and settling for over a hundred years, and by the turn of the twentieth century had developed several larger urban centres. Those who arrived in Alberta at this time, however, had a sense of being in a newly settled land, with a chance to remake society, and break free from outworn traditions (Byrne, 1991; Francis & Palmer, 1992; Palmer & Palmer, 1990).

Although the provinces had some educational circumstances in common, this divergence in perspective may explain why a significant difference in attitude toward curriculum and pedagogic reform developed.

Educational Circumstances in Alberta

Throughout the first three decades of the twentieth century, curriculum development was an ongoing project for the Alberta government. Although "some element of flexibility" (von Heyking, 1996, p. 35) had been included in the original program of 1905, Alberta's educational leaders were soon convinced that it did not meet the needs and interests of Alberta students. Health, agriculture, and a new stress on civics were added to the program in 1910. However, these additions did not represent a profound change in attitude by the Department about what should be taught and learned. Our analysis found very little that reflected methods based on the newer child psychology models of contemporary educational reformers who advocated the education of the whole child through hands-on or activity approaches (Alberta, *Annual Report*, 1913, pp. 81–158; von Heyking, 1996, pp. 46 & 48). After the Great War, the Alberta program underwent a profound and sustained transition, evolving from a more traditional curriculum framework to one of the most progressive in Canada.

Following consultative discussions with a wide variety of stakeholder groups, the Department introduced a revised elementary program (grades 1–8) in 1922 which contained modernized basic subject areas along with new ones; this included citizenship, industrial arts, hygiene, physical education, and household economics (Alberta *Course of Studies*, 1922; McNally, 1922, p. 28). Proud of what was perceived to be an innovative, child-centred curriculum, Deputy Minister of Education G. Fred McNally reported that "requests for copies [of the program] had been received from every province as well as from Newfoundland and the Yukon" (McNally, 1964, p. 63).

Educational Circumstances in Ontario

In contrast to the events unfolding in Western Canada, the focus of Ontario's official curriculum policy changed little between the creation of the Ontario Department of Education in 1871 and the mid-1930s. It adhered to a formalized, discipline-based approach towards education involving a great deal of rote-learning, drill, and memorization (Curtis, 1988, pp. 107–109). Under the direction of the Elementary or Secondary Education Branch, a few subject specialists sporadically updated guidelines that school inspectors then enforced to secure uniform standards throughout the province. In almost all cases, each discipline was closely tied to a specific textbook (Gidney, 1999, pp. 19–21). Even with opposition from teachers' associations, local authorities, and county inspectors promoting changes reflective of the Western reforms, no profound revisions were undertaken until the Conservative government was ousted from power in 1934.[4]

Although conditions between the two provinces seemed similar on the surface, the Ontario government did not experience a period of serious, concerted experimentation with or acceptance of innovative curriculum or pedagogy until the mid-1930s, unlike its counterpart in Alberta, which began making serious changes a decade earlier.

EDUCATORS AND REFORM POLITICS

As the century progressed, political and ideological variations between Ontario and Alberta became more pronounced because shifts in provincial government parties and their links to the educational and intellectual communities affected their attitudes toward curricular and pedagogic reform.

Alberta Progressive Educators and the UFA

Many people who settled in Alberta were seeking a fresh start, believing they could reconstruct a more just society. From this desire grew a number of movements supported by ideologies that advocated deep social and political change. In their political rhetoric, the United Farmers' Association (UFA) reflected these ideals. The UFA began a concerted effort directly after the Great War to improve and advance society through a co-operative, democratic process of social, economic, and political reform (Laycock, 1990, pp. 64–65). Many members of the UFA, which formed the Alberta government between 1921 and 1935, believed that education contributed to the creation of democratic, co-operative citizens and the transformation of society (Patterson, 1968, p. 70).

The Great Depression of the 1930s only intensified the belief that social and economic change were necessary and that curriculum reform was an important avenue for such change. Many UFA members assumed that traditional education perpetuated and promoted an outdated competitive economic system that had led to the Depression. They argued that bringing about desired changes to the economic system required sweeping reforms to school curriculum. This faction within the organization received general support through a resolution passed at the 1934 UFA annual convention. It urged the Department of Education to develop a school program that suggested "throughout the entire curriculum, the idea of the advance of society towards a new form of social organization in which the principle of a struggle for private profit shall be displaced by the principles of equity, justice, mutual aid and social well being" (Patterson, 1968, pp. 70–72).

These beliefs meshed well with American Progressive theories that many Alberta educational leaders advocated (Crawford, 1936; Newland, 1921). During the 1920s and early 1930s, a growing number of these educators had undertaken graduate studies in American universities, many attending Columbia and the University of Chicago, which were both considered hotbeds of progressive education. Armed with new ideas about schooling in a democratic society, these reformers suggested that the elementary curriculum should be based on an activity or project approach and argued further that such socialized activity, with the integration of subject matter through large units of work developed around the genuine life interests and experiences of learners, would be ideal for the one-room schools in Alberta (Patterson, 1968, pp. 92, 120–122, & 129–130; von Heyking, 1996, p. 180 & 185–186).

With the passing of the 1934 UFA resolution and general support of the UFA government, the Department of Education struck a curriculum revision committee composed of one school inspector, William E. Hay, and two normal school instructors, Donalda Dickie and Olive M. Fisher. The group met "for the purposes of preparing an [elementary] activity curriculum to be introduced on a trial basis in the fall term of 1935" (Patterson, 1968, pp. 121–122).[5]

Ontario: Changing Political Parties and Curriculum Reform

Arguing against Ontario's rather inflexible and centralized educational system, several teachers' groups in Ontario pressured the Department for educational reforms to better serve society. Unlike the more radical UFA in Alberta, who openly consulted with a variety of voices within the educational establishment, the Ontario Conservative government tended to refrain from action unless they were directly and vocally petitioned from other levels of the hierarchy. Even then, historian W. G. Fleming (1972, pp. 2–3) maintained that the upper hierarchy of the Ontario education system had become experts in actively turning a deaf ear to dissenting voices (see also Manzer, 1994; Mosely, 1968).

The Ontario Education Association had long advocated the importance of student-centred pedagogy. Although people from Ontario spoke on the subject rather frequently, the most vehement and memorable support for such approaches appears to have travelled to Ontario through circuit tours by progressive speakers and literature brought to the annual conventions.[6] Despite this ferment, comments in newspapers and printed political debates throughout the 1920s and 1930s indicated that these ideas were already impacting educational reform in Alberta. These sources made scathing comparisons between the cutting-edge of educational thought in the Western provinces and the mired conservatism of Ontario's educational system (Patterson, 1970, pp. 377–378).[7] Demonstrating the difference in attitude, one of the members of the UFA Alberta government, C. L. Gibbs (1928), expressed the sentiments of many Westerners, expressing the hope

> that when the [Alberta] Department mountain had finished its labours there would not issue forth some little mouse, grey with Ontario dust and heavy with Ontario prejudice, but that we would have an Act that would really meet our particular needs and be in harmony with progressive ideals now becoming current in the educational world. (p. 3)

By the 1930s, demand in Ontario for progressive reforms became increasingly vehement. The New Education Fellowship, a small but influential organization, pressured the Ontario Education Association for progressive reform. Eventually, an amalgamation of various teachers' federations, parent groups, trustees' associations, and members of the Ontario Education Association itself formed the broad-based Ontario Educational Research Committee. Describing it as "a membership reading like a *Who's Who* of Ontario education at mid-decade,"

Stamp (1982) concluded that this committee's main purpose was "to rip apart current curriculum and instructional practices" (p. 166).

But, only when a new Liberal government ascended to power in 1934 under Mitchell Hepburn did the Department become more receptive to the calls for educational reform. Following remarkably close on the heels of the sweeping changes being broadcast from Alberta, the new Ontario Minister of Education, Leo J. Simpson, announced in 1936 that a committee would be appointed to create a new Program of Studies for the elementary system. Whether influenced by his senior departmental officials, the continued pressure by the Ontario educational elite, or the example put forth from Alberta, Simpson insisted that the new curriculum would be based on more progressive methods.[8] To facilitate this process, two men who were sympathetic to the progressive movement were appointed as co-chairs of the program committee: Thornton Mustard of the Toronto Normal School, and Stanley A. Watson, principal of Toronto's Keele Street Public School. When they issued their final report, the new ideas in the curriculum reflected Alberta's guidelines. In fact, the Alberta Supervisor of Schools, H. C. Newland (in Stamp, 1982) noted with glee, "This is the first time on record that the good old province of Ontario saw fit to import an educational procedure from the West" (p. 167). Although the American progressive movement appeared to heavily influence Alberta's educational reform, committee members for the Ontario curriculum acknowledged Great Britain as the primary contributor to their revisions (Ontario *Programme of Studies*, 1937, pp. 5–6). This difference in influences (or at least the willingness to acknowledge the origins of influence) highlights the divergence in the political and ideological circumstances of the two provinces. Although similar ideas of educational reform influenced both provinces, Ontario, deeply steeped in traditional philosophic idealism, looked more toward Great Britain than the United States for intellectual leadership, and did not appear as deeply committed to social and political change. Alberta, in contrast, experimented with more radical types of political parties and with ideas from American pragmatist philosophical approaches to education for a democratic society. This difference in general philosophical influence may have helped Alberta's progressive curriculum reformers and hindered progressive educators in Ontario.

COMPARING THE REFORMED CURRICULA

When Alberta and Ontario unveiled their new elementary curriculum programs, both documents had all the earmarks of a truly progressive spirit: integrated subject areas, the promotion of child-centred, hands on/discovery pedagogic approaches, and the abolishment of formal promotion examinations at the elementary level (Newland, 1937, p. 15; Ontario, *Annual Report*, 1938).

However, clear differences existed between them in the degree of integration expected and the amount of direction in the documents to guide implementation of the programs.

Alberta Curriculum

The Alberta elementary curriculum (1936) for grades 1 through 6 was ready for trial implementation in September 1935. This curriculum, which closely adhered to the project approach devised by the American progressive scholar W. H. Kilpatrick (1918), was the first official curriculum in Canada to wholeheartedly advocate such a teaching method. Activities were to be directed toward the solving of selected problems in socialized projects labelled enterprises. Within an enterprise, this curriculum broke down traditional subject matter classifications, correlated, and consolidated many different learning units through socialized learning activities and experiences. School learning "embrace[d] not merely the knowledge and skills of the traditional school 'subjects,' but also many appreciations, attitudes, ideals and incidental habits and abilities" (p. 4). The program also stipulated child-centred pedagogy—that is, learning by doing, with the "things to do . . . resid[ing] in the experience of the child" (p. 4).

To ease the transition to the new approach, the finalized elementary program (1936) did not make the enterprise compulsory; it designated instructional materials in a dual manner: subjects (such as reading, arithmetic, science, art, and music), and enterprises (p. 5). Social studies, introduced as a new integrated subject, represented "a fusion of Geography, History and Civics" (Newland, 1936, p. 16). Suggested enterprises were listed alongside subjects in the program (1936), and teachers could "elect as much or as little of the enterprise work as they desire," although teachers were encouraged to attempt at least one or two enterprises per year, to a maximum of six (p. 5).

In 1940, after the new elementary program had been in place for several years allowing teachers to become familiar with its goals and approaches (Newland, 1940, p. 14), the Department issued a revised edition (1940) that involved "a further step . . . towards complete integration of the Program, with the result that the integrated part of the Program now includes History, Geography, Elementary Science, Health and Physical Education" (p. 27).

Ontario: The Little Grey and Blue Books

Contained in the small, grey-covered booklet, the revised curriculum in Ontario entitled the *Programme of Studies for Grades I to VI of the Public and Separate Schools* (1937) soon became known as the "Little Grey Book." Similar to the Alberta program, this curriculum advocated the development of socially desirable qualities and abilities, rather than amassing knowledge. The Ontario document stated that "any education worthy of that name must be planned in accordance with the best available evidence on the nature of the child's development" (p. 5). It determined the function of the school to provide a "stimulating environment" which directed pupils' natural tendencies "into useful and desirable attitudes" (p. 5). The document concluded: "[I]n short, the school must follow the method of nature, stimulating the child, through his own interests, into activities and guiding him into experiences useful for the satisfaction and development of his needs" (p. 6).

Although Ontario reformers did not introduce the Enterprise Method in full-blown description at all grade levels, they took what they considered to be revolutionary action to change the curriculum's traditional fifteen-subject arrangement. Reinforcing the importance of basic reading and inquiry skills, the authors fused the old disciplines into seven broad areas: health, English, social studies, natural science, arithmetic, music, and art. This new program elevated the conventionally fringe subjects of music, art, and physical education from the status of optional subjects or extracurricular activities to the importance of the traditional subjects.

In addition, the curriculum committee introduced the integrated social studies (Ontario, *Programme of Studies*, 1941), using words and set-up almost identical to the Alberta Social Studies model: a mixture of geography, history, and civics, which was to represent 20 per cent of the time spent in school. Rather than the memorization of facts in a chronological fashion grade after grade, children developed desirable social attitudes and inquiring, well-informed minds, interested in understanding their society. They worked their way outward through concentric circles of understanding. Beginning with a study of home and school, students then moved on to study the town, province, then country, followed by other countries, and ultimately to the comparison of ancient and modern social life (p. 60). Although this description seems more structured than that of the Alberta curriculum, teachers were instructed not to worry if students accumulated knowledge in an unsystematic way.

Overall, the program removed restrictions on teachers and pupils by providing latitude for selective emphases and variation in methods, at a teacher's discretion. Outside a common core of knowledge, each student was encouraged to follow his or her "individual talent."[9] Obviously, this meant that a large part of the program was to be delivered using alternatives to the traditional formal lesson. However, when the "Grey Book" came out in Ontario in 1937, it gave little instruction on how to execute the integrated program. Beyond general discussions of the importance of a unified curriculum, it provided no details about the workings of the project method, nor stipulated specific enterprise ideas.

IMPLEMENTATION EFFORTS: ISSUES FOR TEACHERS

Problems with the new programs arose almost immediately in both provinces, particularly with the implementation of the new, activity-based pedagogy. The teachers of the new elementary curricula had great difficulty translating the suggested programs into meaningful learning experiences.

Although the Alberta Department of Education made a significant effort to train teachers in the new approach through summer and normal school sessions, the curriculum developers complained that such efforts focused on pedagogical techniques rather than on the philosophy and theory of the approach. Consequently, in implementing the program, teachers often mistook "the means for the end and . . . allowed the pupils' activity to degenerate into purely mechanical exercises" (Alberta, *Annual Report*, 1937, p. 52). In addition, many teachers believed that the program objectives were too vague. The document focused mainly on attitudes, appreciations, and habits, leaving teachers with no clear idea of expected content knowledge outcomes. The Department's annual reports included notes by school inspectors that, because teachers lacked an understanding of the theory of the activity approach, they tended "to define activity in terms of bodily movements" (Alberta, *Annual Report*, 1938, p. 61). The school inspectors further concluded that enterprises often became "mere pleasant time-filling activity" and even the skill subjects like arithmetic suffered with "far more movement, visiting and consultation than is necessary in a period devoted to mental activity" (Alberta, *Annual Report*, 1941, p. 69).

Alberta teachers also faced two new problems with the progressive program. With the abolishment of all but two formal promotional examinations, teachers were required to devise internal evaluation tools to place "pupils where they can work to best advantage" (Newland, 1937, p. 15). With program goals emphasizing habits, appreciations, and the creation of responsible citizens, teachers were "simply at a loss" (p. 15) about how to measure student achievement. And, with the new emphasis on student freedom and activity, discipline issues increased. The pages of the Alberta Teachers' Association magazine provide evidence of escalating anxiety, where hints for keeping discipline began to appear on a regular basis. In addition, beginning in 1945, the Chief Superintendent of Schools began to devote a section in the Department's annual report to the observations of superintendents about discipline and control (Alberta, *Annual Reports,* 1945, p. 28; 1946, p. 31; & 1947, p.36; von Heyking, 1996, p. 262).

In Ontario, the creators of the 1937 program ran into similar roadblocks. Because the Department had responded to pressures from various interest groups, its officials had expected that the document would be disseminated to a largely young, well-educated generation of teachers who knew the scholarship

surrounding its progressive spirit, and could apply the various approaches needed to reach its goals (Gidney, 1999, p. 32; Ontario, *Annual Report*, 1936, p. 2). Instead, it was faced with numerous teachers who seemed to ignore many aspects
of the reformed program, and who complained that the curriculum documents
did not include details about the workings of the project method or stipulate
specific enterprise ideas. In explaining this apathetic reaction, Patterson (1990)
referred to comments made by V. K. Greer, chief inspector of schools in Ontario:
"Even though young teachers had received training at normal school which was
intended for them for the new curriculum, many of them . . . lacked the courage
to follow the new methods" (p. 106).

The root of the problem was not necessarily a lack of courage, however. As
in Alberta, the problem was related to the misunderstanding of or hostility toward the philosophy of the new method. Although progressive ideas in the form
of Dewey's pragmatic philosophy had been part of the theoretical discourse of
normal schools in Ontario since 1907,[10] such ideas were not adopted in practice.
Although teachers had learned about pragmatic philosophy, the instruction in
normal schools had left most teachers unable to internalize the philosophical assumptions of curriculum integration and the enterprise approach. Phillips (1957)
concluded that these teachers adhered only to the external forms of the progressive approach, thereby losing the significance of such experiences.

> Many teachers thought of enterprises as the material objects produced in pe-
> riods allotted to work with paper, paste, wood, and bits of metal. When these
> teachers ceased having their pupils engage in such nearly useless construction,
> or were told to do so, it appears that enterprise work fell off. (p. 465)

Numerous archival records throughout the late 1930s displayed teachers'
apparent ignorance of progressive approaches or refusal to teach using any approach but traditional methods. In letters sent to the Department, some teachers asked for guidance in undertaking projects; others complained about the
noise levels and lack of discipline associated with the activities. One rural teacher
starkly submitted her resignation, stating that having taught in the system for
forty years she was not going to change now.[11] Some members of the various
grassroots groups that had originally petitioned for the change also began to turn
rather cold towards the new document, arguing that the method was lessening
the emphasis on the three Rs, and weakening discipline and authority (Stamp,
1982). The immediate response of practitioners to the new Ontario program was
unfavourable, if not hostile.

IMPLEMENTATION EFFORTS: RESPONSES FROM REFORMERS AND DEPARTMENTS OF EDUCATION

Between the introduction of the new curricula and their eventual demise, progressive reformers in each province endeavoured to respond helpfully to the implementation problems. However, clear differences occurred in the depth and intensity of the help offered by each province.

The Alberta Response

Believing that appropriately trained educators were the key to proper implementation, Alberta reformers continued their effort to educate teachers in the goals and methods of the activity approach. Normal schools implemented a "new and dynamic type of instruction" to exemplify the new technique, and teachers were encouraged to attend summer school sessions and special programs at teachers' conventions to learn about the new method (Alberta, *Annual Report*, 1940, p. 15). In addition, the Alberta Teachers' Association established professional libraries in school divisions across the province and sponsored numerous local teacher study groups to examine progressive practice.

Although these efforts certainly indicate a strong commitment to implementing the new program and pedagogy, von Heyking (1996) points out that "varying degrees of support for the innovations" (p. 192) occurred among those involved in these pre- and in-service teacher education efforts. For example, a survey of staff at the Edmonton Normal School indicated that opinion among the faculty ranged from those who were completely committed to the deep integration of subject matter and emphasis on development of social attitudes, to those who were "subject-minded" and regarded "the enterprise as merely another, though important, addition to the battery of methods and techniques employed by the progressive teacher" (Doucette, n.d., n.p.). Although teachers may have received a reasonably sound education in the pedagogical techniques, they most likely received mixed and perhaps confusing messages about progressive philosophy and theory.

The education programs for pre- and in-service teachers apparently did not deal effectively with teachers' tribulations in devising internal evaluation tools to measure student achievement. In 1943, the Department of Education, reacting to teachers' continued difficulties with assessment, issued a Supplement to the elementary program of studies (1943) that "set out the *minimum pupil attainments* [sic] that parents, teachers and superintendents should expect to find in the average school" (p. 13). The Department hoped that these attainment targets would establish "a basis for comparing the work of schools in different parts of the Province" (p. 13). In 1946 and 1947, the Department, offering further assistance to teachers in assessing student achievement, introduced a province-wide test-ing program that determined the level of essential skills among grade 6 students. The Department hoped that this examination would maintain a "greater unifor-mity of standards throughout the province" (Alberta, *Annual Report*, 1946, p. 65; 1947, p. 57). Because this assessment program was contrary to the philosophy of the progressive program and pedagogy, this standardized test of skills was incompatible with the theoretical approach that advocated for locally developed, context-specific evaluation.

In contrast, teacher education had enhanced teachers' understanding that progressive practice used a wide variety of resource materials, reference books, and locally developed units. However, despite the efforts of teachers and edu-cation leaders to convince school boards to purchase necessary materials and equipment, school inspector reports into the 1940s indicated that the lack of appropriate resources was problematic (Alberta, *Annual Report*, 1942, p. 29; von Heyking, 1996, pp. 263–264). Hence, despite the fact that progressive the-ory advocated that teachers develop their own units and projects in relation to the particular needs and interests of their students, some members of Alber-ta's Department of Education reasoned that it should assist teachers to develop classroom programs by creating more child-centred, user-friendly textbooks to match program goals (von Heyking, 1996, pp. 254–256). Further, believing that "the lack of teacher reference materials geared particularly to our curricular out-lines may have contributed in part to certain malpractices that have occurred within our Enterprise education" (Alberta, *Annual Report*, 1947, p. 56), some members of the Department (1947) also recommended that the newly estab-lished Teachers' Service Bureau undertake the construction and distribution of "experimental resource units designed to be of direct assistance in handling the topics prescribed or suggested for general use at various grade levels" (p. 56). By 1948, the Bureau had begun the distribution of such resources at no charge, a practice that continued throughout the 1950s.

Overall, despite the relatively intense professional development efforts, Alberta teachers remained generally ill prepared to implement progressive meth-ods. In addition, as various curriculum committees tinkered with the course of studies and as the Department continued to centrally distribute resource materi-als and evaluation tools, the programs and practices actually in use in Alberta schools became an awkward blend of traditional and progressive approaches.

The Ontario Response

By 1941, the Ontario Department of Education realized that teachers were either not employing the new program, or were doing so in a haphazard or formulaic fashion.[12] According to R. M. Stamp (1982), educational leaders in the province may have employed ineffective implementation strategies. For example, little difference appeared at the Normal School level between the list of departmental summer courses before and after the introduction of the curriculum reforms. In fact, courses and examination papers did not particularly stress progressive techniques. Many public school inspectors echoed this lack of emphasis, repeatedly reminding teachers to drill, review, and test student knowledge in the core subjects. Although the Department advised inspectors to familiarize teachers with the new methodology, it gave few details concerning the fine points of the enterprise approach beyond what was found in the "Little Grey Book." As related by Stamp (1982), at least one school inspector's ultimate goal of the new education was merely "to interest the child in his work, so that he wants to do what we want him to do" (p. 169).

Nevertheless, the Ontario Department of Education took some action toward helping teachers implement the new curriculum. The chairs of the curriculum committee, Mustard and Watson, were sent on whistle-stop speaking engagements concerning the innovations. These engagements did not involve actual training sessions and no follow-up information was supplied, leaving teachers with the impression that the new method was nothing more than a fad supported by slogans (Stamp, 1982, p. 171).

To ameliorate implementation problems, the Department re-struck the program committee in 1941 with the goal of updating the curriculum to give teachers concrete guidance in realizing the goals of progressive education. To this end, a new section was added to the document entitled "The Enterprise Method," embodying a truncated version of the techniques put forward in *The Enterprise in Theory and Practice* by Alberta progressive reformer, Donalda Dickie (1940). This section also advised teachers to organize informal meetings to discuss the enterprise approach.

The Ontario curriculum committee's only other addition to the program was a response to media demands for assurance that the Department of Education was cognizant that schooling should reflect the effort to win the war and maintain the Canadian way of life. This addition, extolling the benefits of a democratic society, based on Christian ideals and its bulwark, the British Commonwealth, was repeatedly mentioned in several places: the preamble, the Enterprise, and the Social Studies sections. The Ontario *Programme of Studies* (1941) proclaimed that "national character" could be strengthened only through training students in the rights and responsibilities of citizenship, and concluded that democracy demands "the finest service of which [the child] is capable, and a willingness to make sacrifices for the common welfare" (pp. 5, 16–24, & 71–86).

Beyond the whistle-stop tour and curriculum additions, the Ontario Department of Education did not engage in further efforts to enhance implementation of the enterprise approach, although the Depression had left many schools, especially in rural areas, woefully short of materials needed as teachers' aids, for professional development, or even books for the libraries (Patterson, 1990, p. 110). Although letters from teachers continued to arrive at the Department on a frequent basis, pleading for more concrete aid to understand the progressive techniques, the Department, perhaps distracted by the war effort, offered the same number of training sessions on the Enterprise Method during the early 1940s as it had in the late 1930s. According to Fleming (1971, pp. 9–11), enterprises were never evaluated or used for promotional purposes and only sparse records show that Ontario teachers actually used the approach at this time.

Although both provinces endeavoured to respond helpfully to implementation problems, Alberta clearly made a more profound effort, going beyond making changes to the curriculum document. Nevertheless, Alberta's approach did not prove to be any more successful in sustaining the progressive program in the long run, as compared to Ontario's approach.

LONG-TERM REACTIONS TO THE PROGRESSIVE CURRICULUM AND PEDAGOGIC REFORM

Eventually, both Alberta and Ontario returned to a subject/discipline-based curriculum. Both provinces reacted, in part, to similar negative responses to the progressive program that arose from the broader stakeholder community. However, particular local circumstances also affected the reaction of each Department of Education.

Alberta Reactions

Between 1945 and 1955, an increasing wave of scholarship turned against the progressive ideas embedded in the revised curriculum. Critics, like university professors H. Neatby (1953) and W. G. Hardy (1954), argued that the approach concentrated too much attention on the development of attitudes and behaviours and pleasurable activities and too little on the development of essential basic skills and intellectual rigour. These critics also argued that progressive education was amoral, irreligious, and un-Canadian because it arose out of a materialistic and relativistic American social orientation. Alberta businessmen, politicians, and the general public took up many of these criticisms.[13] Expressing dissatisfaction with the programs and the approach, they were convinced that progressive education had led to falling academic standards. Caught up in the post-war economic boom, parents and the general public were convinced that

schooling should better enable students to participate in the economic opportunities at hand in Alberta; they argued that education should produce high quality technicians and professional people who were in high demand in Alberta's
vigorous economy (von Heyking, 1996).

Although Alberta did not experience a change in government during this
time, there had been a change in personnel at the upper echelons of the Department of Education. H. C. Newland, a vehement anti-traditionalist advocate of
the integrated progressive approach, had resigned as Deputy Minister, replaced
by W. H. Swift, who took a more moderate position. Although Swift (1954) challenged Neatby's more strident claims about the ineffectiveness of progressive
education, he believed "that in some degree theory and enthusiasm have outrun
practice and practicability in instituting changes" (n.p.). Under Swift's leadership, the elementary curriculum committee once again revised the program of
studies in 1955 to re-clarify program goals. Except for social studies, which has
been retained as a compulsory subject in Alberta to the present, this committee
disintegrated the course of studies to re-emphasize content while attempting to
retain child-centred pedagogy.

Ontario Reactions

In 1943, shortly after the dissemination of the new program of studies that included the Enterprise Method, the Ontario Liberals fell from power, replaced by
a Conservative government under Col. George Drew. Rather than promoting a
progressive agenda, the Tories focused on the promotion of an education system
that included the inculcation of patriotism, Christian principles, self-discipline,
the nuclear family, and ethical values for freedom and democracy, re-emphasiz-
ing basic reading and mathematical skills (Drew, 1943–1944). The Department
made no changes to the program documents themselves, however, believing that
another round of curriculum reform would have inserted unnecessary chaos
during a time of great disruption for an administration caught within the strains
of an escalating and costly war effort.

The true end of the first progressive era in Ontario can be linked to the cabinet
shuffle of 1951, which resulted in a newly appointed Minister of Education. In this
move, the progressive Dana Porter was replaced with a long-time Department
and University of Toronto bureaucrat, William J. Dunlop. The complete anti-
thesis of his predecessor, Dunlop put forward a paternalistic view of education.
He maintained that it was the sworn responsibility of Ontario teachers to inculcate a uniform body of knowledge, promulgated by a centralized Department,
based on the will of the populace and established thought (Foley, 1966). Dunlop
repeatedly voiced his antipathy towards the 1941 program of study, stating that

he would not rest until "the last shreds of this so-called progressive education are gone" because it merely encouraged "self-expression and day-dreaming ... to the exclusion of down-to-earth fundamentals" (Dunlop, 1953, p. 63).

He found ample support for his continued battle against progressivism from Neatby's (1953) hugely successful book *So Little for the Mind*. Following her recommendations, Dunlop's plans included the subdividing of social studies into history and geography and the return of Latin to the curriculum. Ontario's mid-century experiment with the integration of disciplines came to a grinding halt.[14] Until the neo-progressive movement of the late 1960s, the Social Studies component of the elementary program up to grade 6 was the only element of the progressive curriculum to survive Dunlop's reactionary reforms.

CHALLENGES TO CURRICULUM AND PEDAGOGIC REFORM

The comparison of the curriculum reform paths taken by Alberta and Ontario reveals conditions that affected the development and implementation of curricula and pedagogy based on propositions put forward by the Canadian progressive education movement. In the Ontario example, the lack of appropriate education for both pre-service and in-service teachers in the new approaches hindered efforts to implement them. At the same time, the Alberta example demonstrates that, although efforts may be exerted to educate teachers, training in pedagogical techniques was practically useless because it was not accompanied by an effort to help teachers internalize the underlying theory and philosophy. The Alberta example also demonstrates that despite a commitment to teacher education, differences in degree of support for reform among teacher educators gave teachers mixed messages about theory and philosophy.

Our examination of the circumstances in both Ontario and Alberta indicates that teachers were not provided with either the education or the financial resources to develop appropriate teaching materials. As a result, teachers relied on materials that did not necessarily match the goals or pedagogy of the program, or the needs of their particular students and projects. Without appropriate education, teachers had difficulty devising strategies to use available materials in ways that were authentic to the new approach.

Added to this issue, Alberta and Ontario progressive reformers did not carefully consider the implications for assessment and evaluation that came with new curricula and pedagogical approaches. This failing implies that development and implementation efforts are hindered if a coherent approach to all aspects of an educational endeavour is not formulated, that is, a coherent epistemology, pedagogy, and evaluation. Without this coherence, the resulting programs in both Alberta and Ontario almost necessarily became a strange patchwork of the traditional and progressive.

This historical study suggests that differences in social and political circumstances and ideology both helped and hindered curricular and pedagogic reform. The Ontario example indicates that a changing political situation, with corresponding changes in ideology, had a dramatic effect on reform efforts: hindering, then helping, then hindering again, depending on the party in power and the minister in charge. The Alberta example demonstrates that the general attitude toward reform and the apparent ideological consensus among education reformers and political reformers proved helpful in the initial development and implementation. However, this example also demonstrates such a consensus, whether apparent or real, was difficult to sustain and that when it disintegrated, the curricular reform effort disintegrated along with it.

Taken together, this comparison demonstrates the connections, contrarieties, and convolutions of curricular and pedagogic reform that unfolded in the two provinces between *c.* 1930 and 1955. If educators were to use these past experiences to inform their current efforts to reform curriculum and pedagogy, they might attend to the conditions that affected these earlier reform efforts to ensure that implementation of the reform remained coherent with its underlying theory, including appropriate teacher education, appropriate funding, and appropriate supporting material. As well, such reformers need to ensure that the philosophical underpinnings of the reform approach are thoroughly understood by teachers, resource developers, and curriculum revisers to ensure a coherent epistemological, pedagogical, and evaluation approach. Moreover, the general social, political, and intellectual environments have a significant impact on how education reformers engage in and sustain the reform effort.

REFLECTIVE QUESTIONS

1. How much influence should the past have on current curriculum decision-making? Why do you feel this way?
2. In your opinion, does curriculum making suffer from a pendulum effect where what is old is new again? Provide examples to support your answer.
3. What can teachers do to create a favourable climate for curriculum change?
4. Do issues such as ineffective professional development, lack of resources, and misunderstanding of theory contribute to resistance when curriculum reform is introduced? Explain your answer using a reform that you have experienced.
5. What lessons can we learn from this period of Canadian curriculum making?

NOTES

1. According to Tomkins (1986) Progressive Education is a "loosely applied label, a complex reality that had both liberal and conservative dimensions" (p. 189). He describes certain subdivisions of the movement based on their dominant characteristics: (a) the "administrative progressives" and "educational scientists" who sought to centralize education for social control and social efficiency and (b) the "pedagogical progressives"—the group we have chosen to examine in our analysis.

2. Note the description of Social Studies in the Alberta Elementary *Program of Studies* (1936): "[Social Studies is a program] . . . where the child is granted a considerable degree of freedom to make decisions and to carry out his [her] own designs. . . . The Social Studies afford experiences in which the teacher progressively aids the pupil to develop an understanding of his relationships to others, and to adjust himself to living in a world of other youths and adults, things, institutions, ideas and aspirations" (pp. 109–110).

3. Statements in the Alberta Ministry's *Bulletin 2* (1949, p. 16) show that health and science continued to be integrated into the enterprise program, while statements made in *Bulletin 2* (1953, pp. 35–36) indicate that there was no need to integrate these subjects.

4. Although educational promoters outside of the inner circle of the Department (for example, the New Education Fellowship and the Ontario Education Association) strongly advanced certain reforms in the school system and local authorities and personalities like Toronto Superintendent James L. Hughes or Hamilton homemaker Adelaide Hoodless even managed to have certain innovations added to the curriculum through their sheer strength of will (Patterson, 1974), Stamp (1982) points out that these new courses were merely piecemeal additions to the curriculum (pp. 164–165) doing little to change the traditional, subject-centred, teacher-centred philosophy in the Ontario program.

5. Although this new curriculum was under development, an election occurred and the Social Credit came to power. This change did not affect the curricular reform in Alberta, and the new government, with William Aberhart as both premier and Minister of Education, continued to support progressive curricular reform. In fact, the curriculum revision of 1940 aimed at an even deeper integration of subjects.

6. As early as 1884, for example, the Ontario Teachers' Association brought in the champion of child-centred education, Colonel Francis W. Parker, to speak at their annual convention (Guillet, 1960, pp. 109–110). For Parker's ongoing connection with Canada, see Campbell (1975).

7. Although the United Farmers of Ontario did win one term in office, they seemed more devoted to extending and improving educational facilities in rural districts than to curriculum reform (Stamp, 1982, pp. 108–109).

8. Both Simpson and his deputy Minister/Chief Director, Duncan McArthur, were well versed in the American, British, and Canadian innovations brought forth by the philosophy of progressivism. For their connection to the educational elite in Ontario, see Wood (1985).

9. A whole section was devoted to this aspect of education in both the *Programme of Studies for Grades 1 to 6* (1941) and the *Programme of Studies for Grades 7 and 8* (1942).

10. Of the four books listed in the first calendar of the Faculty of Education at the University of Toronto, established in 1907, two were written by John Dewey. Even the Ontario Teachers' *Manual on History of Education*, published in 1915, makes mention of Dewey's influence (Phillips, 1957, p. 426).

11. Various authors, "Correspondence to the Superintendent of Elementary Education," RG-2, P-3, Box 244, File 4-815/816, Archives of Ontario.

12. C. C. Goldring, Superintendent of Schools for Toronto in 1937–38, contradicts this statement, claiming that at least 85 per cent of public school teachers encouraged their classes to undertake

enterprises. However, this was in the most urban of school districts with access to more materials (Tomkins, 1986, p. 198). Further, even Goldring warned that he felt the enterprise was being used in an excessively formalized way, as product not process.

13. For examples, see editorial (1946) The three R's, *Lethbridge Herald*, reprinted in *The Alberta School Trustee*, 16/9, p. 28; letter to the editor (November 1947) *Calgary Herald*, p. 20; author unknown (1950), Not enough facts taught in school, *Alberta Home and School News*, 5/9, p. 5; J. J. Brown (1951), Mr. Brown looks at education, *Canadian Business*, 24/11, p. 49 (cited in von Heyking, 1996, pp. 337–339).

14. By 1942, criticisms of progressivism were becoming more pointed during the annual conventions of the Ontario Education Association. See 1943 speeches by Darcy Davidson of Ryerson Public School, Toronto; Dr. J. F. McDonald, the Inspector of Separate Schools for Ottawa; Dr. S. F. Maine of the University of Western Ontario; and the 1952 convention dedicated to rethinking the progressive model, in Guillet (1960).

REFERENCES

Alberta Department of Education. (1907). *Annual report of the Department of Education of the Province of Alberta 1906.* Edmonton: King's Printer.

Alberta Department of Education. (1913). *Seventh annual report of the Department of Education of the Province of Alberta 1912.* Edmonton: King's Printer.

Alberta Department of Education. (1922). *Part I and part II of the course of studies for the elementary schools of Alberta.* Edmonton: King's Printer.

Alberta Department of Education. (1936). *Program of studies for the elementary school grades I to VI*, 109–110. Edmonton: King's Printer.

Alberta Department of Education. (1937). *Annual report of the Department of Education of the Province of Alberta 1936.* Edmonton: King's Printer.

Alberta Department of Education. (1938). *Annual report of the Department of Education of the Province of Alberta 1937.* Edmonton: King's Printer.

Alberta Department of Education. (1940). *Annual report of the Department of Education of the Province of Alberta 1939.* Edmonton: King's Printer.

Alberta Department of Education. (1940). *Program of studies for the elementary school grades I to VI.* Edmonton: King's Printer.

Alberta Department of Education. (1941). *Annual report of the Department of Education of the Province of Alberta 1940.* Edmonton: King's Printer.

Alberta Department of Education. (1942). *Annual report of the Department of Education of the Province of Alberta 1941.* Edmonton: King's Printer.

Alberta Department of Education. (1943). *Annual report of the Department of Education of the Province of Alberta 1942.* Edmonton: King's Printer.

Alberta Department of Education. (1946). *Annual report of the Department of Education of the Province of Alberta 1945.* Edmonton: King's Printer.

Alberta Department of Education. (1947). *Annual report of the Department of Education of the Province of Alberta 1946.* Edmonton: King's Printer.

Alberta Department of Education. (1949). *Bulletin 2, Program of studies for the elementary school.* Edmonton: King's Printer.

Alberta Department of Education. (1953). *Bulletin 2, Elementary school, methods: The Enterprise.* Edmonton: King's Printer.

Barrow, R. (1979). *The Canadian curriculum: A personal view.* London, ON: University of Western Ontario.

Byrne, T. C. (1991). *Alberta's revolutionary leaders.* Calgary, AB: Detselig Enterprises.

Campbell, J. K. (1975). *Colonel Francis W. Parker: The children's crusader.* New York: College Press.

Case, R. (1999). Elements of a coherent Social Studies program. In R. Case & P. Clark (Eds.), *The Canadian anthology of social studies.* Vancouver, BC: Pacific Educational Press.

Crawford, M. (1936). The school and the social order. *The Bulletin of the School of Education Society,* pp. 72–122.

Curtis, B. (1988). *Building the educational state: Canada West, 1836–1871.* London, ON: The Althouse Press.

Dickie, D. (1940). *The Enterprise in theory and practice.* Toronto: W. J. Gage & Company.

Doucette, A. (n.d.). Attitude toward the Enterprise curriculum, n.p., n.d. *Doucette Papers,* file 17.11. Calgary, AB: University of Calgary Archive.

Drew, G. (1943–1944). Addresses & addresses, 1943–1944. *Drew Papers,* files 146, 146 (3b), 314 (3b), and files 249–271. Archives of Ontario.

Dunlop, W. (1952). *Annual report of the Ontario Minister of Education.* Toronto: Queen's Press.

Dunlop, W. (1953). *OSSTF Bulletin.* Publication of the Ontario Secondary School Teachers' Federation.

Fleming, W. G. (1972). *Ontario's educative society. Volume 2: The administrative structure.* Toronto: University of Toronto Press.

Fleming, W. G. (1972). *Ontario's educative society. Volume 3: Schools, pupils, and teachers.* Toronto: University of Toronto Press.

Foley, R. S. (1966). *William James Dunlop: A brief history.* Private publication, available in OISE library.

Francis, R. D., & Palmer, H. (Eds.). (1992). *The prairie west.* Edmonton: Pica Pica Press.

Gibbs, C. L. (1928). Editorial. *A.T.A. Magazine, 8,* p. 3.

Gidney, R. D. (1999). *From Hope to Harris: The reshaping of Ontario's schools.* Toronto: University of Toronto Press.

Guillet, E. C. (1960). *In the cause of education: A centennial history of the Ontario Education Association, 1861–1960.* Toronto: University of Toronto.

Hallman, D. M. (1992). A thing of the past: Teaching in one-room schools in rural Nova Scotia, 1936–1941. *Historical Studies in Education, 4.1,* pp. 113–132.

Hardy, W. G. (1954). Education in Alberta. Articles published in a pamphlet by the *Calgary Herald,* n.d.; articles originally appeared in February 1954 in the *Calgary Herald,* the *Edmonton Journal,* the *Lethbridge Herald,* and the *Medicine Hat News.*

Kilpatrick, W. H. (1918). *The project method.* New York: Teachers College, Columbia University.

Laycock, D. (1990). *Populism and democratic thought in the Canadian prairies.* Toronto: University of Toronto Press.

Manzer, R. (1994). *Public schools and political ideas: Canadian educational policy in historical perspective.* Toronto: University of Toronto Press.

McNally, G. F. (1922). *Annual reports of the Alberta Department of Education.* Edmonton: King's Printer.

McNally, G. F. (1964). *G. Fred.* A memoir recorded and transcribed by H. T. Coutts and B. E. Walker. Don Mills, ON: J. M. Dent and Sons (Canada).

Mosely, H. H. (1968). The philosophy and operation of the grade 13 year. *The Headmaster, 3,* p. 3.

Neatby, H. (1953). *So little for the mind.* Toronto: Clark, Irwin & Company.

Newland, H. C. (1921). The slave mind. *The ATA Magazine,* pp. 20–22.

Newland, H. C. (1936). *Annual report of the Alberta Department of Education.* Edmonton: King's Printer.

Newland, H. C. (1937). *Annual report of the Alberta Department of Education.* Edmonton: King's Printer.

Newland, H. C. (1940). *Annual report of the Alberta Department of Education.* Edmonton: King's Printer.

Ontario Department of Education. (1936). *The Minister's annual report.* Toronto: The King's Printer.

Ontario Department of Education. (1937). *Programme of studies for grades 1 to 6 of the public and separate schools.* Toronto: The King's Printer.

Ontario Department of Education. (1938). *The Minister's annual report.* Toronto: The King's Printer.

Ontario Department of Education. (1941). *Programme of studies for grades 1 to 6 of the public and separate schools.* Toronto: The King's Printer.

Ontario Department of Education. (1942). *Programme of studies for grades 7 to 8 of the public and separate schools.* Toronto: The King's Printer.

Palmer, H., & Palmer, T. (1990). *Alberta: A new history.* Edmonton: Hurtig Publishing.

Patterson, R. (1968). *The establishment of progressive education in Alberta.* Unpublished doctoral dissertation, Michigan State University.

Patterson, R. (1970). Society and education during the wars and their interlude: 1914–1945. In J. D. Wilson, T. Stamp, &. L. P. Audet (Eds.), *Canadian education: A history* (pp. 360–384). Toronto: Prentice Hall.

Patterson, R. (1974). *Profiles of Canadian educators.* Toronto: D. C. Heath.

Patterson, R. (1990). The Canadian experience with progressive education. In E. B. Titley (Ed.), *Canadian education: Historical themes and contemporary issues* (pp. 95–110). Calgary, AB: Detselig Enterprises.

Phillips, C. E. (1957). *The development of education in Canada.* Toronto: W. J. Gage and Company.

Stamp, R. M. (1982). *The schools of Ontario, 1876–1976.* Toronto: University of Toronto Press.

Swift, W. H. (1954). Pendulum or synthesis? Address to the Edmonton teacher convention. *Swift Papers.* Accession no. 69-29, file 3/6/1, University of Alberta Archives.

Thomson, G. E. (2000). A fondness for charts and children: Scientific progressivism in Vancouver schools, 1920–50. *Historical Studies in Education, 12,* 111–128.

Titley, E. B. (1990). *Canadian education: Historical themes and contemporary issues.* Calgary, AB: Detselig Enterprises.

Tomkins, G. (1986). *A common countenance: Stability and change in the Canadian curriculum.* Scarborough, ON: Prentice-Hall Canada.

von Heyking, A. J. (1996). *Shaping an education for the modern world: A history of the Alberta Social Studies curriculum, 1905 to 1965.* Unpublished doctoral dissertation, University of Calgary.

Wood, B. A (1985). *Idealism transformed: The making of a progressive educator.* Kingston & Montreal: McGill-Queen's University Press.

9

Getting Things Done:
Donalda J. Dickie and Leadership
Through Practice

REBECCA PRIEGERT COULTER

Donalda James Dickie (1883–1972) was a progressive educator whose career illustrates how women provide leadership in education even as they are excluded from positions of formal authority. A normal school instructor for most of her paid working life, Dickie educated teachers, wrote textbooks for students and teachers, developed programs of study and curriculum materials, and actively participated in the wider educational and women's communities. She exercised what can be called the power of practice to provide direction to the education of children and teachers across Canada. Indeed, Dickie marshalled a capacity for intellectual work, a deep understanding of the actual nature of classrooms, and an ability to sustain a lifelong commitment to the heavy demands of teaching, research, and writing to become one of Canada's most influential educational leaders during the first half of the twentieth century.

Although democratic, populist, and feminist impulses have extended the meaning of leadership to include roles well beyond formal positions of authority held by appointment within a hierarchical structure, we know remarkably little about how female educators exercised leadership historically. Dickie's story opens up questions about the nature and form of women's leadership in state systems of schooling, forcing us to consider how women in the past "did leadership" while being denied recognition as leaders. Indeed, so strong was the discursive exclusion of women from notions of public leadership that Dickie probably did not even recognize herself as a leader; rather, like so many women, she would have described herself as a person who "just got things done."[1] Certainly this is how she was described by her colleagues who saw her as a "doer" or, as a younger male contemporary put it, "the little red hen" of Alberta education,[2] a reference simultaneously laudatory and derisive and reminding us of the ambivalence that confronts women of ambition. Dickie, herself, claimed to be "just a teacher."[3] Precisely as a "doer" and a teacher, however, she provided leadership within an increasingly self-conscious teaching profession, a reason why she was so widely recognized in her time as a central player in the progressive education movement.

Dickie was successful because she based the instructional leadership she offered on two important principles. First, she situated herself within the largely female teaching force and respected those with whom she worked. She was continuously involved with a network of teachers who collaborated with her on new textbooks, tested materials she developed, and provided feedback about new programs or curricula. Her links to the field also provided her with the passion and the power to negotiate from a position of strength within the wider national network of normal school instructors, university professors, education officials, and school trustees. Put another way, she could work "down" with the mostly female teaching force or "up" with the almost wholly male administrative structure. A second hallmark of her leadership was her ability to combine an understanding of a better, more just, and peaceful world with usable curriculum content and practical teaching ideas. That is, Dickie had a conscious political philosophy that leaned towards humanism and social reform, and an educational philosophy that valued both subject matter knowledge and child-centred pedagogy. Dickie devoted much time and effort to sharing this perspective with teachers both during initial preparation and through in-service programs. She spoke directly to teachers in professional journal articles, teacher-education textbooks, and various instructional manuals. She embedded her own curriculum design and personal pedagogical approaches within the textbooks she wrote. Over several decades, she developed concrete, child-friendly learning materials along with specific pedagogical strategies, thereby offering classroom teachers practical methods for carrying through on more abstract principles. In these ways, Dickie utilized many commonly recognized leadership strategies including collaboration, networking, and mentoring.

Yet even as she modelled an active agency, she was caught in the contradictions facing women carving out professional careers within the institutions of the state. As a teacher, she was expected to educate the young for citizenship while, by virtue of her sex, she was denied even the right to vote.[4] As a graduate student, she entered Oxford University at a time when she could not supplicate for a degree because she was a woman.[5] She toiled for nearly thirty-five years as a normal school instructor but never held an administrative post or a position of formal authority with her employer, Alberta's Department of Education. And despite playing a central role in the development of progressive education and writing the recognized teacher-education text in the field, her contributions have been rendered almost invisible in Canadian educational history.[6] Dickie, then, is one of those female educators who stood hip-deep in cultures saturated with phallocentric knowledges, in institutional structures ruled epistemologically and procedurally by men and masculinist signifiers, and in a discipline which, despite its historical terrain as "women's work" . . . remains [in] the theoretical and administrative custody of men.[7]

How she negotiated these circumstances, not of her own choosing, to actively create a realm of influence and some power, and how she used specific strategies to survive and even flourish in a world she could only partially understand because of her location within it, is the subject of this article.

EARLY INFLUENCES

Apart from a short autobiographical note written for her family and a collection of clippings and letters, Dickie left no personal papers.[8] Her life must be reconstructed from her published writing, from the scant records left in various archives, and from the recollections of others. In this regard, the difficulties of reclaiming Dickie's life are not unusual for as Heilbrun points out, women's biographers have too often been forced "to reinvent the lives their subjects led" from "what evidence they could find."[9] It remains true that although I was able to find many of the "facts" of Dickie's existence, her thoughts and feelings about that experience are elusive and her life constantly slips into the shadows. But perhaps, slipping in and out of the shadows is an appropriate metaphor for Dickie, who evaded the normative script to live the ambiguous life of a professional woman, claiming a small enclave in the foreign territory of male hegemony.

In common with the rest of us, the circumstances of Dickie's early years proved crucial to her identity. Her origins in a Scottish Presbyterian family and community with a high regard for reading and learning almost certainly shaped her views about the importance of education in one's life[10] and her own life modelled the continuous pursuit of knowledge. Born in Hespeler, Ontario, on October 5, 1883, the eldest child of Hannah (Anne) Shepherd Hall Dickie and William Stewart Dickie, a school teacher,[11] Dickie was orphaned at four years of age.[12] She and her two younger brothers fell under the care of their paternal grandmother, Mrs. James Dickie, a widow who likely offered a model of female independence and courage. Although Dickie described her grandmother as "a clever, interesting and very entertaining woman" and her childhood as "happy and stimulating," it also appears true that as the eldest of the three orphaned siblings, Dickie came to feel a special responsibility for the care of her brothers and a close attachment to them.[13] She also spent time working in various families in the community, assisting with child care and other household tasks. This, along with the care of her brothers, may have been part of the practical experience that encouraged the rapport with children and understanding of childhood often noted by others reviewing her later work and accomplishments.[14]

Dickie's sense of Canadian nationalism and connection to place which so shaped her writing on citizenship and country also went back to her early life in southwestern Ontario. She had strong ties to the farm where she had spent her first years, claiming that "under those grey roofs people of my blood have lived for generations, out of that earth I sprang."[15] She went on to observe,

> My feeling for that bit of earth is more than love. It has in it something of the sacredness of love for a mother, something of the passion that flares between man and woman, something that is deeper than either. Here are my roots. This is my land.[16]

As an adult she was an anglophile, but she was also a descendant of the Dickies who had come to Canada from Scotland to escape poverty after the Napoleonic Wars and the Land Clearances.[17] The cultural memory of hardship and immigration that passes from one generation to the next must at least partially account for Dickie's positive rendering of Canada's multicultural heritage and her support for the development of a social safety net to counter the worst effects of poverty and unemployment.

BECOMING A TEACHER

Like many Canadians of the day, Dickie also had the experience of migrating from one region to another. While still in elementary school, she moved to Souris, Manitoba, with her grandmother and then to Moose Jaw, in what is now Saskatchewan, to enter high school.[18] In 1901, taking up one of the few occupational choices open to women, she attended the Regina Normal School. In its souvenir magazine which she co-edited, Dickie is described as "one of our cleverest junior members both in spheres of literature and teaching."[19] This evidence provides the earliest indication we have that people were beginning to take note of Dickie's intelligence, her abilities to master both content and pedagogy, and her willingness to roll up her sleeves and get things done. While at normal school, Dickie made important contacts and at least one of her classmates, H. C. Newland, would go on to join her in playing a leading role in progressive education in Alberta.[20]

When she completed her normal school training, Dickie was eighteen years old and an independent young woman with a Second Class Interim Certificate. She began to teach in a small school at Westview, just outside Moose Jaw, for a salary of $45 per month, gaining her permanent professional certificate on December 30, 1903.[21] But further education was never far from her mind. When she had saved enough money, she returned to Ontario to take her senior matriculation at Galt Collegiate,[22] and then registered at Queen's University in 1906. For three academic years (1906–1909) she completed her coursework extramurally, but for the 1909–1910 term she was in-residence to meet the degree requirements set by Queen's University.[23] To fund her academic studies, she engaged in a common practice for Ontario university students and went west in the summer to teach.[24] Her school teaching experiences were important for they provided Dickie with an understanding of the difficulties of rural education, a reality she was to keep in mind for the rest of her career. Her identification with the women working alone in one-room schools scattered across the Canadian landscape shaped her approach to pedagogy and made her a strong, though not uncritical, advocate for women teachers when she served on curriculum committees or confronted male academics. Her teaching in southern Saskatchewan may also have been key to the special sensitivity she developed to the situation of Canada's First Nations, a sensitivity that would later make its way into many of the textbooks that she wrote.

While a student at Queen's, Dickie excelled academically. In 1909 she won the University Medal for English and in 1910 the University Medal for History.[25] Arthur G. Dorland, who became a respected Canadian historian, knew Dickie at Queen's and recalled,

> I did not get the gold medal [in history]. This was awarded instead to a brilliant woman student, Donalda Dickie, who having won the medal in English extramurally the previous year (the first time—and so far as I am aware the last time—it was ever won by an extramural student) entered Queen's for her final year, and also captured the history medal. This was a very proper recognition of unusual merit. Miss Dickie was not only more mature in her thinking, but she surpassed the rest of the class also in the quality of her writing and in her powers of expression.[26]

In fact, because of her exceptional academic achievements, Dickie was awarded the M.A. degree in humanities in 1910, rather than the baccalaureate.[27]

Queen's was a post-secondary setting that provided "the kind of comfortable and intimate environment that appealed to academically bright students from 'homes of moderate means.'"[28] More importantly it was an institution that encouraged its students to take up lives of public service.[29] Many leading progressive educators of the twentieth century were Queen's graduates, among them John Harold Putnam.[30] William Aberhart, a fellow teacher who graduated the same year as Dickie, went on to become Premier and Minister of Education in Alberta's first Social Credit government in 1935, precisely at the time when the province was introducing a new curriculum co-authored by Dickie.[31] For Dickie, the Queen's connection offered a shared background and contacts with many like-minded educators and others in public service, thus according her a place in what we now call a network of influence.

THE EDUCATION OF A NORMAL SCHOOL INSTRUCTOR

Although she probably did not know it, Dickie was poised to exercise leadership in the educational community. Someone in Alberta had recognized her gifts, for immediately upon graduation from Queen's, Dickie was offered a position on the staff of the Practice School affiliated with the Calgary Normal School, and then, in 1912, she was appointed to teach at the new Provincial Normal School in Camrose, Alberta. Her memories of this period were typically upbeat: "For the first year Dr. James Miller, the principal, and I were the only members of staff and each taught half the subjects. It was hectic, but great fun."[32] In that year she also published her first article in a professional journal, "Dramatization as a Method in Composition," followed shortly after by two articles on the teaching of Canadian history.[33] The pattern of her professional career was established. She was to teach at all of Alberta's three normal schools, being transferred from one to another as enrolments and provincial finances dictated, until her retirement in 1944[34] while also producing journal articles, school textbooks, workbooks, and teacher manuals in several subject areas.

Although she now held a job of high status for a woman, Dickie's desire for academic achievement persisted. Having completed her M.A., she almost immediately began post-graduate work by taking summer classes in history and English at Columbia University.[35] Then, in April, 1916, she entered a B.Litt. program at Somerville College at Oxford University.[36] She wrote about this experience revealing the wonder and joy she felt at being in England and, especially, at Oxford. It is as though she could not believe her good luck and her enthusiasm for the rituals of student and college life was unbounded. She spoke of the libraries with awe, calling them "an inspiration" and proclaiming her mornings in the Bodleian "unforgettable." And she was completely taken with the history and beauty of the university and its surroundings. She was not oblivious to the war raging in Europe, had experienced fear during the crossing of the Atlantic and, while at Oxford, helped with the care of the wounded who were housed in some of the colleges. But despite the material shortages and harsh realities of war, Dickie remained enthralled with the possibilities of the intellectual life she found at Oxford.[37]

While there, she met and became fast friends with Eglantyne Jebb, who went on to become principal of the Froebel Institute at Roehampton, and whose cousin of the same name founded the Save the Children Fund.[38] This lifelong friendship undoubtedly provided an entrée to a rich world of educational debate in England, including the New Education Movement, and positioned Dickie in the wider international discourses of progressive education.[39] It is also reported that Dickie was acquainted with Vera Brittain, Winifred Holtby, Dorothy Sayers, and other prominent women who were students at Somerville College in the same period[40] and hence we might conclude that Dickie was exposed to what Brittain called "a universal tide flowing so strongly toward feminism."[41]

On April 9, 1917, Dickie's youngest brother, Thomas, was killed at Vimy Ridge[42] and in June she left Oxford, forty-two days short of completing her residency.[43] Whether this was because she was required to return to her post at the Camrose Normal School or because she wished to join her fiancé who had been gassed at the front and was in hospital in Winnipeg, Manitoba, where he ultimately died, is unclear.[44] She did return to Somerville College in 1921 to complete her residency and continue work on her thesis. Before she had completed her thesis, her supervisor died and she decided to transfer to the doctoral program at the University of Toronto in 1926 and complete her graduate work there.[45]

During the 1926–1927 academic year, Dickie took a leave of absence to complete her residency at the University of Toronto, although it was described inaccurately and a bit dismissively by the (male) principal of the Calgary Normal School as a year "partly of rest and partly of further research work abroad."[46] It would not have been surprising if Dickie had required some rest at this point because she had just completed a text on teaching composition, compiled a book of poetry for student use, developed an elementary school language arts series called *Learning to Speak and Write,* and prepared a series of eight Canadian history readers.[47] She also was working full-time as a teacher educator, doing research for and writing a dissertation, continuing to supervise extracurricular activities at the normal school, and speaking at teachers' conventions. In this context, "just getting things done" was a mind-boggling feat!

In 1929 she successfully defended her dissertation, *John Foxe's Acts and Monuments of the Church,* and convocated in the spring of 1930, making her one of only six women to earn a University of Toronto Ph.D. in history prior to 1960.[48] She also became a member of a very small and select group of educators who held doctorates in Canada. With the Ph.D., Dickie now had an additional credential to enhance her intellectual authority and her academic credibility, an increasingly important consideration in the field of education.[49]

Earning a Ph.D. was a remarkable accomplishment, not only because Dickie did so while maintaining a commitment to her teaching and to her publishers, but because, as Mary Kinnear points out, at that time doctorates were rare and university teaching, let alone normal school teaching, did not require an advanced degree.[50] Despite her stellar academic record, nowhere is there a hint that Dickie was ever considered for a post in a history department, a result, no doubt, of the fact that at the time the hiring of new faculty was done informally with department chairs seeking "good men" and senior male professors recommending their male graduate students.[51] As Boutilier and Prentice argue, the professionalization of history by the first half of the twentieth century meant that the discipline became, by definition, one that "privileged male experience and preserved most permanent academic jobs for university-trained men."[52] Donald Wright is even more blunt: "Sexism not only protected the status of history as a masculine discipline but protected the academic labour market for men."[53] It is, of course, possible that Dickie, herself, did not wish to teach at a university and that she did not actively seek work there. But why then did she complete a doctorate in history rather than education? Surely the paucity of female professors in history departments, in general, suggests that more than personal preference was at work here.[54]

In a world of systemic and overt sexism, academic achievement can signify both a woman's recognition that she must be exceptional and her hope that merit would trump gender. In Dickie's case, achievement pulled her towards the centre of power, but gender pushed her to the margins, leaving her to lead from the middle as it were, through the strategy of "practical action."[55] However, this leadership strategy was a two-edged sword. Women were exploited but received neither monetary recognition nor appointment to administrative positions. Yet there was power in practice. Through action or work, often done collectively, women made change and asserted control over their world. Put another way, practical action did not offer extrinsic rewards at the individual level, but paid large social dividends.

INSTRUCTIONAL LEADERSHIP THROUGH TEXTBOOK WRITING

In her mid-thirties, Dickie was ready to embark on what would become one of her major leadership projects. When she returned to Canada from Oxford in 1917 and took up her position at the Camrose Normal School, she was asked to teach history but "found the history text books in use by the children in the Practice School not only uninteresting but literally incomprehensible to most of their young readers." She concluded "that I probably could not do worse and determined to try my hand."[56] As a result of this decision, Dickie began a writing and publishing effort that extended into the 1960s. If she were to be denied opportunities to lead from a formal position of authority, she would shape education in another way and promulgate a progressive and meliorist reading of the world along with a child-centred pedagogy through teaching materials. Textbooks were, and are, the ubiquitous tools of state education. In the first half of the twentieth century, when teachers had few other resources to rely on, especially in the isolated rural schools, textbooks regularly determined what would be taught and became particularly significant instruments for developing a national identity and Canadian citizenship.[57] Textbooks, and the guides for teachers that came with them, could also shape teaching methods. Furthermore, because the majority of Canadians did not complete high school in the early decades of the twentieth century, what they learned in elementary school can be seen as especially important in shaping political consciousness and notions of citizenship. In this context, Dickie's textbooks take on particular significance because through them she structured what teachers taught and children learned about their nation and their social responsibilities. Her purpose was clear: "[W]e in Canada have our own traditions, our own ideals, and our own history. This is what we want our children to know."[58] Of course, Dickie was not alone in seeking this goal. In general, school textbooks promoted a distinct kind of Anglo-Canadian nationalism that did not wholly reject but provided some distance from the British connection, while carefully mediating the links between Canada and the United States.[59] The Canadian state also turned to schools to assimilate an immigrant population, extinguish "foreign" languages, erase ethnic identities, and teach the young how "Canadians" lived. As a result, textbooks often contained racist content, downplayed social conflict, and reinforced traditional patterns of gender relations[60] and Dickie's work was not completely free of these flaws. However, her books were more open to diversity and difference, subtly challenging hegemonic beliefs and leading readers towards tolerance and understanding.

Although she spoke out against hyphenated Canadianism,[61] Dickie also pointed out the advantages of a multicultural population and encouraged teachers to help children appreciate the richness immigrants brought to their new country. She emphasized the hard work and harsh conditions immigrants faced in their desire for a better life. In her portrayal of the peoples of Canada's First Nations, Dickie made a commendable effort to provide accurate and fair information. Her textbooks included Aboriginal stories as well as information about traditional and contemporary life in First Nations communities. She showed Aboriginal children living in loving families with home routines comparable to those of other children. Dickie was very open minded about the role of medicine men, natural healing processes, and Native spirituality. And in a sly turn of the table, through which we can appreciate Dickie's humour, she compared the Chicken Dance Society to other men's service clubs, the Masons and Elks.[62]

Dickie scattered positive comments about Aboriginals throughout her books. In a language arts text, for example, she noted that "Indians were fine speakers" and exhorted students to emulate their model.[63] In her introduction to a story about an Aboriginal man, she asked, "Do you admire clever people? You will find a hero in this tale if you do."[64] Thus she troubled racist stereotypes by naming the man both clever and heroic. In her history texts, Dickie was critical of the treatment of Aboriginal peoples in Canada. In contrast to her usually pro-government renderings of events, she recognized that Canada's "actions were not always fair or wise"[65] and that the treaties "did create many difficulties and problems for the Indians, problems which have not yet been met successfully."[66] Indeed, she calls the Canadian government "negligent" in its treatment of the Indians and Métis.[67] Dickie's unique contribution in textbook writing was the preparation of two readers, a pre-primer and a primer, featuring Aboriginal children as protagonists.[68] These two readers are likely the first Canadian examples of what we would now call inclusive curriculum material. Both readers offer a very positive, albeit somewhat sentimental and anglicized, view of Aboriginal children and their families.

Dickie also challenged the dominant gender discourse of the day, not by hammering home the political history of women's struggle for the right to vote, but by making apparent women's efforts to secure the future of Canada. For example, students learned that mothers and fathers worked equally hard to clear the land and build farms. She informed youngsters about the important work of the nuns in schools, hospitals, and social services and reminded them that "housekeepers spent their lives in crushing toil."[69] Sixth graders read about Madame La Tour who, in the absence of her husband, took command over a group of men to defend an Acadian fort. They also learned about the possibility of male anger when a woman was successful. They could not have missed Dickie's admiration as they read about Marie Maisonat who went from the pranks and fun of girlhood to politics when she "discovered that she loved power, knew how to win it, knew how to use it."[70] Similar woman-positive material can be found in the readers Dickie compiled and they contain clear examples of what we might now call a critical anti-sexist pedagogy. For example, after students read Longfellow's poem, "Stay at Home, My Heart," with its claim that for women "To stay at home is best," they find this question: "Nowadays girls are nurses and teachers and stenographers and doctors. Do the girls of today think that staying at home is the best?"[71]

I do not claim that Dickie's texts were overtly feminist or even consistent in their portrayal of girls and women because much of her material is more conservative and traditional. But it is clear that girls using Dickie's texts would find affirming material and all students would be required to think about gender relations. It is also true that because of Dickie's interests in the lives of ordinary people, past and present, young people using her texts were exposed to stories about workers and farmers, about the technologies of work, and the various elements of daily living. Housework was recognized as work and as part of the economy, a rather forward idea for the time. More than other textbook writers of the period, Dickie appeared sensitive to class issues and much in sympathy with hard-working people trying to make ends meet. She compared possessive individualism unfavourably with co-operative community values and even pointed out to school children the way in which competitive practices in education created adults who cared only for personal success. She explained the systemic nature of poverty and unemployment and warned young people not to blame the victims. By 1950, she was very supportive of the growing welfare state, speaking positively of the family allowance program, unemployment insurance, old age pensions, and other health and welfare initiatives. She retained her cheery optimism about Canada, often emphasizing that although mistakes were made, governments tried to do their best for the people. In this regard, she revealed a progressive conviction about the benevolent state and fostered the Canadian commitment to peace, order, and good government.

It is difficult to assess the influence of Dickie's textbooks on young Canadians because we cannot know with certainty how teachers used the material, nor what students learned from it. Nonetheless, we do know that Dickie's textbooks were commended to use by leading educators. For example, Thornton Mustard of the Toronto Normal School wrote a glowing introduction to Dickie's series, *Junior Language*, which ended with the exuberant claim, "A new day, my masters, in the teaching of English Composition!"[72] Textbooks authored or compiled by Dickie were authorized or approved for use in many provinces and often over several decades. Selections from Dickie's Canadian history readers, chosen and compiled by Helen Palk, a Manitoba teacher and normal school instructor, appeared under the title, *Pages from Canada's Story*. This textbook was used in Alberta, Saskatchewan, Manitoba, Ontario, Prince Edward Island, and Quebec and may have been used in other provinces. It first appeared in 1928, was reprinted at least twenty-five times by 1961, with revisions in 1936, 1949, and 1951.[73] The title page of *The Great Adventure* indicates it was authorized for use in Alberta and Newfoundland and approved for use in Ontario. It likely was used elsewhere, as well, because it was favourably reviewed in the popular media and in academic journals and won the Governor General's Award for the best book of juvenile literature published in 1950. This book sold more than 50,000 copies in its first year and also went through many successive printings after its first appearance. As late as 1977, five years after Dickie's death, it appeared as a sound recording in Alberta.[74] Similarly, the Canadian Parade reading series, compiled by Dickie and three teachers, went through many reprintings after first appearing in 1947. Authorized for use in Alberta and British Columbia and approved for permissive use in Ontario, this series was supported by teacher manuals and workbooks, additions which further ensured that the textbooks would become the curriculum. Sutherland notes that these readers were used in three provinces for a twenty-year period.[75] Thus the evidence points to a very influential role for Dickie's textbooks for a large part of the twentieth century. It was no accident that the federal government called on her to write the remedial reading program for soldiers during World War II.[76]

Despite Dickie's advanced degrees and obvious competence, taken-for-granted gender norms and masculinist organizational practices denied her opportunities to hold formal leadership positions in the education system. Like other women excluded from the hierarchy of educational administration, she was forced to look for alternative arenas in which to play out her capacities and skills and introduce the reforms she thought necessary. From among her limited options, she chose textbook writing as an important means to provide instructional leadership. Here was a form of power open to her and she fully exercised it even after she retired as a normal school instructor in 1944. Revealing her lively sense of humour she wrote, "Now that I have retired and can write all the time, the only hope I can see for Canada is reforestation."[77] In the 1960s, she was working on a history of the Commonwealth nations when old age caught up with her and robbed her of the mental acuity needed to complete that task.[78]

EXERCISING LEADERSHIP THROUGH CURRICULUM DEVELOPMENT

By the time she was fifty, Donalda Dickie had gained enough credibility to move closer to the centre of power and become an educational insider. She was highly educated and widely recognized for her textbook writing and her progressive pedagogical approaches, which she had championed for many years as part of a larger transnational movement. She worked quietly and persistently for change from within the educational system, but was not seen as a threat to the existing relations of power or established modes of operation. She got along well with men and was among the few women who were admitted to membership in the Education Society of Edmonton, a group of senior stakeholders in education who met on a regular basis to study new developments and discuss future directions for the province. It is not surprising, then, that Dickie became centrally involved in Alberta's grand experiment with progressive education in the 1930s.

Between 1921 and 1935, Alberta was governed by the United Farmers of Alberta (UFA), a political party built on the principles of agrarian populism, group government, and co-operation.[79] Education was a key concern for the party and there was a conscious desire to improve opportunities for rural children and support the teaching of co-operation in the schools. The United Farm Women of Alberta (UFWA), whose local and provincial leaders were often former teachers, played an important role in promoting the school reforms proposed by the progressive education movement in North America and England. The UFWA, for example, supported the Dalton Plan and encouraged its use in Alberta.[80] The convergence between the interests of the governing party and Alberta's educational leaders, several of whom had done graduate work at Teachers College, Columbia, and the University of Chicago where they were influenced by the pantheon of American progressivists, resulted in the decision to bring progressive education to Alberta. An important outcome of this decision was the wholescale revision of the school curriculum.[81] Designed under a UFA government, the new revisions were implemented with the support of another populist party, Social Credit, after the farmers lost the 1935 election.

According to a colleague in the Edmonton Normal School, Fred McNally, the provincial supervisor of schools, drew Dickie into the curriculum revision process in the early 1930s.[82] McNally, who became Deputy Minister of Education in 1935, had attended Teachers College, Columbia, where he found John Dewey's lectures incomprehensible but enjoyed his course with William Heard Kilpatrick, "one of the greats both as a teacher and a scholar."[83] He liked Kilpatrick's project method and called upon Dickie, whom he had supervised while serving as principal of the Camrose Normal School, to speak to a conference of school inspectors about the methods of progressive education. Well received by the inspectors, Dickie was then appointed in 1934 as one of three members of a committee assigned the task of drafting a framework for a new elementary school curriculum that would reflect an activity-oriented and integrated approach. The core committee supervising the work was almost wholly male in membership and the senior administrator assigned to oversee the revision process was Hubert C. Newland, the Chief Inspector of Schools, but the committee named to actually do the work was two-thirds female, with Olive Fisher of the Calgary Normal School joining her friend Dickie, along with William Hay, a school inspector.

In short order, this three-person committee presented a plan for curriculum reorganization to Newland. Central to the plan was the enterprise, the term the committee came up with to describe an interdisciplinary, child-centred, activity method of education. Dickie herself saw the enterprise as "the co-operative achievement of a social purpose that a teacher presents to her class with a view to having them use it as an experience in intelligent social behaviour."[84] Newland "was well pleased with the vision of the plan" and believed it would provide "an opportunity for learning the ways of democratic living, since pupils and teachers would participate in the planning of the work to be undertaken."[85] The implementation process began in 1935 when seventy-five teachers from across the province were brought to a summer school to learn about the new curriculum with the expectation that they would return to the field to proselytize their colleagues.

Over the next few years, Dickie was the most prominent activist in the cause of progressive education. A younger contemporary working in the Department of Education described her leadership in this way:

> Dr. Dickie did more than any other single person to make the implementation of the activity movement in Alberta education a reality. She wrote, she spoke, she demonstrated. She published, she edited, she revised, she evaluated. She gathered around her a group of energetic, young, competent teachers. In her classes, both during the academic years and during summer schools, she produced dozens of young enthusiasts who went out singly and in pairs to sell the gospel of the activity program. In a matter of a few short years, the "enterprise method" had reached into every corner of the province; into every teachers' convention; into every curriculum guide.[86]

Dickie's teacher-education textbook, *The Enterprise in Theory and Practice,* first published in 1940, solidified her leadership in action, as did the many articles she published in a wide range of journals.[87] All told, Dickie's ability to think, write, work with others, and prepare useful teaching materials proved crucial to attempts to implement progressive education reforms in Alberta. She was adroit in argument, able to shift ground easily to draw from the various strands of progressivism to make a case for each particular audience she addressed. She "sold" progressive education to teachers, school trustees, businessmen, and the women's organizations whose membership she enlisted in the cause.[88]

Although Dickie has been labelled variously as a pedagogical, child-centred, or child freedom progressive,[89] her own life story and her body of work reveal a woman who was also committed to traditional scholarship and the pursuit of knowledge. She did not see theory and practice as binaries and believed that children could come to learning with joy and pleasure but still master content and skills. Like feminist scholars of the late twentieth century, Dickie was concerned with the interconnectedness of knowledge, with the stories of the silenced in history, and with the making of knowledge and the role of experience in that process. She was interested in using education to promote social improvement and thought that this could be done by offering students active, purposeful learning activities designed to prepare them for democratic citizenship.

However, as she neared the end of her employment as a normal school instructor and faced retirement in 1944, Dickie began to appear less than sanguine about the likely success of the progressive experiment in Alberta. A tone of increasing desperation can be discerned in her writing as she resorted to expediency to fight for the curriculum she had worked so hard to develop. Particularly jarring is her turn towards emphasizing the vocational and social control dimensions of progressive education as she tried to mollify critics.[90] Only after retirement did she return to stating what had clearly been her goal all along: "To teach the young where and how to get information for themselves and how to use it to solve their social problems and make a useful contribution to the solution of the problems of the community."[91]

There were real difficulties posed for the smooth implementation of progressive reforms. Access to a variety of learning resources, especially books, was essential, yet many schools lacked such materials. The enterprise method required well-educated and skilled teachers,[92] but classrooms were too often staffed with poorly educated or young and inexperienced teachers, unable to cope with the demands of an integrated curriculum. World War II only exacerbated the problem.[93] Dickie, usually so supportive of teachers, was sharp in her condemnation of those she called "down-at-the-heel" conservatives who "do not, and will not, read."[94] In many cases, classrooms were filled with activity for activity's sake and little real learning took place, at least partly because the provisions for the professional development and re-education of teachers were inadequate. And, of course, many teachers resisted progressive education and disagreed with this new approach to schooling.[95]

At the same time, the Social Credit government became increasingly right wing and more oriented to fundamentalist moralism, and the administration in the Department of Education was changing and becoming more reliant on educational psychology to define educational purpose.[96] Elements of the business community and the media began an attack on progressive education that found support in the universities.[97] Some of the educators who had been strong supporters of progressive education changed sides.[98] Finally, even Dickie herself hinted at some second thoughts about the revised school curriculum. In the foreword to the 1950 history textbook, *The Great Adventure,* she commends the important work being done in social studies but admits that history "appears in bits and patches" and students "lose much of the significance of many social studies topics" and "leave school without ever having read a complete, connected history of their country."[99]

CONCLUSION

Dickie's work in curriculum reform in the 1930s and 1940s came closest to modelling leadership as it is commonly understood in the educational literature. More
than at any other point in her career, she moved to the centre of formal power
in education and had the opportunity to shape the provincial school system as a
whole. She worked indefatigably over a ten-year period for the implementation
of the enterprise approach, using the full range of strategies commonly thought
necessary to successfully introduce curriculum reform. It is hard to see how she
could have done more. It is surprising, then, that in her brief autobiographical
notes, Dickie makes no mention whatsoever of the work she did in curriculum
revision or the part she played in Alberta's experiment with progressive education. Was she soured on top-down change-making, or did she dislike the political machinations that went on behind the scenes? Did she come to realize that
many educational leaders did not understand progressive education and consequently were not deeply committed to curriculum reform? Was she overcome
with disappointment when she realized that her vision of change was becoming
so watered down that it bore little resemblance to its original conceptualization?
Or did Dickie come to realize that the curriculum and pedagogy she proposed
were unattainable in the existing bureaucratic educational system? It is impossible to know, but she certainly turned back to textbook writing with a vengeance
when she retired in 1944 and said no more about the enterprise. Indeed, in her
autobiographical notes, she emphasized textbook writing as her major achievement in life, a fact which should encourage a further reconsideration of the way
in which educational leadership is too often read as synonymous with educational administration.[100]

In 1925, Dickie offered the following words of advice to the students gradu-
ating from the Calgary Normal School. Almost certainly as a reference to her
grammar classes and the use of comparatives and superlatives, she observed,
"Play is pleasant; Work is pleasanter; Achievement is pleasantest of all."[101] She
might have been speaking of her own life because, although she could play and
did so by golfing, hiking, climbing, and travelling, she devoted the best part of
her years to work. As a result, she achieved recognition as an author, an educator, and as a woman who provided "leadership and inspiration" to teachers.[102]
Thus it was that Dickie exercised power. She claimed the right to be heard in the
educational discourse, and moved into spaces where action mattered and where
getting things done made a difference.

REFLECTIVE QUESTIONS

1. How has Donalda Dickie's work influenced your educational practice today?
2. Do you feel you have a "voice" in education? Tell a story about your experience to support your answer.
3. Do you see the issues identified in this reading in current curriculum? Why might that be the case?
4. Coulter claims that textbooks were significant instruments for developing a national identity and Canadian citizenship. Is this still the case today? Provide examples to support your response.
5. How does the description of the progressive movement in Alberta showcase the issue of political influence on curriculum decision-making?

ACKNOWLEDGEMENTS

I wish to acknowledge the financial support of a Faculty of Education, University of Western Ontario Internal Research and Development Grant and the Social Sciences and Humanities Research Council of Canada Standard Research Grant No. 410-2000-0357. The assistance of archivists and librarians including Pauline Adams (Somerville College Archives, Oxford University); Elaine Atwood (Alberta Teachers' Association Library); Paul Banfield (Queen's University Archives); Rachel Canada (University of North Carolina at Chapel Hill); Marnee Gamble (University of Toronto Archives and Records Management); James Gorton (Archives of Ontario); Kathryn Ivany (City of Edmonton Archives); Tim Novak and Ted Sheard (Saskatchewan Archives Board); Jim Quantrell (Cambridge City Archives); Claude Roberto (Provincial Archives of Alberta); and Raymond Frogner (University of Alberta Archives) was invaluable.

NOTES

1. Jill Blackmore, *Troubling Women: Feminism, Leadership and Educational Change* (Buckingham: Open University Press, 1999); Carol Harris, "Innovative Leadership in Community Context: Elizabeth Murray and the History Plays in Tatamagouche, Nova Scotia," in *Women and Leadership in Canadian Education*, eds. Cecilia Reynolds and Beth Young (Calgary: Detselig, 1995), 173–192.
2. J. Oviatt to [P. Oviatt], July 7, 1970. Letter reproduced in R. S. Patterson, comp., *Progressive Education* (Edmonton: Faculty of Education, University of Alberta, n.d.). Original held by R. S. Patterson in his personal files.
3. Elizabeth Donalda Harris, telephone interview with author, December 2001. "Betty Don" Harris is Dickie's niece.
4. As a resident of Alberta, Dickie got the provincial vote in 1916 and, as the sister of someone in the armed forces, the federal franchise in 1917. She was not recognized legally as a "person" in Canada until 1929. See Alison Prentice et al., *Canadian Women: A History*, 2nd ed. (Toronto: Harcourt Brace, 1996).
5. Women gained the right to supplicate for degrees at Oxford in 1920. See Paul Berry and Mark Bostridge, *Vera Brittain: A Life* (London: Chatto and Windus, 1995), 154.

6. Donalda Dickie, *The Enterprise in Theory and Practice* (Toronto: W. J. Gage, 1940). For histories of progressive education in Alberta see, R. S. Patterson, "The Establishment of Progressive Education in Alberta" (Ph.D. diss., Michigan State University, 1968); R. S. Patterson, "Progressive Education: Impetus to Educational Change in Alberta and Saskatchewan," in *Education in Canada: An Interpretation*, eds. E. Brian Titley and Peter J. Miller (Calgary: Detselig, 1982), 169–192; Nick Kach, "The Emergence of Progressive Education in Alberta," in *Exploring Our Educational Past*, eds. Nick Kach and Kas Mazurek (Calgary: Detselig, 1992), 149–174; Amy von Heyking, "Selling Progressive Education to Albertans, 1935–53," *Historical Studies in Education* 10, nos. 1 and 2 (1998), 67–84. Dickie receives only the briefest of mentions in all these studies of progressive education in Alberta.

7. Carmen Luke and Jennifer Gore, "Introduction," in *Feminisms and Critical Pedagogy*, eds. Carmen Luke and Jennifer Gore (New York: Routledge, 1992), 2.

8. I am grateful to Dickie's niece, Elizabeth Donalda Harris, and her son, Dave Harris, for sharing this material with me. The originals remain in their possession.

9. Carolyn Heilbrun, *Writing a Woman's Life* (New York: Ballantine, 1988), 31.

10. Andrew C. Holman, *A Sense of Their Duty: Middle-Class Formation in Victorian Ontario Towns* (Montreal & Kingston: McGill-Queen's University Press, 2000).

11. Charles G. D. Roberts and Arthur Leonard Tunnell, eds., *The Canadian Who's Who*, vol. 2, 1936–37 (Toronto: Murray Printing, 1936); University of Toronto Archives (UTA), School of Graduate Studies (SGS), Acc. No. A84-0011/026, Dickie, Donalda file, Application for Admission, March 17, 1926.

12. City of Cambridge Archives, Transcript of Dickie Family Grave Marker, New Hope Cemetery. The Harris interview indicated that new information has come to light recently which suggests that Dickie's father did not die in Australia in 1889, as his family concluded when he failed to return from a trip to that country. Rather, it appears he failed to inform his Canadian family that he was staying in Australia, where he remarried and started a second family.

13. Donalda Dickie, autobiographical notes, unpublished typescript in possession of Harris family, n.d. Harris interview revealed that Dickie spent most of her vacations with her brother and his family, and that she provided financial support to the family during the Depression.

14. For comments on Dickie's understanding of children see, for example, "Who's Who Among Educationists," *Edmonton Bulletin*, July 8, 1936 and book reviews in UTA, Ace. No. A73-0026/083 (94), Clipping File, Dickie, Donalda James. Information about working out comes from Harris interview. See, also, Holman, *A Sense of Their Duty* about the practice of children working in the homes of others in the Galt, Ontario, region where Dickie was born.

15. Donalda Dickie, "Can We Teach Love of Country?" *Chatelaine*, April 1945, 57.

16. Ibid.

17. Laraine Sole. *Waverley: The Early Families* (Wanganui, NZ: H & A Print, 1996).

18. Harris interview; Dickie, autobiographical notes.

19. Saskatchewan Archives Board, Regina (SAB,R), Collection R-E 238, *Regina Normal School Magazine: Souvenir Number*, 1901, 17.

20. Patricia E. Oviatt, "The Educational Contributions of H. C. Newland" (M.Ed. thesis, University of Alberta, 1970).

21. SAB,R, Collection R-I77.11, File 5: Certificates Granted by Dept. of Education, NWT, 1903–1905; File 20: Inspector's Reports, 1899–1904; File 11: Index of Teachers, 1908–1927; School Officials' Registers, Westview S.D. No. 256.

22. Dickie, autobiographical notes.

23. Queen's University Archives (QUA), Office of the University Registrar fonds, Student Registers series, Locator #1161, Vol. 10.

24. Dickie, autobiographical notes; SAB,R, Collection R-177.11, File 11: Index of Teachers, 1908–1927 and School Officials' Registers, Clarilaw S.D. No. 685. On university students going west each summer to teach see Rosalind Rowan, "The Eastern Student as the Western Teacher," *The School 5*, no. 2 (1916), 97–101.

25. QUA, Office of Advancement, Advancement Business Office *fonds*, Deceased Alumni series, Locator #3599, Box 6.1, Donalda James Dickie.

26. Arthur G. Dorland, *Former Days and Quaker Ways: A Canadian Retrospect* (Picton: Picton Gazette Publishing Co., 1965), 175–76. I am grateful to Paul Banfield at the Queen's University Archives for drawing this quote to my attention.

27. QUA, Queen's University Printed Collection, "Calendar of Queen's College and University, Kingston, Canada, For the Year 1909–1910."

28. P. T. Rooke and R. L. Schnell, *No Bleeding Heart: Charlotte Whitton, A Feminist on the Right* (Vancouver: University of British Columbia Press, 1987), 10.

29. A. B. McKillop, *A Disciplined Intelligence: Critical Inquiry and Canadian Thought in the Victorian Era* (Montreal: McGill-Queen's University Press, 1979).

30. B. Anne Wood, *Idealism Transformed: The Making of a Progressive Educator* (Kingston & Montreal: McGill-Queen's Press, 1985).

31. John Irving, *The Social Credit Movement in Alberta* (Toronto: University of Toronto Press, 1959), 10. R. D. Gidney first pointed out this university connection between Aberhart and Dickie.

32. Dickie, autobiographical notes.

33. D. J. Dickie, "Dramatization as a Method in Composition," *The School 1*, no. 3 (1912), 185–188; "Teaching Canadian History," *The School 3*, no. 1 (1914), 37–41; "Methods of Teaching Canadian History," *The School 3*, no. 5 (1915), 337–340.

34. Alberta Department of Education Annual Reports trace the relocation of normal school instructors. Dickie was at the Calgary Practice School in 1910, then employed at the Camrose Normal School in 1912, transferred to the Edmonton Normal School in 1920, Calgary Normal School in 1923, back to Edmonton in 1928, Camrose in 1933, Edmonton in 1935.

35. Dickie, autobiographical notes.

36. Pauline Adams, email to author, October 5, 2001, conveying information about Dickie contained in the Somerville College Register.

37. D. J. Dickie, "Life at an English University," Part 1, *The School 6*, no. 3 (1917): 213–217; Part 2, *The School 6*, no. 4 (1917), 274–277; Part 3, *The School 6*, no. 5 (1918), 346–349.

38. Harris interview; Francesca M. Wilson, *Rebel Daughter of a Country House: The Life of Eglantyne Jebb, Founder of the Save the Children Fund* (London: George Allen and Unwin, 1967).

39. Celia Jenkins, "New Education and Its Emancipatory Interests (1920–1950)," *History of Education 29*, no. 2 (2000), 139–151; Peter Cunningham, "Innovators, Networks and Structures: Towards a Prosopography of Progressivism," *History of Education 30*, no. 5 (2001), 433–451.

40. "Who's Who Among Educationists."

41. Vera Brittain quoted in Heilbrun, *Writing a Woman's Life*, 105.

42. The exact date of death is recorded on the dedication page of Donalda Dickie, *The Great Adventure: An Illustrated History of Canada for Young Canadians* (Toronto: J. M. Dent, 1950).

43. Adams, email.

44. Harris interview.

45. UTA, SGS, Acc. No. A84-0011/026, Dickie file.

46. Alberta Department of Education, *Annual Report, 1926* (Edmonton: King's Printer, 1927), 22.

47. Donalda J. Dickie, *Modern Practice in the Teaching of Composition* (Toronto: W. J. Gage, 1923); Donalda J. Dickie, comp., *The Canadian Poetry Book: A Book of Modern Verse* (Toronto: J. M. Dent, 1922); Donalda J. Dickie, *Learning to Speak and Write: Book I, Grades I, II, III, and IV and*

Book II, Grades V, VI, VII, and VIII (Toronto: Educational Book Company, 1924); Donalda J. Dickie, *Dent's Canadian History Readers,* 8 vols. (Toronto: J. M. Dent, 1924–26).

48. Donald Wright, "Gender and the Professionalization of History in English Canada Before 1960," *Canadian Historical Review 81,* no. 1 (2000), 29–66.

49. See, for example, R. S. Patterson, "Hubert C. Newland: Theorist of Progressive Education," in *Profiles of Canadian Educators,* eds. Robert S. Patterson, John W. Chalmers, and John Friesen (n.p.: D.C. Heath, 1974), 289–290; H. T. Coutts and B. E. Walker, recorders, *G. Fred: The Story of G. Fred McNally* (Don Mills, Ontario: J. M. Dent, 1964). Newland went to the University of Chicago and earned a doctorate in 1932. McNally notes he was sent to Teachers College, Columbia, on full salary but never completed his degree. There is no evidence to suggest that Dickie received any support from her employer to attend a doctoral program.

50. Mary Kinnear, *In Subordination: Professional Women, 1870–1970* (Montreal & Kingston: McGill-Queen's Press, 1995), 33.

51. Wright, "Gender and the Professionalization of History."

52. Beverly Boutilier and Alison Prentice, "Introduction: Locating Women in the Work of History," in *Creating Historical Memory: English-Canadian Women and the Work of History,* eds. Beverly Boutilier and Alison Prentice (Vancouver: UBC Press, 1997), 4.

53. Wright, "Gender and the Professionalization of History," 31. Wright notes the specific sexism of two professors who were involved in supervising Dickie's work.

54. See, Wright, "Gender and the Professionalization of History" and Alison Prentice, "Laying Siege to the History Professoriate," in *Creating Historical Memory,* 197–232.

55. Randi R. Warne, *Literature as Pulpit: The Christian Social Activism of Nellie L. McClung* (Waterloo: Wilfrid Laurier University Press, 1993), 186.

56. Dickie, autobiographical notes.

57. B. Anne Wood, "Canadian Citizenship for a Progressive State," in *Canada and Citizenship Education,* ed. Keith A. Macleod (Toronto: Canadian Education Association, 1989), 19–26; Ken Osborne, "Public Schooling and Citizenship Education in Canada," *Canadian Ethnic Studies 32,* no. 1 (2000), 8–37; Penney Irene Clark, "'Take It Away Youth!': Visions of Canadian Identity in British Columbia Social Studies Textbooks, 1925–1989" (Ph.D. diss., University of British Columbia, 1995).

58. Elizabeth Bailey Price, "Calgary Has Four Women Authors," *Canadian Bookman 8,* no. 3 (1926), 94.

59. Ken Osborne, "'Our History Syllabus Has Us Gasping': History in Canadian Schools—Past, Present, and Future," *Canadian Historical Review 81,* no. 3 (2000), 404–435; George S. Tomkins. *A Common Countenance: Stability and Change in the Canadian Curriculum* (Scarborough, Ontario: Prentice-Hall, 1986).

60. See, for example, Osborne, "Public Schooling and Citizenship Education"; Kenneth W. Osborne, *"Hard-working, Temperate and Peacable"—The Portrayal of Workers in Canadian History Textbooks* (Winnipeg: University of Manitoba, 1980); Neil Sutherland, *Growing Up: Childhood in English Canada from the Great War to the Age of Television* (Toronto: University of Toronto Press, 1997); Clark, "'Take It Away Youth!'"

61. Donalda Dickie, "The Anglo-Canadian Problem," *Canadians All 3,* no. 4 (1945), 13, 68–69.

62. The most sustained discussion can be found in Donalda Dickie, *All About Indians,* Book 2, Dent's Canadian History Readers (Toronto: J. M. Dent, 1925).

63. Donalda Dickie and Frederick S. Cooper, *We Talk and Write of What We Do* (Toronto: W. J. Gage, 1955), 95.

64. Donalda Dickie, comp., *Ships of Araby,* The Fifth Reader in the Far Horizons series (Toronto: J. M. Dent, 1936), 301.

65. Donalda Dickie, *The Great Golden Plain: A History of the Prairie Provinces* (Toronto: W. J. Gage, 1962), 194.

66. Ibid., 215.

67. Ibid.

68. Donalda J. Dickie and George Dill, *Two Little Indians* (Toronto: J. M. Dent, 1933); D. J. Dickie, *Joe and Ruth Go To School* (Toronto: J. M. Dent, 1940).

69. Donalda Dickie, *When Canada Was Young*, Book 5, Dent's Canadian History Readers (Toronto: J. M. Dent, 1925), 211.

70. Donalda Dickie, *In Pioneer Days*, Book 6, Dent's Canadian History Readers, rev. ed. (Toronto: J. M. Dent, 1927), 59.

71. Dickie, *Ships of Araby*, 103.

72. Thornton Mustard, introduction to *Junior Language, Book A*, by Donalda Dickie (1938; reprint Toronto: Gage, 1944), iii.

73. Donalda J. Dickie and Helen Palk, *Pages from Canada's Story* (Toronto: J. M. Dent, 1928). It is difficult to tell how many printings this book went through but I have been able to confirm the following publication history. Reprinting occurred in 1931, 1932 (twice), 1933, 1935. A slightly revised edition appeared in 1936 and was reprinted each year from 1937 to 1943. The book was "reset and electrotyped" and issued in 1947, revised and issued in 1949 and 1951, and then reprinted each year from 1952 to 1959 and again in 1961.

74. Donalda Dickie, *The Great Adventure: An Illustrated History of Canada for Young Canadians* (Toronto: J. M. Dent, 1950; reprinted 1951, 1952, 1953, 1954, 1955, 1956, 1957, 1958); sound recording (Edmonton: Alberta Education, 1977). The book may also have had further reprintings. Dickie's publisher also contacted the J. Arthur Rank Company to explore making a film of the book for use in Commonwealth countries. See [signature indecipherable], J. M. Dent and Sons (Canada) to Dr. Donalda Dickie, October 30, 1951. On circulation numbers see letter from J. M. Dent and Sons (Canada) to Dr. Donalda Dickie, October 23, 1951. Originals of both letters in possession of Harris family. For reviews of this book, see, for example, UTA, A-73-0026/083 (94), Clipping File, Dickie, Donalda James; J.E.P., "Review of *The Great Adventure*," *Saturday Night 66* (December 5, 1950), 45; n.a., "La Grande Aventure," *La revue de l'université Laval VII*, no. 2 (1952): 187–189. On the Governor General's Award see, Canadian Cultural Information Centre, *The Canadian Literary Awards, Part 1: Governor General's Literary Awards* (Ottawa: Author, 1966).

75. Donalda Dickie, Belle Ricker, Clara Tyner, and T. W. Woodhead, comps., *Young Explorers; Gay Adventurers; Proud Procession*; Canadian Parade Readers (Toronto: J. M. Dent, 1947; reprinted 1948, 1949, 1950, 1951, 1952, 1953, 1954, 1955, 1957) with teacher guides and workbooks; Neil Sutherland, *Growing Up*, 217.

76. "Dr. D. Dickie Retiring from Normal School; Widely Feted," *Edmonton Bulletin*, June 5, 1944. Glenbow Archives and Library, Library Clipping File, "Donalda Dickie."

77. "Notes About Authors," *Chatelaine*, April 1945, 2.

78. Harris interview.

79. See, for example, Leroy John Wilson, "Perren Baker and the United Farmers of Alberta— Educational Principles and Policies of an Agrarian Government" (M.Ed. thesis, University of Alberta, 1970); James Rennie Bradford, *The Rise of Agrarian Democracy: The United Farmers and Farm Women of Alberta, 1909–1921* (Toronto: University of Toronto Press, 2000); Tom Monto, *The United Farmers of Alberta: A Movement, A Government* (Edmonton: Crang Pub., 1989).

80. L. J. Wilson, "Educational Role of the United Farm Women of Alberta," in *Shaping the Schools of the Canadian West*, eds. David C. Jones, Nancy M. Sheehan, and Robert M. Stamp (Calgary: Detselig, 1979), 124–135.

81. See, Patterson, "The Establishment of Progressive Education in Alberta"; von Heyking, "Selling Progressive Education."

82. University of Alberta Archives (UAA), Ace. No. 69-29, Series l, Box 4, Item 3/1, File 1, Interview transcript, W. D. McDougall.

83. Coutts and Walker, *G. Fred*, 41.

84. Dickie, *The Enterprise*, 125.

85. UAA, Ace. No. 69-29, W. D. McDougall Collection, Box 4, 3/1, File 5, Donalda Dickie and Olive Fisher, "Some Events Leading to the Re-Organization of the Curriculum of the Department of Education of the Province of Alberta in 1933." Unpublished typescript, n.d.

86. Oviatt to [Oviatt].

87. Dickie, *The Enterprise*; see, also, articles by Dickie in a wide range of journals, including "New Lamp for Old," *Alberta School Trustee,* December 1939, 13–15; "Education via the Enterprise," *The School 21,* no. 9 (1940), 3–6; "Enterprise Education in Alberta," *Understanding the Child,* April 1940, 7–11; "Democracy and the Enterprise," *The School 31,* no. 6 (1943), 464–469; "Enterprise Education—Part 1," *The BC Teacher,* September 1940, 18–20 and Part 2, October 1940, 75–77; "A Comment on the New Course of Study for Elementary Schools," *The ATA Magazine,* November 1936, 35–36.

88. Shelley Anne Marie Bosetti-Piche, "The Interest of Edmonton Club Women in Education, Health and Welfare, 1919–1939" (Ph.D. diss., University of Alberta, 1990).

89. See, Patterson, "The Establishment of Progressive Education in Alberta"; von Heyking, "Selling Progressive Education"; University of Calgary Archives (UCA), UARC 86.034, A. L. Doucette fonds, Box 17, File 17.11, "Attitude Towards The Enterprise Curriculum." This document is an undated, anonymous assessment of the position on the enterprise taken by each of the normal school instructors. Here Dickie is put in the "child freedom group."

90. See, for example, Dickie, "Democracy and the Enterprise."

91. Donalda Dickie, "Improving Techniques in Social Studies," *The School 33,* no. 8 (April 1945), 673.

92. Alberta Department of Education, *Annual Report, 1935* (Edmonton: King's Printer, 1936), 19.

93. Robert S. Patterson, "History of Teacher Education in Alberta," in *Shaping the Schools of the Canadian West,* eds. David C. Jones, Nancy M. Sheehan, and Robert M. Stamp (Calgary: Detselig, 1979), 192–207.

94. Dickie, *The Enterprise*, 435.

95. Patterson, "Progressive Education: Impetus to Educational Change"; R. S. Patterson, "Voices from the Past: The Personal and Professional Struggles of Rural School Teachers," in *Schools in the West,* eds. Nancy M. Sheehan, J. Donald Wilson, and David C. Jones (Calgary: Detselig, 1986), 99–111.

96. Patterson, "Hubert C. Newland"; Oviatt to [Oviatt].

97. The attack most often cited is Hilda Neatby, *So Little for the Mind: An Indictment of Canadian Education* (Toronto: Clarke, Irwin & Co., 1953). See, also, W. G. Hardy, *Education in Alberta* (Calgary: Calgary Herald, n.d.). For a thorough discussion of the opposition, see Campbell A. Ross, "The Neatby Debate and Conservative Thought in Canada" (Ph.D. diss., University of Alberta, 1989).

98. UCA, UARC 86.034, A. L. Doucette *fonds,* Box 1, File 1.5, General Correspondence. Material in this file indicates that Doucette, an instructor at the Calgary Normal School, had actively supported progressive education reforms, but later recanted.

99. Dickie, *The Great Adventure*, vii.

100. Blackmore, *Troubling Women.*

101. UCA, UARC 0.2, Calgary Normal School Yearbooks, Box l, File 1924–25, "The Comet," 9.

102. UTA, Office of the President, Acc. No. A68-0007, Citation for Donalda James Dickie, June 6, 1952.

10

"There is no magic whereby such qualities will be acquired at the voting age":
Teachers, Curriculum, Pedagogy and Citizenship

LORNA MCLEAN

> I want my students to be aware of the world and its problems. I want them to be trained, and able, to take their share in good creative living, at community, national, and international levels. And I know that if they are to do this they must learn in their youth to take responsibility, to bear willingly their share of the tasks to be done, to live in mutual respect with others. These things must happen in my own classroom. There is no magic whereby such qualities will be acquired at the voting age.[1] (*Blanche Snell, teacher, York Memorial Collegiate, 1929–1961*)

Blanche Snell was an exceptional teacher. In the early 1950s, she taught English, social studies, and guidance for three hours each day to a class of twenty-five grade 9 students. She began her course by discussing what each student hoped to get out of the year at high school. Together, they outlined the rights and responsibilities of each member of the group, including the teacher. They documented their decisions and agreed upon the principles by which they would work. Students divided up tasks and set up a planning committee. At first, Miss Snell reported, "it appears sheer fun. Shortly after it becomes full of serious problems. . . . so, with the ups and downs, we go through the year, trying to understand why we behave as we do, trying to become self-motivated and controlled."[2]

In a subsequent article on curriculum planning, Miss Snell wrote about student-centred learning:

The teacher who cannot stand commotion and has little patience, who is unable to fail and start again, who cannot give others the right to plan, who cannot, after initial failures, continue to have faith in the capacity of youth to use good judgement, is not the one to attempt this type of teaching. It is a kind of teaching to be believed in, not legislated into. Once attempted, there is no turning back.[3]

In evaluating the effectiveness of her approach, Miss Snell was modest: "The only evidence of difference, at the moment, is the unsolicited incidental comment [by former students], for they drop in to chat, and when in larger groups we draw together as if by instinct." She elaborates further, "To attempt to measure this kind of learning is to attempt to assess the intangible. The culmination of the test will come only when we see these young people as adults, assuming their share of the world's tasks."[4]

In addition to her work in the classroom Miss Snell sought to influence students' interests beyond Canadian borders by forming a United Nations Club in the 1950s and organizing a United Nations Model Assembly, wherein students were faced with the "problem of learning the points of view of the countries they represented, of conducting discussion in true United Nations manner, and of familiarizing themselves with the UN charter." Preparation for the Assembly entailed a good deal of work under the guidance of their teachers.[5] To further develop their understanding of international issues, in 1959, Miss Snell sponsored a radio broadcast involving four students from two schools to discuss the topic: "Should Canada increase its aid to the underdeveloped countries in the world?"[6] Furthermore, she spearheaded projects to support education around the world; for example, her school raised $1,000 for the Pubvnan Technical School fund in Korea.[7] Blanche Snell's advocacy for what would be termed today global education or global citizenship education extended beyond fundraising projects in schools, however. In 1960, she was one of several judges invited to select the winners of the Agnes Macphail essay contest, which was sponsored by the Women's International League for Peace and Freedom.[8]

I highlight Miss Snell's life story here because her insights about citizenship, youth, and democracy suggest reasons to question what it meant to be a good citizen in Canada in the late 1940s through to the 1950s. This study of formal citizenship education for adolescents offers an opportunity to explore how citizenship training related to notions of identity, nationalism, belonging, and global citizenship education within a postwar liberal democracy. To better understand these relationships, I applied a critical discourse analysis to the Ontario curriculum and pedagogical materials, reviewed promotional materials prepared by the federal government (including the CBC Archives website and the records of the

Canadian Council for Reconstruction through UNESCO), analyzed a collection of high school yearbooks and studied the publications of the Canadian Teachers' Federation (CTF), and the Ontario Secondary School Teacher's Federation (OSSTF) over two decades. This research on formal citizenship education and youth suggests reasons to re-evaluate our understanding of what is considered the legitimate domain and purpose of citizenship education along with the possibilities of teaching citizenship within a high school setting.

While other scholars have examined the nature of education in this time period,[9] extra-curricula activities,[10] the role of the federal government,[11] teachers' experiences,[12] and how notions of citizenship have intersected with diversity,[13] as yet, no one has probed the way in which these multiple experiences inform the nature of citizenship education, postwar ideals and objectives for Canadian national and international identity, especially as they pertain to young people. For this research, I draw upon the theoretical framework of historian Kenneth Osborne. According to Osborne, four themes dominated the teaching of citizenship in the social studies curriculum in the twentieth century: identity, political efficacy, rights and duties, and social and personal values.[14] Throughout the postwar period, the emphasis on rights and duties, and social and personal values dominated education, alongside a sustained attention to issues of national identity and, to a lesser extent, political efficacy.

Like Miss Snell, Osborne believes that citizenship must be learned:

> It is based on a body of knowledge, skills and values that can never be taken for granted . . . This is what makes schools so important . . . [democracy depends on] the existence of a vital civil society—that network of non-political institutions (unions, associations, clubs, organizations of all kinds) in which people participate and practise such democratic skills as holding office, dealing with disagreement, working with others, exercising tolerance, and so on. In other words, democratic activity takes place in two settings: the formal institutions of the state and the ostensibly non-political life of civil society.[15]

This article will explore the formal and quasi-government institutions of the state; a second follow-up study will examine informal associations and youth groups.

INTRODUCTION

Increasing nationalism and unity in post–World War II Canadian society encouraged burgeoning interest in Canadian citizenship and education, leading to the introduction of a new Citizenship Act on January 1, 1947.[16] Secretary of State Paul Martin signalled this enthusiasm in the House of Commons when he declared, "[c]itizenship means more than the right to vote; more than the right to hold and transfer property; more than the right to move freely under the protection of the state; citizenship is the right to full partnership in the fortunes and the future of the nation."[17] The belief that citizenship was an instrument of nation building underlay the 1947 act.[18] Canadians shared a sense of urgency for teaching citizenship among the youth of the day. C. R. MacLeod, a professor at the Normal School in London, Ontario, captured this sentiment in the introduction to his 1949 book, *Citizenship Training: A Handbook for Canadian Schools*: "The World Today, is faced with a crisis—a crisis in human relations. Educators are becoming more and more conscious of the responsibility of schools to help overcome this crisis."[19] The threat of a "crisis" was, and is, used frequently to frame the rhetorical approach of citizenship education projects, but, in this instance, given the devastation of World War II, for many it was also a reality.

Equally important was the adoption of the Universal Declaration of Human Rights by the United Nations on December 10, 1948. It espoused non-discrimination based on race, colour, sex, language, religion, and politics. Its impact on society and global citizenship education is worthy of further consideration. During the parliamentary hearings on human rights in 1947 and 1950, "measures were justified on the basis that they would provide better protection of basic rights and would help to educate citizens in the values of tolerance and mutual respect of rights."[20] Likewise, Christopher MacLennan argues that "[t]he international concern in the 1940s and 1950s for universal human rights invaded not only the conference rooms of the United Nations but also the newsrooms, classrooms and living rooms of Canadians."[21]

Profound demographic shifts and population growth following World War II contributed to the growing sense of urgency for educating newcomers to become good citizens. Canada's population expanded from 12.1 million in 1945 to 18.2 million in 1961. Part of this increase was due to the 1946–62 baby boom: more than a demographic category, this "generation" acquired a social and political dominance that would define the 1960s in profound ways.[22] However, the arrival between 1951 and 1956 of 791,930 immigrants,[23] including persons displaced by the war, also contributed to growth. Their impact on Canadian culture was due not only to their numbers but also their origins: in the immediate postwar years, most came from Britain; between 1948 and 1951, many also arrived from eastern Europe. From 1951 to 1957, there was increased immigration from northern and western Europe, while origins shifted to southern Europe between 1958 and 1961. National security concerns, heightened by the Cold War and the revelation of Soviet espionage by Igor Gouzenko in 1945, affected immigrants suspected of having communist sympathies.[24] As well, there is some evidence to suggest that Cold War fears may have shaped the way teachers approached topics such as citizenship.

As the country was also becoming more urbanized, immigrants were drawn to urban areas where the population of students burgeoned. Of the 1,055,818 non-Canadian citizens in 1961, about 70 per cent lived in metropolitan areas with a population of 100,000 or more, and 70 per cent of these were located in the three largest metropolitan areas.[25] Ontario was increasingly attractive.[26] The population growth had significant implications for education: between 1946 and 1961, elementary enrolment jumped 116 per cent and secondary placements by 141 per cent. The number of classrooms in Ontario doubled, and school boards launched recruiting drives for teachers from across Canada and Britain.[27]

The Federal Government

In keeping with Liberal Prime Minister St. Laurent's stated goal of "making Canadian citizens of immigrants and making Canadian citizens of as many as possible of the descendants of the original inhabitants of this country,"[28] in January 1950, the government created the Department of Citizenship and Immigration, with four central offices including the Citizenship Branch.[29] The Branch was responsible for promoting knowledge of Canada—its society, institutions, culture, and languages—among Canadians and newcomers through educational, training, and community development projects.[30] As Cynthia Commachio observes in her study of youth from the period, "public discussions about youth labour emphasized training, not merely in terms of job-related skills, but just as much in terms of character formation, self-management, and citizenship, the latter encompassing these other individual traits in their most expansive productive sense. Canada's youth held the key to its national prosperity and to its international standing."[31] Unlike many other western countries that have enacted federal citizenship policies—Australia and the United States, for instance—Canada does not have a national or federal bureau of education.[32] Despite the lack of a government agency, and the positioning of educational jurisdiction within provincial boundaries, the federal government's flourishing bureaucracy pursued dynamic strategies to shape citizenship education among Canadian high school students. Along with funding research and training teachers, the federal government cooperated with the provinces in developing materials. As Alan Sears contends, "the state used the argument of compelling national interest to override constitutional niceties and influence aspects of Canadian citizenship education."[33]

From the 1940s to the 1960s, thousands of booklets and film strips designed to introduce immigrants to Canada were distributed through immigrant language classes and volunteer organizations for use with both immigrants and Canadian youth.[34] As a case in point, in the 1950s and again in the early 1960s, the Department of Citizenship and Immigration distributed a discussion guide titled "Let's Take a Look at Prejudice."[35] The supplementary reading list targeted social and personal values, tolerance, respect for minorities, and compassion—the hallmarks of liberalism. The ideological orientation of the guide, which depicted prejudice as a state of mind and discrimination as the action, offered suggestions for denouncing societal failings through education, legislation, and community action combined with workshops to study the Canadian Bill of Rights. Such materials shared a common view of the time that prejudice and discrimination were "learned" and therefore could be "unlearned" through effective teaching strategies.

The federal government attempted to ensure that it did not overstep jurisdictional bounds by using "surrogate" organizations such as the National Film Board (NFB) or Canadian Broadcasting Corporation (CBC) and provincial programs to carry out citizenship education. Because of their quasi-government status, surrogate organizations could tackle more controversial issues and take greater risks than an elected government: for example, John Grierson, NFB director, "was certain that a powerful national experience could be kindled through the medium of film." Appointed by Prime Minister King, Grierson sought to develop the NFB as, in his words, "more of a Ministry of Education than anything else," in which "the new citizenship of the co-operative state is even now, in spite of confusion, asking to be articulated."[36] By the 1940s, NFB films promoted working in and for the community locally, nationally, and internationally. Films such as *Lessons in Living* (1944) featured public school settings to articulate the "new citizenship of the co-operative state."[37] *Youth Is Tomorrow* (1939), one of the NFB's first documentaries, encouraged youth in the post-Depression world to think globally; postwar films such as *Tomorrow's Citizens* (1947) promoted themes of world citizenship. By the 1950s, the NFB was producing documentaries on racism and prejudice for use in schools and amongst community groups.[38] One example, *No Longer Vanishing*, promoted citizenship among Canada's First Nations and featured First Nations integration into Canadian society.

Throughout this period, the federal government marshalled its spending power to induce the provinces to offer programs consistent with federal citizenship policy and to build the capacity to carry out that policy in public schools. Although the provinces complained that the conditions attached to federal money "constituted undue interference by the federal government in a provincial area of responsibility," they did not refuse the funds.[39] Surrogate organizations, which relied on state resources to carry out citizenship education, extended the capabilities of the relatively small federal department by venturing into areas beyond the state's reach. The Federation of Women Teachers of Ontario (FWTAO) offers one such example. The February 1947 issue of the FWTAO's publication, *The*

Educational Courier, featured an article which recommended "visual aids on intercultural relations" prepared by the Citizenship Branch with the NFB on topics such as "Peoples of Canada."[40]

Attempts at influencing educational practice in the schools drew upon other forms of media to garner attention among youth. Working alongside the Canadian Association for Adult Education (CAAE), the CBC broadcast the national radio program *Citizens' Forum*, which modelled interactive, progressive forms of education that instructed the audience on basic civic literacy skills and provided opportunities to apply these skills through participation in civic affairs. The program, which began in 1945, continued for twelve years and was later adapted for television. Although the program was intended for adults, weekly panel debates were transmitted from different provinces at various locations, including schools, where they were often held in conjunction with the Home and School Association. Topics ranged from national issues such as the death penalty to the question of "how we acquire prejudices." NFB documentaries on related topics were announced in the *Citizens' Forum Bulletin*, which included background information "as well as opposing views and attitudes and suggestions for further reading."[41]

Experienced educators, like Miss Snell, contributed their pedagogical and curriculum expertise as part of the *Citizens' Forum* organizational team. Among the representatives on the *Forum's* committee were a number of teachers, including Emma Carr, who resigned as secretary of the FWTAO in 1944 to become secretary of the *Forum*, and later Evelyn MacDonald, a teacher from Bloor Collegiate Institute who represented the CAAE.[42] Not surprisingly, teachers took advantage of the programs by incorporating them into their classroom planning. Miss Rutherford, a secondary teacher in Kirkland Lake, joined the *Citizen's Forum* and devoted a weekly history class to a discussion of the issues raised by the broadcasts.[43]

The Citizens' Forum and the NFB offer evidence of critical civic engagement among quasi-governmental organizations that provided a pedagogical model for public debate through documentaries and radio broadcasts, much as today's blogs or interactive social networking websites do. As Janine Brodie reminds us, in postwar states "social liberalism prescribed that all citizens could make claim to a measure of equality, social security, and collective provision as a right of citizenship, independent of their status in the market or their personal character. Social citizenship required positive obligations from the collective to provide resources for the welfare of individuals."[44] While the *Citizens' Forum* and the NFB did not focus solely on citizenship education, they did succeed in addressing issues of (in)equality, social justice, and international development by modelling innovative models of instruction for teaching citizenship literacy skills and for generating public debate subscribing to the belief that personal enlightenment might or might not lead to action.[45]

PROVINCIAL CURRICULUM AND THE GOOD CITIZEN

Throughout the fifties, citizenship education was a primary focus of the social studies curriculum. In Alberta, for example, it "encompassed a wide range of desirable outcomes, from 'displaying democratic attitudes and behaviours in all social situations' to 'developing consumer competence.'"[46] In Nova Scotia, the *Guidelines on Citizenship* took a more pragmatic approach and stated that "People must not only *know* what constitutes good citizenship, they must *practice* being good citizens." Citizenship was taught in schools: assigned tasks required students to make a list of the important qualities of a good citizen.[47] Articles in the federations' publications, *The Education Courier* and *The Bulletin* promoted teaching intercultural relations as part of the curriculum to help students overcome fears of other people.[48]

According to the Ontario *Intermediate Division, 1951 Curriculum: Grades VII, VIII, IX, X*:

> Social Studies is the study of man [sic] in relationship to his environment and to other people. This central theme embraces in one subject history, geography, civics, and guidance.... Social Studies should help the pupils to understand and to improve the democratic way of life ... We must define and meet our responsibilities to society more effectively.[49]

Much like the categories suggested by Osborne, the curriculum set out four themes: knowledge and understanding, skills, attitudes, and behaviour—with few references to political efficacy.[50] Knowledge and understanding encompassed values of tolerance and respect.[51] Skills included critical thinking and group discussions, but not, interestingly, preparing an argument, debating, or other forms of dissension—abilities that are part of the democratic process. The component of the curriculum incorporating attitudes called for respect unprejudiced by qualities of race, colour, class, creed, or national origin, but said nothing about discrimination; gender was not mentioned. Finally, "acceptable social behaviour" included "co-operation with individuals and groups without regard to nationality, religion, or social position."

Curriculum is written by educators and sanctioned by the Ministry. Like texts, curriculum is produced out of, and is positioned "within complex sets of relationships and processes in particular times and places."[52] The social studies curriculum's guiding principles frame my analysis:

It is better for pupils to find out the information for themselves and draw con-
clusions under the teacher's guidance than to have information given to them.
The habit of judgement can be fostered in pupils by leading them to think and
reason for themselves. . . . ; Democracy should be presented not as an ideal
which has been attained but as a desirable way of life in which improvements
are continually being sought; and Citizenship is not a subject to be taught but a
spirit to be engendered. Social Studies provides many opportunities for arran-
ging activities which develop the qualities of good citizenship.[53]

To better understand how the curriculum represented citizenship in relation to nationalism and belonging alongside Osborne's four themes of identity,
political efficacy, rights and duties, and social and personal values, I selected key
topics across all grades of the 1951 Ontario secondary social studies curriculum
from history, geography, government of Canada, world history, and present-
day global political, economic, and social relationships. To analyze the textual
content, I drew upon Walt Werner's eight concepts for interpreting authorship
in texts: representation, the gaze, voice, intertextuality, absence, authorship,
mediation, and reflexivity.[54] For a definition of progressive education, I base my
understanding on student-centred learning theory, which focuses on studying
contemporary problems to better prepare children for the real world through
interactive, experiential classroom learning experiences. I define a more traditional approach as teacher-centred, with structured teacher-led lessons focusing on textbook assignments based on literacy competencies.

The grade 7 social studies curriculum on "Living in a Democracy" introduces its objective "To appreciate the freedoms we enjoy." The curriculum
speaks from the perspective of those who have benefitted from "Our freedoms." Under "*our* freedoms" (emphasis mine) students are invited to "collect newspaper clippings which illustrate our possession of these freedoms."[55]
Nowhere are students asked to search out examples of "people" who do not
share "our" freedoms, such as First Nations, African Canadians, or women.
In fact, the possessive "our" explicitly marginalizes dissenting voices. The accompanying exercise instructs teachers to "read or dramatize events in Canadian history by which these freedoms were won." The implicit interpretation of
such an activity champions a past history of hard-won freedoms, not deplor-
able losses, such as the then-recent, government-imposed, forced relocation of
Japanese-Canadians.

In the grade 8 curriculum, titled "How the British People Laid Foundations
for Our Social Life," the objectives centre around the larger narrative of imperialism, privileging the "contribution of British standards of conduct."[56] Likewise,

under the section "How Britain Laid the Foundation for Modern Industry," students are directed to research the topic and "appreciate Britain's contribution to the world in developing modern industry, transportation, and communication"; there is no question that Britain's contribution is anything but worthy of celebration. Although the goal of teaching students about "the social problems which arise from industrialization" offers opportunities to denounce unequal power relations and worker dissent, there are only two opportunities for such discussions: the directive to "Dramatize complaints of a merchant about goods" conceals a power imbalance between merchants and workers; the assignment to "list improvements that have been made in factory and home conditions of the worker of today" deflects attention from the workers' historic contempt, to the "improved" conditions of modern society.

The topic of slavery in grade 9 appears under the unit title "How the American people occupied half a continent and preserved their unity."[57] Title, subtitles, and pedagogical tasks circumscribe slavery within a storyline of American nation building and economic expansion. The unit first focuses on the labour demands of the cotton industry with recommendations for students to "show how Whitney's cotton gin increased the demand for slaves," and explain why "in the South cotton was king." Thus, when slavery is introduced, it is positioned first as an American, economic (rather than moral) issue, and then within the freedom movement (thus linking Canada with freedom): "How did the underground railway operate? Why was Windsor a terminal?" The day-to-day degrading experiences of slavery are represented only by the bewildering directive to "Dramatize a slave auction scene." It is uncertain how this unit might teach "democracy . . . not as an ideal which has been attained but as a desirable way of life in which improvements are continually being sought," given the orientation of the research assignments.

For the study of First Nations, the curriculum introduces students to "Indians" under the topic "How the environment affected our earliest inhabitants";[58] the objectives do not identify who these "inhabitants" were. Rather, the prominence of place, not people, is reinforced by two themes: first "to understand the broader geographical features of Canada and to examine the ways in which this environment affected life in typical regions"; and second, "to appreciate the culture of these early inhabitants." Although the topics open up the possibility of discussing "differences that are not seen as inferior" when students are invited to "report what they know of Indian life from previous reading and from first hand knowledge," there is limited opportunity to develop this theme because the following assignment has students "contrast the natural conditions in the area of those times with its present state by means of a picture display" and "make a sand-table display of a typical area." After dealing with topics related to "how the open plain shaped its own particular pattern of living," students "*attempt a discovery* of the ways in which members established social customs, enforced order and justice" (my emphasis); the unit then concludes with the section "the Indian as a citizen of Canada today."[59] Here, students are encouraged to explore categories of analysis that prescribe particular assumptions about integration: occupations, health, famous Indian citizens, and reservations. Finally, the invitation for pupils to collect "items from newspapers" and investigate "the citizenship status of Indians" creates a key learning moment to teach "respect for people and individuals unprejudiced by qualities of race, colour, class."

As Werner notes, texts do more than convey facts; they represent power by privileging some voices and silencing others. Curriculum authors decide what gets put in and what is left out.[60] With few exceptions, women of any race, colour, or creed are not represented as historical actors in the 1951 curriculum. Likewise, Canadian men and women of African, Chinese, Japanese, Indian, and many European nationalities are not represented, despite their long-term presence in Canada. Although curriculum units on the "Local Community" and "How Different Peoples Formed One Nation" invite teachers "to identify the national origins of families represented in the class" and "review ethnic groups found in your class or community," it would have been difficult for many of these pupils to see their identity represented in the curriculum. Thus, despite progressivist policy aims and guidelines governing student-centred learning, the 1951 curriculum presented Canadian identity and values through a storyline of national progress and linear social, economic, and political developments. At the same time, however, the range of topics and pedagogical strategies also offered creative space for teachers like Miss Snell to challenge these exclusionary narratives.

PEDAGOGICAL PRACTICE

The diversity of approaches to teaching social studies across Canada has been the topic of much debate. Some historians claim that the 1950s were conservative years in education while others have seen opportunities for progressive practices. Bob Gidney states that "Progressivism made far less headway in Canada . . . still it provoked equally fierce opposition in newspapers, magazines, and speeches from both educators and the laity"[61] as evidenced by Hilda Neatby's much-quoted *So Little for the Mind*. While Penney Clark has observed that, because social studies had been introduced during the progressive era of the 1930s, it was frequently seen to be child centred.[62] In her study of social studies curriculum in twentieth-century Alberta, Amy von Heyking concludes that "It was simply impossible to find a synthesis of traditional and progressive approaches in a subject area that was progressive by its very nature."[63] More recently, Paul Axelrod called for historians of education to consider an analysis beyond the paradigms of progressive/traditional polarities to a more nuanced understanding of education in the fifties.[64] Reva Joshee and Lauri Johnson's study is an example of this approach. Their study of the Welland Citizenship Program, which was adapted from the Springfield Plan in Massachusetts, concludes that this Plan which connected values of cultural diversity with tolerance and citizenship was taught for several years in northern Canadian schools and communities and contributed to "a pivotal time in the development of diversity and equity policies in Canada."[65] As well, from other sources we know that the film, *It Happened in Springfield*, was promoted across Ontario by the teachers' federation as an instructive model for "Teaching good citizenship to youngsters. . . . [through] interest and enlist[ing] sympathy."[66]

It is difficult to determine the extent to which any teacher, as exemplified in the profile of Blanche Snell, practised student-centred learning strategies. As Kathleen Weiler has observed, in the classroom people can "assert their own experience and contest or resist the ideological and material forces."[67] Von Heyking reports that, in Alberta, "There is some evidence that . . . teachers were slowly incorporating some of the new techniques."[68] However, a 1960s survey "found that most teachers relied on lecturing, question and answer, class discussion and written exercises. . . . classroom discussions were usually around material presented in textbooks."[69] In Ontario, a study of teaching in the sixties confirmed a teacher-centred approach, relying heavily on textbook assignments.[70] While progressive methods were a subject of debate in the Toronto school boards between 1948 and 1951, implementation of such practices remains uncertain.[71]

A review of the provincial federations' monthly publications, over two decades, reveals a scattering of articles featuring student-centred classroom planning. In one instance, an elementary teacher initiated a project with her class of students who originated from eleven different nationalities; every Friday, she set up a geography class in which students "travelled" to different countries and parents brought in materials for the "trips." The teacher reported a change in attitude and a new comradeship as admiration for the "talents and achievements of other nationalities developed."[72] If a secondary teacher wanted to engage in citizenship education, among the reference books cited in the Ontario curriculum was MacLeod's *Citizenship Training: A Handbook for Canadian Schools*. Claiming that "Citizenship must be acquired through practice," part 2 of the book documents eighteen techniques for integrating citizenship with other subjects.[73] Likewise, a study of women teachers in Toronto secondary schools suggests that Miss Snell was not alone in her commitment to teaching citizenship and democracy through classroom practice. Kristina Llewellyn's study of the "performance" of women teachers in Toronto secondary schools reveals how some teachers negotiated the gender hierarchy of the postwar liberal "democracy" in schools.[74]

GLOBAL CITIZENSHIP EDUCATION

As chronicled in the teaching experience of Blanche Snell, the 1950s witnessed interest among Canadian educators, federations, and politicians in addressing human rights and world issues. Educational leaders such as G. Blair Laing, chairman of the Toronto Board of Education, stated in a speech at the Empire Club in 1950[75] that the main purpose of education is democracy; calling for "education for World Brotherhood or World Citizenship." Similarly, Lester B. Pearson in speaking to the members of the FWTAO in 1948 on the "Role of the Teacher in International Affairs" prevailed upon teachers to instruct their students about other countries as the key to "peaceful and progressive relations."[76] As well, within federations' publications, teachers were routinely encouraged to support various causes such as the Canadian Appeal for Children to provide food and clothing for children and books for schools.[77] By 1962, teachers were invited to expand their knowledge of other countries and promote educational opportunities by signing up for CTF's international development program, Project Overseas, to teach children in the Caribbean, Africa, and Asia.[78]

Because Canada lacks a federal agency to oversee education, no central government agency coordinated UNESCO's postwar education programs;[79] instead, they were funnelled through surrogate organizations. In 1947, the Canadian Council for Reconstruction was founded as a voluntary, non-profit organization to assist war-torn countries; a constitution was adopted by representatives of thirty organizations, including the Canadian Education Association, the Boy Scouts, and the YWCA, at a conference convened by the Department of External Affairs.[80] In 1948, Grace Dolmage, coordinator of the Winnipeg Child Guidance Clinic, reported to the Canadian Education Association on a recent UNESCO seminar on world understanding through childhood education; that same year, Dr. Fletcher Peacock, director of education in Fredericton, spoke about UNESCO's seminar on teaching about the UN's work for "world understanding . . . to remove prejudices."[81] It wasn't long before teachers from across Canada were drawn into the organization. In 1950, Gladys Voycheshin, a Winnipeg teacher, attended the UNESCO seminar as the CTF's representative,[82] and a UNESCO seminar promoting geography and international understanding was held for teachers at Macdonald College of McGill University.[83] The Canadian Council for Reconstruction dissolved in the mid-1950s, just before the creation of the Canadian Commission for UNESCO in 1957.[84] In 1953, UNESCO undertook a large-scale project with a number of secondary schools to "determine to what extent mutual understanding and the elimination of prejudice can be fostered by education"; but it wasn't until 1965 that Oakwood Collegiate in Toronto became the first UNESCO-associated school in Canada.[85] The lack of a central government agency in the 1950s to promote

UNESCO in the schools may account for the low profile of the organization among the federal departments and within the provincial curriculum.

The United Nations, however, was featured in the Ontario curriculum in 1951. For the final unit in grade 10 social studies, students were invited to discuss the role of the United Nations under the heading "cooperation is essential for world security."[86] The last assignment in the curriculum, "Canada's place and responsibility in the United Nations," required students to "assemble in a special section of the class loose-leaf scrapbook evidence of Canada's faith and support of United Nations. Discuss the personal responsibility of each Canadian to United Nations." If at the end of a busy year teachers were able to schedule this assignment, then the students might have discovered that the United Nations Declaration of Human Rights was written by a Canadian, John Humphrey.[87]

SCHOOL CULTURE AND CITIZENSHIP

School culture played a vital role in shaping a student's daily experience of formal education. As we shall see, the four strands of Osborne's model of citizenship teaching were reproduced within student-led clubs in secondary schools in the postwar period. Political efficacy and rights and duties were central to students' understanding of human rights and global citizenship in the United Nations (UN) Clubs that formed after the incorporation of the UN Association in Canada in 1946.[88] Historian Kenneth Dewar recalls competing in a public-speaking competition sponsored by the UN Association as a formative experience of his schooling in the late 1950s. His public-speaking coach, a social studies teacher, was also a staff sponsor of the school's UN Club.[89] The UN Clubs' existence seemed to rely on the commitment of a teacher-sponsor, such as Miss Snell. At Lisgar Collegiate in Ottawa, under the supervision of the head of the history department, a UN Club was formed in 1945 to promote "a better understanding of world affairs." It flourished for several years with up to thirty members who organized films, public speaking, and lively debates, but declined in the mid-fifties, shortly before its staff sponsor retired; it was resurrected in 1967 when Lisgar became a certified UNESCO school.[90]

Outside service organizations, such as the Rotary Club, also played a part in fervently promoting global citizenship education among secondary students. Its popular, and highly contested, school-wide public-speaking contests attracted the attention of students, teachers, and school officials. In 1955, for example, Adrienne Poy (later Adrienne Clarkson, Governor General of Canada), was one of two winners of the Rotary Club's public-speaking contest who was chosen to represent Canadian students at the student UN Model Assembly.[91]

The Red Cross was another organization which prevailed upon students to increase their awareness of global issues and to act as "good citizens." In 1946,

80,150 student members belonged to the Canadian Junior Red Cross, whose objectives included "health, service and good citizenship." Junior Red Cross branches in Canada were in correspondence with members of the society in forty-nine countries of the world, promoting "International friendliness" as one of the "essentials of good citizenship." They conducted meetings according to parliamentary procedure, practised public speaking, and took "their responsibilities as young citizens seriously."[92] In a way that was different and similar, charitable giving was promoted through UNICEF's Halloween fundraising campaign. By the mid-1950s, various communities across Canada encouraged schools to coordinate the successful drive "to eliminate disease, want and misery from the lives of children in less privileged countries."[93]

Other clubs continued to thrive as teenage school culture blended social events with service. For example, throughout the 1950s, at one Ontario high school, four of the eight non-athletic school clubs educated members about good citizenship through fundraising projects such as school dances, benevolent events, and information sessions. The Boys and Girls Hi-Y (affiliates of the YM-YWCA) were involved in charitable services such as purchasing gifts and organizing game nights for the children in a local orphanage and at the hospital, and engaging in political discussions with invited speakers and films. The Welfare Club, formed in 1946, sent money to destitute families in postwar Europe. By the 1950s, this small group of mostly girls promoted "International good will" and "the problems faced by under-privileged people." They annually raised money with dances and the Welfare Tea to send to CARE, UNICEF, and the Unitarian Service Committee.[94]

CONCLUSION

Dominique Clement's study of social movements and social change reminds us of the importance of understanding the dynamics of public opinion. As he argues,

> Human rights are ultimately linked with changes in the law, yet at the same time they are informed by the cultural context of the community they serve. . . . Human rights are a powerful force because the source of human rights lies not in the law but in human morality. A society with a strong rights culture allows individuals to make rights claims even though, at the time, they are not recognized by the state or even the community around them.

To underscore his argument, Clement remarks how "Canadians have come to view themselves as rights-bearing citizens, and this has had a profound impact on the relationship between the state and civil society."[95]

In this paper, I am not claiming that the forties and fifties were decades of rampant social justice; systemic barriers to equality and human rights in the postwar period resulted in multiple forms of discrimination in Canada. Even within the material cited here, human rights for the most part was racialized, but not systemically gendered.[96] Rather, what I am suggesting is that despite the traditional rhetoric of the provincial curriculum, there existed school clubs, quasi-government organizations, and some educators, like Miss Snell, who exposed youth to a range of ideas about social justice, human rights, international development, and discrimination at an age when they clearly understood concepts of (in)equality and (in)justice. Within the lived experience of the culture of secondary school clubs, many students gained first-hand knowledge of Canadian identity, political efficacy, rights and duties, and social and personal values. Through the routine practice of organizing meetings, taking minutes, preparing reports, inviting speakers, debating topics, resolving conflicts, seeking consensus, fundraising, and a host of other tasks, students learned how to take responsibility "in good creative living, at community, national and international levels." As well, this research profiles ways that schooling in the fifties may have influenced, in part, citizens in the 1960s and 1970s to embrace political and social actions. Finally, this study suggests that exposure to ideas of tolerance and individual rights may have contributed to a later understanding of diversity and difference, as expressed in the multiculturalism policies in the 1970s and 1980s, as Canadian.

REFLECTIVE QUESTIONS
1. Is citizenship something that can be taught and learned? Justify your response.
2. What do you believe the purpose of citizenship education is and how do you see it being most effectively implemented in the classroom?
3. What are the democratic freedoms we are privileged to have? Does our curriculum content emphasize them? Can you find an example?
4. Where do you see a "recycled curriculum" as discussed in this reading?
5. How do we ensure that the voices of all groups in our society are heard and considered? Can we?

ACKNOWLEDGEMENTS
The author sincerely thanks Alessandra Iozzo-Duval, Kelly Brand, and Heather Brittain for their diligent research.

NOTES

1. Blanche Snell, "Operating the 'Core' Curriculum," in *Education: A Collection of Essays on Canadian Education*, vol. 1, 1954–1956 (Toronto: W. J. Gage, 1956), 53–56.

2. Ibid., 55.

3. Ibid., 55.

4. Ibid., 56.

5. *York Memo* [yearbook] (Toronto: York Memorial Collegiate Institute, 1955), 43.

6. *York Memo*, 1959, 66.

7. *York Memo*, 1961, 8.

8. "Students Honoured at Tea," *Globe and Mail*, March 31, 1960, 19. Following Miss Snell's death in 1972, the Ontario Teachers' Federation created the Blanche E. Snell Estate Fund—recipients of the award must be citizens of a developing country and must return to their own country to work in education; see Ontario Teachers' Federation, "OTF Initiatives: International Assistance," *Ontario Teachers' Federation: Your Voice, Your Strength*, www.otffeo.on.ca/english/init_assist.php.

9. Robert Gidney, *From Hope to Harris* (Toronto: University of Toronto Press, 2002); Robert Stamp, *The Schools of Ontario* (Toronto: University of Toronto, 1999); Amy von Heyking, *Creating Citizens* (Calgary: University of Calgary Press, 2006); Paul Axelrod, "Beyond the Progressive Education Debate: A Profile of Toronto Schooling in the 1950s," *Historical Studies in Education* 17, 2 (2005), 227–41.

10. Cynthia R. Commachio, *The Dominion of Youth: Adolescence and the Making of Modern Canada* (Waterloo: Wilfrid Laurier University Press, 2006), 129–159. See also Michael Gauvreau, "The Protracted Birth of the Canadian 'Teenager': Work, Citizenship, and the Canadian Youth Commission, 1943–1955," in *Cultures of Citizenship in Post-War Canada, 1940–1955*, eds. Nancy Christie and Michael Gauvreau (Montreal: McGill-Queen's University Press, 2003), 201–202.

11. Alan Sears, "Instruments of Policy: How the State Influences Citizenship Education in Canada," *Canadian Ethnic Studies 29*, 2 (1997).

12. Rebecca Coulter and Helen Harper, eds., *History Is Hers: Women Educators in Twentieth Century Ontario* (Calgary: Detselig, 2005); Kristina R. Llewellyn, "Gendered Democracy: Women Teachers in Post-War Toronto," *Historical Studies in Education / Revue d'histoire de l'éducation* 18, 1 (2006), 1–25.

13. Reva Joshee and Lauri Johnson, "Historic Diversity and Equity Policies in Canada," in *Transformations in Schooling: Historical and Comparative Perspectives*, ed. Kim Tolley (New York: Palgrave MacMillian, 2007).

14. Ken Osborne, "Citizenship Education and Social Studies," in *Trends and Issues in Canadian Social Studies*, eds. Ian Wright and Alan Sears (Vancouver: Pacific Educational Press, 1997), 45; and Ken Osborne, "Public Schooling and Citizenship Education in Canada," in *Educating Citizens for a Pluralistic Society*, eds. Rosa Bruno-Jofré and Natalia Aponiuk (Calgary: Canadian Ethnic Studies, 2001), 11–48.

15. Osborne, "Citizenship Education and Social Studies," 49.

16. William Kaplan, *The Evolution of Citizenship Legislation in Canada* (Ottawa: Multiculturalism and Citizenship Canada, 1991), 20.

17. Cited in Kaplan, *The Evolution of Citizenship Legislation in Canada*, 17–18.

18. On the significance of this legislation for immigrants, see Harold Troper, "Citizenship Education in Urban Canada," in *Citizenship in Transformation in Canada*, ed. Yvonne M. Hébert (Toronto: University of Toronto Press, 2002), 150–161.

19. C. R. MacLeod, introduction to *Citizenship Training: A Handbook for Canadian Schools* (Toronto: J. M. Dent, 1949). See also Alan Sears and Emery J. Hyslop-Margison, "The Cult of

Citizenship Education," in *Troubling the Canon of Citizenship Education*, eds. George Richardson and David Blades (New York: Peter Lang, 2006), 13–24; Robert Adamoski, Dorothy E. Chunn, and Robert Menzies, eds., *Contesting Canadian Citizenship: Historical Readings* (Peterborough, ON: Broadview, 2002); and Yvonne M. Hébert, ed., *Citizenship in Transformation in Canada* (Toronto: University of Toronto Press, 2002).

20. R. Brian Howe, "Human Rights in Hard Times: The Post-war Canadian Experience," *Canadian Public Administration / Administration Publique du Canada* 35, 4 (1992), 466.

21. Christopher MacLennan. *Toward the Charter: Canadians and the Demand for a National Bill of Rights, 1929–1960* (Kingston: McGill-Queen's Press, 2003), 3.

22. Madga Fahrni and Robert Rutherdale, introduction to *Creating Postwar Canada: 1945–75*, eds. Magda Fahrni and Robert Rutherdale (Vancouver: UBC Press, 2008), 3–5; Doug Owram, *Born at the Right Time: A History of the Baby-Boom Generation* (Toronto: University of Toronto, 1996).

23. Warren Kalbach, *The Impact of Immigration on Canada's Population* (Ottawa: Dominion Bureau of Statistics, 1961), 348–349.

24. From 1946 to 1958, more than 29,000 prospective immigrants were rejected as "security risks," and 8,572 people were deported over the same period; Ninette Kelley and Michael Trebilcock, *The Making of the Canadian Mosiac: A History of Canadian Immigration Policy* (Toronto: University of Toronto Press, 1998), 314; Franca Iacovetta, *Gatekeepers: Reshaping Immigrant Lives in Cold War Canada* (Toronto: Between the Lines, 2006).

25. Kalbach, *The Impact of Immigration*, 419.

26. Kelley and Trebilcock, *The Making of the Canadian Mosiac*, 314.

27. Robert Gidney, *From Hope to Harris* (Toronto: University of Toronto Press, 2002), 27–28. On the postwar objectives of secondary schools, see Robert Stamp, *The Schools of Ontario* (Toronto: University of Toronto, 1999).

28. Cited in Heidi Bohaker and Franca Iacovetta, "Making Aboriginal People 'Immigrants Too': A Comparison of Citizenship Programs for Newcomers and Indigenous Peoples in Postwar Canada, 1940s–1960s," *Canadian Historical Review* 90, 3 (September 2009), 428–429.

29. In addition to its mandate, the citizenship branch was responsible for immigration, Indian affairs, the Canadian Citizenship Branch, and Canadian Citizenship Registration Branch. For an analysis on the similarities in immigration and Indian citizenship, see Iocovetta and Bohaker, "Making Aboriginal People 'Immigrants Too,'" 428–429. For an analysis of wartime citizenship policy, see Ivana Caccia, *Managing the Canadian Mosaic: Shaping Citizenship Policy, 1939–1945* (Kingston: McGill-Queen's University Press, 2010).

30. Michael Gauvreau claims that, throughout the 1940s, it was "the emphatically 'public' qualities of youth as producer and citizen, rather than the 'private' nature of the teenager as consumer of leisure and personal relationships, that defined the attitudes of Canadians between the end of World War II and the early 1950s." Michael Gauvreau, "The Protracted Birth of the Canadian 'Teenager': Work, Citizenship and the Canadian Youth Commission," in *Cultures of Citizenship in Post-War Canada, 1940–1955*, eds. Nancy Christie and Michael Gauvreau (Montreal: McGill-Queen's Press, 2003), 203.

31. Commachio, *The Dominion of Youth*, 129. See also Michael Gauvreau, "The Protracted Birth of the Canadian 'Teenager,'" 201–238.

32. Lorna McLean, "No Short Cuts to Better Days": Education, identity and citizenship in early modern Canada, 1900–1930. *Journal of Canadian Studies* 41 (2007), 2–26.

33. Alan Sears, "Instruments of Policy: How the State Influences Citizenship Education in Canada," *Canadian Ethnic Studies* 29, 2 (1997), 7.

34. Ibid., 1.

35. The guide was originally published in the 1950s in the Citizenship Branch's monthly journal, *The Citizen*. Ottawa. Department of Citizenship and Immigration. *Let's Take a Look at Prejudice, Citizenship Guide*. Reprinted, 1961.

36. Brian Low, NFB *Kids: Portrayals of Children by the National Film Board of Canada, 1939–89* (Waterloo, ON: Wilfrid Laurier University Press, 2002), 28.

37. Ibid., 29–30.

38. Ibid., 29–40.

39. Sears, "Instruments of Policy," 10.

40. *Educational Courier*, "Visual Aids on Intercultural Relations," February 1947, 22.

41. To hear a selection of the broadcasts, visit CBC Digital Archives at http://archives.cbc.ca.

42. *Educational Courier*, "The Editorial Slant . . . ," October 1944, 3; see also CBC Digital Archives at http://archives.cbc.ca.

43. W. D. Rutherford, "Are student discussion groups worth while?" *The Bulletin*, Ontario Secondary School Teachers' Federation (OSSTF) 28(1) February, 1948, 31–32.

44. Janine Brodie, "Reforming Social Justice in Neoliberal Times," *Studies in Social Justice* 1, 2 (2007), 98.

45. Ronald Faris, *The Passionate Educators: Voluntary Associations and the Struggle for Control of Adult Educational Broadcasting in Canada, 1919–1952* (Toronto: Peter Martin, 1975), 101–111.

46. Amy von Heyking, *Creating Citizens* (Calgary: University of Calgary Press, 2006), 106–107.

47. Eveleen Burns, *Civics and Citizenship, Grades 7, 8, and 9: A Guide for Teachers*, Tentative ed. (Halifax: Department of Education 1957, rev. ed. 1958), 8, 10.

48. Alice Miel, "The School's Fourth R—Relationship," *The Educational Courier*, December 1946, 5, 34. Reprinted from OHIO schools; "Better Human Relations" *The Bulletin* (December 1949), 256.

49. Ontario Department of Education, *Intermediate Division, 1951 Curriculum: Grades VII, VIII, IX, X* (Toronto: Minister of Education, 1951), 58. For an analysis on how the dominant culture continues to pervade social studies curricula, see Kurt W. Clausen, Todd Horton, and Lynn Lemisko, "Democracy and Diversity: A Content Analysis of Selected Contemporary Canadian Social Studies Curricula," *Citizenship Teaching and Learning* 4, 1 (July 2008), 435–449.

50. Ontario Department of Education, *Intermediate Division, 1951 Curriculum*, 58–60.

51. Ibid., 58–59.

52. Walt Werner, "Reading Authorship into Texts," *Theory and Research in Social Education* 28, 2 (Spring 2000), 194.

53. Ontario Department of Education, *Intermediate Division, 1951 Curriculum*, 60–61.

54. Werner, "Reading Authorship into Texts," 194.

55. Ontario Department of Education, *Intermediate Division, 1951 Curriculum*, 73–74.

56. Ibid., 85–87.

57. Ibid., 104–106.

58. Ibid., 64–65.

59. Ibid., 66.

60. Werner, "Reading Authorship into Texts," 73.

61. Gidney, *From Hope to Harris*, 35.

62. Penney Clark, "'Home-Grown Product' or 'Made in America'? History of Social Studies in English Canada," in *Trends and Issues in Canadian Social Studies*, eds. Ian Wright and Alan Sears (Vancouver, BC: Pacific Educational Press, 1997), 68–99.

63. Von Heyking, *Creating Citizens*, 107.

64. Paul Axelrod, "Beyond the Progressive Education Debate: A Profile of Toronto Schooling in the 1950s," *Historical Studies in Education* 17, 2 (2005), 227–241.

65. Reva Joshee and Lauri Johnson, "Historic Diversity and Equity Policies in Canada," in *Transformations in Schooling: Historical and Comparative Perspectives*, ed. Kim Tolley (New York: Palgrave MacMillian, 2007), 111, 114. For an American perspective, see Clarence Chatto and Alice Halligan, *The Story of the Springfield Plan* (New York: Barnes and Noble, 1945).

66. *Educational Courier*, "Visual Aids on Intercultural Relations," 22.

67. Kathleen Weiler, *Women Teaching for Change* (South Hadley, MA: Bergin and Garvey, 1988), 1; see also Rebecca Coulter and Helen Harper, eds., *History Is Hers: Women Educators in Twentieth Century Ontario* (Calgary: Detselig, 2005).

68. Von Heyking, *Creating Citizens*, 110.

69. Ibid., 111–112.

70. A. B. Hodgetts. *What Culture, What Heritage?* (Toronto: OISE, 1968). On racism in history textbooks from post–World War II to the 1990s, see Ken Montgomery, "Imagining the Antiracist State: Representations of Racism in Canadian History Textbooks," *Discourse: Studies in the Cultural Politics of Education* 26, 4 (December 2005), 427–442; and José Igartua, *The Other Quiet Revolution* (Vancouver: UBC Press, 2006), 63–88.

71. Frank K. Clarke, " 'Keep communism out of our schools': Cold War Anti-communism at the Toronto Board of Education, 1948–1951." *Labour / Le Travail* 49 (Spring 2002), 93–119. On teachers' fears of using progressive teaching methods during the Cold War years in the United States, see Gerard Giordano, *Wartime Schools: How World War II Changed American Education* (New York: Peter Lang, 2004).

72. C. Slater, "Citizenship—A Class Enterprise," *Educational Courier*, October 1945, 17, 36.

73. MacLeod, *Citizenship Training*, 54–64.

74. Kristina R. Llewellyn, "Gendered Democracy: Women Teachers in Post-War Toronto," *Historical Studies in Education / Revue d'histoire de l'éducation* 18, 1 (2006), 1–25. See also Alison Prentice and Marjorie Theobald, eds., *Women Who Taught: Perspectives on the History of Women and Teaching* (Toronto: University of Toronto Press, 1991); and Rebecca Priegert Coulter, "Getting Things Done: Donalda J. Dickie and Leadership through Practice," *Canadian Journal of Education* 28, 4 (2005), 669–699. For a biographical account of an activist teacher's career, see Kate Rousmaniere, *Citizen Teacher: The Life and Leadership of Margaret Haley* (Albany, NY: State University of New York Press, 2005).

75. G. Blair Laing, "Education Today—Are We in Tune with the Times?" In *The Empire Club of Canada Addresses* (Toronto: Empire Club Foundation, 1951), 41–50. Rpt. online *The Empire Club of Canada*, http://speeches.empireclub.org/details.asp?r=vs&ID=61330&number=1.

76. Pearson, L. B., "Role of the Teacher in International Affairs," *Educational Courier*, December 1948, 7–8, 34, 36–37.

77. Claire Slater, "A Hand across the Sea," *Educational Courier*, February 1948, 17, 36.

78. Rebecca Priegert Coulter, " 'Girls Just Want to Have Fun': Women Teachers and the Pleasures of the Profession," *History Is Hers: Women Educators in Twentieth Century Ontario*, ed. R. P. Coulter and H. Harper (Calgary: Detselig, 2005), 220.

79. In 1950, Canada paid $300,000 a year toward UNESCO's expenses. *Montreal Gazette*, "Limited Resources Spread Too Thin?" September 7, 1951.

80. Library and Archives Canada (LAC), Canadian Council for Reconstruction through UNESCO (1947–1952) fonds, MSS2245, MG28-I45, R7680-0-0-E.

81. *Winnipeg Tribune*, "Train Children at Three for Peace, Says Director," September 29, 1948.

82. *Montreal Gazette*, "Far East Held 'Neglected' in History School Books," September 8, 1950.

83. *Montreal Daily Star*, "Delegates Attend First UNESCO Seminar," July 18, 1950.

84. LAC, Canadian Council for Reconstruction through UNESCO (1947–1952) fonds; Canada Council for the Arts, *Milestones: Forty Years in the Life of the Canada Council* (Ottawa: CCA, 1999).

85. LAC, Canadian Council for Reconstruction through UNESCO (1947–1952) fonds, MG 28 197, vol. 28, folder 3, bulletins 1965–70, UNESCO Associated School in Canada bulletin, n.d.

86. Ibid., 136–139.

87. The previous suggestion recommends that students "prepare biographical sketches of outstanding Canadians such as Dr. Brock Chisholm and H. L. Keenleyside, who hold high posts in UN organizations." Ibid., 139.

88. LAC, Canadian Council for Reconstruction through UNESCO (1947–1952) fonds, MG 28, I202, vol. 20, United Nations Association in Canada. Provinces are organized into branches with the central office in Ottawa. In 1961, for example, V. M. Knight of the Halifax Branch, United Nations Association in Canada, requested that the committee "start organizing immediately to provide the necessary leadership for the community and the schools when the new school term opens in September." Nova Scotia Archives and Records Management (NSA), MG1, vol. 2910, no. 36.

89. Kenneth C. Dewar, "Hilda Neatby's 1950s and My 1950s." *Journal of Canadian Studies 40*, 1 (2006), 213.

90. *Vox Lycei* [yearbook] (Ottawa: Lisgar Collegiate 1966–67), 83.

91. *Vox Lycei*, 1955–56, 19.

92. George Tuttle, *Youth Organizations in Canada: A Reference Manual*, prepared for the Canadian Youth Commission (Toronto: Ryerson Press, 1946), 102–103.

93. NSA, Duckworth Collection, MG1, vol. 2910, no. 34, "Organizing Program for Hallowe'en Drive," newspaper clipping, n.d.; Memo to Halifax School Principals from Halifax Hallowe'en UNICEF Committee, n.d.

94. *Vox Lycei*, 1946.

95. Dominique Clement, *Canada's Rights Revolution* (Vancouver: UBC Press, 2008), 34.

96. Llewellyn, "Gendered Democracy"; Joan Sangster, *Transforming Labour* (Toronto: University of Toronto Press, 2010), 35.

11

Characteristics of Canadian Curricula

DAVID PRATT

PROVINCIAL CURRICULUM DEVELOPMENT

Curriculum development is a large-scale operation in Canada. Each province maintains curricula for the numerous programs offered in its schools: Alberta, for example, lists over 200 curricula for grades 10–12 alone (Alberta Education, 1978). Periodic revision and innovation produces hundreds of new or revised provincial curriculum documents each year. Many school boards publish detailed curricula based on provincial guidelines, and individual schools, departments, and teachers produce curriculum documents as course outlines and descriptions.

This investment in curriculum writing may represent the triumph of hope over experience. There is little evidence that the quality of classroom teaching is much influenced by curriculum writing at the state or provincial level. Provincial guidelines do offer parameters for selection of subject matter and this may have some impact. But provincial curriculum reviews frequently express dismay at the low level of implementation of official guidelines (Ontario Ministry of Education, 1982). The study of curriculum implementation has arisen in recognition that many variables intervene between adoption of official guidelines and realization of change in schools.

This is not to say that curriculum planning is unimportant. Research on school and classroom effectiveness shows that dedicated planning of learning conditions is a major factor in student achievement (Bloom, 1984; Walberg, 1984). Such considerations apart, curriculum documents merit attention for two reasons. First, they are fascinating cultural artifacts. Like authorized textbooks, they imply the values of a society through definition of subject matter, objectives, and curriculum rationales. Second, provincial curricula indicate how well curriculum development is currently being done and serve as models. This study is concerned with the second, the state of the art in curriculum planning in Canada as embodied in provincial curriculum documents.

Few studies of Canadian curricula across disciplines have been conducted on a national basis. Provincial curriculum guidelines have been extensively studied only in science education (Orpwood & Souqué, 1984; Finegold & Mackeracher, 1986). The Council of Ministers of Education has published descriptions of curricula in Canada in various subjects (Council of Ministers, 1979, 1981, 1982, 1983, 1985). Critiques by Neatby (1953) and Barrow (1979) were until recently virtually the only serious general studies of aspects of Canadian curricula. This paucity of scholarship was to a considerable degree remedied by the publication in 1986 of Tomkins's *A Common Countenance: Stability and Change in the Canadian Curriculum*. This book provides a diachronic basis for understanding curriculum in Canada and is distinguished by its thoroughness, balance, and incisiveness. Students of the Canadian curriculum will for long be in Tomkins's debt.

The question remains: What are the characteristics of curricula developed at the provincial level in Canada?

For the purposes of this paper, a curriculum may be defined as "an organized set of educational intentions." These intentions include not only what students are expected to learn, but also such other factors as recommended instructional strategies and materials, prerequisite learnings, management of individual differences, required facilities and personnel, and so on. The definition implies two primary sets of considerations for curriculum planning. On the one hand, there are questions about the validity, significance, and meaning of the intentions. These are questions of value that cannot be reduced to questions of technique. On the other hand, there are questions about the organization of these intentions, their completeness, coherence, clarity, and practicality. These questions are both ideological and technical. The concern of this paper is with the second set of questions. Questions of the nature and quality of themes, concepts, and topics included in Canadian curricula, while in urgent need of attention by scholars, are not the primary focus of this study. It is my more modest intention to produce a first description of Canadian provincial documents in terms of what they include and what they omit.

In March 1986, I wrote to the Director of Curriculum or equivalent in each of the provinces and territories to request copies of general curriculum regulations and of official curricula in science, history, English, and family studies. Both territories and all but one province replied.

THE SAMPLE

About half of the one hundred documents reviewed here came as hard copy, and the rest from an ONTERIS (Ontario Education Research Information System) file containing microfiche copies of provincial and territorial curricula.[1]

Since the Yukon and Northwest Territories produce very few of their own curricula, instead using British Columbia and Alberta curricula, no Yukon or NWT curricula were included in the sample.

To obtain provincial samples comparable in terms of curriculum subject and with a balance of traditional and newer disciplines, the sample from each province contained at least one curriculum in each of history or social studies, language arts, science, mathematics, physical education and health, and family studies. The distribution of subjects in the sample is shown in TABLE 1. In each provincial sample, at least four of the curricula came from elementary grades, and at least four from secondary grades. The median date for each province ranged from 1979 to 1983, and for the total sample, 1981.

TABLE 1: Subject areas of documents

History/social studies	18
Language arts	14
Science	14
Physical education/ health	11
Mathematics	10
Family studies	10
Drama	7
Geography	3
Music	3
Other*	10

*Accounting, art, Christian ethics, computer studies, driver education, economics, French, lifestyles, personal life management

DOCUMENT CHARACTERISTICS

Production Characteristics

Production characteristics of curricula—format, illustration, and so on—by province are shown in TABLE 2. In general, curriculum documents were less attractive than they could be. A typed, stapled document does not carry the same message as a glossy, illustrated, printed publication.

The Authors

More than 500 educators were named as members of writing committees in the sample. In all Quebec documents, as in most Nova Scotia documents, authorship was anonymous. Elsewhere names and affiliations of members of the writing committees generally were given. The size of the committees ranged from a median of three persons in Prince Edward Island to thirteen in Ontario, with a national median of nine.

TABLE 2: Production characteristics

Province	Mean pages	Number printed	Number illustrated	Usual binding
British Columbia	101	6	4	Sewn
Alberta	57	9	1	Sewn or loose leaf
Saskatchewan	74	3	2	Corner staple
Manitoba	144	0	2	Loose leaf
Ontario	74	10	5	Sewn or magazine
Quebec	68	10	0	Magazine
New Brunswick	78	0	0	Corner staple
Nova Scotia	66	1	0	Plastic spiral
Prince Edward Island	33	0	0	Plastic spiral
Newfoundland	47	0	0	Not ascertainable
Total		39	14	

Authors were predominantly educators, most often teachers and typically with one or two representatives of the Ministry or Department of Education. Professors sat on most committees in Manitoba, Ontario, Saskatchewan, and Alberta, but on few elsewhere.

Non-educators were shown as committee members for only eight curricula. For example, the committee for the Newfoundland *Family Living 2200 Curriculum Guide* (1983) contained a physician and a social worker, and the Newfoundland *Theatre Arts 2200 Course Description* (1982) committee included a theatre director. Only two committees, both in Saskatchewan, listed a school trustee among their members. The writing of school curricula in Canada was apparently controlled by purveyors of services to the exclusion of consumers of services. The clients of the schools—parents, employers, students, and taxpayers—were unrepresented.

Needs Assessment

Over the past two decades, the practice of needs assessment has developed in social and educational policy making as a means of collecting information on which to base planning decisions (Witkin, 1984). A needs assessment typically collects two kinds of data. Empirical information is gathered on relevant social indicators, such as employment, health, consumption, literacy, student achievement, and so on. Opinion data is also collected from three main classes of people: experts, who have special information or expertise; clients, who have a right to be consulted; and gatekeepers, whose political status gives them potential control over implementation of the curriculum.

Scholars do not universally accept needs assessment in developing curricula (Barrow, 1984). It becomes a cynical political stratagem if used to put curriculum to referendum. Needs assessments should inform, but not necessarily determine curriculum decisions. Although it is judicious to determine public opinion prior to making public proposals, the fundamental ethic of needs assessment is respect for the client. Apart from its ethical significance, such respect, as Fullan (1982) points out, is critical to successful implementation of change. Only Quebec curricula mentioned needs assessment. Those provinces not reporting needs assessments rarely gave any full explication of the sources from which their proposals derived.

Rationale

Sixty-five of the one hundred documents, including at least half of the documents from each province, contained an explicit rationale. Rationales in the provincial documents ranged from four pages in the Ontario *Dramatic Arts Curriculum* (1981) and the Manitoba *Science 100 Guide* (1982) to brief one-paragraph statements found in most documents.

Aims and Objectives

Aims in the curricula I examined were multiple rather than singular. Although the point is disputable, I take the position that it is good communication and good discipline for curriculum designers to make a single statement expressing the purpose of a curriculum. Current practice in successful corporations (see Peters & Waterman, 1982, especially pp. 65, 153) supports this position. Singular aims were found in only thirteen of the one hundred documents. All Quebec documents contained a single aim (*objectif terminal*) for each of the modules of which they consisted, and the most recent Quebec documents also included an aim (*objectif global*) for the curriculum as a whole. Some examples of singular aims follow.

> Quebec: *Programme d'études: Secondaire; Art dramatique* (1983)
> La programme d'art dramatique veut rendre l'élève apte à utiliser la langue dramatique comme moyen d'expression, de communication et de création tant sur le plan individuel que collectif. (p. 9)

> New Brunswick: *Elementary Health Education* (1981)
> The overall objective of the Health Education program should be to develop citizens who are able to incorporate health information and principles into life situations so as to achieve and maintain the highest level of well-being. (p. 3)

Nova Scotia: Geography Grades 10–12 Revised Guidelines (1979)
The main aim of the course is to develop in students an awareness of the processes that have contributed and continue to contribute to the shaping of our physical environment, both at a local level and across the globe. (p. 10)

The nature and use of objectives varied widely in the documents. In some cases, objectives were explicit and tightly coupled with content. This was notably the case with the Quebec *Programmes d'études*, which consisted essentially of hierarchies of an *objectif global, objectifs généraux, objectifs terminaux,* and *objectifs intermédiares,* the last explicitly linked with subject matter. In many curricula from other provinces, objectives were indistinguishable from lists of subject matter.

Objectives embodied a positivist epistemology in their almost exclusive attention to cognition. As TABLE 3 shows, only twenty documents contained objectives referring to the development of the self—meaning, identity, or relationships—in ways that transcended the cognitive, and they were mainly in such non-traditional subjects as theatre arts, family living, or health. Even then, phraseology is often in terms of cognition.

British Columbia: Family Management: Curriculum Guide and Resource Book, Grade 11 (1985)
To develop an understanding of self in relation to others. (p. 2)

Alberta: Elementary Health Curriculum (1983)
Learns how to make and keep friends. (p. 71)

Manitoba: Lifestyles 205 Interim Guide (1982)
Develop an understanding of self as a sexual being. (p. 5)

New Brunswick: Family Living 122 (1976)
To appreciate that rewarding relationships depend on nonexploitation and positive concern for others. (p. 5)

Despite extensive mention of objectives, priorities among them were rarely given. The implication is that all objectives were equally important, and that all teachers and all students should seek to achieve all of them. Only four Quebec curricula classified objectives as *obligatoires* and *facultatifs*. Orpwood and Souqué (1984) observed that Canadian science curricula often contained a multiplicity of aims, priorities among the aims were rarely clear, many aims appeared to have only rhetorical value, and aims and objectives often did not match. My findings suggest this to be true of Canadian curricula in general.

TABLE 3: Rationale, aims, and objectives

Number of curricula with:

	Rationale	Singular aim	Personal/social objectives
British Columbia	7	1	2
Alberta	7	0	5
Saskatchewan	7	0	1
Manitoba	5	0	3
Ontario	8	1	3
Quebec	7	5	0
New Brunswick	6	1	2
Nova Scotia	5	2	1
Prince Edward Island	5	0	0
Newfoundland	8	3	3
Total	65	13	20

TABLE 4: Evaluation of learner achievement

Number of curricula providing evaluation:

	Suggestions	Examples	Criteria
British Columbia	5	4	0
Alberta	2	2	0
Saskatchewan	7	1	0
Manitoba	4	2	1
Ontario	8	3	2
Quebec	10	0	1
New Brunswick	3	2	1
Nova Scotia	8	3	0
Prince Edward Island	2	2	0
Newfoundland	10	1	0
Total	59	20	5

Evaluation of Learner Achievement

Of one hundred documents, fifty-nine made suggestions on evaluation of student learning; twenty gave examples of tests or test items; only five provided clear and explicit criteria for evaluation. A summary by province is shown in TABLE 4.

Some provinces provide information and guidance on evaluation separately from curricula. In Ontario, the Ontario Assessment Instrument Pool offers collections of test items to teachers of most subjects. British Columbia publishes an annual *Table of Specifications*, which provides detailed descriptions of the provincial grade 12 examinations in core subjects and shows numerous sample questions. In at least one subject, a Saskatchewan curriculum guide (*English: Student Evaluation*, 1980) offered highly practical information and recommendations for teachers in evaluating student achievement. Quebec gives evaluation advice in *Programmes d'études* and teachers in each school-leaving subject receive a *Guide pédagogique*, a *Guide d'évaluation en classes*, and an *Information Document* (Gouvernement du Québec, 1987, p. 4).

Description of the Learners

Any reader of a curriculum will ask for whom it is planned. Almost all curriculum documents identified prospective learners by grade level but only eighteen described learner characteristics in any detail. Perhaps designers believed teachers were so intimately involved with students that such description would be redundant, or that the diversity of students defied generalization. Although some of the sample curricula asked for completion of previous courses or grades, none offered detailed guidance on prerequisites or pretesting.

Curriculum Content

Curriculum content—the subject matter and methods of instruction—is traditionally the major and sometimes the only area detailed in curriculum documents. Despite the research and rhetoric on objectives, curriculum content expresses most directly the developers' intentions and has most impact on teachers' instructional decisions.

Almost invariably, the documents in this sample gave detailed lists of topics, concepts, or themes. Most also suggested pedagogical strategies, although some published objectives and subject matter separately from teaching strategies. Quebec's *Guides pédagogiques* include detailed recommendations for instruction as well as sample lessons and learning situations. Ontario, Nova Scotia, and British Columbia have similar publications.

APTITUDE DIFFERENCES

One aspect of student diversity that interests teachers is variation in aptitude. Aptitude, reflected most clearly in speed of learning, varies widely in any given subject area from student to student, and this presents teachers with numerous questions. Must slower learners master all the same objectives as faster learners and, if so, how? What strategies would help slower learners avoid failure and frustration? How can underachievement be diagnosed and remediated? How can curriculum content be adapted and what special teaching methods are most appropriate for slower and faster learners? How can the marginal time of faster learners be used effectively? What enrichment materials are provided in the curriculum? What provisions are there for acceleration?

Such questions were dealt with in only a minority of provincial curricula. A total of eleven curricula referred to the special needs of slow learners, typically those in such special programs as the Basic Program in Ontario and the Adjusted Program in Nova Scotia. Only three curricula mentioned the special needs of faster learners. The absence of attention to aptitude differences in a curriculum implies an official position that learners at a given level are homogeneous in aptitude and that all learners can and should master the same objectives. Since teachers find both positions untenable, those positions can only weaken the credibility and impact of official curricula.

Learning Materials

One of the primary factors affecting the implementation of curricula is whether the curriculum contains or is accompanied by high-quality practical instructional materials (Fullan, 1982; Werner, 1981). In some provinces, learning materials were not dealt with in curricula but in supporting documents (*Guides pédagogiques* in Quebec; *Circular 14* in Ontario; *Media Resources Guides* in British Columbia). As TABLE 5 shows, about half of the curricula listed textbooks or teacher references and about a quarter listed audiovisual materials.

Ten curriculum documents included some learning materials. The Manitoba *Social Studies Grade 11 Interim Guide* (1984), for example, included map outlines ready for duplicating. The British Columbia *Junior Secondary Science Curriculum Guide and Resource Book* (1985) contains several "Student cards" that provide detailed instruction, illustrations, and assignments on such topics as measuring mass, focusing the microscope, and writing a lab report.

An omission of some significance was that ninety-nine of the one hundred documents listed no supporting computer software. The sole exception was the New Brunswick *Accounting 122 Curriculum* (1982), which listed fourteen programs. There are now thousands of computers in Canadian classrooms. But the computer is unlikely to be integrated into instruction until it is integrated into curriculum documents.

TABLE 5: Learning materials

Number of curricula:

	Listing texts	Listing teacher references	Listing AV materials	Listing computer software	Including materials in document
British Columbia	3	6	2	0	1
Alberta	8	4	1	0	0
Saskatchewan	6	4	2	0	0
Manitoba	1	8	3	0	2
Ontario	0	4	2	0	1
Quebec	0	7	0	0	1
New Brunswick	7	9	2	1	2
Nova Scotia	5	9	5	0	0
Prince Edward Island	8	5	3	0	2
Newfoundland	3	6	4	0	1
Total	41	62	24	1	10

Consumables, Equipment, and Facilities

Many a battle has been won or lost by logistics (Van Creveld, 1977), and such curriculum logistics as materials and facilities, though relatively unglamorous, can make or break a curriculum. Consumables are materials used up in instruction that have to be replaced—paint, paper, chemicals, modelling clay, typewriter ribbons, and so on. Only four curriculum documents mentioned consumables.

Almost every curriculum requires equipment, whether an overhead projector, a tape recorder, microscopes, a globe, or a volleyball net. Fourteen documents mentioned equipment. The British Columbia *Elementary Science Curriculum Guide* (1981) is a model in this regard, containing a twelve-page list of consumable and non-consumable materials and equipment for teaching science, and the quantity required for each school.

Facilities are the teaching space required for a particular program. A program in swimming or auto repair has special requirements for facilities. So do programs in theatre arts, physical education, art, music, and science. Although architectural features can rarely be modified, several environmental factors can be manipulated, including classroom layout, noise, temperature, lighting, and decor. Teachers do not always give such factors much thought, which is a good reason for making pertinent suggestions in the curriculum. Unfortunately, provincial curriculum planners do not appear to give these factors much thought either. Eleven curricula, mostly in drama and physical education, mentioned facility requirements.

Personnel

The success or failure of a curriculum will depend primarily on teachers who instruct it. At the same time, teachers undertaking to implement a new curriculum need to know exactly the extent of their responsibilities. Only six curricula indicated qualities required of teachers, and only six what responsibilities would be entailed.

Despite the critical role of the school principal in curriculum implementation, much discussed in recent research (Fullan, 1982; Leithwood & Montgomery, 1982), none of the documents in the sample mentioned the role of the principal.

No document mentioned the support that such persons as guidance counsellors or teachers of other subjects might provide. Despite the advocacy of integration of school resource centres into curricula and programs in such statements as Ontario's *Partners in Action* (1982), no document indicated a role in the curriculum for the school resource centre or librarian. No document mentioned people outside the school who could be recruited to assist or enrich the instructional program.

Time and Cost

Time is the principal resource consumed by schooling. Most curricula in Canada are planned for a one-year time format, typically about 100 to 120 hours per year. Detail regarding the allocation of these hours to the components of the curriculum was given in twenty-five of the documents.

Instructional hours are not the only time a curriculum requires. Students may be required to commit further amounts of time for homework or field trips. Teachers will usually have to commit time outside of class for planning, administration, remediation, and evaluation. Non-instructional time requirements were not dealt with in any of the curriculum documents.

Time is the most significant cost involved in schooling, but most curricula entail financial costs as well. When a curriculum requires special expenditures, these need to be shown in documents so that the funds can be allocated in advance. Only one curriculum dealt with costs, the Newfoundland *Theatre Arts 2200 Course Description* (1982).

Program Evaluation and Field Testing

Just as schools need guidance in evaluating student learning, they also need advice on evaluating the success of a curriculum as a whole. Without such evaluation, systematic improvement of curricula after adoption is unlikely. Only fourteen of the documents suggested criteria for the evaluation of the program.

The success of a curriculum innovation will depend to some degree on "debugging" the program through pilot (small-scale) and field (typical use) tests conducted prior to wide-scale implementation. Unless a program is adequately tried out, the costs of defects will usually be passed downwards to users and consumers, that is, to teachers and students. Only four documents referred to pilot and field tests. At the most detailed, these four documents listed the names of schools and teachers who piloted the curriculum, but the results of these trials were not given. Information about field tests—where they were conducted, by whom, with what results, and how the document was subsequently modified—would add greatly to the credibility of a curriculum and would indicate sources from which implementers could seek information and advice.

One curriculum paid serious attention to the desirability of feedback from teachers for further refinement of the curriculum. This was the draft document for British Columbia's *Family Management Curriculum Guideline and Resource Book Grade 11* (1985), which provided several pages on which teachers could submit suggestions.

CONCLUSIONS

Provincial curriculum documents vary widely in content and quality, both among and within provinces. Virtually the only commonality among Canadian curriculum documents is that almost all are approximately the same shape (8.5″ × 11″ in nine provinces, 21 × 30 cm in Ontario). If the best features of the best Canadian curricula were combined, the resulting documents would be excellent by any standard.

This raises questions about the provinces developing curricula in isolation. Local curriculum development is likely to increase local commitment to curricula, but there is no reason why all local curriculum development has to start *de novo.* There was little evidence in the documents in this sample that curricula from other jurisdictions had been read or used. This parallels the lack of international co-operation in curriculum development. Possible explanations include the time, cost, and effort of such co-operation; the subsequent need to share ownership of and credit for curriculum innovation; and the low political value of such intangibles as improved classroom instruction. Some interprovincial exchange of curricula does take place, however, and is facilitated by meetings of provincial Directors of Curriculum, which are convened periodically by the Council of Ministers of Education (C. K. Brown, Director of Instruction, Newfoundland, Personal Communication, February 1987).

TABLE 6: Selected characteristics by date

	1970–1981 (N = 50) %	1982–1986 (N = 47) %
Rationale	52	79
Singular aim	12	13
Evaluation of learning	56	83
Description of learners	12	28
Time allocation	24	32
Program evaluation	16	9

In general, provincial curriculum documents are abreast of the state of the art in curriculum development of about 1970. **TABLE 6** summarizes the differences on selected characteristics between the documents published in and prior to 1981 and those published since 1981 (three documents bore no date). The more recent documents are more likely to include a rationale and to contain some discussion of evaluation of student learning. Otherwise there has been little change. Provincial curricula have yet to take advantage of the advances in curriculum development of the past decade, particularly those evolving from research in such areas as Needs Assessment, Mastery Learning, School Effectiveness, and Program Evaluation. This report has indicated many curriculum components which provincial documents usually deal with cursorily or omit altogether. One of the most significant areas of weakness is the absence of priorities and of clear criteria, qualitative or quantitative, for evaluation of either learner achievement or program success. During the period 1975–1985, when most of these guidelines were produced, issues of evaluation suffered considerable neglect in many Canadian jurisdictions. And, in fact, the separation of instruction and evaluation has been an unfortunate feature of the history of curriculum. But to leave decisions in this area to individual teachers appears to vitiate a central concept of provincial curriculum planning, the provision of a minimal education for all. This is particularly the case as measurement of achievement is a notoriously weak area of teacher education programs and a field in which most teachers feel insecure.

The other major area of concern in Canadian curricula has deeper implications. It was noted earlier that the clients of the schools—parents, employers, taxpayers—are ordinarily excluded from curriculum committees. Nor are their views accessed by means of needs assessment. Curriculum development is a process carried out almost entirely by educators, and the need for client opinion is ignored. Also ignored is the need for empirical data, both from needs assessment before the curriculum is developed and from field testing after development. The approach therefore is almost entirely bureaucratic and political: the development of curriculum is viewed as a quasi-legislative activity of writing rules and regulations.

Over the past fifteen years, many detailed curriculum decisions have been made behind closed doors in provincial cabinet meetings and in the offices of provincial Ministers of Education. Such decisions are often made in response to pressure from individuals, special interest groups, and the media. This is an invisible influence in official curriculum documents. Its assessment awaits badly needed participant observation studies of curriculum development at the provincial level.

There are practical and ethical concerns with the bureaucratic model of curriculum development. Practically, the best decisions are unlikely to emerge from ignorance of relevant data. But, more significantly, if democracy means anything at all, it must entail the principle that those affected by decisions have the right and the opportunity to contribute to the formulation of those decisions. This principle has not as yet much affected curriculum decision-making in Canada.

REFLECTIVE QUESTIONS

1. Pratt argues that, "There is little evidence that the quality of classroom teaching is much influenced by curriculum writing at the state or provincial level." What does this say about the importance of curriculum?

2. What do you think of Pratt's definition of curriculum as "an organized set of educational intentions"?

3. Do you concur with Pratt that, "It is good communication and good discipline for curriculum designers to make a single statement expressing the purpose of a curriculum"? Can you find such a statement in one of your provincial/territorial curriculum documents?

4. Is a "positivist epistemology" still evident in our current curriculum documents? If yes, locate an example. If no, explain why not.

5. Do we still use a "bureaucratic model of curriculum development" in Canada? Justify your response.

NOTE

1. Exigencies of space prevent inclusion of the titles of the one hundred documents analyzed. The list may be obtained from the author.

REFERENCES

Alberta Education. (1978). *Program of studies for senior high schools.* Edmonton: Alberta Education.

Barrow, R. (1979). *The Canadian curriculum: A personal view.* London, ON: University of Western Ontario, Faculty of Education.

Barrow, R. (1984). *Giving teaching back to teachers: A critical introduction to curriculum theory.* London, ON: Althouse Press.

Bloom, B. S. (1984). The 2 Sigma problem: The search for methods of group instruction as effective as one-to-one tutoring. *Educational Researcher, 13*(6), 4–16.

Council of Ministers, Canada. (1979). *Provincial mathematics programs in Canada as of 1978–1979.* Ottawa: Council of Ministers of Education.

Council of Ministers, Canada. (1981). *Analysis of science curricula in the provinces.* Ottawa: Council of Ministers of Education.

Council of Ministers, Canada. (1982). *Social studies provincial curricula.* Ottawa: Council of Ministers of Education.

Council of Ministers, Canada. (1983). *Arts: Provincial curricula.* Ottawa: Council of Ministers of Education.

Council of Ministers, Canada. (1985). *Physical and health education: A survey of provincial curricula at the elementary and secondary levels.* Ottawa: Council of Ministers of Education.

Desjarlais, L. (1975). *Needs and characteristics of students in the intermediate years, ages 12–16.* Toronto: Ontario Ministry of Education.

Finegold, M., & Mackeracher, D. (1986). Meaning from curriculum analysis. *Journal of Research in Science Teaching, 23,* 353–364.

Fullan, M. (1982). *The meaning of educational change.* Toronto: Ontario Institute for Studies in Education.

Gouvernement du Québec, Ministère de l'Éducation, Direction générale des programmes. (1987 May 21–22). Information document. Meeting of Curriculum Coordinators, Toronto, Ontario.

Leithwood, K. A., & Montgomery, D. J. (1982). The role of the elementary school principal in program improvement. *Review of Educational Research, 52,* 309–339.

Neatby, H. (1953). *So little for the mind.* Toronto: Clarke Irwin.

Ontario Ministry of Education. (1982). *Partners in action.* Toronto: Ontario Ministry of Education.

Orpwood, G. W. F., & Souqué, J.-P. (1984). Introduction and curriculum analyses. *Science education in Canadian schools* (Background Study 52; vol. 1). Ottawa: Science Council of Canada.

Peters, T. J., & Waterman, R. H., Jr. (1982). *In search of excellence: Lessons from America's best-run companies.* New York: Harper & Row.

Tomkins, G. S. (1986). *A common countenance: Stability and change in the Canadian curriculum.* Scarborough, ON: Prentice-Hall.

Van Creveld, M. (1977). *Supplying war: Logistics from Wallenstein to Patton.* Cambridge: Cambridge University Press.

Walberg, H. J. (1984, May). Improving the productivity of America's schools. *Educational Leadership, 42,* 19–30.

Werner, W. (1981). *An interpretive approach to curriculum implementation.* Paper presented at the Canadian Association for Curriculum Studies invitational conference, Toronto, Ontario.

Witkin, B. R. (1984). *Assessing needs in educational and social programs.* San Francisco: Jossey-Bass.

12

A Topography for Canadian Curriculum Theory

CYNTHIA CHAMBERS

Northrop Frye (1971) claims that for Canadians the answer to the question "Who are we?" cannot be separated from the answer to the question "Where is here?" (p. 220). The classic existential question—"Who am I?"—can be posed only by people for whom "where" they are is not an issue, the place itself apparently being fully known and well defined. These would be people from places such as Europe and the United States. Posing the question "Where is here?" implies a preoccupation with where we are in relation to other places. It also implies asking: "How do I find my way around here? Can I survive here? How can I survive here? Who were the people here before me?"

Robert Kroetsch (1994), a Canadian poet and novelist, has described growing up in Alberta on the Canadian prairies in the 1930s, a time when the school curriculum and the body of literature it referenced were strangely silent about the place he was living. Kroetsch read books at school but he neither read, heard, nor learned anything about Alberta itself. The school curriculum was a colonial curriculum in that home was either somewhere else or not worth consideration. It was as if there were no Alberta, no landscape, no life, or no Alberta writers to name and describe the place where he lived then and where I live now.

The situation did not improve much in the next couple of decades. In a creative documentary of his return to the prairies, Mark Abley (1986) realizes the school curriculum always turned his attention, his vision, elsewhere, beyond the prairie landscape and history where he was living. When he drives into

Lethbridge, Alberta—the place of his childhood and the place where I now live and work—he suddenly recollects:

> I grew up ignorant of the little city; I grew up hardly knowing where I was. . . . My schooling taught me nothing about place. I could hardly have expected my teachers to mention that in the 1920s, Lethbridge contained one of the largest brothels on the prairies; but they might at least have talked about Fort Whoop-Up. For me, as for Wallace Stegner in the Eastend of 1918, "Knowledge of place, knowledge of past, meant . . . knowledge of the far and foreign." I remember studying in painful detail the geography of the Hudson Bay Lowlands; I remember compiling a scrapbook about New Zealand; but I recall no lessons about Southern Alberta. Its literature, its history, even its sundry landscapes remained a closed book. (pp. 213–214)

In the Canadian north where I grew up in the late 1950s and 1960s, the silence—in response to the question "Where is here?"—was even more pervasive. There was no radio or television, no curriculum or textbooks, no trade books or comic books that spoke of the place I lived and knew, the place that has formed my memories, shaped my sensibilities as a woman, a Canadian, and a curriculum writer. Whereas the children I went to school with, our families, and I lived without central heating, running water, or sewage systems, the textbooks we read were illustrated with children living in suburban homes delineated with cement sidewalks, rows of evenly trimmed hedges, and white picket fences. Whereas we sat in classrooms heated by diesel or wood-burning stoves in our snow pants, mukluks, and parkas trimmed with wolf fur, knowing our parents at home were not dressed much differently, the textbooks were illustrated with children dressed in sunsuits, oxfords, and dress pants. Father went off to work in a grey suit, carrying a brown leather briefcase, while Mother stayed at home, cooking and baking in a dress, an apron, and high heels. Outside our northern classroom windows, the tiny leaves of the all-too-sparse birch and poplar fell to the ground and were ignored in a brief autumn that came and went before school was even in full swing. In our *Fun with Dick and Jane* and *We Work and Play* basal readers (Gray & Hill, n.d.; Gray, Baruch, & Montgomery, n.d.-b) and *Think-and-do* workbooks (Gray, Baruch, & Montgomery, n.d.-a), a hired man named Zeke raked up the large red and orange maple leaves that threatened the moral correctness of the rational, suburban order assumed in the textual narrative.

Kroetsch (1994) contrasts his childhood in the 1930s with the present, when there are so many Alberta writers that there is cacophony rather than silence: fiction writers such as Merna Summers, Rudy Wiebe, W. P. Kinsella, Greg Hollingshead, and W. O. Mitchell; poets such as Kristjana Gunnars, Alice Major, and Robert Hilles; nonfiction writers such as Myrna Kostash and Hugh Dempsey; speculative fiction writers such as Dave Duncan and Candas Jane Dorsey; children/young adult fiction writers such as Monica Hughes and Martin Godfrey. I can contrast my northern childhood of the 1950s and 1960s with the present, when there are at least two northern writers in print: Michael Kusugak (1990, 1993, 1998), an Inuit from Repulse Bay, and Richard Van Camp (1996, 1997, 1998), self-described as "half Dogrib and half white" (cited in Perren, 1999, p. 1), both of whom collaborate with illustrators to produce beautiful northern children's literature. There is the well-known Yukon-born nonfiction writer Pierre Berton as well as southern writers such as Rudy Wiebe (1994) with a literary interest in the north.

Thus, there appears to be an explosion of writing, not only in Alberta but in all of Canada, in all genres. For example, the amount of Canadian speculative fiction being published has increased dramatically in the last decade. However, as Canadian speculative fiction critics (Runté & Kulyk, 1995) point out, the growth spurt cannot be disconnected from the realization that Canadian speculative fiction is distinct, particularly from its American counterpart. Two characteristics of Canadian speculative fiction pertinent to curriculum theorizing are first, the critical role that setting plays in the stories, and second, the theme of the Alienated Outsider. In their stories, Canadian speculative fiction writers speculate about how humans are shaped by their environment and the effects, both manifest and potential, of ignoring the intimacy of this relationship. Dorsey, a speculative fiction writer from Alberta, observes that "in some cases the protagonist's relationship to the environment is the story, more so than the tendency in American SF for characters to collect 'plot coupons' to get out of the story" (cited in Runté & Kulyk, 1995, p. 16). Writers of speculative fiction continue the Canadian literary tradition of wondering "Where is here?" and "How do we survive living here?" When the characters of these novels battle the environment, they inevitably lose, giving voice to the deeply held belief that Canadians are shaped by the climate and geographies of where they live, and that they are always ultimately subordinate to nature.

THEMES EVIDENT IN CANADIAN FICTION
Survival

In *Survival: A Thematic Guide to Canadian Literature*, the classic criticism of what has fondly and irreverently been named Can-Lit, Margaret Atwood (1972) claims that "there"—America, England, and France—has always been more important than "here." Whatever is produced "there" eclipses what is produced here, rendering "invisible the values and artifacts that actually exist 'here' . . . so people can look at a thing without really seeing it, or look at it and mistake it for something else" (p. 18). Thus, as Canadians, we may not recognize our own literature, land, and history, our uniqueness—our own curriculum and its theory—even when we are living in the midst of it. This invisibility is even more poignant, and dangerous, perhaps, in that it keeps us from seeing what is here as being of any value. Atwood decided that those living north of the forty-ninth parallel needed "a geography of the mind" to navigate and traverse the *terra incognita*, the unknown land that is Canada, and that Canadian literature could provide such a map.

> We need such a map desperately . . . we need to know about here, because here is where we live. For members of a country or a culture, shared knowledge of their place, their here, is not a luxury but a necessity. Without that knowledge we will not survive. (p. 19)

Atwood's manifesto may seem a bit old fashioned now, written as if there was a single Canadian culture or identity. Perhaps she was a bit hegemonic and colonizing herself: writing from Ontario, the deeply resented capital of the Canadian culture and knowledge industries, a site that rarely seems to question its own right to speak for others—for those of us who speak languages other than English, and who live on the prairies, in the mountains, or by the oceans, particularly the Arctic Ocean. But her prophecy that Canadians must find a way to share their knowledge of this place in order to survive sounds neither old fashioned nor quaint. Although apocalyptic, I suspect it is closer to the truth than what we might want to imagine.

Particular countries have specific and central symbols which identify their literature (Atwood, 1972). For England, the predominant symbol is the island with its allusions to the body-as-island (with the monarchy being the head and the peasant class the feet), the island as self-contained and self-sufficient society. For the United States of America, the central symbol is the frontier. This image infuses American literature, and consciousness, with the hope of continual expansion and redemption through the conquest of new lands, the ever-present possibility of Utopia and the fantasy of its realization. Since Fredrick Jackson Turner's 1920 essay "The Significance of the Frontier in American History," claim social historians such as Jill Conway (1974), the frontier has been the key symbol of American mythology because in the wilderness:

> a man first throws off the artificial values of European culture, reverts to primitive savagery or simplicity, and then emerges from the conflict with nature literally metamorphosed into the archetypal American whose masculine virtues must forever be tempered by some form of struggle or conquest. (p. 76)

Conway, an Australian immigrant who was vice-president of the University of Toronto before leaving for the United States to be president of Smith College, claims there is striking similarity between the national ethos of Australia and that of the USA. Whereas most Australians live in urban centres, it is the bush that offers opportunity to reject the social restraint of European culture, the hegemony of colonialism. The mythical Australian swagman and the American dime-novel western hero share the ethos that human beings will always triumph in their conflict with the wilderness.

For reasons of imagination, as well as of ideology, geography, and history, Canadians have always been much more ambivalent about their relationship to the unknown, to the wilderness. Frye claims that for Canada, the dominant motif, particularly of our early literature, has been survival: bare survival in the face of a hostile environment and hostile people; grim survival in the face of disaster and crisis; cultural survival for all of Canada in the shadow of the United States' cultural imperialism; political survival for a country recently emerged from the long shadow of British colonialism to find itself in the deeper shadows of a political, economic, and military machine to the south; and, finally, for spiritual survival that might allow Canadians to imagine and forge a life beyond the minimal or perhaps to live well where they are right now.

A few years ago I had the pleasure of working with a Dene curriculum team from the Government of the Northwest Territories. In preparing the rationale for an elementary curriculum that was to integrate Dene language learning with knowledge about Dene culture (Northwest Territories Education, Culture and Employment, 1993), the team struggled with the age-old curriculum question: "What knowledge is of most worth?" with the addendum "of most worth *here*, for the Dene?" Fibbie Tatti and Mistu Oishi, the team's key leaders, posed this question to Dene elders in a series of workshops throughout the Mackenzie River valley. The Dene elders stated unequivocally and repeatedly that education and the curriculum must teach children survival, survival not only of the Dene people and their language and way of life, but survival of all living beings and the world in which they live. As a latecomer to the team, and someone charged with helping the team to articulate the philosophical rationale for the curriculum, I resisted what I perceived, at the time, to be a simplistic and utilitarian answer to a complex and philosophical question. Survival seemed too basic, too mundane a concept around which to organize a curriculum.

It took me several years to understand that the Dene elders were saying that without education there can be no survival. I then realized that the elders on the curriculum team were echoing the claims of the 1,000 witnesses to the Mackenzie Valley Pipeline Inquiry twenty years earlier. These witnesses stood up and spoke out publicly against the world's largest proposed megaproject, a 48-inch natural gas pipeline that, from its origin in Prudeau Bay, Alaska, to its destination in the American Midwest, would traverse primarily Canadian and Dene land. In making his case that such a pipeline would be dangerous and should not be built, Eddie Cook, a Dene who had been schooled by the Oblates of Mary Immaculate missionaries, told the Inquiry, "The land was the best teacher I ever had" (cited in Chambers, 1989, p. 140). So perhaps the speculative fiction writers, as well as Canadian nature writers such as Sharon Butala (1994) and the Dene elders, have it right: the aim of curriculum is survival, the survival of children and of all that sustains them. And, they tell us, this survival comes not from grand forms of theorizing and memorizing abstractions, but from human beings learning and living in a respectful relationship to their lived topos of here.

The *Dene Kede* curriculum team faced the task of finding an image, a metaphor, a metonym that would highlight the educative responsibility of adults to children implied by the notion of survival. In the curriculum discussions that followed, the team arrived at the hand drum as a central metaphor for survival; the beat of the drum was a metaphor for the beat of the human heart and a metonym for life itself. On the front of the hand drum, caribou hide is stretched tautly so that when it is struck a musical note radiates out, in concentric circles of sound, from the drum to the people listening and dancing. The beat of the hand drum resonates with the beating of the human heart. At the back of the drum are four babiche thongs, woven into the edges of the hide and pulled to the centre from the four directions, at once drawing tight the hide and creating a handle. The outer rim of the drum was the child and each of the four thongs represented a key spiritual trait that children must be taught in their relationship to all living things, including the land and each other, such as respect. Following these four spiritual codes made it possible that the child and his/her community could survive. Thus the babiche handgrip at the centre of the thongs, the hub by which a drummer holds the drum, was survival itself. The curriculum team had found a metonym for life and survival that was at once particular and universal, from here but able to speak to there.

Although curriculum guides and school materials of the 1990s may better reflect the land in which students live than they did in Kroetsch's Alberta of the 1930s or Abley's of the 1960s or my Yukon and Northwest Territories of the 1950s and early 1960s, curriculum theory in Canada may not. Although there is more homegrown curricula in all Canadian provinces and territories than in the past, when they read and try to apply curriculum theory to practice, Canadian educators and students have a harder time seeing themselves and the place where they live than they ought to. (This is especially true when they look beyond the social studies curriculum, with its traditional focus on human and physical geography.) And although some fine Canadian works such as Milburn and Herbert's (1973) *National Consciousness and the Curriculum: The Canadian Case* and Tomkins's (1986) classic *A Common Countenance: Stability and Change in the Canadian*

Curriculum, do, in a way, address the question of "Where is here?" in Canadian curriculum, by and large they still tend to speak from an imaginary space derived from and created by the cognitive habits of Europe. More than anything else, my interest is precisely to cultivate a new kind of curricular imagination that not only honours the multitude of ways the Canadian landscape shapes how Canadians "see" things, but, more importantly, that explores how such shaping itself is an active process that cannot be simply described through the Eurocentric instrumentalities of previous generations.

Colonialism and Beyond

Atwood (1972) claims that in Canadian literature "victim" is a sister preoccupation to that of survival. There is no question that the land now known as Canada has a long history as a colonized nation—with the French and the English, as well as much earlier the Scots, driving their flags into the soil—and that shaking off colonial status [has] occurred only in the last few decades of the twentieth century. The Union Jack was exchanged for the Maple Leaf on the country's flag in the 1960s and the Canadian constitution made its (final) journey across the Atlantic in the early 1980s. Ven Begamudré (1994), a Canadian short story writer, claims Canadians as a whole are a marginalized people. We live on a continent dominated by the United States; we are a country of women living in a culture dominated by men; we are a country of recent immigrants of colour dominated by former immigrants who forget that white is a colour too; and we are a country of linguistic multiplicity dominated by the English language and a political fiction of linguistic duality.

Until recently, writers preoccupied with the experience of victimization at the hands of a hostile environment dominated English-Canadian literature. On the other hand, French-Canadian writers wrote of being victims of internal colonization, of political and cultural survival in the colony within. The hostile topos of which francophones wrote included not just the landscape, weather, and the "Indians," but British cultural, economic, and political power, which constantly threatened and continues to threaten what it means to be French and to live in Canada. With the exception of a very few writers such as Pauline Johnson, the nineteenth-century romantic poet born of a Mohawk father and an English mother, there were no Aboriginal literary voices. Certainly, there were no published descriptions of the Aboriginal experience of colonization either as survival or as victimization.

Recently, the marginal space of Canadian literature has become quite crowded, not just with male francophones but with women writers from all backgrounds, recent immigrants for whom neither English nor French is mother tongue, gays and lesbians, Aboriginal writers, and even a few of us from Canada's other colonies, the Yukon, Northwest Territories, and Nunavut. There is a similar trend in Canadian curriculum theory and writing, a trend that must be followed if we are to survive, as Atwood reminds us. These writers and theorists have reconfigured the margins, the place of survival, as a topos filled with life worth living and at certain times worth talking and writing about. Just as our primarily English-speaking literary ancestors found the ferocity of Canadian winters—as well as the immensity of the prairies—rich fodder for writing, the most recent generation of Canadian writers finds our marginality, as individuals and groups, provides grist for the literary mill. Thus not only writers in marginalized genres such as speculative fiction explore the theme of the Alienated Outsider; recently, mainstream writers such as Atwood (1996), Timothy Findley (1995), and Jane Urquhart (1993) have written historical novels excavating the immigrant experience for crazy and/or poor women of Irish descent. Social scientists, feminists, and political philosophers may continue to theorize marginalization primarily as a form of oppression and thus inherently unjust (Young, 1990). Canadian writers (many of whom are themselves feminists) are working creatively, as well as critically, within the location of Alienated Outsider. Perhaps the Canadian experience of marginalization as a site of both critique and creativity opens the possibility for sensitivity to otherness, difference, life, and seeing the world simultaneously from multiple intersecting latitudes and longitudes. Perhaps, just as the characters in Canadian speculative fiction discover and as much Canadian fiction suggests to its readers, living in the hinterland is in many ways superior to living in the centre, for exactly this reason.

Just as Canadians need a literature about "here" because this is where we live, Canadians also need a form of curriculum theorizing grounded in "here," which maps out the territory of who we are in relation to the topography of where we live—the physical topos as well as the sociopolitical, historical, and institutional landscape of our lives. Canadians need a curriculum theorizing that helps educators and students come to grips with how Canada, such as it is, has survived to date, and how we who occupy this multi-variegated landscape called Canada can continue both to survive and—to move beyond grim survival—to find our way together in this place.

To accomplish such a task, Canadian curriculum theorists will have to reshape tools inherited from others and make them our own. I suggest that like the four babiche thongs stringing the drum together for survival, four challenges face us.

FOUR CHALLENGES FACING CANADIAN CURRICULUM THEORISTS

Writing from This Place

Our first challenge will be to name where we are, and what it looks and feels like to be in this place, even when we feel "out of place." Canadian curriculum theorists may need to experiment with tools from the indigenous Canadian intellectual tradition and incorporate them into our theorizing. For example, a homegrown curriculum document, theory, or inquiry might draw more extensively upon the rich Canadian traditions of journalism and creative documentary (Kostash, 1994). Canadian curriculum theorists could even explore the poetic voice, in the tradition of down-to-earth Canadian poets such as Lorna Crozier (1992, 1995, 1999), who are often accused of dragging prairie dust through their poems. T. E. Hulme, an Englishman who came to the Canadian prairies in the late nineteenth century, eventually returned to England to write poetry then called modern. Hulme (cited in Abley, 1986) wrote:

> The first time I ever felt the necessity or inevitableness of verse, was in the desire to reproduce the peculiar quality of feeling which is induced by the flat spaces and wide horizons of the virgin prairie of Western Canada. (p. 123)

With poetry forged on the vastness of the landscape outside my studio window, Hulme helped overturn the dominance of the Romantic tradition in English poetry. Experiencing the Canadian prairies, as either a visitor or a lifelong resident, calls a poet to write gritty verse shaped by that landscape, to craft words and images that purport not to explain the enormity of the world but to turn readers to face the very place where they live. The Canadian prairies never let writers forget how difficult it is to simply hang on to their pen and hat in the dry, relentless wind. As prairie writers and other Canadians explore how it is we can possibly survive here, they also find themselves humbled by the task of creating down-to-earth art rather than theorizing grandly. By reading and following their example, Canadian curriculum theorists can write from this place, of this place, and for this place.

A Language of Our Own

The second challenge will be to find and create a language of our own, and to turn to our own for that language. Perhaps we can begin to meet this challenge by reading *Saturday Night, Geist: The Canadian Magazine of Ideas and Culture*, and *Event* as well as—or, when time is tight, instead of—*Harper's, The Atlantic Monthly*, and *The New Yorker*. Canadian curriculum scholars can make more diligent efforts to seek out the work of other Canadian scholars: political philosopher Charles Taylor, metallurgist and philosopher of technology Ursula Franklin, media theorist Marshall McLuhan, and Blackfoot lawyer and philosopher Leroy Little Bear. These Canadian scholars have retooled philosophy, politics, technology, and media in ways that can help Canadian curriculum scholars map the territory of the sociopolitical and cultural "here." Perhaps those of us writing curricula and curriculum theory can turn to prolific Canadian postmodernists such as Arthur Kroker and Linda Hutcheon to trace the postmodern divide through the Canadian consciousness. And of course "here" is not just the academy. To listen to, and to hear, the languages and the stories of the landscape, imagination, and vast otherness that is Canada, curriculum writers may need to turn to Canadian poets, novelists, and writers of nonfiction, including Aboriginal writers of fiction and memoir, prairie poets, and northern journalists.

Understanding and drawing upon Canadian literary and scholarly traditions may not be enough to ensure survival in any of its various forms. If, as Atwood suggested thirty years ago, Canadians must take survival for ourselves and our children seriously, then we may be compelled to move beyond our official languages and theories as well as our traditional ways of taking care of business in curriculum. Finding, creating, and using a curriculum language of our own may require listening (for which curriculum theorists are not known), learning, and using the language of our neighbourhoods, the languages and dialects that both predate and follow the arrival of English and French. If we cannot learn to speak to each other, at least we can begin by learning to hear each other. Following the example of Canadian literature, finding our own language may mean blurring the lines between fiction and nonfiction, mixing languages within a single text, or crossing genres. Perhaps Aboriginal writers can provide an example the rest can follow. For example, Louise Halfe (1994) carefully juxtaposes English and Cree words in her poems to heighten the meaning of the words in each language, as well as the overall effect and significance of the poem. Maria Campbell, who articulated the agony and beauty of growing up Métis in her classic *Halfbreed* (1973) recounts the bawdy and humorous stories of her community of origin in *Stories of the Road Allowance People* (1995). She partially translates these stories so that English speakers can understand the narrative and the humour, but retains enough of the original Michif for the reader to be acutely aware that she or he is hearing another language, another way of speaking the world. Perhaps Canadian curriculum theorists can experiment with creating a linguistic hybrid such as Michif.[1] A new hybrid trade language of curricular and linguistic multiplicity could offer Canadian curriculum scholars the possibility of both creating and locating a curricular landscape of our own. This language of our own might bear a much closer relationship to the imaginary landscape of Canadian fiction and creative nonfiction, as well as to the physical landscape in which Canadian educators and their students live and work, than most contemporary curriculum discourses.

Interpretive Tools of Our Own

Our third challenge will be to seek out or create interpretive tools that allow Canadian curriculum theorists to write and interpret who Canadians are, what we know, and where we want to go, all the while remaining cognizant of an important truism: there will be no single answer to these questions. "The flats of Canada," Hulme once observed of the Canadian prairies, "are incomprehensible on any single theory" (cited in Abley, 1986, p. 122).

When she attempted to write a biography of her mother's working-class English life as well her own autobiography in a single narrative, Steedman (1986) found that the interpretive tools for analyzing exclusionary narratives of class, childhood, and girlhood—as well as the studies these tools produced—had not and could not account for the particularities of either her own life or her mother's. Traditional Marxist analysis of working-class life, for example, "denies its subjects a particular story, a personal history, except when that story illustrates a general thesis," writes Steedman (p. 10). She makes a case for the need for a new set of interpretive tools, ones that do not deny the particularities of place or personal history for the sake of the explanatory or universal.

Most interpretive devices Canadian curriculum theorists have inherited are from the European imaginary space, tools meant to dislodge, to show what is behind and beyond what is taken for granted, to make individuals uncomfortable with society and possibly with themselves. As Theodor Adorno said, "It is part of morality not to be at home in one's home" (cited in Abley, 1986, p. 134). Perhaps Canadians, preoccupied with ourselves as Alienated Outsiders, have learned this lesson too well. From our literature it appears that home is a very ambiguous notion for most English-speaking and immigrant Canadians. Many of us are unsure where we come from, where here is, and whether we belong. This ambiguity about home has not necessarily improved our morality, as Adorno might have hoped. Although this ambiguity has played a large part in the birth of our rich literary tradition, a certain malaise, which might be described as spiritual, has been the twin in this birth, and this malaise has left many Canadians longing to know who we are and where our home is. The single most important task for Canadian curriculum theorists may be to search within the physical and imaginary landscape of Canada for the tools we need to see our home, to help us understand how we have come to be "out of place" in this home, and how we can finally come home here.

Topography for Canadian Curriculum Theory

If anything offers the possibility for community and commonality in this era of multiplicity and difference, it is the land that we share. When Atwood (1972) wrote *Survival*, she wanted to write a geography of mind to guide Canadians through their own literature, to aid us in understanding ourselves and others, and ultimately to ensure that we survive, as a society, a people, and a nation. In its original meaning, *geo-graphy* was to write or scribe *geo*, the world, a rather grand task. Perhaps Canadian curriculum theorists would be content to begin with the slightly more humble but no less difficult task of beginning a topography, rather than a geography, of curriculum theory. We need to write in a detailed way the topos—the particular places and regions where we live and work—and how these places are inscribed in our theorizing, as either presence or absence, whether we want them there or not. Through recovery of an understanding of the topos, especially of imaginary and physical landscape and our history within it, we may find a place to begin the difficult work of reaching into and across the territories of difference. And thus our fourth challenge will be to write a topography for curriculum theory, one that begins at home but journeys elsewhere. When the Dene elders spoke of survival, they meant survival for us all, not just Dene people; when the Cree elders hold a pipe in a ceremony and pray, they pray for us all, not just for Cree people. So too curriculum theorizing must begin at home but it must work on behalf of everyone.

CONCLUSION

Canadian curriculum theorists and practitioners—on behalf of all Canadians—must continue to ask the question "Who are we?" And as curriculum scholars and practitioners, they can only begin to answer the question as they write from here, from this particular place, even if they are not writing it directly. Perhaps they can turn to such tools as indigenous Canadian languages and literatures, in their efforts to better understand how topos writes us rather than how we write it. In their quest for a way of offering the possibility of survival for us all, curriculum writers are not alone; Canadian novelists, poets, essayists, and (creative) nonfiction writers have made this journey before and have left a map to follow. If Canadian curriculum theorists meet their challenge, curriculum Canadiana will live out the question "Who are we?" in relation to the questions "Where are we?" and "Who are they?" and bear witness to the possibilities for us all of doing so. Such writing and theorizing may elucidate how for the Dene of northern Canada, the French both inside and outside Quebec, and all Canadians in the era of North American and Asia-Pacific free trade, it is possible to survive and to thrive in—and possibly even to subvert—the economic and political shadow of others. To accomplish this, Canadian curriculum theorists must come to understand that the topos from which they write is the physical, imaginary, and sociopolitical landscape they share with the communities and children on behalf of whom they work and write.

REFLECTIVE QUESTIONS

1. Is developing or further developing a sense of what it means to be Canadian a focus in our teaching? Is it reflected in our curriculum and teaching resources?
2. How might we bring more Canadiana into our curriculum?
3. How important is where we live—the geography of our understanding—to teaching curriculum in the twenty-first century that engages all learners?
4. Chambers wrote this article in 1999. Does the curriculum today address "where is here" any differently? In today's global village, does it still need to?
5. How is cultural identity important in analyzing beliefs about schooling and in determining what knowledge is most worthy to be included in the official curriculum?
6. Do you think it is possible to write a curriculum that can work for and reflect the experiences of all Canadians given the diverse experiences of topography, culture, language, and heritage that exist in Canada today? Is there one unifying ideal that Canadians should embrace or define ourselves by?

ACKNOWLEDGEMENTS

I thank David Geoffrey Smith and Robert Runté as well as three anonymous reviewers for their helpful suggestions in revising this manuscript. I also thank David Jardine for his initial encouragement to publish this article and David Sumara for organizing the conference session for the *Journal of Curriculum Theorizing* at which an early version of this paper was first presented.

NOTE

1. Michif is a language that combines Cree syntax, particularly verbs, with French and Cree nouns as well as more recently with English words that have migrated into the language. Two kinds of Michif exist: Michif French, a variety of French spoken by Métis people in Métis communities (Douaud, 1985; Lavallee, 1991), and Michif, in which the syntax is Cree and most nouns and modifiers, as well as prepositional phrases, come from French (Crawford, 1983; Bakker, 1997).

REFERENCES

Abley, M. (1986). *Beyond forget: Rediscovering the prairies.* Vancouver: Douglas & McIntyre.

Atwood, M. (1972). *Survival: A thematic guide to Canadian literature.* Concord, ON: House of Anansi Press.

Atwood, M. (1996). *Alias Grace.* Toronto: McClelland & Stewart.

Bakker, P. (1997). *A language of our own: The genesis of Michif, the mixed Cree-French language of the Canadian Métis.* New York: Oxford University Press.

Begamudré, V. (1994, September). *Through Indian eyes.* Paper presented at the annual meeting of the Writers Guild of Alberta, Calgary.

Butala, S. (1994). *The perfection of the morning: An apprenticeship in nature.* Toronto: Harper-Collins.

Campbell, M. (1973). *Halfbreed.* Toronto: McClelland & Stewart.

Campbell, M. (Trans.), & Racette, S. E. (Illus.). (1995). *Stories of the road allowance people.* Penticton, BC: Theytus Books.

Chambers, C. (1989). *For our children's children: An educator's interpretation of Dene testimony to the Mackenzie Valley Pipeline Inquiry.* Unpublished Ph.D. dissertation, University of Victoria, Victoria, BC.

Conway, J. K. (1974). Culture and national identity. In G. Milburn & J. Herbert (Eds.), *National consciousness and the curriculum: The Canadian case* (pp. 71–81). Toronto: Ontario Institute for Studies in Education.

Crawford, J. (1983). Speaking Michif in four Métis communities. *Canadian Journal of Native Studies, 3*(1), 47–55.

Crozier, L. (1992). *Inventing the hawk.* Toronto: McClelland & Stewart.

Crozier, L. (1995). *Everything arrives at the light.* Toronto: McClelland & Stewart.

Crozier, L. (1999). *What the living won't let go.* Toronto: McClelland & Stewart.

Douaud, P. (1985). *Ethnolinguistic profile of Canadian Métis* (National Museum of Man Mercury Series, Canadian Ethnology Service Paper No. 99). Ottawa: National Museums of Canada.

Findley, T. (1995). *The piano man's daughter.* Toronto: Harper-Collins.

Frye, N. (1971). *The bush garden: Essays on the Canadian imagination.* Toronto: Anansi Press.

Gray, W. S., & Hill, M. A. (n.d.) *Fun with Dick and Jane* (E. Campbell & K. Ward, Illus.). Toronto: W. J. Gage.

Gray, W. S., Baruch, D., & Montgomery, E. R. (n.d.-a). *Think-and-do book to accompany the new Fun with Dick and Jane* (The New Basic Readers, Curriculum Foundation Series). Toronto: W. J. Gage.

Gray, W. S., Baruch, D., & Montgomery, E. R. (n.d.-b). *We work and play* (E. Campbell, Illus.) (Basic Readers, Curriculum Foundation Series). Toronto: W. J. Gage.

Halfe, L. (1994). *Bear bones & feathers.* Regina: Coteau Books.

Kostash, M. (1994). Creative nonfiction and me. *WGA [Writers Guild of Alberta] WestWord, 14*(5), 1, 7.

Kroetsch, R. (1994, September). Keynote address presented at the annual meeting of the Writers Guild of Alberta, Calgary.

Kusugak, M. A. (1990). *Baseball bats for Christmas* (V. Krykorka, Illus.). Toronto: Annick Press.

Kusugak, M. A. (1993). *Northern lights: The soccer trails* (V. Krykorka, Illus.). Toronto: Annick Press.

Kusugak, M. A. (1998). *Arctic stories* (V. Krykorka, Illus.). Toronto: Annick Press.

Lavallee, G. (1991). The Michif French language: Historical development and Métis group identity and solidarity at St. Laurent, Manitoba. *Native Studies Review, 7*(1), 81–93.

Milburn, G., & Herbert, J. (Eds.). (1973). *National consciousness and the curriculum: The Canadian case.* Toronto: Ontario Institute for Studies in Education.

Northwest Territories Education, Culture and Employment. Education and Development Branch. (1993). *Dene Kede: Education, a Dene perspective.* Yellowknife: Government of the Northwest Territories.

Perren, S. (1999, March 6). Counting Canada, and horses, beavers, dead ducks and dogs [Review]. *The Globe and Mail* [online], p. 1. Accessed at http://www.chaptersglobe.com/reviews

Runté, R., & Kulyk, C. (1995). The northern cosmos: Distinctive themes in Canadian SF. In A. Paradis (Ed.), *Out of this world: Canadian science fiction and fantasy* (pp. 150–164). Kingston, ON: Quarry Press/Ottawa: National Library of Canada.

Steedman, C. (1986). *Landscape for a good woman: A story of two lives.* New Brunswick, NJ: Rutgers University Press.

Tomkins, G. (1986). *A common countenance: Stability and change in the Canadian curriculum.* Scarborough, ON: Prentice-Hall Canada.

Urquhart, J. (1993). *Away: A novel.* Toronto: McClelland & Stewart.

Van Camp, R. (1996). *The lesser blessed.* Vancouver: Douglas & McIntyre.

Van Camp, R. (1997). *A man called Raven* (G. Littlechild, Illus.). Markham, ON: Fitzhenry & Whiteside.

Van Camp, R. (1998). *What's the most beautiful thing you know about horses?* (G. Littlechild, Illus.). San Francisco: Children's Book Press.

Wiebe, R. (1994). *A discovery of strangers.* Toronto: Knopf.

Young, I. M. (1990). *Justice and the politics of difference.* Princeton, NJ: Princeton University Press.

13

Curriculum as Cultural Practice:
Postcolonial Imagination

YATTA KANU

The opportunity to take familiar curriculum concepts/ideas and reimagine and rearticulate them in ways that facilitate the development of new habits of mind is exciting for me for a number of reasons. First, it brings to the forefront what I have been "preaching" in my academic work for some time now, namely, that alternative sites for curriculum theorizing could be generated from already established curricular metaphors/concepts and their reflections in practice. Second, the move itself is a recognition that multiple modes of theoretical representation emerge from genuinely valuing alternative insights and perspectives grounded in a dynamic variety of human experiences, thereby adding richness and complexity to curriculum and curriculum discourse. Third, it is an opportunity for me to closely examine a popular and taken-for-granted curriculum metaphor—"curriculum as cultural practice"—and demonstrate how, historically, it has been mediated through a colonial imagination "contrived to the disbenefit of the other" (London, 2001, p. 45). The intent here is to reimagine and retheorize this metaphor and its function in a postcolonial context. This third reason subsumes the first two and will be explored more fully as a focus of this paper. I will begin by articulating the senses in which the terms "postcolonial" and "imagination" are used here.

The "postcolonial" yokes a diverse range of experiences, cultures, and problems, resulting in a looseness in meaning that has confounded many and triggered considerable debate over the precise parameters of the field. Locations from which the "postcolonial" has been interpreted and explored in the recent past have included not only the period after independence which marked the departure of the imperial powers from their former colonies but that before independence—where the focus is on the formation of the colony through various mechanisms of control and the various stages in the development of anticolonial nationalism—and even the period prior to colonization in which the cultural productions and social formations of the colony before colonization are used to better understand the experience of colonization. Furthermore, "postcolonial" sometimes includes independent colonies that now contend with neocolonial forms of subjugation through expanding forms of capitalism and globalization, and minority populations in First and Third World countries experiencing repression and exploitation. What these locations have in common is that they signify a position against imperialism, and while this paper admits of all these locations, it is the "postcolonial" as a stance against Eurocentrism, as evidenced by the dominance of Western knowledge/cultural production and dissemination, that is important here. From this stance, "postcolonial" becomes the site where a variety of assumptions accepted on individual, academic, and political levels are called into question in the struggle for more democratic social relations.

While this engagement of the postcolonial provides a framework for critique, "imagination," a construct often used in recent discourses on globalization and education, is used here to help explain how people come to know, understand, and experience themselves as members of a community and citizens of a nation-state (Popkewitz, 2000). Imagination, according to Popkewitz, functions to "form individuals into the seam of a collective narrative" (p. 168) and help them generate conceptions of personhood and identity. In this paper, the term is used in ways similar to Rizvi (2000) who writes:

> Imagination is the attempt to provide coherence between ideas and action, to provide a basis for the content of relationships and the creation of categories with which to understand the world around us. What is imagined defines what we regard as normal. (pp. 222–223)

In Rizvi's formulation, imagination is not an attribute possessed by a few en-dowed individuals but instead "denotes a collective sense of a group of people, a community that begins to imagine and feel things together" (p. 223). Thus de-fined, imagination serves two purposes in this paper. First, it provides a frame-work for understanding how curriculum has been mediated and to what effect, and second, it signifies possibilities for alternative means of curriculum con-struction for a more democratic future. The construct is therefore used here, on the one hand, as an analytical framework for historically examining "curriculum as cultural practice" where the curriculum has been employed to neutralize difference, assimilate, and establish for the "other" a world view and a concept of self and community (London, 2001), and on the other, for proposing reform where curriculum could be reconstructed to become more responsive to the demands of education in today's contexts where diversities have outstripped the meaningfulness of any homogenizing models.

THE NEED FOR CULTURAL INQUIRY IN UNDERSTANDING CURRICULUM REFORM

My choice of the familiar concept "curriculum as cultural practice" as a focus for the CACS (Canadian Association for Curriculum Studies) Presidential symposium was deliberate. First, it was intended to place culture at the centre of curriculum analysis and reform, and second, to stress practice as an important context for these endeavours. Curriculum has been and will always remain a cultural practice, making cultural inquiry very important in contemporary understandings of educational reform, especially as reform relates to social inclusion and exclusion, and to the relation of knowledge and power. This assertion is amply supported by the literature on cultural politics and principles of reform. For example, Dirlik (1987), arguing against the notion that culture ought to be subsumed or replaced by other seemingly more radical approaches to understanding education and social lives, posits that we need culture as one, if not the, primary source for radical inquiry, for culture shapes our ways of seeing, and it is these we must question first if we are to make changes in action at either the micro or macro levels. Diane Hoffman, among others, sufficiently recognizes the important relationship between cultural knowledge and power to argue, in a brilliant article on reconceptualizing education in the new millennium, for "a recentered discourse on culture in comparative education that recognizes the value of cultural inquiry, in particular, of cultural inquiry as a source of destabilization of taken-for-granted categories, representations and truths" (1999, p. 464). For Hoffman, one of the traditional and principal uses of culture in comparative education has been as a source of positive destabilization of the categories brought to analysis. She therefore argues that:

> A form of inquiry (i.e., cultural inquiry) that encourages us to look with a critical eye at the categories that we are using is of utmost importance in the comparative analysis of education, for it is only when we do so that we can generate alternatives to what already exists. (p. 481)

Hoffman's position on the relevance of cultural inquiry to educational reform finds support in Maseman's (1990) suggestion that cultural inquiry emphasizes the uncovering of the particularities of lived experiences across different groups, particularly in schools and classrooms, and hence acts as an antidote to theoretical abstractions and generalities that do not account for cross-cultural variation.

Recent developments in anthropology, especially in the domains of "practice theory" and "situated learning," provide useful insights on the importance of practice in cultural inquiry. Given the social situatedness of learning and its implications, and the cultural assumptions that underlie practices, proponents of practice theory and situated learning posit practice as the most appropriate unit of analysis in understanding education, curriculum, and pedagogy. Thus, it is the position of this paper that an analysis of curriculum as cultural practice, past and present, along with the imagination through which it has been mediated, will provide an appropriate beginning place for curriculum reform. In the next section, therefore, I provide some historical insights into how curriculum as cultural practice, filtered through a colonial imagination, has constituted a basis for social relationships deemed to be required in defining the world for the "other," specifically the "colonized other."

CURRICULUM AS CULTURAL PRACTICE: COLONIAL IMAGINATION

Like the postcolonial, colonialism has been defined in several ways (e.g., Nandy, 1983; Spivak, 1990; Willinsky, 1998), with each definition linking colonialism with notions of power, superiority, and greed on the part of the West. Here, it is colonialism as a "civilizing mission" and as an ideological formation intended to establish for the "other" a view of the world and a concept of self and community, especially through the production, representation, and dissemination of knowledge, that is the focus of my analysis. In that sense, the "colonized other" refers to not only the former colonies that formed the periphery at the receiving end of dispensations from metropolitan centres in Western Europe during the colonial period, but also minority populations experiencing repression and discrimination in dominant culture societies.

Historically, curriculum imagination has been mediated by the nation-state which, faced with the impossibility of incorporating its "surplus" (i.e., those who cannot fit) into the symbolic realm of national identity, appeals to "a fantasy structure or scenario through which it perceives itself as a homogeneous entity" (Salecl, 1994, p. 15) with a common history, language, and culture. Cultural theorists Homi Bhabha and Stuart Hall have called attention to the ambivalence of the nation in the production of national identity. For example, in the introduction to his book, *Nation and Narration*, Bhabha (1990) refers to "the impossible unity of the nation as a symbolic force ... [in spite of] the attempt by nationalist discourses persistently to produce the idea of the nation as a continuous narrative of national progress" (p. 2). Stuart Hall (1992) also locates the attempt to create a "sense of nation" in discourses that constitute what he calls "the myth of cultural homogeneity" within the nation-state, asserting that:

> Instead of thinking of national cultures as unified, we should think of them as constituting a discursive device which represents difference as unity or identity. They (national cultures) are cross-cut by deep internal divisions and differences, and are unified only through the exercise of cultural power. (p. 297)

A recognizable theme in the discourse of the nation as continuous narrative of national harmony and progress and the production of "unifying" national cultures is the role of the school as an "ideological state apparatus" (Aronowitz, 1992; Bourdieu & Passeron, 1977), that is, the school as the state's vehicle for ideological assimilation and homogenization. Schools, according to this theory, function not only to normalize those whose attitudes, norms, values, and behaviours are different from what is constructed as the norm and as normal, but also to inscribe particular rationalities in the sensitivities, dispositions, and awarenesses of individuals to make them fit into a single set of imaginaries about national citizenship (Popkewitz, 2000). The contention is that school is a constitutive part of these relationships and its purpose is to create a form of consciousness that enables the inculcation of the knowledge of dominant groups as "official knowledge" for all students, and the maintenance of social control without the dominant groups necessarily resorting to overt mechanisms of domination—what Althusser (1971) calls the "repressive state apparatus." According to Apple (1993), the "politics of official knowledge" works not through coercion but through accords and compromises that favour the dominant groups. Apple elaborates:

> These compromises occur at different levels: at the level of political and ideological discourse, at the level of state policies, at the level of knowledge that is taught in schools, at the level of the teachers and students in classrooms, and at the level of how we understand all of this. (p. 10)

Power and control, then, are exercised through a formal corpus of knowledge which the school distributes through curriculum, rules, and regulations. Thus, schools are said to not only control people and meaning but also confer cultural legitimacy on the knowledge of specific groups (Giroux, 1983).

For an illustration of how curriculum as cultural practice worked to the benefit of the colonialists and the disenfranchisement of the colonized during colonial administration, I turn to Norrel London's (2001) recent analysis of how the state (in this case, Britain), as a privileged entity, contrived and mediated colonial imagination during the process of Empire building, using curriculum and pedagogy to control the mind of the colonized. London's insights, more than any other recent scholarship, have added much to our understanding of how education and schooling can be "deliberately twisted to minister to subversive ends" (London, 2001, p. 45). The context of London's analysis is British colonialism in Trinidad and Tobago during the nineteenth and first half of the twentieth centuries, and he discusses how ideology became the primary agent for the internalization and acceptance of British and Western culture, and how education and schooling were used as the medium for developing in the "colonized other" the required sense of psychological subordination. London describes the curriculum canvas during the period as drawing from the universe of educational ideologies available in the metropolitan arena (Britain), enhanced by thinking which had prevailed both in the United States and in parts of Europe—ideologies such as mental discipline, humanism, child study, and social efficiency. He writes:

> In each of these traditions the choice of content and of delivery practices was subjugated to the colonial ideal. Congruence with established objectives for domination and acceptance of a defined worldview was a major requirement. (p. 55)

For example, because of its mindless characteristics such as drill and rote memorization, London points out that mental discipline became an appropriate vehicle for the colonial purpose, the essence of the doctrine being in conformity with colonial desire to throttle creativity and critical thinking in the education of the "other." Instructive is London's observation of how humanism, the tradition that most emphasized the promotion and maintenance of what was considered the best of Western cultural heritage and values, was put to work as the arsenal of the colonizer in Trinidad and Tobago. Because it exemplifies British colonial education almost everywhere during Empire building, the observation is worth quoting at length here:

> The heroes exalted in the history books, the norms and mores presented for inculcation (the cadence of public holidays established, for example), and the standards of excellence and gallantry paraded for emulation (as depicted in the story of Odysseus and the Cyclops, for example) were contrivances for the colonial purpose. Emphasis on these, to the exclusion of all others, was an attempt to obliterate the existentialist past of the colonized and to present an alternative and preferred view of reality. A 1948 evaluation report on the work in one school encouraged teachers, for example, to teach "the songs that the world

would sing", understandably at the expense of developing local talent. The official pronouncement meant that students did not have a voice, nor were they encouraged to develop one—in singing or speaking. They were the "voiceless" objects in a socio-political sense, a position which gestures in the direction of Gayatri Spivak's (1988) concern: "Can the subaltern speak?" (p. 68)

Elsewhere (Kanu, 1993), I have documented foreignness of curriculum and voicelessness in pedagogy in my analysis of colonial education in another former British colony, Sierra Leone. In that piece, I wrote:

> The subject-matter taught was foreign and had no relevance or bearing on students' lived experiences and it was taught in ways that stifled critical thinking and creativity. The main interest of the colonizer was to ensure that the "uncivilized natives" digested the new cultural reality that their official knowledge was imparting. . . . Students received knowledge but were perceived as incapable of producing or changing knowledge. Teaching was a monological process that lacked any theory about students' capacity to interpret reality and bestow it with multiple meanings. (p. 2)

It appears therefore that, though recent discourses on education and administration in the former British Empire point to local variations from territory to territory (Willinsky, 1998), in general the overall intent of colonial education, as Bacchus (1994) has pointed out, was to instill in the colonized "a worldview that would develop in them a voluntary subservience to the white ruling groups and a willingness to continue occupying their positions on the lowest rung of the occupational and social ladder" (p. 308).

The same observation can be made about the state's use of education/curriculum in the process of national identity formation in other European states in the nineteenth and early part of the twentieth centuries. For instance, Osborne (1995) has pointed out that the aim of formal education in Europe during this period was to create an institutionalized cultural identity by shaping curriculum, writing history, formalizing languages, establishing literatures, inventing traditions, assimilating minorities, instilling nationalism—in short, creating citizens. In the words of a nineteenth-century Italian nationalist, "We have made Italy; now we must make Italians" (quoted in Osborne, 1995, p. 17).

In a recent article (Kanu, 2002b), I argued that what was true of European states in the nineteenth and early twentieth centuries was essentially true of the United States and Canada in their formative period. For example, American cultural historian Randolph Collins (1979), placing the legacy of homogenization and conformity in education in a historical context, has pointed out that the impetus for compulsory schooling in the United States was rooted in the need to control the socialization of the children of European immigrants and to perpetuate the values of the middle class and the knowledge base of the traditional Anglo-Protestant culture. Similarly, Canadian social historians (e.g., Axelrod, 1997; Osborne, 1995; Strange & Loo, 1997) have argued that the enthusiasm for compulsory public schooling in Canada was fuelled by the desire to perpetuate Anglo-Celtic, Protestant, and French Catholic ideals. Though at the time Canada was struggling with its own identity, wavering between asserting a unique Canadian identity and remaining tied to the majesty and power of Britain and the British Empire, Canadian elites showed no uncertainty of purpose when it came to the critical role they assigned to state institutions in shaping the identity of its citizens. For instance, Richardson (2002) points out that Vincent Massey, the first Canadian-born Governor General, explicitly laid out the responsibility of schools in the realization of an ideal-type Canadian when he said:

> In a country with so scattered a population as ours and a vast frontier exposed to alien influences, the tasks of creating a truly national feeling must inevitably be arduous but this is the undertaking to which our educational systems must address themselves, for by true education alone will the problem be solved. To our schools we must look for the good Canadian. (1926, p.11)

Thus the state proceeded to build the Canadian nation by regulating the education (and the moral behaviours) of those not considered ideal types. After Confederation, for example, through the introduction of the Indian Act (1879) and the establishment of the Department of Indian Affairs (1880), the state became unabashedly involved in transforming the character of all Aboriginals, "protecting" them on reserves, and civilizing and assimilating the "savages" into Anglo-Saxon norms (Strange & Loo, 1997). Believing that the best chances for lasting results would be achieved with First Nations children, the federal government decided, in 1879, to take a more direct role in their education by setting up their own residential schools where children could be assimilated from the allegedly corrupting environments of their homes and families. The curriculum offered in these schools was intended to break First Nations students of their "nomadic habits" and prepare them for employment befitting their status, and make them "good Christians." Thus, the curriculum consisted of religion and trades (apprenticeships) in carpentry, tin-smithing, boot-making, and tailoring for boys, and sewing, laundering, cleaning, and cooking for girls to prepare them for employment as domestics. When Indian chiefs attempted to resist an education that offered children only a slim possibility of economic advancement, yet was based on alien languages, faith, and culture, and completely out of step with Indian traditional forms of learning, the federal government reacted by appointing truancy officers in 1930, who were empowered to impose penalties to compel all Indian children between the ages of seven and sixteen to attend school (Strange & Loo, 1997).

Compulsory schooling of children was also an indirect route to regulating non-native parents and families, with non-English immigrants especially being made the objects of assimilation. According to Strange and Loo (1997), the Doukhobors, a radical Christian sect which rejected all forms of state intervention in civil life, were the group that suffered the most coercive attempt to impose state education during the interwar period. Maclaren (1995) informs us that Doukhobors, like professional educators, believed children should be taught how best to regulate themselves: "To us, education means being a good Doukhobor. That is, to love all living things and do no evil, not to shoot, not to eat meat, not to smoke, not to drink liquor" (p. 6). The only problem was that Doukhobors (like the Indian chiefs who did not want schools, Christianity, or the law on their reserves) thought that traditional communities, not the state, knew best how to carry out this mission. However, according to Strange and Loo (1997), Doukhobor parents were frequently fined, even jailed, and goods belonging to entire Doukhobor communities were seized by the police for violation of school attendance laws.

In the Canadian West where a massive influx of non-British/French immigrants arrived between 1901 and 1921 to settle the "Last Best West," the choice between cultural accommodation and cultural change was decided in favour of aggressive assimilationist policies. For instance, Axelrod (1997) states that in response to the question of how the diverse cultures of the newcomers were to be accommodated, Northwest Territory School Superintendent, Arthur Groggin, sought to address what he saw as "the pressing educational problem posed by a foreign and relatively ignorant population" this way:

> To gather the children of different races, creeds, and customs into the common school and "Canadianize" them. . . . Though they may enter as Galicians, Doukhobors, or Icelanders, they will come out as Canadians. . . . A common school and a common language will produce that homogeneous citizenship so necessary in the development of that greater Canada lying west of the Lakes. (quoted in Axelrod, 1997, p. 85)

Thus, mass schooling and the curriculum were the vehicles through which the accomplishment of the cultural and psychological colonization of the "other" was imagined. Despite successive post-1945 immigrations, first from war-torn Europe and, since 1960, from non-traditional sites of immigration such as South Asia, the Caribbean, and, more recently, Africa, and the subsequent introduction of multiculturalism since the early 1970s, this "common imagining" of the Canadian nation is still alive in the curriculum of schools across Canada, as documented in recent analyses of homogenizing nationalist discourses in the K–12 social studies curriculum in the provinces of British Columbia (McDonald, 2002) and Alberta (Richardson, 2002). It is also evident in continued calls for a coherent national history for all immigrant children to learn in school (Bliss, 2001; Granatstein, 1998), and in the recent (2000) warning by the Dominion Institute (a history organization that periodically sponsors questionnaires that test the historical literacy of Canadians aged eighteen to twenty-four years) that the lack of knowledge of Canada's history means that Canada's youth lack the "cultural currency" that is critical to the development of a national identity. To remedy this "crisis," the Institute recommends a mandatory history course in each province that includes a minimal list of people and events critical to Canadian history (Richardson, 2002).

As the foregoing historical analysis of "curriculum as cultural practice" shows, curricular encounter with the "other" has been unequal, unethical, and anchored in racism and violence. McCarthy and Dimitriadis (2000) have categorized these practices as "resentment" which they describe as "the specific practice of identity displacement in which the social actor consolidates his identity by a complete disavowal of the merits and existence of his social other" (p. 193). Thus, a sense of self is only possible through an annihilation or "emptying out" of the other, whether discursively or materially. These practices have not always met with anticipated success as values deemed good by the colonizer/nation-state have been constantly repudiated by those on whom they have been imposed. In the former European colonies, for example, repudiation took the form of nationalist movements that eventually led to independence for these countries. Independence, however, has been followed by the march of neocolonialism in the guise of modernization and development in an age of globalization and transnationalism. This reinvention of imperialism implies that schools and school curriculum cannot separate themselves from the task of neocolonization.

In Canada and the United States, the new waves of non-traditional immigrants and the refusal of these immigrants to become "carbon copies" of the dominant groups within their countries have meant that the tropes by which the elites construct and maintain a single set of national identity are no longer sustainable. Given these developments, how can democratic, ethical curricular relationships be formed? In the rest of this paper I once again engage the metaphor "curriculum as cultural practice"—the intent, this time, is to reimagine its function in a postcolonial context, and theorize curricular intentions and practices that are inclusive and, therefore, ethical and democratic. In doing so, I appeal particularly to "hybridity," a construct used by postcolonial theorists Homi Bhabha and Stuart Hall to describe the ambiguity that characterizes the postcolonial.

CURRICULUM AS CULTURAL PRACTICE:
POSTCOLONIAL IMAGINATION

The recent addition of curriculum internationalization to the educational discourses of reform and research should be thought of not only as exhortations of change but also constructions of imaginaries that potentially embody "a deep reshaping of the images of social action and consciousness through which individuals are to participate" (Popkewitz, 2000, p. 172). Underlying the new discourse of internationalization is curriculum imagination that, as was quoted earlier, "denotes a collective sense of a group of people, a community that begins to imagine and feel things together" (Rizvi, 2000, p. 223). This imagining of ourselves as a community participating, interpreting ourselves, and creating knowledge together is critical to curriculum reform in a postcolonial context. "Hybridity" becomes crucial in the formulation of the agenda of reform, for its politics embody fluid, pragmatic, and multiple power relations, unlike the relations of domination documented in the foregoing section of this paper.

Postcolonial theorist Homi Bhabha has argued that one of the consequences of imperialism has meant that, in an intellectual sense, the colonizer and the colonized have been brought together in identity formation that is continually in a process of hybridity. Bhabha (in an interview published in Rutherford, 1990) describes hybridity as the "third space" where the meaning of cultural and political authority is negotiated without eliding or normalizing the differential structures in conflict. Elsewhere, I have referred to Bhabha's "third space" as the place for the construction of identities that are neither one nor the other (Kanu, 2002b). I have argued that because of centuries of Western European impact on Africa (from missionary and trade activities to outright colonization), for example, it is no longer possible to postulate a unitary Africa over/against a monolithic West—a binarism between a distinct self (as African) and "other" (as European). That is, there is no longer a single set of discourse about progress and change; rather, there is a hybrid—a third space—where local and global images meet in a weaving that has its own configurations and implications. This overlay is best highlighted in Spivak's (1990) response to critics who fault her on not seeking possibilities of discovering/promoting "indigenous theory." She writes:

> I cannot understand what indigenous theory there might be that can ignore the reality of nineteenth century history. . . . To construct indigenous theories, one must ignore the last few centuries of historical involvement. I would rather use what history has written for me. (p. 69)

Indeed, education itself in the former colonies occurs within an overlay of discourses that move in the interstices of the colonial and the colonized. The rapid movements and collision of peoples and media images across the world have further disrupted the traditional isomorphism between self, place, and culture. The Eurocentric (e.g., Bennett, 1994) and Afrocentric (e.g., Asante, 1993) debates that have emerged in discourses about curriculum reform are themselves driven by nostalgia for a past in which Europe and Africa are imagined without what McCarthy and Dimitriadis (2000) call "the noise of their modern tensions, contradictions and conflicts" (p. 195). These debates refuse the radical hybridity that is the reality of today's major metropolitan societies everywhere.

Curriculum reform as postcolonial imagination, grounded in the reality of hybridization, would allow the influences of history and global migration to inform new responses to teaching, and invite curriculum workers to rethink the production, representation, and circulation of knowledge so that these do not remain the monopoly and privilege of one group. This way, the subjugated memories and histories of those hitherto marginalized can become part of the curriculum conversation. Thus imagined, curriculum reform does not involve opposing Western culture against the cultures of the non-West, but is instead founded on the principle of the heterogeneous basis of all knowledge and the need to find abiding links that connect groups across ethnic affiliations, geographical origins, and locations. Cameron McCarthy (1998) would refer to the knowledge that results from such interaction as "an alloy of racial, cultural and ethnic metals." Bacchus (2002) has pointed out that this emerging approach to knowledge production is already being recognized in the field of medicine where greater efforts are being made to explore the value of multiple sources of knowledge. For example, Bacchus argues, traditional health practices such as acupuncture and chiropractic remedies (now known as alternative medicine) are increasingly being utilized in Western societies while pharmacologists, in the development of new drugs, are seeking traditional cures that have been used in different societies. It is my fervent hope that more of this "alloyed" approach to knowledge production and dissemination would be engaged in curriculum work.

The space from which I theorize curriculum construction based on hybridity can be explained by my history as a postcolonial subject who was born and raised in Sierra Leone, a former colony of Great Britain, but who has studied and lived extensively in the West. Growing up in Sierra Leone in the 1960s and 1970s, I existed in a constant state of negotiation between the cultural form of England and that of my emerging postcolonial country. This first-hand experience of cultural ambiguity was what triggered and maintains my interest in postcolonial theory compatible with postmodern formulations of hybridity, intertextuality, third space, in-between-ness, and native rearticulation. Using "what history has written for me," I draw on these formulations to theorize postcolonial curriculum and education based on a new kind of intercultural hermeneutic whereby the diverse traditions, ways of knowing, and knowledge production of different peoples are brought to a new conversational interface, for, as McCarthy (1998) has argued, any single narrative or identity at the core of the curriculum—whether African, Asian, or European—is in fact a dangerous confinement.

My effort in this hybrid or alloyed approach to curriculum reform has, therefore, focused on finding out what knowledge, understanding, and cultural capital others have that can be brought to the curriculum conversation. My most recent work in this search has focused on culture and Aboriginal students' learning in Canada's formal school system. More precisely, my work focuses on the investigation of specific aspects of First Nations (Ojibway, Cree, and Métis) culture that could be integrated (infused) into the planning and teaching of the school curriculum to enhance and enrich learning for not only First Nations students but for non-native students as well (Kanu, 2002a).

Coming to this work with the experience of colonization, I have been encouraged by Kierkegaard's argument (in Caputo, 1987) that no matter how much is subtracted from the individual there is always a "remainder" that could embrace the task of constituting the self as a self. This constituting process involves what Kierkegaard refers to as "repetition" which, for him, is a forward rather than a backward movement. Through the process of repetition, the individual is able to press forward,

> ... not toward a sheer novelty which is wholly discontinuous with the past, but into the being which he himself is. . . . Repetition is that by which the existing individual circles back on the being which he has been all along, that by which he returns to himself. (quoted in Caputo, 1987, p. 12)

The experience of colonization has taken a lot away from the colonized, and different forms of neocolonialism continue to influence and affect decisions and practices in the former colonies. In multicultural societies with minority populations, the struggles over identity have produced new exclusions as monolithic notions of identity clash with convictions of identity that are heterogeneous. In the midst of such incessant dispersal of the self, there is need for people to define themselves in terms of new memories by which they come to know, understand, and experience themselves—memories dissociated from the old collective identities, and reimagined with another collective narrative (Balibar & Wallerstein, 1991). As Wald (in Popkewitz, 2000) points out, "Older identities are estranged and one's 'home' (identity) is no longer located where one thought it was" (p. 170). If, indeed, we are serious about the construction of another narrative, then curriculum reform needs to be grounded in "imagined communities" where relations are no longer unidirectional or univocal, flowing from the colonialist to the colonized. The challenges we face in the twenty-first century transcend national boundaries and single sets of discourses. We could call them "supranational or transnational challenges," as Parker, Ninomiya, and Cogan (1999) have suggested. Addressing these challenges requires hybrid/multinational curriculum thinking and acting consisting of overlays of multiple discourses, and plural assumptions and strategies.

REFLECTIVE QUESTIONS

1. Canadian classrooms are becoming increasingly diverse. Is it possible for all students to feel their cultural views are represented in the curriculum? How might this occur?
2. What might a hybrid, multinational curriculum look like?
3. Is there opportunity for you as an educator to allow for the "heterogeneous basis of all knowledge"? Provide an example.
4. Do we accept "other" knowledge as valuable? How would valuing alternative perspectives in the curriculum add richness to learning experiences for students?
5. If our national identity is one of "difference," can Canada ever feel like a cohesive country? Defend your position.

REFERENCES

Althusser, L. (1971). *Lenin and philosophy.* New York: Monthly Review Press.

Apple, M. (1990). *Ideology and curriculum.* New York: Routledge.

Apple, M. (1993). *Official knowledge: Democratic education in a conservative age.* New York: Routledge.

Aronowitz, S. (1992). *The politics of identity.* New York: Routledge.

Asante, M. (1993). *Malcolm X as cultural hero and other Afrocentric essays.* Trenton, N.J.: Africa World Press.

Axelrod, P. (1997). *The promise of schooling: Education in Canada, 1800–1914.* Toronto: University of Toronto Press.

Bacchus, M. K. (1994). *Education as and for legitimacy: Development in West Indian education between 1846 and 1895.* Waterloo, ON: Wilfrid Laurier University Press.

Bacchus, M. K. (2002, March). Curriculum, education and globalization, with special reference to the developing countries. Keynote address at the Conference on Problems and Prospects of Educational Development in Developing Countries, University of the West Indies, Barbados.

Balibar, E., & Wallerstein, I. (1991). *Race, nation, class: Ambiguous identities* (Chris Turner, Trans.). New York: Verso.

Bennett, W. (1994). *The book of virtues.* New York: Simon and Schuster.

Bhabha, H. K. (1990). Introduction: Narrating the nation. In *Nation and narration* (pp. 1–7). London: Routledge.

Bliss, M. (2001, October). Teaching Canadian national history. Address at "Giving the Future a Past" Conference, Association for Canadian Studies, Winnipeg.

Bourdieu, P., & Passeron, J. C. (1977). *Reproduction in education, society and culture.* Beverly Hills, CA: Sage Publications.

Caputo, J. (1987). *Radical hermeneutics: Deconstruction and the hermeneutic project.* Bloomington: University of Indiana Press.

Collins, R. (1979). *The credential society: An historical sociology of education and stratification.* New York: Academic Press.

Dirlik, A. (1987). Culturalism as hegemonic ideology and liberating practice. *Cultural Critique, 6* (Spring), 13–50.

Dominion Institute Releases. (2000, June 20).

Giroux, H. (1983). Theories of reproduction and resistance in the new sociology of education: A critical analysis. *Harvard Educational Review, 53,* 257–293.

Granatstein, J. L. (1998). *Who killed Canadian history?* Toronto: Harper Perennial: Harper-Collins Publishers Ltd.

Hall, S. (1992). The question of cultural identity. In S. Hall, D. Held, & T. McGrew (Eds.), *Modernity and its futures* (pp. 292–297). Cambridge, England: Polity Press.

Hoffman, D. M. (1999). Culture and comparative education: Toward decentering and recentering the discourse. *Comparative Education Review, 43*(4), 464–488.

Kanu, Y. (1993). *Exploring critical reflection for postcolonial teacher education: Sierra Leone.* Unpublished Ph.D. dissertation, University of Alberta, Edmonton.

Kanu, Y. (2002a). In their own voices: First Nations students identify some cultural mediators of their learning in the formal school system. *Alberta Journal of Educational Research, 48*(2), 98–121.

Kanu, Y. (2002b). Understanding curriculum and pedagogy as attunement to difference: Teacher preparation for the 21st century. *Journal of Professional Studies, 9*(2), 50–60.

London, N. A. (2001). Curriculum and pedagogy in the development of colonial imagination: A subversive agenda. *Canadian and International Education, 30*(1), 41–76.

Maclaren, J. (1995). Creating "slaves of Satan" or "new Canadians"? The law, education and the socialization of Doukhobor children, 1911–1935. In J. Maclaren (Ed.), *Essays in the history of Canadian law: British Columbia and the Yukon.* Toronto: Hamar Fisher and John Maclaren.

Maseman, V. (1990). Ways of knowing. *Comparative Education Review, 34*(4), 465.

Massey, V. (1926). "Introduction." In C. N. Cochrane & W. S. Wallace, *This Canada of ours.* National Council of Education (Canada).

McCarthy, C. (1998). *The uses of culture: Education and the limits of ethnic affiliation.* New York: Routledge.

McCarthy, C., & Dimitriadis, G. (2000). Globalizing pedagogies: Power, resentment, and the re-narration of difference. In N. C. Burbules and C. A. Torres (Eds.), *Globalization and education: Critical perspectives* (pp. 187–204). New York: Routledge.

McDonald, K. (2002). Post-national considerations for curriculum. *Journal of Curriculum Theorizing, 18*(1), 95–110.

Nandy, A. (1983). *The intimate enemy: Loss and recovery of self under colonialism.* Delhi: Oxford University Press.

Osborne, K. (1995). *In defense of history: Teaching the past and the meaning of democratic citizenship.* Toronto: Our School/Ourselves Education Foundation.

Parker, W. C., Ninomiya, A., & Cogan, J. (1999). Educating world citizens: Toward multinational curriculum development. *American Educational Research Journal, 36*(2), 117–145.

Popkewitz, T. S. (2000). Reform as the social administration of the child: Globalization of knowledge and power. In N. C. Burbules & C. A. Torres (Eds.), *Globalization and education: Critical perspectives* (pp. 157–186). New York: Routledge.

Richardson, G. H. (2002). *The death of the good Canadian: Teachers, national identities and the social studies curriculum.* New York: Peter Lang.

Rizvi, F. (2000). International education and the production of global imagination. In N. C. Burbules & C. A. Torres (Eds.), *Globalization and education: Critical perspectives* (pp. 205–225). New York: Routledge.

Rutherford, J. (Ed.) (1990). The third space: Interview with Homi Bhabha. In J. Rutherford (Ed.), *Identity, community, culture and difference* (pp. 301–307). London: Lawrence & Wishart.

Salecl, R. (1994). *The spoils of freedom: Psychoanalysis and feminism after the fall of socialism.* New York: Routledge.

Spivak, G. (1990). The postcolonial critique. In S. Harasym (Ed.), *The postcolonial critique: Interviews, strategies, dialogues* (pp. 67–74). New York: Routledge.

Strange, C., & Loo, T. (1997). *Making good: Law and moral regulation in Canada, 1867–1939.* Toronto: University of Toronto Press.

Willinsky, J. (1998). *Learning to divide the world: Education at Empire's end.* Minneapolis: University of Minnesota Press.

14

Reflecting Today, Creating Tomorrow:

The Dual Role of Public Education

JON YOUNG

> The only hope for curing the ills of the world is that young people may picture a better one and strive to realize it. To frame this picture and to cultivate that ambition is the greatest duty of the school.[1]

Education, as Terry Wotherspoon reminds us, is a social activity concerned with the development and transformation of people's lives.[2] Fundamentally, it is about self-knowledge and identity: about coming to know ourselves—who we are, where we are in time and space, where we have been, where we are going, what we can become, and what our responsibilities are to ourselves and to others. Recognizing that a great deal of what we know, believe, and can do is *not* learned in schools, it is nonetheless the school—particularly the public school—where society's most sustained and systematic efforts to structure and direct that process for our youth takes place. With governments spending some $37 billion in 1999–2000 on elementary and secondary schooling for more than 5 million students, the nation's education system constitutes not only one of its major public assets but also an expensive, highly visible instrument of social policy that shapes both our individual and our national identities as Canadians living in a pluralist/multicultural, capitalist democracy. It is where the interests of individual children and families meet the interests of the state, and it is where the past and present meet the future. Given this, it is inevitable that schools become the focus of a never-ending curriculum debate as to what knowledge and whose cultures constitute the appropriate and necessary basis for this process of identity formation. In Paquette's words:

> Control over both the form of schooling and its academic and moral content is the symbolic battlefield wherein ideas, beliefs and cultures struggle perpetually for more control of what societies will look like in the future.[3]

THE SOCIALIZING ROLE OF SCHOOLS

To state that a role of schools is to contribute to the preparation of young people for adult roles and active citizenship in Canadian society masks the complexities of the task. What knowledge, skills, and dispositions any one of us needs to live a fulfilling, successful, and productive adult life is not something that lends itself readily to a "once-and-for-all" definition—either by any one individual or collectively by the state. Today the increasing recognition of Canadian cultural diversity and the uncertainties associated with technology and a changing global economy serve only to add to the ambiguity associated with this agenda. Yet this is the task of schools. Three questions help to illustrate the complexity of the school's socializing role: Where do the responsibilities of the school end and other socializing agencies take over? How do schools prepare different students for different roles? What knowledge and skills are deemed essential to this purpose?

WHERE DOES THE SCHOOL'S ROLE END?

We live within a complex web of different social and cultural relationships and networks that range from the local and familial to the national and the global, many if not all of which play a part in our total education. Yet the public school is not only universally available and publicly funded, it is also compulsory. Since the introduction of compulsory attendance legislation in Quebec in 1943, young people in Canada have been required by law to go to school (although across the country there are different legislative provisions relating to compulsory school ages, definitions of what constitutes a school, and the grounds on which one might be exempt from attending).

In the last half century the public school has been asked to take on more and more responsibility for shaping people's lives and addressing perceived social problems and challenges—from human sexuality and HIV/AIDS awareness to conflict resolution and education. This broadening of the school curriculum invites further debate and raises concerns from professionals that, when carried too far, it distorts the primary purpose of schools. Expecting teachers to be "all things to all people," they argue, prevents schools from successfully focusing on their traditional intellectual responsibilities. It also invites criticism from those parents and communities who see this expanding role as encroaching on, and undermining, the proper authority of the family and the community.

This debate over the appropriate scope of the socializing influences of the school curriculum has a long and vigorous history of both accommodation and confrontation in Canada. It has seen parents jailed and their children taken from them for not sending them to school; it has given rise to a range of different legal provisions for home schooling; and it is reflected in the array of different provincial regulations providing for the establishment, and sometimes public funding, of private/independent schools.

HOW DO SCHOOLS ALLOCATE STUDENTS INTO AN UNEQUAL AND COMPETITIVE SOCIAL ORDER?

To talk of preparing young people for adult lives requires us to give attention to how schools prepare particular students for particular roles in adult life, for whether we are discussing the labour market and our public lives or the social, emotional, and cultural aspects of our private lives, the diversity of adult roles is great. Within the sociology of education literature, the role of schools in allocating young people to positions within the existing economic structures is seen as a major purpose of the education system. Furthermore the public school is generally seen as an appropriate agency for doing this in a way that is acceptable and fair. Two views dominate the analyses of what schools do—and should do—in this regard. The meritocratic perspective sees schools as the neutral and benign vehicle through which students explore their interests and, based on individual talent and effort, acquire the skills and credentials appropriate to different occupations and statuses in society. The social reproduction perspective sees schools serving to perpetuate and legitimize existing inequities in terms of people's access to higher status occupations. According to this interpretation, family circumstances rather than individual talent and effort are the primary determinants of school success.

While both of these analyses offer insights into the ways schools currently function, they also serve to frame quite different visions of the role of the public school in Canadian society. It is possible to argue that while the 1960s, 1970s, and early 1980s saw a greater commitment to creating a pluralistic, inclusive, and meritocratic system, the more recent "market-driven" orientation to public education in a number of jurisdictions will increase the degree to which family circumstances impact upon school success. [4]

WHAT KNOWLEDGE? WHOSE KNOWLEDGE?

Notwithstanding the existence of home schooling provisions across the country, the private school system, and federally funded schools in First Nations' communities, close to 95 per cent of Canada's diverse student population attend provincially funded public schools and follow a curriculum prescribed by the provincial governments. As Canada has, in the second half of the twentieth century and the beginning of the twenty-first century, shifted from being a country with an explicitly assimilationist and Anglo-conformist (outside of Quebec) social policy to a multicultural society in which equality rights are embedded in the Constitution, the school curriculum has been expected to reflect this new reality.

Building a new public school curriculum that can simultaneously value and incorporate the diversity of experiences that children bring to the school as well as pay attention to the perceived demands of an increasingly technological and global social order is a challenge to policy-makers, curriculum designers, and teachers alike. On occasion this has led to pressures to develop culturally focused schools within the public school system, such as the Aboriginal-focused Niji Mahkwa and Children of the Earth high schools in Winnipeg. On other occasions it has seen the development of bilingual and trilingual public schools.

However, for many people the ideal of "the common school" where children from all walks of life come together and learn from one another still dominates much of our thinking about public schooling, and despite the fact that in many cities neighbourhood house prices serve to enforce their own forms of segregation, priority is given to developing curricula that are truly inclusive—which draw in/on the richness of knowledge and human experience in our diverse society and which support learning and school success for all students.

THE TRANSFORMATIVE ROLE OF SCHOOLS

For all of the challenges schools face to prepare society's young for the world as it is today, preparing them for the future magnifies the task in hand. Yet the role of schools has always been about building the future at the same time as it reflects the past and maintains the present. This is the notion reflected in the quote from the principal of the Winnipeg Normal School some seventy years ago at the beginning of this article and in Osborne's vision of the democratic ideal of public schools as "socializing children into a society that has yet to be created and by doing so make its creation possible."[5]

At a time when rapid and large-scale change is characterizing many aspects of our lives, preparing students for an uncertain future invites several different responses. For some, at least some aspects of Canada of the future are readily apparent, if not inevitable, and require an educational response—the call, for example, from Canada's business leaders for schools to pay greater attention to developing the skills they associate with a highly skilled, globally competitive labour force, or the need for schools to better prepare students to appreciate the cultural diversity that has long been and will increasingly become a hallmark of Canadian society. For others, little is either apparent or inevitable, and the task of schools is, more critically, to help create the future. It is in this context that the educative ideals of public school—more than just socialization—become of central importance. is by introducing students to the broadest possible range of knowledge and experiences and engaging them in an ongoing exploration of the "big questions" of life that we equip the next generation to recognize and challenge the failings and injustice within our present world and in doing so work to build a better one.

The challenge, then, is for schools to look beyond present values and priorities, to try to envision what the future will require. Ken Osborne, in his valuable discussion of citizenship education, argues that: Canada's existence requires special qualities in its citizens: acceptance of diversity, a willingness to live with ambiguity, an understanding of the nature of the country and a familiarity with its history and, not least, the ability to enter into the continuing debate that characterizes Canadian public life.[6]

If Canada's public schools are to nurture these qualities, it is important that they resist pressures of the neoconservative reform agenda to privilege labour market training over all other educational purposes and reaffirm the broader educational purposes of self-knowledge and democratic citizenship. If they fail to resist those pressures, says Osborne, "we will be neither individual men and women seeking to make the best of our lives, nor citizens engaged with others in a common enterprise, but only workers and consumers, fodder for the technological future."[7]

CONCLUSION

Finding the right balance between various pressures for socialization and the need to prepare for—and help to create—an unknown future demands that we engage in a public dialogue on public education that fosters support for public schools and public solutions to the challenges that they face. These debates need to take place at the individual school, school board, provincial and national levels, and they must be truly public, including—but not dominated by—the teaching profession. Paquette (1991) reminds us of both the uncertainty and the importance of this dialogue on public education when he says:

> Inevitably these solutions [to the complex challenges of public education policy] will be tentative and evolutionary, but they will be nonetheless important for the fact [that], since the quality of life that our children experience is intimately and inextricably related to the quality of the solutions we devise.[8]

REFLECTIVE QUESTIONS

1. Would you agree with Young that the school is a "highly visible instrument of social policy"? Explain why you think this is a good or a bad thing.

2. What have been some of the issues in the "never-ending curriculum debate" that Young identifies?

3. How important is the socialization role of schooling? Do Young's arguments support Kieran Egan's views on socialization in the article "What is curriculum?"

4. Do the two views of the purpose of schooling that Young describes resonate with your experience? Provide examples of each.

5. What do you envision that "the future will require" of an educated person?

NOTES

1. W. A. McIntyre (Winnipeg Normal School principal), 1932, p. 45, quoted in Ken Osborne, "Education for Democratic Citizenship," in *The Erosion of Democracy in Education: From Critique to Possibilities,* eds. John Portelli and R. Patrick Solomon (Calgary: Detselig, 2001), 56.

2. T. Wotherspoon, *The Sociology of Education in Canada* (Toronto: Oxford University Press, 1998).

3. J. Paquette, *Social Purpose and Schooling: Alternatives, Agendas and Issues* (London: Falmer Press, 1991), 2.

4. See D. Henley and J. Young, "An Argument for the Progressive Possibilities for Public Education: School Reform in Manitoba," in *The Erosion of Democracy in Education: From Critique to Possibilities,* eds. John Portelli and R. Patrick Solomon (Calgary: Detselig, 2001), 297–328.

5. Osborne in Portelli and Solomon, 51.

6. Ken Osborne, *Education: A Guide to the Canadian School Debate* (Toronto: Penguin, 1999), 21.

7. Ibid., 22.

8. Paquette, 178.

Part III

Contemporary Issues and Trends in Canadian Curriculum

Contemporary Issues
and Trends in Canadian
Curriculum

Understanding what is meant by "curriculum" and how it developed in Canada is important, but no overview of Canadian curriculum would be complete without examining issues that have affected the implementation and understanding of curriculum over the last decade and will likely continue to do so for some time. This last section of the book attempts to bring the discussion about curriculum in Canada to a more contemporary state of affairs. Some questions that you may wish to consider as you read the chapters in this section are:

- Where is curriculum and where should curriculum go in the twenty-first century? What will children really need to know?
- What do we value in Canadian society and does our education system reflect what we claim to value?
- What evidence is there of the push-and-pull between local, regional, and federal education bodies and other stakeholders who are currently influencing our curriculum?

The articles selected for inclusion in Part III of this anthology represent a wide range of contemporary issues and trends in Canadian curriculum including: multiculturalism; Aboriginal, global, and religious education; environmental stewardship; and gender and sexuality. These readings are but a sample of the articles that explore contemporary issues in curriculum development. They are not meant to be a comprehensive overview of all aspects of the issues under investigation but rather to provide you with a starting point for examining both the issues highlighted here as well as others that may arise, depending on your particular educational situation.

The first article in this section speaks to Aboriginal education. "In Their Own Voices: First Nations students identify some cultural mediators of their learning in the formal school system" begins by looking at the influence of culture on learning through the experiences of a group of First Nations high school students in Winnipeg. The author, Yatta Kanu, then identifies five themes that she feels should be addressed in pre-service education in order to enhance beginning teachers' socio-cultural communication with Aboriginal students.

Ethnic diversity is examined from a broader perspective in "Critical and Emerging Discourses in Multicultural Education Literature: A Review." In this article, Anna Kirova looks at current multicultural education practices in Canada. She identifies what she sees as major conceptual flaws in both multicultural theory and practice that work against the Canadian Multiculturalism Act. She then lays out some suggestions for addressing these flaws, including new ways of thinking about the meaning of culture, cultural difference, and cultural and national identities.

Louis Volante's "Equity in Multicultural Student Assessment" turns to the issue of assessment, specifically from the perspective of promoting cultural equity. It is argued that standardized tests narrow the curriculum by assessing what is easily measured, which erodes the teaching of higher-order thinking skills. Volante concludes that this issue is multifaceted and that to be truly equitable for all students, any decisions about assessment must include the broader community in order to better reflect home-related influences on learning.

Broadening the issue further to a global perspective, Lynette Shultz reviews variations in the approaches to global education in "Educating for Global Citizenship: Conflicting Agendas and Understandings." In this article, she compares and contrasts three approaches to globalization: neoliberal, radical, and transformational. Shultz argues that since the choice of approach taken can greatly influence the type of global citizen created, educators need to be clear about their goals when addressing global citizenship in the curriculum.

As Canadian curriculum developers consider issues of global citizenship, a related issue that comes up is what to teach, or how to teach, students about the environment. In "Transformative Environmental Education: Stepping Outside the Curriculum Box," Julie Johnston takes on the issue of environmental education by looking at what is currently being done in the name of environmental education, which the author feels is sorely lacking in the school curriculum. She also provides suggestions for encouraging transformative environmental education with a focus on sustainability.

Of course, some students will come to the classroom with different ideas about the environment and other issues. This is in part because the curriculum experienced by students is not confined to the classroom—outside life experiences influence students' understanding of any number of topics that infuse the curriculum. As Kelly Young points out in "Curriculum of Imperialism: Good Girl Citizens and the Making of the Literary Educated Imagination," outside organizations can play an important role in identity formation. In this article, she examines specifically the issue of gender in the curriculum as she discusses the ways in which organizations such as the Girl Guides teach the dominant view of what it means to be a good Canadian.

Sometimes when the topic of gender is raised, this can lead to a parallel discussion about sexuality. In " 'People who are different from you': Heterosexism in Quebec High School Textbooks," Julia Temple considers the issue of human sexuality through her examination of heterosexism in the content of Quebec high school textbooks. She demonstrates how textbooks can be used to portray dominant, hegemonic ideologies while ignoring other realities; in this case, forms of sexuality. She contends that heterosexism in textbooks and in the curriculum needs to be addressed by providing more attention to diverse ways of being.

The final article in this collection, "Religion, Public Education, and the Charter: Where do we go now?" addresses the issue of religious education in the curriculum. The overarching question asked is: "What role, if any, should religion have in Canada's public schools?" Clarke presents arguments both for and against the inclusion of religious education with the acknowledgement that the values and principles of the Canadian Charter of Rights and Freedoms need to be respected in any choices made. He provides several case studies to show how the Charter has been used to guide and resolve some religion-in-education issues.

As our society develops, there is no doubt that new trends will emerge that will need to be considered by those who develop and those who use curriculum. After all, to remain current, curriculum must not only change with the times but also imagine what is to come and respond to new issues and opportunities as they emerge.

15

In Their Own Voices:

First Nations students identify some cultural mediators of their learning in the formal school system

YATTA KANU

INTRODUCTION

The overall goal of the research reported in this article was the achievement of inclusivity in the classroom, more precisely how an improved understanding of the influence of culture on Aboriginal students' learning could result in more inclusive teaching and, therefore, higher academic achievement and school retention rates among Aboriginal students. The major premise undergirding the conceptual framework for this research was provided by socio-cultural theories of cognition that link the development of children's thinking, communication, learning, and motivational styles with the culture into which they are socialized and that argue that an intricate connection exists between culture and students' learning (Ramirez & Castañeda, 1974; Vygotsky, 1981; Wertsch, 1991; Winzer & Mazurek, 1998). According to Wertsch, for example, all forms of cognition are socially situated in the contexts of small groups and in the broader social and institutional settings, and cultural mediation constitutes one way by which cognitive processes become contextualized. Vygotsky asserts that various semiotic systems are used to negotiate meaning between individuals and to mediate higher mental functions. These systems develop in specific ways in different cultures and act as negotiators of meaning and as agents that transform mental functions. Winzer and Mazurek echo these claims in their argument that children's conceptual framework—their learning and thinking processes—are deeply embedded in their own cultures and that difficulties in classroom learning and interactions arise when there is a mismatch between a child's culture and all the intricate subsets of that culture and the culture of the teacher and the classroom, setting up that child for failure if the school or the teacher is not sensitive to his or her special needs. Cultural socialization, therefore, influences how students learn, particularly how they mediate, negotiate, and respond to curriculum materials, instructional strategies, learning tasks, and communication patterns in the classroom.

Although the link between cultural socialization and students' learning has been fairly well established in the academic literature, there is a dearth of research knowledge on the specific aspects or areas of culture that consistently mediate or influence the thought processes and learning of particular groups of students and that might provide insights for developing more appropriate instruction for pre-service teachers for the enhancement of cross-cultural communication, the design and implementation of assessment strategies, and the creation of effective instructional materials. Winzer and Mazurek (1998) have suggested that for investigating cultural differences in learning, three aspects of learning are especially significant: cognitive or learning style, communication style, and language differences.

Abundant empirical knowledge exists on how the outward manifestations of culture such as the customs, traditions, and behaviour codes of particular cultures affect the learning-teaching processes. Cultural variables such as the conception of time and how this affects teachers' assessment and evaluation of students' performance (Hamayan & Damico, 1991; Samuda, 1989), norms regarding competition and interdependence (Philips, 1983), proximity (Shade & New, 1993), nonverbal norms of communication as they assist teachers in comprehending the intended meanings of students (First, 1988; Yao, 1988), notions of fate and how this determines achievement (Lee & Krugly-Smolska, 1999), visual cues, ways of responding to persons in authority, and differences in the extent to which students are brought up to accomplish things on their own and arrive at their own independent opinions and decisions (Dao, 1991; Grossman, 1995) have all been identified as variables that must be understood by teachers. However, studies on cultural knowledge involving the understanding of the tacit variables that underlie these outward manifestations and that are seen to affect human cognition, identity, and people's modes of perception (Lee & Krugly-Smolska) are sparse. Notable among studies in this latter category found in the literature review are Kleinfeld and Nelson's (1991) study, which found no empirical support for the common conclusion that adapting instruction to Native Americans' learning styles—defined in terms of visual cognitive abilities—will increase academic achievement, and Kanu's (2001) more recent study that identified five cultural mediators of teacher learning in South Asia.

In Canada, a pluralistic and multicultural country with enormous diversity, this dearth of research-based knowledge to help teachers and teacher educators in their effort to achieve more culturally appropriate teaching has sometimes resulted in teachers' use of curriculum materials, teaching strategies, and learning tasks "intended to include all students," but which in fact inhibit participation and conceptual understanding for some students (Manitoba Teachers' Society, 1998), thereby excluding or marginalizing those students and hence severely curtailing their opportunities in life.

This study was undertaken in order to address this knowledge gap by investigating the influence of cultural socialization on the classroom learning of a particular group of students—students of Aboriginal ancestry—consistently perceived as failing in the high school classroom because of cultural differences between them and the formal school system.

THE RESEARCH PROBLEM

Beginning with the Hawthorn report (1966/67) and its claim that 97 per cent of Indian [sic] children dropped out of the public school system, research and other reports have consistently pointed out that public education has continued to fail Aboriginal youth. They leave the school system without the requisite skills to participate in the economic life of their communities and Canadian society, without the language and cultural knowledge of their people, with their identities and self-worth eroded, and without realizing the Aboriginal vision of culturally and linguistically competent youths ready to assume the responsibilities of their nations (Canadian Communication Group [CCG], 1996). This failure has been largely explained in terms of the rupture between the home culture of Aboriginal students and the processes and environments of the formal school system. The Royal Commission on Aboriginal Peoples (RCAP) reports that the efforts of Aboriginal educators and communities are currently directed towards restoring continuity between the home culture and the school, and significant strides in this area are reported. For example, First Nations Tribal Councils and locally elected school committees that have assumed local control and leadership of band-controlled schools; Aboriginal first language instruction and the teaching of Aboriginal languages; the staffing of schools with Aboriginal teachers; the inclusion of Aboriginal elders as teachers; and the development of curriculum grounded in the values, history, and traditions of Aboriginal peoples are all attempts to reduce the cultural discontinuity experienced by Aboriginal students in the formal education system (CCG, 1996). Provincial governments and school boards have also put many initiatives in place to create positive learning environments for Aboriginal students. For example, schools have hired Aboriginal teachers and Aboriginal support staff, and curriculum has been reviewed to eliminate obvious racism.

What are the overall results of all these efforts? According to the RCAP (CCG, 1996), gains have been modest, and much more needs to be done. Most success has been noticed in band-controlled schools that are located on reserves and that serve more homogeneous groups of students in terms of linguistic and cultural heritage (Haig-Brown, Hodgson-Smith, Regnier, & Archibald, 1997). According to Brady (1995), these schools often experience greater autonomy in responding to students' needs than schools in urban and rural settings where control remains in the hands of "paternalistic" bureaucracies (Corson, 1992). In provincial schools where most Aboriginal students outside of the territories attend school (Department of Indian Affairs and Northern Development [DIAND], 1994), parents and Aboriginal community members have little direct access to decision-making (Brady, 1995); no special effort is made to make them feel part of the life of the school, and the vast majority of teachers in these schools belong to the dominant mainstream culture. The lack of Aboriginal cultural knowledge among these teachers has generally resulted in pedagogical and interaction patterns that have resulted in negative learning experiences for Aboriginal students.

Since the 1960s Aboriginal people have responded by lobbying for programs that would bring Aboriginal teachers into public school classrooms. However, although there are many more Aboriginal teachers in Aboriginal and non-Aboriginal school systems and many more Aboriginal teacher education programs than a decade ago, the numbers remain far too low relative to current and projected needs (CCG, 1996). For the foreseeable future, therefore, efforts need to be made to infuse the preparation of teachers from mainstream culture with the history, languages, and pedagogical traditions of Aboriginal peoples, especially in provinces such as Manitoba where it is reported that the Aboriginal population has increased by 19 per cent, that Winnipeg has the highest concentration of Aboriginal persons in an urban area in Canada, and that Aboriginal youths make up a large proportion of the school-aged population in Winnipeg (Manitoba Bureau of Statistics).

The inspiration for this study arose from my experience as a teacher educator consistently observing pre-service teachers from dominant Euro-Canadian culture in high school classrooms in Winnipeg using teaching processes and curriculum materials that either ignored the Aboriginal students in their classrooms or elicited minimal participation from them. From conversations with a number of these pre-service teachers, I learned that they did not possess the cultural knowledge needed to adapt classroom materials and processes to ensure meaningful participation for the Aboriginal students in their classrooms.

It has been suggested that it is incumbent on teacher education programs to provide the sort of preparation that teachers need in order to work successfully with Aboriginal students in Canada's public schools (CCG, 1996). This research was premised on the belief that the beginning point for such teacher preparation is the interface between culture and students' learning.

The research had two specific purposes. The first was to identify specific aspects of Aboriginal cultural socialization that consistently influenced or mediated the way the Aboriginal students in the study received, negotiated, and responded to curriculum materials, teaching strategies, and learning tasks in their high school classrooms, specifically social studies classrooms. Knowledge of some cultural mediators of the learning of these Aboriginal students is critical to our understanding of how teachers could best adapt classroom materials and processes to enable similar groups of students to have generous and positive access to their heritage culture while also acquiring knowledge of, and confidence with, the content and codes of mainstream culture (Ellis, 1999).

A second purpose was to develop recommendations for teaching and teacher education that have the potential to provide the cultural support needed by Aboriginal students to succeed in their learning in the high school classroom.

For this study, culture was defined as those shared beliefs, values, and meanings that inform the educator about a learner's culturally determined learning and thought processes. As the process of the production of meaning on which different groups draw to make sense of their world, culture is socially and historically located (Kanu, 2001). Because economic status affects the influence of culture on cognition and learning, it is important to point out that all the students in the study came from low-income backgrounds, a factor that could account for any mismatch between their cognitive and learning experiences and the content and processes of the formal school system.

In line with Statistics Canada's (1996) definition, the term *Aboriginal* was used in this study to mean students of First Nations, Métis, and Cree ancestry. The Aboriginal students who participated in the study identified themselves as First Nations Ojibwa, Cree, and Métis.

RESEARCH QUESTIONS

The following questions guided the study:

1. What are some of the curriculum materials, learning tasks, and teaching strategies currently used by teachers who have been identified as successful with, and committed to, inclusivity in high school social studies classrooms with Aboriginal students? (Data collection method for this question consisted of classroom observations.)

2. What learning goals do teachers wish to achieve by using these materials, strategies, and learning tasks? (Data collection method: research conversations with teachers.)

3. How do these materials, strategies, and learning tasks facilitate class participation and conceptual understanding for Aboriginal students? (Data collection methods: research conversations with Aboriginal students; Aboriginal students' journals.)

4. What aspects of Aboriginal cultural socialization contribute to enhance or inhibit Aboriginal student participation and understanding when these materials, strategies, and learning tasks are used in the social studies classroom? (Data collection methods: research conversations with Aboriginal students; Aboriginal students' journals.)

5. What are the preferred classroom teaching and learning strategies of Aboriginal students? (Data collection method: research conversations with Aboriginal students.)

6. How are such classroom methods or strategies similar to or different from the dominant methods through which Aboriginal children learn in indigenous Aboriginal culture? (Data collection methods: research conversations with Aboriginal students; Aboriginal students' journals.)

7. What cultural support systems are teachers providing, and could provide, to enhance participation and conceptual understanding for Aboriginal students in the high school social studies classroom? (Information for this question came from the overall data collected during the research.)

Research Procedures and Methods

The site for this study was an inner-city high school in urban Winnipeg, selected because of its high Aboriginal student population and its interest in working with the Faculty of Education at the University of Manitoba to find teaching methods, processes, and curriculum materials that reach all students in the classroom. According to the vice-principal, the school is one of the toughest schools in the inner city. Every year over 600 students register, but only 300 complete the school year. Most of the students are teenage parents on welfare. Seventy-nine per cent of the students' parents are unemployed, and many of the students have experienced little success in their lives and need to be persuaded to come to school. In a school like this, courses are used more to improve the quality of students' lives than to transmit purely academic knowledge.

Data for the study were collected between April and June 2000 in an integrated grade 9 social studies classroom with 80 per cent Aboriginal students and teachers who had been identified as successful teachers of Aboriginal students and who had expressed a willingness to enhance their understanding of cross-cultural instruction.

There were three reasons for selecting a social studies classroom for this study.

First, social studies in one form or the other is a required course in all high school grades and was, therefore, likely to have a fair mix of Aboriginal and non-Aboriginal students in the classes. Second, I am a social studies instructor and was, therefore, more likely to understand the goals, concepts, and teaching processes targeted in these classrooms. Third, because social studies derives its subject matter from the social science disciplines, it offers opportunities for the use of a variety of curriculum materials, teaching strategies, and learning tasks that apply across a large number of subject areas.

Research participants for the study included ten students of Aboriginal ancestry (seven Ojibwa, two Cree, and one Métis) in a grade 9 social studies class and two teachers from the classroom involved in the study. One teacher was Caucasian and had taught grade 9 social studies for twenty-three years. The other was a black (African-Canadian) teacher who taught mainly science but provided support through individualized instruction during social studies lessons.

The total number of participants in the research was twelve, selected on the basis of their willingness to participate in the study. Because the research involved extensive intrusion into the classroom of the teachers and the lives of the students participating in the study, a great deal of sensitivity was brought to the research process. In line with Archibald's (1993) call to conduct research with mutual respect, trusting relationships were built between me (the researcher) and the research participants long before the research began. Entry into the school and the social studies classroom was negotiated through the help of the vice-principal (a Métis), who introduced me and my research intent to the teachers and students of the grade 9 social studies class. This introduction was followed by several visits to their classroom, first simply as a visitor sitting in on their classes. My intent was to make the students and the teachers feel comfortable with my presence in the class and for the teachers to realize that I was not there to be critical of their work or devalue what they were doing in their classroom. Rather, the intent was for us to work together as educators to find ways of arriving at more inclusive classroom teaching. Free and informed written consent of the teachers, students, and the parents of the students was obtained before starting the research, and research participants were given the option to withdraw from the study at any time.

This was an ethnographic study for which multiple data collection methods such as classroom observations, research conversations, and students' journals were used. According to Bogden and Biklen (1998), multiple data collection strategies lend credibility to a study because when data from multiple sources are triangulated, they increase the validity and reliability of results. The ethnographic method also offered me enhanced opportunities to understand the research participants in their own context and the reasons behind the data generated. In addition, ethnography offered the flexibility to follow and document events as they arose during the research, and provided substantially more complete and complex data on the questions under investigation (Cohen & Manion, 1985). Data collection methods for the study are described below.

Classroom observations. Classroom observations of curriculum materials, teaching strategies, and learning tasks used in the social studies classroom under study were carried out. There were ten one-hour classroom observations. Data collected through this means were later used as material for research conversations with participants.

Research conversations. Two sets of research conversations (each lasting one hour) were held with Aboriginal students in the study. The first set of conversations was intended to obtain participants' initial responses to the research questions and to the data from the classroom observations. The second set provided me with the opportunity to probe specific responses in more detail and explore any new questions and ideas that emerged. Research conversations were selected because, according to Gadamer (1984), such conversations have no predetermined answers and, therefore, offer the openness occasioned by the desire of the researcher and the research participant to know about a topic of mutual interest to them. "It is only during genuine conversation that the subject matter of the topic begins to emerge and take on recognizable meaning and adequate intelligibility. In this sense, conversation is not simply an incidental condition of inquiry, but . . . it is the very life of inquiry, discovery and truth itself" (p. 33).

Students' journals. Aboriginal students participating in the study were asked to maintain a journal where they documented the cultural experiences that influenced or mediated how they received, negotiated, and responded to curriculum materials, teaching strategies, and learning tasks in the social studies classroom.

The research conversations were audio-recorded, and field notes were written during classroom observations. Research conversations were transcribed verbatim, viewed, and returned to the participants for "member checks" (Lincoln & Guba, 1985) before being analyzed. Important sections of data collected from the multiple sources described above were highlighted and summarized. Doing so enabled me to gain an overview of what they offered concerning the research questions. As well, I was able to see whether the data gave rise to any new questions, points of view, and ideas. All data were coded and categorized using both deductive and inductive methods. Coded data were read and organized according to themes emerging from the data (Miles & Huberman, 1994). The themes were examined collaboratively with the participants in order to understand what certain data meant and how certain facts could be explained. Data analysis and interpretation, therefore, incorporated both emic and etic perspectives (Jones, 1979). Research narratives based on the collected data were constructed. To address the concern expressed in the RCAP (CCG, 1996) report that "Aboriginal people have had almost no opportunity to correct misinformation and to challenge ethnocentric and racist interpretations" (p. 235) and to give voice to the *other*, a key concern in this study, the research narratives were returned to the research participants for comments, changes, and/or confirmation before being included in the final report. According to Te Hennepe (1993), "Returning the text is to move the conversation into an outer circle and ask the people there if, in their opinion, the reconstructed conversation has integrity" (p. 236). Te Hennepe also writes, "the integrity of the speaker's words can be lost as the text writer creates a new telling of what was said" (p. 236). An attempt has been made to respect the participants' words or contributions by including them as quotes where appropriate to enrich the research narratives.

Where participants are quoted in the report, pseudonyms have been used to protect their identities. Therefore, the ten students are referred to as Mike, Ned, Kem, Rich, Liz, Joe, Don, Andy, Tim, and Jon. The teachers are referred to as Mrs. B. and Mr. X.

FINDINGS AND DISCUSSION

Analysis of the data generated from the research instruments revealed several findings related to the two major concerns of the research:

1. curriculum materials, learning goals, teaching methods or strategies, and student learning tasks currently used by successful social studies teachers of Aboriginal students;

2. aspects of Aboriginal cultural socialization that enhanced or inhibited Aboriginal student participation and conceptual understanding when these materials, strategies, and learning tasks were employed in the social studies classroom.

The curriculum materials, learning tasks or activities, teaching methods or strategies, and learning goals observed in the social studies classroom during the research are presented in TABLE 1.

The following section discusses the themes that emerged from my conversations with the Aboriginal students about the aspects of their culture that helped or hindered their learning.

Caveat. The study recognized the diversity present in Aboriginal cultural values and traditions, a few of which emerged in the research conversations with the Aboriginal students in this study who came from Ojibwa, Cree, and Métis backgrounds. However, there were sufficient common elements among them that appeared to conflict with the values, culture, and processes that are dominant in the conventional classroom. These common elements in the data provided the bases for the construction of themes.

TABLE 1: Curriculum materials, teaching methods or learning tasks, and learning goals in a grade 9 social studies class

Curriculum materials	Teaching methods or learning tasks	Learning goals
No prescribed textbooks were used. Materials were selected according to needs and interests of students, but of relevance to successful living in mainstream Canadian society. Materials used included the following:		
Stories with moral messages from the book *Chicken Soup for the Soul*.	Reading of the stories by the teacher; teacher-led discussion of questions on the stories (questions ranged from recall to higher levels of thinking).	To develop students' listening and comprehension skills; to develop higher level thinking; to provide student motivation through the moral lessons in the stories (e.g., perseverance, respect for self and others).
Concepts such as *stereotyping, discrimination, prejudice, racism, lazy* that depicted some of the lived experiences of many Aboriginal students. Concepts of more general relevance and application, for example, *supply and demand, critical consumer decision-making factors, advertising, motives for purchasing goods and services, human rights*.	Small-group discussion of concepts; two teachers and one teacher aide in the room provided support to students as they worked in groups; sharing of insights through oral presentations; teacher input through further discussion, examples, probing questions (scaffolding), and notes.	For students to understand the ignorance and discrimination present in stereotyping; for students to recognize their own prejudices; for students to improve their discussion and public speaking skills; to relate curriculum to students' daily lives.
Pictures of accomplished Aboriginal people in respected professions.	Whole-class teacher-led discussion through higher-level thinking questions that encouraged student participation (expression of ideas and opinions).	To make the curriculum relevant to the Aboriginal students (students see themselves in positive ways in the curriculum); students will be motivated by positive role models.
"The Canadian Scrapbook: Looking back on Aboriginal early lives."	Independent and small-group worksheet activities; scavenger hunt locating information from pages already identified by the teacher (scaffolding research work); individualized instruction by teachers; whole-class discussion of student responses.	For Aboriginal students to understand their rich history; for students to develop research skills.
Teacher's notes on transparencies and other visual aids.	Visual aids were used by the teacher to explain certain concepts. Notes provided lesson summaries for students.	To support student learning through visual examples.

THEMES RELATING TO CULTURAL INFLUENCES ON ABORIGINAL STUDENTS' LEARNING

Theme 1: Traditional Aboriginal Approaches to Learning

Four traditional (meaning Aboriginal indigenous approaches to learning practised outside the formal school system) practices in Aboriginal culture were found to have enhanced or hindered the participation and conceptual understanding of the Aboriginal students in the social studies classroom where the research was conducted, as follows.

Learning through stories. All the students in the study agreed that the story reading method adopted by their social studies teacher was effective in helping them understand the concepts and messages contained in each story. Consistent with claims by Cruikshank with Sidney, Smith, and Ned (1990) and Haig-Brown (1997) that in Aboriginal culture narratives are often used for teaching about cultural norms, the students provided the following cultural reasons for the effectiveness of the storytelling method.

In indigenous Aboriginal culture traditional stories, legends, songs, and many other forms of knowledge are passed on among generations by continual retelling (through stories) by elders and leaders who carry the knowledge of these spoken forms in their memories. As one research participant put it,

> My grandmother knows these stories inside out. My parents also know them and I learn the stories from them all. We all know the songs that go with each story. (Don)

Armstrong (Kirkness with Bowman, 1992) affirms these claims when she writes, "Aboriginal traditional education is a natural process occurring during everyday activities (such as storytelling)...ensuring cultural continuity and survival of the mental, spiritual, emotional and physical well-being of the cultural unit and of its environment" (p. 7).

Children develop a sense of morality by observing parents and elders modelling certain behaviours and through stories and legends they hear from parents and elders.

> We learn what is right and wrong from these stories. For example, many stories of hunting my grandpa has told me are about being honest about the number of catches each person had on a group hunting trip. (Jon)

Stories offer important ways for individuals to express themselves safely (e.g., convey messages of chastisement without directly preaching the message or specifically moralizing or blaming the culprit). According to Archibald (1993), First Nations peoples' stories are shared with the expectation that the listeners will make their own meaning, that they will be challenged to learn something from the stories. Stories, therefore, appear to contain layers of meaning that listeners decode according to their readiness to receive certain teachings.

> You just get the message as you listen to the story and you loosen up and improve your behaviour, if you want to. (Ned)

Learning through observation and imitation. A second learning approach that appeared to have a strong basis in Aboriginal culture emerging from the study was observational learning. Probing questions during our research conversations revealed a close link between learning by observation and imitation and some traditional childrearing practices that have survived in many Aboriginal families. It appears from these conversations and others I had with four of my own university students (two white and two Aboriginal) that whereas white children, for example, by virtue of their upbringing and their linguistic overexposure are oriented toward oral communication as a vehicle for learning, Aboriginal children have developed a learning style characterized by observation and imitation as children and adults in the extended family participate in everyday activities. Joe, a student in the study, elaborated on this approach to learning:

> When they [parents, grandparents, or teachers] actually show you and you see it in action, it's easier for you to grab.

Kem, another student, linked this learning method to preparation for adult responsibility:

> Actually seeing how something is done, instead of reading how it's done, that's hard to remember. When you watch how it is done it automatically clicks in your head. It's like making bannock, you learn to make it by watching the older people and then making it by yourself.

By contrast, students in the study pointed out that the "talk approach" to much of school instruction actually inhibited classroom learning for them. In an effort to reconcile these data with the benefits of oral instruction earlier touted by these participants during our discussion about storytelling, I asked them for clarification. Liz's comment below reflected those made by the rest of the students:

> Do you remember how I said some teachers explain too much and too fast? That really confuses me. I get lost in the explanation. But Mr. X., he cuts it down to size, right to the chase, works the formula on the board, which I watch step by step. I like that.

It appears that although oral instructional methods such as storytelling are an important cultural approach to learning for these students, the verbal saturation that characterizes much of school instruction, especially when this instruction is fast-paced and delivered in a different language, is not conducive to academic success for them. Haig-Brown et al. (1997) support this finding with their description of the concise communication style of the Aboriginal mathematics teacher they observed at Joe Duquette High School, an Aboriginal community school. They write:

> His directions are minimal, short, almost abrupt: "Put your name at the top. Straight multiplication. Maximum, five minutes and there is a table at the top. Five seconds. Start." There are no words wasted, no wasted time. One might think of the speaker in another class telling the students of his learning that the Cree language is a gift of the creator to be used wisely. (p. 110)

This finding is significant because such learning style differences have far-reaching consequences in the formal education of Aboriginal students, particularly in view of the fact that the formal education system almost always favours those who are highly verbal.

Community support encourages learning. Learning through verbalization was also disparaged by the students for another reason: the perceived lack of support in the integrated classroom community. All but one Ojibwa participant pointed out that the teaching-learning method they found most uncomfortable was when they were called on to make an oral presentation in front of the class. The students revealed that they were intimidated by the direct criticism that this method entailed in the formal (Western) school system. Jon's comment on this point is instructive:

> It's like they are looking out for the mistakes you make and they pounce on you. Even the teachers sometimes make you feel dumb by the questions they ask after you have presented something. . . . It's like they don't believe you, because they don't understand.

I probed further to see how learning might be different in the Aboriginal community, and Ned said:

> In the [Aboriginal] community, if you don't have the right answer you are not criticized directly, and you ask for some help because you know the people that are around you, so you feel secure. Also, in the community you are doing it for the community so everyone pitches in. . . . In school, although you know the teacher and the other class members, you are on your own. You are doing it for your own education as an individual. As far as school is concerned, I don't look forward to sharing my responses.

This finding is consistent with Brant's (1990) documentation of parenting and social interaction in some Aboriginal cultures as entailing *non-interference*, meaning refraining from directly criticizing the individual. It is also consistent with Collier (1993) who, based on her research on teaching Aboriginal students, made a suggestion: "never put Native students on the spot [by] asking them directly by name to answer a question in public" (p. 114).

For these Aboriginal students silence seemed to be the best defence mechanism in an integrated class where they felt they were among white strangers whom they have been raised to believe are constantly critical of them. Chris's comment spoke to this point:

> Yeah, that's why I prefer to remain silent in class. . . . It's just that I don't really know and trust people here. At home and in my community, I know and trust people, so I just blabber along without fear of making mistakes or being criticized. But when school starts, I don't talk, period, so they leave me alone.

Te Hennepe (1993), in her study of the experiences of First Nations students in university anthropology classrooms, quotes one of her interviewees, Mary, on how Native students deal with the breakdowns that occur when the expected respect and authority of their voices are violated in the learning process.

> When a Native student goes into a classroom, part of you is removed and sort of your Indian spirit is put apart from you, so you are separated so you can deal with the mainstream societal values. You try to talk about Native matters that are in the text without using the eyes of your Indian spirit. . . . When you look at it with your wholeness all that emotional stuff wells up. You try to see it through their eyes. When you leave the room your spirit is back. This is how I deal with the pain. Remove yourself from your body. Your spirit is up there waiting for you. You are up there and looking at yourself. You look back and you see compliance. You comply. (p. 257)

Some researchers have explained the classroom silence of Native students in terms of *interference theory*, which states that Native children in non-school contexts "talk a mile a minute" and that their silence in class derives from the culture of the classroom because the instructor and context require a different language to learn material that is foreign (Whyte, 1986). Whyte writes, "The problem (of classroom silence) lies not with the child but rather is an educational problem of designing a learning setting which is right for the children—in which children feel comfortable and secure enough to participate verbally" (p. 297).

The Ojibwa participant who said he was not uncomfortable with oral classroom presentations is a clear indication that membership in a certain group does not predict behaviour; it only makes certain types of behaviour more probable.

This shows that culture is not a unified whole, and although there may be distinctive learning patterns among cultures, great variations exist among individuals within groups (Winzer & Mazurek, 1998).

Learning through scaffolding. When asked about the type of support they needed to help them learn most in social studies, the data indicated that all the students in the study required some form of scaffolding or temporary framework of support, at least until they were able to develop the skills to learn independently. Forms of scaffolding identified included: direct guidance and support from the teacher through detailed and slow explanations (Jon, Liz, Rich, Mike); numerous examples (Jon, Ned, Andy); and explicit steps to follow in the performance of a given task (all except Ned). Data from the classroom observation showed that the two teachers and one teacher's aide in the classroom provided these structures to enhance Aboriginal students' learning.

These three forms of support appear to have direct foundations in childrearing practices among certain Aboriginal peoples where children are socialized to accomplish tasks largely through the support, direct guidance, and feedback from parents and other significant adults. Don compared this classroom support to what he obtained at home:

> Mrs. B., Mr. X., and Ms. T. always go round when we are working on our own, to explain more about what we are to do. It helps a lot, just like at home.

Learning through visual sensory modes. Eight of the ten participants in the study pointed out that they were better able to understand and retain concepts when these were presented through visual images. Ned, for example, said:

> Mrs. B. can explain something verbally over and over and many of us still ask her for further clarification. But when we see it in pictures or on transparency, when the overhead comes on, it is different, probably because it is bright. It does grab your attention and then you see the material as she is talking about it. It's like a different way of learning.

Liz agreed:

> For me too. I understand better when I actually see an image or picture of something, which the teacher is talking about.

Rich added,

> She [Mrs. B.] gets our attention better with things we actually get to see. Most of the students stop fooling around when the transparency comes on, for example. That's why many of us also like to learn on the computer. We actually see the images in front of us and then understanding becomes less difficult.

However, although these findings are consistent with Grossman's (1995) assertion that Native American and Alaskan Native youth tend to be visual learners, the claims to elevated visual abilities need to be established by further research. Psychological research is still inconclusive about whether visualization abilities are higher among Aboriginal groups than among comparative groups. For example, Berry (1966) in several studies found that Canadian Inuit indeed scored considerably higher on various spatial and visual tests than comparative groups from West Africa and Scotland, but Mackinnon (1972) failed to replicate this finding in a small study of Canadian Inuit students. Berry (1969), however, theorizes that the ecological demands of a particular environment, along with the cultural group's adaptation to that environment, may press for the development of a particular pattern of cognitive abilities.

Kleinfeld (1971), in a study conducted in the United States, also found that Inuit village students exceeded urban students of the same ages on a modified version of the Memory for Designs Test. However, because the students in my study were neither Inuit nor village students, further research is needed to develop a theoretical basis for their claims to elevated visual abilities. Furthermore, there is a dearth of reviews in the literature on the effects of instruction adapted to the ability patterns and learning styles of Native groups in both Canada and the US. Of the three studies found by Kleinfeld and Nelson (1991) on the proposition that adapting instruction to Native groups' learning styles would increase achievement, two studies did not show that Native groups learn more with visually based instruction. Another study found support for the proposition in one site but not in another, and the visually based instruction was even more effective for Caucasian students. These findings called into question the notion that instruction was effective because it was "culturally adapted" and established the need for further research into the hypothesis that instruction adapted to Native groups' visual learning style will enhance learning.

Theme 2: Effective Oral Interaction Between Teacher and Aboriginal Students Assist Learning

This theme emerged from our conversations about cultural and socio-economic class differences in patterns of oral interactions between parents and children. Heath (1983), from a study conducted on linguistic interactions among different cultural and socio-economic groups, established that white middle-class parents communicate with their children largely through indirect statements (e.g., "Is this where the scissors belong?") whereas working-class whites and African-American parents from all socio-economic classes are more likely to use directives such as "Put the scissors back on the shelf."

The data in my research suggest that Aboriginal parents also communicate with their children mainly through the use of such directives. Two of the research participants, for example, said:

> They [parents] tell me directly what they expect me to do; they do not leave it up to me to figure out what they mean. (Liz)

> Mr. X. [the black teacher] tells you straight what he requires from you. I like that. (Don)

Because teachers in Canadian classrooms are mainly white and come from middle-class backgrounds, Aboriginal students are less likely to understand what to do if the teacher uses indirect statements. Research (Heath, 1983; Philips, 1983) has shown how a mismatch between a child's linguistic culture and that of the teacher and the classroom can adversely affect learning and academic achievement. Clarity is important to school success because students are judged by what they produce in class and on tests. Such product, based as it is on the specific codes of a particular culture (English or French in the case of Canada), is more readily produced when the directives of how to produce it are made explicit. The study data strongly suggested that effective teachers of Aboriginal students offer clarity about what they demand, and they provide structures that help students produce it.

Theme 3: Concepts of Self

This finding refers to notions of the self, how the self is constructed and understood, and how this construction mediates the learning process in different cultures. Bearing in mind that any ontological boundaries of the self are primarily theoretical (most theorists propound hybrid concepts of what constitutes the self), the research revealed that the Aboriginal students in this study understood and described notions of the self and how the self is constructed in Aboriginal culture largely in terms of interdependence, communality, and social relatedness more than, say, Caucasian groups who frequently de-emphasize the relationship between personality and culture and tend to treat the self as a relatively self-contained agent. Because these Aboriginal students viewed themselves less as a separate psychological unit and more as a part-function of the cultural forces from which they emerged, they identified a cultural model of learning that is grounded in Aboriginal cultural values such as co-operation, collaboration, group effort, and group rewards. In school these values would lend themselves well to group work and co-operative tasks, and it was, therefore, not surprising that eight of the ten research participants disclosed that they thrived better as learners in co-operative, collaborative, or group work situations. However, they also pointed out that because group work and co-operative learning tasks in school were not usually organized effectively for productive work, group work had actually hindered rather than promoted learning for them. Several of them elaborated on this point, as the following quotes demonstrate.

> You see, it's different in school than in the [Aboriginal] community. In the community everybody participates equally or almost. You have a bunch of people who carry an equal share of the task and they know it is for the good of the community. So everyone does their part and you learn from each other. In school no one in the group cares, really. Group members do not share their opinions or ideas. (Don)

> And they make a lot of noise during group work. (Liz)

> Yes, and if you have someone smarter than the other people in the group, then they are going to rely on that one person for all the ideas. (Mike)

> So I think what we need is better group work organization from them [the teachers]. I like group work because you can talk to others. You can discuss your ideas if you don't understand something, like in the community. . . . But in class that does not happen in groups. (Ned)

Haig-Brown et al. (1997) have pointed out that communal work is integral to life and each day in the Aboriginal community and that community members work together, each taking on the responsibilities appropriate to their knowledge abilities.

However, caution is needed in interpreting this finding as specific only to Aboriginal students. In a study conducted into the learning styles of various cultural groups in the US, Cox and Ramirez (1981) found that many culturally diverse students are more group-oriented, more sensitive to social environments, and more positively responsive to adult modelling than are Euro-American students.

It is clear from these discussions that more needs to be done in the area of co-operative group work in schools to enable Aboriginal students to benefit from it academically by drawing on the co-operative, collaborative, and communal aspects of their culture to enhance their learning. Boyle-Baise and Grant (Ellis, 1999) have reported that teachers did not generally acknowledge group membership as an important part of some students, insisting that all students are individuals with individual differences.

Theme 4: Curriculum Relevance Enhances Aboriginal Students' Learning

Relevant curricula have long been acknowledged as supporting and promoting successful learning for all students, and according to the RCAP (CCG, 1996) report, this requirement is seen by Aboriginal people as one of three fundamental issues in the education of Aboriginal children and youth (the others are Aboriginal language education and Aboriginal control and parental involvement). Curriculum relevance for success in school learning is particularly important for minority students such as those of Aboriginal ancestry for two reasons. First, educationists (Greene, 1993) have observed that despite all the exposure to difference in the world today and the increasing interest in pluralism and the existence of multiple realities, Eurocentric and patriarchal views still persist where curriculum and learning are concerned. Second, minority students continue to be treated largely as invisible when they are made to experience textbooks and linguistic conventions considered to be neutral but that in fact assume a subject from the dominant white culture (Ellis, 1999). Furthermore, as one of the students in the study said during one of our conversations relating to photographs of successful Aboriginal professionals that Mrs. B. had used as curriculum material for two of her social studies lessons,

> Aboriginal people are seen [in white society] as backward, stupid, and responsible for their own failure. When one individual fails to make it, everyone in the culture is called a failure. (Rich)

For this reason, although the research participants said they would appreciate exposure to non-Aboriginal curriculum content because, as Liz put it, "the exposure helps us learn about other perspectives and cultures," they overwhelmingly agreed that seeing positive representations of themselves (Aboriginal people in general) more regularly in the school curriculum would validate their identity, motivate them to participate more in class, and help them develop pride in their own culture and people. According to one student, such a curriculum would also nurture their aspiration for the future:

> Yeah, these pictures [of successful Aboriginal people] make you feel like you have a chance. You walk downtown Winnipeg any day and all you see is [sic] Aboriginal people lying on the ground either completely drunk or asking for change. That feels really depressing and hopeless. But when you see pictures of Aboriginal people who have succeeded—police officers, lawyers, and all that—you feel you have a chance and you push yourself more in school to be like them. (Ned)

Research participants also pointed out that in addition to positive images of Aboriginal people, curriculum should include Aboriginal perspectives, histories or traditions, and interests, all of which have foundations in their cultural heritage but which have been largely denied them in the formal school system:

> In my previous school, there was nothing in grade 7 or 8 social studies about us [Aboriginal people]. We learned about people through different ages—Greeks, Romans, Egyptians, but nothing really about Aboriginal people or if there was, we did not cover it in class. (Mike)

> Here in this school at least, Aboriginal students are in the majority and sometimes in social studies, some of our lessons have Aboriginal material. But in my former school, the teachers generally did not talk about us as part of the lesson. . . . Yeah, maybe they were scared to offend us. (Liz)

Referring to the importance of cultural heritage in learning, Bintz (Ellis, 1999), after teaching language arts to mature-aged Aboriginal students in an Aboriginal studies program in Australia, wrote:

> I began to see how they operated from and through a cultural heritage, that is, from a deeply embedded and culturally defined system of values, beliefs and meanings about the social world. More importantly, I learned that this system significantly influences and reflects what students value and why they value it and, therefore, is central, not peripheral, to creating curriculum in the classroom that is culturally relevant and personally meaningful. (p. 177)

As Ellis (1999) elaborates, without the knowledge or the interest to begin planning curriculum from an appreciation of who students are or what they know or care about, teachers tend to seek diagnostically and remediate what they think is missing in students.

Theme 5: Teacher's Interpersonal Style

Under this theme are subsumed many subthemes that emerged to describe those dimensions of teacher interpersonal style that are effective in eliciting intellectual participation from the Aboriginal students in the study. These dimensions, in order of importance to the study participants, are as follows.

Respect

All the research participants identified respect as the most important dimension of the teacher's interpersonal style. Because research on cultural difference has found that various cultures may hold different views of behaviours that express such feelings as respect (Wax & Thomas, 1961, in Kleinfeld & Nelson, 1991), participants were asked to elaborate on what they meant by respect in teacher-student interactions. For them respect referred to the following teacher behaviours.

> Not stereotyping me as the drunken, failed Indian whose image the teacher already has in mind. (Ned)

> Treating me like I already have something the teacher respects. (Liz)

> Not making me feel dumb in front of the whole class. Treat me like I know something which the teacher may not know . . . everybody knows something. (Don)

> It is as simple as valuing and understanding me as a person. Like, just teach the way you want to be treated. . . . You know, teach with respect for us as individuals and do not treat us like we are all the same. (Rich)

This finding supports the interview conducted by Haig-Brown et al. (1997) with sixteen students of Aboriginal ancestry (Cree, Ojibwa, Métis, and Saulteaux) from Joe Duquette High School, in which all the students identified respect as "the number one rule" for successful interactions among the teachers, staff, and students in the school. According to these researchers, respect is integral to traditional Aboriginal values. They write: "Respect encompasses the understanding that children are complete human beings given as gifts from the Great Spirit on loan to adults who share with them the responsibility for preparing them for life's journey" (p. 46). They also quoted what a member of the school's Parent Council said about respect during an interview: "You are born as equal and you are born with respect . . . every individual has it [respect] and you don't have to earn it" (p. 46).

Strictness

Although earlier research (Brant, 1990) has documented the practice of non-interference (meaning not attempting to control the behaviour of others by direct intervention) as a prominent characteristic of parenting and social interaction in many Aboriginal cultures, the image of the teacher as a strict disciplinarian emerged as the second most important characteristic of the teacher's interpersonal style. With one exception (the Métis student in the study who said he was being raised by his Cree grandmother), participants seemed to expect their teachers to be strict, intolerant of nonsense, and act like the authority figures they are. Otherwise the message is sent that this adult has no authority, and the students react accordingly. As the following quotations show, the Aboriginal students in this study firmly believed in this strict image of the teacher.

> I think Mrs. B., I don't know what it is, but she should be tougher with us. After all she is the teacher, she has the authority. (Jon)

> I agree with Jon. She needs to be stricter to keep the class more in order. Some people call her down and treat her anyhow . . . whatever, and she just stands there. (Mike)

> Some of the things kids do in her class, I know I can never get away with at home. I know my boundaries and how far I can take my family, especially my dad. If I go past that boundary I know I am in trouble . . . probably get grounded for days or something, without any argument. I was surprised at first at what she [Mrs. B.] was tolerating from them. (Ned).

From the above quote from Ned, it appeared that his surprise had foundation in the teaching traditions of some First Nations where elders and parents, as respected teachers, convey to the young the acceptable rules of behaviour and the values to be honoured through subtle verbal and nonverbal communication (CCG, 1996). Such a teacher is a role model whose own behaviour and attitudes are absorbed by the children.

Another possible reason why these Aboriginal students expected an authority figure to act with authority is that in Aboriginal culture, authority is earned through effort and exhibited by personal characteristics, as opposed to authority being achieved by the acquisition of an authoritative role. According to Mike,

> In the community, like the chief—this is just an example—like the chief is chief because he has done many good things in his personal life and in the community to deserve to be chief. He has that authority. The teacher is the same . . . I mean she has qualifications, and therefore, the authority. She should act with authority.

Many middle-class teachers do not perceive authority in this way and may attempt to reduce the implications of overt power in order to establish a more egalitarian and non-authoritarian classroom atmosphere. However, if the students operate under another notion of authority, as the Aboriginal students in this study seemed to be doing, they may perceive the middle-class teacher as weak, ineffective, and incapable of taking on the role of teacher.

However, as indicated above, the image of the teacher as a strict individual wielding authority in the classroom did not seem to hold for the Métis participant, suggesting that the cultural values and traditions of Aboriginal peoples are diverse. In response to Ned's comments about behavioural boundaries he had to observe at home, this Métis student said:

> Jeez, I can never live like that. My grandmother lets me do what I want. I go and come as I like, no questions asked. Sometimes, I go for two days . . . as long as I stay out of trouble. (Chris)

Chris's comment is consistent with Brant's (1990) claim that in some Aboriginal cultures,

> the principle of non-interference predominates. The child's will is respected, and adults do not interfere in the choices made by the child. The imposition of the adult's will on the child is inappropriate except, of course, in instances where the child may encounter harm. (CCG, 1996, p. 454).

English-Currie's (1990) description of her upbringing as a member of the Blackfoot Nation in what is now Alberta also echoes this claim. She writes:

> This non-interference, non-directive approach determined a basis for a future lifestyle. We matured rapidly and we became adept at determining our own actions and making our own decisions, while being sensitive to the expectations of the collective and to our elders. (p. 50)

The contrast between this laissez-faire approach and the regimentation of the classroom experience, including the exertion of the teacher's authority, may constitute a discontinuity between the school and the child's home environment. This cultural conflict has been cited in several documents as a threat to the Aboriginal child's identity in the formal education system and a major cause of school failure (Wuttunee, in CCG, 1996).

Personal Warmth

The data revealed that nine of the ten participants in the study expected their teachers to treat them with emotional warmth and have personal relationships with them. This finding is consistent with the report of Haig-Brown et al. (1997) that teachers at Joe Duquette High School referred to their students as "extended families" (p. 142), and students referred to their teachers as "friends," "second parents," and "sensitive" (p. 122). It is also consistent with Collier's (1993) position that Native students like to have personal relationships with their teachers.

Warmth as a teacher attribute emerged during our conversation about the effectiveness of the individualized instruction each student regularly received from the two teachers and one teacher's aide present during each lesson. Ned's comment on this point was typical and instructive:

When she [Mrs. B.] is teaching from in front of the room, she is kind of far from you and she is usually talking to everyone, not to any of us in particular except if she is addressing a question to someone specifically. But when we are working on our own and all three of the teachers go round and help us individually, that helps a lot.

Wishing to find out more about how this personal contact or closeness, as opposed to the professional distance teachers typically maintained in the classroom, enhanced Aboriginal students' learning, I asked Ned to elaborate on his comment and he said,

Well, I mean, the close contact means personal attention. When they come close to you, sometimes they bend down to your seat level and you tell them your specific problem and they explain and help you. When you get the point right, sometimes they pat you on the back. They are also more friendly one on one.

Research shows that individualized instruction has a positive effect on student academic achievement in general. For Aboriginal students in particular, individualized instruction appears to carry added benefit because of its significance in communicating the warmth that these students perceived as important in interactions between them and their teachers. Joe expressed this feeling best in his closing comment on this aspect of our conversation:

When they [the teachers] are that close and personal you get the feeling they care.

However, the effect of personal warmth on Aboriginal students' intellectual performance needs to be further investigated. Many studies with white students have also found warmth to be a central dimension of teacher behaviour related to outcomes such as student attentiveness (Ryans in Kleinfeld & Nelson, 1991), productivity (Cogan in Kleinfeld & Nelson, 1991), and achievement (McKeachie & Lin in Kleinfeld & Nelson, 1991).

Data from my study do not suggest that all "respectful," "strict," and "warm" teachers are good teachers of Aboriginal students. They do, however, suggest that there are different notions among different cultural groups about which characteristics make for a good teacher. It is, therefore, impossible to create a model of the good teacher without taking issues of cultural and community contexts into account.

TENTATIVE RECOMMENDATIONS

Based on the above findings and discussions, the following tentative recommendations were developed for teaching and teacher education that have the potential to enable Aboriginal students to draw generously and positively on their cultural heritage to acquire the school knowledge and mainstream cultural codes they need to succeed in Canadian society.

1. The use of indigenous Aboriginal approaches to teaching and learning, such as storytelling and learning through observation and imitation, should be encouraged in classrooms with Aboriginal students. Storytelling especially has been found to be a most powerful teaching tool for making abstract ideas intelligibly concrete to students (Osborne, 2000) and should, therefore, be used more often to arouse the interest not only of Aboriginal students, but all students in the classroom.

2. Teaching methods largely characterized by fast-paced talk as a main vehicle for bringing about students' learning should be minimized. The verbal saturation characterizing current teaching in schools appears to impede Aboriginal students' learning.

3. Until they have developed the skills for independent learning in the formal education system, Aboriginal students should be provided with learning scaffolds in the form of detailed explanations, numerous concrete examples of concepts under classroom discussion, and explicit steps to follow in the performance of a given learning task.

4. Until conclusive research evidence emerges to disprove the claim that instruction adapted to Native groups' visual learning style will increase learning, visually based instruction should be maximized in classrooms with Aboriginal students.

5. Because of the existence of cultural differences in patterns of oral interactions, classroom communication by teachers should offer clarity (preferably in directive language) about what is required (the product) from Aboriginal students in the classroom.

6. Without belittling the importance of independent thinking and independent work in the teaching of Aboriginal students, as many opportunities as possible should be provided for co-operative and collaborative group work. In doing so, care must be taken to build the elements of accountability and equitable distribution of work into co-operative or collaborative tasks to increase their academic benefits for all students, but more so for Aboriginal students for whom this approach to learning seems to have a cultural basis. Collier (1993) endorses this recommendation when she posits that an added benefit of small-group work for Native students is that it provides them with easier opportunities to speak and go over the material than larger-class situations.

7. To increase motivation for learning among Aboriginal students, curriculum materials and classroom teaching-learning processes must include Aboriginal

perspectives, histories, cultures, and successes and should nurture high aspirations for Aboriginal students while also exposing them to non-Aboriginal curriculum materials. Here infusion rather than once-in-a-while add-on materials and activities should be stressed. As Banks (1994) has pointed out, culturally sensitive education is a dynamic and ongoing process. Add-on programs often trivialize ethnic cultures and view ethnic content from the perspective of mainstream culture.

8. Aboriginal students seem to expect their teachers to be strict, show personal warmth toward them, and show respect for them and for their own knowledge and experiences. Teaching and teacher education aimed at enhancing Aboriginal students' learning must, therefore, encourage the development of these teacher characteristics.

9. Supportive classroom environments should be created to increase opportunities for oral participation by Aboriginal students. Whyte (1986) states that the verbal capacity of Indian or Métis students may have been underestimated, with the end result in some cases of their being streamed away from academic programs, which emphasize verbal skills.

SUGGESTION FOR FURTHER RESEARCH

This was a small-scale exploratory study undertaken to identify Aboriginal cultural aspects that mediate or influence the learning of some students of Aboriginal ancestry in the formal school system. Some specific hypotheses concerning such cultural mediators have been developed as a result of this study. As the above discussions of the study's findings indicate, research is still largely inconclusive about many claims relating to specific or predominant Aboriginal cultural ways of learning, highlighting the difficulty in arriving at any final "formula" for helping a cultural group perform better in an educational setting. Indeed, researchers still have to resolve whether optimal results are achieved when the learning styles of any cultural group or individual are systematically matched to curriculum and instructional methods (Curry, 1990). Some (Franklin, 1992; Miller-Lachman & Taylor, 1995) have pointed out that accommodating cultural learning styles of at-risk students consistently has resulted in increased academic achievement, increased attendance and retention, and gains in reading and mathematics (Carbo & Hodges, 1991). Others (Kleinfeld & Nelson, 1991), however, have concluded that although ample evidence documents that certain learning styles tend to be predominant in certain cultures (i.e., patterns exist in how members of different groups approach tasks), there is no demonstrable impact on achievement when teachers try to match specific teaching strategies to specific aspects of students' cultural learning style preferences.

At this point, further research designed to test rigorously the key findings of my study in a larger population needs to be carried out in order to develop more informed recommendations to guide teacher education and teaching.

REFLECTIVE QUESTIONS

1. What evidence does the author provide in this article of the "intricate connection [that] exists between culture and students' learning"?
2. What does Kanu suggest would be "culturally appropriate teaching" for Aboriginal youth?
3. In your teacher training program, what preparation did you have for teaching Aboriginal students? Was the acquisition of "cultural knowledge" a part of your program?
4. How do the findings from Kanu's study inform your understanding of working with Aboriginal students?
5. What implications does this study have for curriculum development?

REFERENCES

Archibald, J. (1993). Researching with mutual respect (editorial). *Canadian Journal of Native Education, 20,* 189–192.

Banks, J. A. (1994). *Multicultural education: Theory and practice* (3rd ed.). Boston, MA: Allyn & Bacon.

Berry, J. W. (1966). Temne and Eskimo perceptual skills. *Journal of International Psychology, 1,* 207–299.

Berry, J. W. (1969). Ecology and socialization as factors in figural assimilation and the resolution of binocular rivalry. *International Journal of Psychology, 4,* 271–280.

Brady, P. (1995). Two policy approaches to Native education. Can reform be legislated? *Canadian Journal of Education, 20,* 349–366.

Brant, C. (1990). Native ethics and rules of behavior. *Canadian Journal of Psychiatry, 35,* 534.

Bogden, R. C., & Biklen, S. K. (1998). *Qualitative research for education* (3rd ed.). Boston, MA: Allyn & Bacon.

Canadian Communication Group. (1996). *Gathering strength: Report of the Royal Commission on Aboriginal peoples.* Ottawa: Author.

Carbo, M., & Hodges, H. (1991). Learning styles: Strategies can help students at risk. *ERIC Excerpt 13.* ERIC Clearinghouse on handicapped and gifted children.

Cohen, L., & Manion, L. (1985). *Research methods in education* (2nd ed.). New York: Croom Helm.

Collier, L. (1993). Teaching Native students at the college level. *Canadian Journal of Native Education, 20,* 109–117.

Corson, D. J. (1992). Minority cultural values and discourse norms in majority culture classrooms. *Canadian Modern Language Review, 48,* 472–496.

Cox, B. G., & Ramirez, M. (1981). Cognitive styles: Implications for multicultural education. In J. A. Banks (Ed.), *Education in the '80s: Multiethnic education* (pp. 122–134). Washington, DC: National Education Association.

Cruickshank, J., with Sidney, A., Smith, K., & Ned, A. (1990). *Life lived like a story: Life stories of three Yukon Native elders.* Vancouver, BC: University of British Columbia Press.

Curry, L. (1990). A critique of research on learning styles. *Educational Leadership, 48,* 50–56.

Dao, M. (1991). Designing assessment procedures for educationally at-risk Southeast Asian–American students. *Journal of Learning Disabilities, 24*, 594–601.

Department of Indian Affairs and Northern Development (DIAND). (1994). *Basic department data, 1994.* Ottawa: Ministry of Supply and Services.

English-Currie, V. (1990). The need for evaluation in Native education. In J. Perrault & S. Vance (Eds.), *Writing the circle: Native women of Western Canada* (pp. 47–60). Edmonton, AB: NeWest.

Ellis, J. (1999). Children and place: Stories we have, stories we need. *Interchange, 30(2), 171–190.*

First, J. M. (1988). Immigrant students in the US public schools: Challenges with solutions. *Phi Delta Kappan, 70*, 205–210.

Franklin, E. A. (1992). Learning to read and write the natural way. *Teaching Exceptional Children, 24*, 45–48.

Gadamer, H. G. (1984). *Truth and method.* New York: Crossroads.

Greene, M. (1993). Diversity and inclusion: Toward a curriculum for human beings. *Teachers College Record, 95*, 211–221.

Grossman, H. (1995). *Special education in a diverse society.* Boston, MA: Allyn & Bacon.

Haig-Brown, C. (1997). *Coyote learns to make a storybasket: The place of First Nations stories in education.* Unpublished doctoral dissertation, Simon Fraser University.

Haig-Brown, C., Hodgson-Smith, K. L., Regnier, R., & Archibald, J. (1997). *Making the spirit dance within: Joe Duquette High School and an Aboriginal community.* Toronto: James Lorimer.

Hamayan, E., & Damico, J. (1991). *Limiting bias in the assessment of bilingual students.* Austin, TX: University of Texas Press.

Hawthorn, H. B. (Ed.). (1966/67). *A survey of the contemporary Indians of Canada: A report on economic, political and educational needs and policies.* Ottawa: DIAND.

Heath, J. (1983). *Ways with words: Language, life and work in communities and classrooms.* New York: Cambridge University Press.

Jones, S. (1979). Integrating emic and etic approaches in the study of intercultural communication. In M. Asante, E. Newmark, & C. Blake (Eds.), *Handbook of intercultural communication* (pp. 57–74). Beverly Hills, CA: Sage.

Kanu, Y. (2001). Curriculum, culture and teacher learning: A case study of an innovative teacher education program in Pakistan. *Canadian and International Education, 29(2)*, 21–45.

Kirkness, V. J., with Bowman, S. S. (1992). *First Nations and schools: Triumphs and struggles.* Toronto: Canadian Education Association.

Kleinfeld, J. S. (1971). Visual memory in village Eskimo and urban Caucasian children. *Arctic, 24*, 132–138.

Kleinfeld, J. S., & Nelson, P. (1991). Adapting instruction to Native Americans' learning styles: An iconoclastic view. *Journal of Cross-cultural Psychology, 22*, 273–282.

Lee, M., & Krugly-Smolska, E. (1999). Cultural understanding in prospective overseas teachers. *Canadian and International Education, 28(1)*, 1–16.

Lincoln, Y., & Guba, E. (1985). *Naturalistic inquiry.* Newbury Park, CA: Sage.

Mackinnon, A. A. (1972). *Eskimo and Caucasian: A discordant note on cognitive perceptual abilities.* Unpublished manuscript, Saskatchewan Department of Health, Saskatoon.

Manitoba Teachers' Society. (1998). *Position paper on initial teacher education in Manitoba.* Winnipeg, MB: Teacher Education, Certification and Evaluation Committee.

Miles, M. B., & Huberman, A. M. (1994). *Qualitative data analysis.* London: Sage.

Miller-Lachman, L., & Taylor, L. S. (1995). *Schools for all: Educating children in a diverse society.* New York: Delmar.

Osborne, K. (2000). Voices from the past: History as storytelling. *Canadian Social Studies, 35(1).* Accessed at http://www.quasar.ualberta.ca/css

Philips, S. U. (1983). *The invisible culture: Communication in classrooms and community on the Warm Springs Indian reservation.* New York: Longman.

Ramirez, M., & Castañeda, A. (1974). *Bicultural democracy, bicognitive development and education.* New York: Academic Press.

Samuda, R. J. (1989). Psychometric factors in the appraisal of intelligence. In R. J. Samuda, S. L. Kong, J. Cummings, J. Pacuale-Leone, & J. Lewis (Eds.), *Assessment and placement of minority students* (pp. 25–40). Toronto: Hogrefe.

Shade, B. J., & New, C. A. (1993). Cultural influences on learning: Teaching implications. In J. A. Banks & C. A. Banks (Eds.), *Multicultural education: Issues and perspectives* (2nd ed., pp. 317–331). Boston, MA: Allyn & Bacon.

Statistics Canada. (1996). *Census of population questionnaire.* Ottawa: Bureau of Statistics.

Te Hennepe, S. (1993). Issues of respect: Reflections of First Nations students and experiences in postsecondary classrooms. *Canadian Journal of Native Education, 20,* 193–260.

Vygotsky, L. S. (1981). The genesis of higher mental functions. In J. V. Wertsch (Ed.), *The concept of activity in Soviet psychology* (pp. 144–188). Armonk, NY: Sharpe.

Wertsch, J. V. (1991). A sociocultural approach to socially shared cognition. In L. S. Resnick, J. M. Levine, & S. D. Teasely (Eds.), *Perspectives on socially shared cognition* (pp. 85–100). Washington, DC: American Psychological Association.

Whyte, K. (1986). Strategies for teaching Indian and Métis students. *Canadian Journal of Native Education, 13*(3), 33–40.

Winzer, M. A., & Mazurek, K. (1998). *Special education in multicultural contexts.* New York: Prentice-Hall.

Yao, E. I. (1988, November). Working effectively with Asian migrant parents. *Phi Delta Kappan, 70,* 223–225.

16

Critical and Emerging Discourses in Multicultural Education Literature:

A Review

ANNA KIROVA

INTRODUCTION

Multicultural education in Canada was conceived as a response to cultural pluralism in society. It is linked to immigration and represents a shift in Canadian social policy that parallels dramatic shifts in immigration policy (Ghosh & Abdi, 2004). As a result of Canada's historical immigration patterns and policies, as well as public responses to immigration, Canadian social and educational institutions differ significantly from those of other immigrant-receiving countries such as the United Kingdom, the United States, Australia, New Zealand, and France, among others. Although these unique patterns influenced the singular development of Canadian educational policies, research, and practices (Lund, 2003), a noticeable cross-fertilization of theoretical frameworks has developed in these countries, both in their implications for multicultural education practices and the critique of these practices. Mitchell (2001) states that most contemporary liberal thought in educational theory deems that democratic practice in Western education occurs in and through communal efforts to work through problems in an essentially multicultural student body. She points out that: "within this theoretical framework, by virtue of collective, plural education, Americans and Canadians simultaneously endorse both democratic possibility and the ongoing maintenance of national unity and identity" (p. 68).

In Canada, educational institutions are seen as having the obligation to provide continuity and content to the ongoing dialogue about the nature of multiculturalism and the management of diversity (Elliston, 1997). Indeed, periodically, educational reforms are identified as one of the initiatives needed for the integration of immigrants into majority-language institutions (Kymlicka, 2001).

In the past decade, however, concern has increased among the general public, researchers, and practitioners that schools are poorly equipped to cope with increased diversity and that instead of playing a role in facilitating equity and belonging, they may become locations that foster isolation and replicate racialized forms of injustice (Wideen & Barnard, 1999). The fact that racism in schools is persistent and is afflicted with denial and defensiveness (Dei, 2005); that stereotyping Tamil youth, for example, with the *gang* label or *Paki* name-calling; and the pervasiveness of gendered Islamophobia and the politics of veiling women point not only to how the negative stereotypes constitute violence to bodies in the post-9/11 context (Zine, 2004), but also raise the general question of how effective multicultural education is in integrating minority students. Recent attention to the challenges faced by second-generation immigrant youth (e.g., Filipino-Canadian youth) who still experience a sense of dislocation and restrictions on belonging enforced by daily racism in the Canadian system (Pratt, 2002) provides evidence that multiculturalism is unable to provide protection from the sense of exclusion.

Furthermore, the expectation that multicultural education policies and practices will result in equal participation of all students in education and thus allow for equal participation in the public and economic spheres has been challenged by the fact that visible-minority students' dropout rates exceed those of the Canadian born (Derwing, DeCorby, Ichikawa, & Jamieson, 1999; Watt & Roessingh, 2001) and that some racial groups are overrepresented in the criminal system (Wortley, 2003). Furthermore, a number of studies (Li, 1998; Gee & Prus, 2000; Kazimapur & Halli, 2003) show that "non-White origin creates a penalty for visible minorities in the labour market" (Li, 1998, p. 126). The findings of these studies indicate that the idea of liberal multiculturalism has not been achieved if measured by household income, and, as a result, racialized groups are more highly represented among the poor than are white Canadians (Galabuzi, 2005).

The ability of multicultural education to become a vehicle for achieving justice, liberty, and equality that pervade the social, economic, and political life of society (Giroux, 2001) has been challenged since its inception. The purpose of this article is threefold:

1. to examine the critical discourses in the academic literature on multicultural education pointing to the major conceptual flaws in multicultural education theory that have led to practices that have achieved effects opposite to the intent of the Canadian Multiculturalism Act;

2. to identify some of the suggestions being made in the context of the post-multiculturalism discourse defined as alternatives to multiculturalism (Vertovec, n.d.) on how to address these flaws in multicultural education theory and practice; and

3. to discuss some possible implications of the key findings of the review for multicultural education.

METHODS AND PROCEDURES

In order to identify and articulate the most common criticisms of multicultural education, a critical review and analysis were conducted of the English-language academic education literature. The focus was on journal articles, books, dissertation abstracts, book reviews, reports, policies, and other documents. Databases researched included ERIC, Academic Search Premier, Proquest, Web of Science, and Google Scholar. Some repetition eventually became evident, and saturation was reached in these sources.

The keyword searches were multicultural* or post-multicultural* with multiple other search terms that were variable, for example, critic* or critique*, or problem* (the asterisk ending on a keyword expands the search to include other endings) and the limits of years between 1996 and 2006. Some seminal works prior to this period were also included in this article in order to provide a historical context for more recent criticisms.

Each search began with a broad base, and limits were added and combined to produce a manageable data set. The initial search produced sixty salient pieces. For the purposes of this article, from this data set, forty-eight academic peer-reviewed articles, four books, seven book reviews, and five reports that focused on a theoretical critique of multicultural education—rather than on providing evidence of racism, discrimination, and the failure of immigrant students or the need to improve teacher preparation programs in order to meet the needs of the diverse student body—were analyzed in depth.

Analysis of the above sources enabled the identification of the most common theoretical perspectives which most of the authors have used to critique various aspects of multicultural education in the past ten years: anti-racism, critical pedagogy, and critical race theory. These theoretical perspectives emerged as oppositional discourses to mainstream multicultural education theory, policies, and practices and thus provide a distinct yet somewhat overlapping array of criticisms or concerns about multicultural education.

Following a brief historical overview of multicultural education in Canada, the criticisms articulated in the English-language literature about the problems of multicultural education are organized into three major sections. The first focuses on the criticisms of multicultural education; the second focuses on emerging propositions in the post-multiculturalism discourse on potentially productive directions for multiculturalism policy and multicultural education. The third section provides a summary of the key findings of the review of literature and discusses some implications for multicultural education.

A BRIEF HISTORICAL OVERVIEW OF MULTICULTURAL EDUCATION IN CANADA

The emergence of multicultural education in the Canadian educational system is influenced by the implementation of the 1971 federal Multicultural Policy statements (James, 2003; James & Shadd, 2001), the 1982 Canadian Charter of Rights and Freedoms, and the 1988 Canadian Multiculturalism Act. From its inception, multicultural education is linked to the goals of the original federal multiculturalism policy, which promotes ethnocultural retention, fosters appreciation of the cultural heritages of others, and assumes increased intergroup harmony (Lund, 2003).

Willinsky (1999) identifies the effect of the Multiculturalism Act on education as follows:

- government sponsorship of cultural community groups, ethnic events, and related school programs, creating a hyphenated mode of being among the nation's citizenry;
- initiation of heritage language programs in a number of Canadian communities, extension of Anglo–North American traditions of English literature to a new range of voices and experiences, and inclusion of non-European inventors, scientists, and mathematicians in mathematics and science lessons; and
- implementation of anti-racist programs to help students deal with the racism they encounter in school and community.

A major problem of the implementation of Canadian multicultural education is that "the Multiculturalism clause [of the federal Multicultural Policy] for education is vague" and that the "lack of federal control over education, and provincial legislation in general, has limited federal ability to influence education in this direction to any meaningful degree" (Ghosh & Abdi, 2004, p. 45). Because education is a provincial responsibility, multiculturalism as a federal policy is interpreted differently by the provincial educational authorities and is translated into varying forms of educational policies. Currently, five provinces have officially accepted multiculturalism in education, with Saskatchewan being the first to implement this policy in 1975, followed by Ontario in 1977, and Quebec with its own intercultural education perspective. The other two provinces are Alberta and Manitoba.

Despite the differences among multicultural educational policies across Canada, a synthesis of the components of multicultural education identifies three specific goals:

1. equivalency in achievement;
2. more positive intergroup attitudes; and
3. developing pride in heritage.

(Kehoe & Mansfield, 1997, p. 3)

These goals are to be achieved using a number of strategies including, but not limited to, teaching English as a second language while encouraging retention of heritage languages; removing ethnocentric bias from the curriculum; providing information about other cultures, which follows the criteria of teaching about similarities, institutionalizing in-school cultural celebrations as well as those of the Anglo-Celtic majority; and acquainting all students with their own and other cultures through the exchange of literature, art, dance, food, clothing, folk rhymes, religion, and so forth.

The Report on the State of the Art of Multicultural Education in Canada led by Keith A. McLeod from 1992 to 1996 identifies the following major tasks in the field of education: (a) to develop a more inclusive conceptualization and (b) to improve curriculum and pedagogy. The report stresses that the current climate has reopened the debate on multiculturalism and Canadian identity (Elliston, 1997). From a Canadian perspective, the future of multiculturalism, as McCreath (1997) suggests, needs to be seen in the context of the question of "whether there is a future for Canada" (p. 24). Although the concept of multiculturalism in the Multiculturalism Act is seen as valid, it is described as untried in education (McCreath, 1997). Similarly, most recently Ghosh and Abdi (2004) conclude that multicultural and intercultural education programs only theoretically give access to all ethnocultural groups and that these programs have not resulted in equal participation in the educational or economic spheres. Thus they claim, "Canadians cannot afford to ignore the implications of a failed multicultural policy, and now face a challenge of redefining meaning in the quest for peace and collective prosperity" (p. 139).

CRITICISMS OF MULTICULTURAL EDUCATION

The first criticisms of multicultural education come from anti-racist theorists, who are typically seen as holding opposing views to those of multiculturalists, particularly in the UK (Brandt, 1986; Troyna, 1987), in the US (Nieto, 1992; Perry & Fraser, 1993; Sleeter & Grant, 1998), and in Canada (Dei, 1996; Tator & Henry, 1991). Anti-racist education theorists stress that multicultural education ignores

racial differences and racial discrimination and fails to challenge the organizational structures of institutions as a basis for this discrimination. The debate
between the two views on the focus of multicultural education is described as
harmful (Tomlinson, 1990) because it diverts educators' attention from making
practical curriculum changes.

The gap between theory and practice is also identified as a major weakness of
multicultural education by critical pedagogy theorists (Brown & Kysilka, 1994;
Cole, 1986; May, 1994; Wilhelm, 1994). Although Canadian anti-racism education
connects with critical pedagogy and African-centred pedagogy (Dei, 1996), the
boundaries between anti-racism and multicultural education are clearer at the
level of rhetoric than of pedagogical practice (Carrington & Bonnett, 1997).

The gap between theory and practice is not the only weakness in the field
of multicultural education. The existence of conceptual differences regarding
multiculturalism held by anti-racist, anti-discrimination, human rights,
languages, and intercultural and transcultural advocates and the fact that each
claims that his/her view or interpretation is correct creates one of the most
critical challenges of multicultural education (McLeod, 1997) as it results in
confusion and frustration among educational practitioners. In their review of
multicultural education research from 1990 to 2001, Grant, Elsbree, and Fondrie
(2004) confirm an earlier description of the field as "troubled" (p. 185), which is
traced to "conceptual confusion, research epistemological bias, funding, [and]
research acceptance in the academy" (p. 200). Kincheloe and Steinberg (1997)
describe the field as involving conservative, liberal, pluralist, left-essentialist, and
critical multiculturalism, and McLaren (1997) adds to the list critical/resistance
and revolutionary multiculturalism.

The review of the academic literature related to multicultural education
critiques presented here indicates that the field is still divided in terms of
conceptualization of the main theoretical categories including culture, power,
agency, race, identity, social class, oppression, and difference. Divisions among
the three theoretical perspectives reviewed in this article—anti-racism, critical
theory, and critical race theory—result partly from varied histories and are
variably motivated and positioned among scholars with diverse political agendas.
Nevertheless, there are some commonalities among these critical perspectives,
which are outlined in the following sections.

Emphasizing Exoticized, Knowable ("Other") Cultures Solidifies the Boundaries Between Majority and Minority Cultures

As noted above, multicultural education in Canada is premised partly on the idea
of the importance of preserving heritage. Critics point out that this emphasis

results in "reductive striving for cultural simplicity and knowability" (Walcott, 1997, p. 122). The need for learners to "study 'foreign' cultures, participate in multicultural days or go on field trips to 'cultural communities' and community centres" (Pon, 2000, p. 284) is viewed by multicultural educators as a remedy for the racism and ethnic hostilities that stem from people's lack of familiarity with other cultures (Gosine, 2002).

Teaching students about the similarities and differences of many cultures is encouraged. Activities tend to focus on cultural celebrations, and thus remain at the superficial level of food, dance, and music represented in the "*piñata* curriculum or the *snowshoe* curriculum" (Hoffman, 1996, p. 550). Multicultural education is defined as the celebration of difference on special occasions or dates, which is typically accomplished as an add-on to the regular curriculum. As a result, the practice of multicultural education is characterized by folklorization.

Critics (Stables, 2005; Troyna, 1987) argue, however, that increased knowledge of other groups might, in fact, enhance the feeling of difference, may not necessarily lead to critical examination of the dominant culture, and thus does not encourage dialogue among groups about how to work through differences. In some instances, as Flecha (1999) shows, the emphasis on the concept of difference can also be used, as in the case of the neo-Nazis in Europe, for the development of hate programs.

Another outcome of the emphasis by multicultural education on cultural heritage, critics argue, is that the concept of culture is simplified and reified to fit multicultural discourses that support visions of personal, ethnic, or national cultural identity that are fixed, essentialized, stereotyped, and normalized (Bateson, 1994; Perry, 1992; Musgrove, 1982; Turner, 1993; Wax, 1993). However, "the tendency to view non-Western cultures as stable, tradition-bound, timeless entities shifts us dangerously back towards viewing others as beings who are profoundly and inherently different from ourselves" (Perry, 1992, p. 52). Difference, then, is not only assumed in multicultural educational theory and practice, but is created in relation to the "norm." Therefore, treating cultures as discrete units strengthens the boundaries between majority and minority cultures. Not surprisingly, then, as Mitchell (2001) suggests, non-white, non-Western "citizens" cannot be part of the nation-building project because the nation is constituted by their exclusion.

Critics in Canadian education academic literature trace the above outcome of multiculturalism back to Trudeau's (1971) pluralistic notion of the Canadian "mosaic" that is still "the favored metaphor of Canadian education administrators and policy makers when seeking to underline the pluralistic nature of their national culture and society" (Carrington & Bonnett, 1997, p. 412). They show that despite the commitment of educational and social policies in promoting "race" and ethnic equality, responses at the provincial level have been varied, and developments in practice have been uneven. Comparing race equity education in Ontario and British Columbia, for example, Carrington and Bonnett observe that regional devolution ensures varied responses to multiculturalism at the provincial level that result in uneven developments in praxis and so "it may be erroneous to conceive of just one Canadian mosaic" (p. 412).

A related criticism of multiculturalism is that in the mosaic metaphor, and in other popular representations of diversity such as quilts, salads, tapestries, and so forth that purport to recognize difference, the unity of cultures is a given. "Difference is thereby diluted or made to support overarching frameworks of shared values or worldview firmly enshrined in that privileged existential space called '*culture*'" (original emphasis; Hoffman, 1996, p. 550).

By Renaming the Difference from Racial to Cultural, White Dominance Is Reproduced

Overemphasis on culture has ideological ramifications as it shifts the naming of difference from racial to cultural. This, critics point out, represents a shift in the epistemic site of racism. Willinsky (1999), for example, suggests that "renaming the difference" (p. 95) obscures the important social processes that shape education, and thus "it fails to make clear the relationship between racial and cultural difference" (p. 97). Renaming the difference also results in changing the common code for racial difference in Canada, which is currently *cultural difference* (original emphasis; Schick & St. Denis, 2005): a quality that racial minority children, especially Aboriginal children, are said to have and that is given as the reason for any lack of school success.

Other critics (Bannerji, 2000; James & Shadd, 2001) also challenge multicultural education for equating race with ethnicity and culture. For them, in the multicultural perspective, race is no more salient than ethnicity in matters of socio-economic and political inequalities. Thus, insofar as racial inequality is seen to exist, multicultural educators play down structural explanations in favour of explanations about cultural differences (Pon, 2000). According to Ghosh and Abdi (2004), rejection of the biological definition of race and consequent cultural conceptions of race, "indicates a shift in the strategies of racism from overt to covert forms" (p. 58). They assert that using the official Canadian expression to refer to non-white groups, namely *visible minorities,* clearly indicates that: "minorities are defined by skin colour in a society where whiteness is taken to be the norm" (p. 58).

The shift from racial to cultural difference is viewed as serving the "ideology of racelessness," which is consistent with a "national mythology that Canada is not a racist country" (Backhouse; 1999, p. 14). Schick and St. Denis (2005) also assert that forgetting about the salience of race is not merely a passive letting go. They stress that a multicultural approach to education sanctions the ignorance of racializing systems, including the production of white identities and the taken-for-grantedness of racial dominance. Multiculturalism, therefore, "has failed to question the norm of whiteness and the domination of white culture by making it invisible. By remaining concealed, and removing the dominant group from race and/or ethnicity, the focus on difference is depoliticized" (Ghosh & Abdi, 2004, p. 34), and asymmetrical relations of power are maintained. Cultural difference rhetoric, then, connects educational failures to the "other" by de-emphasizing how dominant (white) identities are implicated in the production of difference.

Multiculturalism's View of the Self/Culture Relationship Reiterates the Cultural Hegemony Associated with Eurocentrism

The essentialized views of culture assumed in multicultural education lead to understanding self/cultural identity and self-esteem as fundamentally the same in all cultures and ethnic groups (Hoffman, 1996). This view is found both in Taylor's (1994) and in Kymlicka's (1995) conceptualizations of self as a property of human nature animated by those human qualities assumed to be universal. In multicultural education theory and practice, it is assumed that "there is a one-to-one relationship between self and culture characterized by a clear, fixed commitment to a particular cultural or ethnic identity" (Hoffman, 1996, p. 557). The argument goes further to suggest that the ownership formulation of identity as something one has (i.e., "all students have an ethnic identity" or "every student has a culture") represents the relationship between person and culture as one of possession, which reflects notions of property rights and makes ethnicity compatible with the dominant economic structure of society. This argument is supported by Appiah's (1997) assertion that most of the social identities that make up our diverse society do not actually have independent cultures that need to be represented in school curricula. He maintains that what are frequently coded as cultural identities are, in fact, social identities that cannot be understood as independent cultures. Thus by being told that everyone should have a clear ethnic or cultural identity, minority children are not only forced to choose their identity, but also to "live within separate spheres defined by the common culture of their race, religion, or ethnicity" (p. 34). Similarly, Ghosh and Abdi (2004) state that for visible minorities, the self-definition not only brings a sense of discomfort, but also produces conflict in identity formation because they are forced to define themselves and because "traditions are being reconstructed through fragmentation" (p. 71). In their critique of multicultural education, critical race education theorists trace the notion of property in the historical construction of whiteness in relation to the concept of individual rights—the so-called "property issue" (Ladson-Billings, 1995, 1998).

Related to the self/culture property assumptions are identity politics as a response to minority cultures' demands for political and cultural recognition that are articulated with the supposition of the authenticity of minority identity assumed to be an already formed or pre-given stable identity constructed in relation to whiteness. When "recognition" is understood and practised as a form of tolerance, it masks or even reiterates the cultural hierarchization associated with Eurocentrism (Cornell & Murphy, 2002).

Multiculturalism's Culturalist Ideology Reinforces Existing Inequalities

Critical theorists challenge multicultural education for its obsessive concern with culture, which they claim masks political and socio-economic conditions that contribute to real inequity in contemporary plural societies, thereby making multiculturalism a safe way of sidestepping the important issues. Cole (1986), May (1994), McLaren (1995), McCarthy (1994), and Watkins (1994), among others, claim that, because it often occurs in the absence of a transformative political agenda, this culturalist orientation can serve only to reinforce the domi-nant Western ideology that supports existing inequalities. For example, in his early critique of multicultural education discourses, Giroux (1983) stated that power and domination were sometimes "reduced to misunderstandings that can be corrected by providing accurate information" (p. 31). Thus, critical theorists (Giroux; McCarthy, 1994; McLaren, 1995) assert that multicultural education locates discrimination in individuals' lack of sensitivity and knowledge and as-sumes that it can be changed by efforts to reduce prejudice, promote cultural awareness and knowledge, and achieve equal accessibility. As a result, multi-cultural education views these measures as substitutes for structural change, which in turn leaves the status quo intact.

In contrast, anti-racist education challenges systemic racism, which consists of the policies and practices of organizations that directly or indirectly operate to sustain the advantages of people of certain "social races" (Henry, Tator, Mattis, & Rees, 2000). Anti-racist is defined as an "action-oriented strategy for institutional, systemic change to address racism and the interlocking systems of social oppression" (Dei, 1996, p. 25). However, as Willinsky (1999) points out, although "the move from multicultural to anti-racist education is a promising step in pursuit of how collectives are constructed," what remains is "the history of the learned investment in the significance of the differences and divides among humankind" (p. 393).

Critical race educational theorists also argue that equity of opportunity is meaningless to children from unequal conditions with unequal social capital. Schools thus reinforce existing inequalities when they ignore social differences that affect learning and achievement. Moreover, because both educational institutions and teachers possess the all too important intercultural competence in varying degrees (Bennet, 2001), some students are not treated equally in a system that perpetuates the dominant culture, values, and norms through its curriculum and organization.

Multicultural Education Is Assimilationist in Creating National Citizenship and Identity

In reviewing the role of the school in revealing national Canadian culture and identity, Diakiw (1997) indicates that the discussion is fraught with dangers because Trudeau proclaimed in 1971 in the House of Commons that "while we have two official languages, we have no official culture, no one culture is more official than another." In defence of multiculturalism, Diakiw stresses that this proclamation has "contributed to a backlash manifested in the Reform Party, Quebec Separatism, and a fundamentalist resurgence across Canada" (p. 27). However, Diakiw agrees with the view of critical theorists that: "multiculturalism posits a serious threat to the school's traditional task of defending and transmitting an authentic national history, a uniform standard of cultural literacy, and singular national identity" (Giroux, 1992, cited in Diakiw, p. 27).

Critical theorists argue that multicultural education theory creates problems, contradictions, and dilemmas for members of minority groups living in a liberal democracy. There are two reasons for this. First, liberal democracy is based on principles of liberal theory regarding the importance of respecting individual rights and individual actions, but multicultural education tends to focus on group rights and actions. Second, they argue that multicultural education theory directs minority group members into "trying to belong to [both] their cultural community and national community" (Rosaldo, 1989, p. 44). This has created dilemmas and difficulties for people who find it difficult to reconcile some of the cultural norms and values of two communities. In turn, this contributes to self-alienation and consequent problems with citizenship and national identity.

Similarly, the promotion of a homogeneous vision of Canada, regardless of the diversity of its citizens, is identified by Strong-Boag (2002) as a sign of Canada's inability to address the shortcomings of citizenship education based on universal citizenship. In her view, women, Native people, and working-class people have suffered exclusion from this kind of citizenship education that has resulted in even greater inequalities for these groups. A similar critique is offered by Cecille dePass and Shazia Qureshi (2002) who explore how people of colour exist in the spaces between citizen and non-citizen in Canadian society. They reject the term *visible minority* in favour of *people of colour,* viewing the former as an externally imposed definition and the latter as a self-selected term for self-definition.

The primary challenge to existing models of citizenship education in Canada is identified by Hébert and Wilkinson (2002) as the need to respect differences while identifying and nurturing commonalities. Thus, although acknowledging that certain individuals and groups experience limited sociopolitical participation in liberal democracies, Hébert and Wilkinson suggest that social cohesion is both a desirable goal and a nebulous concept that may never be fully resolved because societies and human beings are always in a state of flux. However, they suggest that research on citizenship in Canada lacks coordination and has been undertaken largely as a result of "personal preferences, interests, affinities, and whims" and has been "subject to continuous ideological winds" (p. 228).

It is important to emphasize that none of the sources reviewed here suggests dismissing the idea of multiculturalism as a desired characteristic of educational theory or practice. On the contrary, the emerging post-multiculturalism discourse in the academic education literature offers theoretical suggestions about rearticulating the main concepts of multicultural education in order to reflect their complexity and to create an education system that is inclusive of all students. The key postulations of the post-multiculturalism discourse are presented in the following section.

EMERGENT POST-MULTICULTURALISM DISCOURSE ON MULTICULTURAL EDUCATION

In addition to identifying the main criticisms of multicultural education, the review of the academic literature reveals an emerging post-multiculturalism discourse that indicates some significant shifts in understanding and articulating central concepts such as culture, power, and cultural, national, and civic identity. Similar trends are also observed in the literature outside the field of education. For example, in her recent comparison of Canadian multiculturalism and Quebec interculturalism policies, Nugent (2006) observes that in the last ten years, the initial emphasis on difference that was strongest in the 1988 Multiculturalism Act has shifted to a stronger focus on integration, civic participation, social justice, and national security (Abu-Laban, 1999; Kymlicka, 2001; Labelle, 2005). In addition, in the latest annual report on the implementation and direction of the act, identity is defined as belonging and attachment to Canada rather than to any particular subgroup in the country (Canada, 2004; Abu-Laban & Gabriel, 2002;

Nugent, 2006). The following section outlines trends in post-multiculturalism discourse in the English-language academic education literature.

The Shift in Understanding Culture and Cultural Difference

As indicated above, one of the main criticisms of multiculturalism and multi-cultural education is that culture is simplified and reified to fit multicultural dis-courses that support visions of personal, ethnic, or national cultural identity that are fixed, essentialized, stereotyped, and normalized. This, in turn, solidifies the boundaries between cultures and, by extension, between cultural groups. To ad-dress this issue, the current conceptualization of culture is drawn from cultural studies (Hall, 1996; Williams, 1976) and critical anthropology (Clifford, 1988, 1992). Culture is defined as the whole way of life of a society or group in a partic-ular period and as a dynamic, rather than static, phenomenon (Hartman, 1997). Human culture is now understood as "both historical ('backward-looking') and dynamic ('forward-looking')" (Shi-Xu, 2001, p. 283). Culture is also seen as being able to "re- and trans-form itself " (p. 283). From this point of view, the purpose of multicultural education now is "to create possibilities in confronting the views in which we see the world" (Ghosh & Abdi, 2004, p. 31), and, thus, it represents a site of struggle.

Ghosh and Abdi (2004) maintain that postmodern thought resists the idea of culture as an organizing principle that creates borders around ethnicity, class, and gender. Such borders falsely homogenize cultures within a culture. Building on Bhabha's (1994) notion of the third space, they suggest developing broader horizons where we negotiate new ideas and vocabularies to enable us to make comparisons partly through transforming our own standards. They describe the third space as one of renegotiation of cultural space that offers the opportunity to create conventions and practices in and between varied modes of meaning. It is a harmonization of cultures, not their dissolution, disappearance, or disintegration. The fusion of cultures in the third space, then, does not mean difference-blindness or homogenization; rather, it emphasizes identity because individuals see the world from their own perspectives and have multiple identities, some of which may be contradictory. Therefore, validating cultural, social, and gender differences and developing individual identities should be the focus of multicultural education.

Gosine (2002) suggests that adopting a critical, non-essentialist approach to cultural difference in schools would provide students with theoretical tools to challenge the racist discourses that construct exoticized and stigmatized "others" and help them to develop a more complex and thorough understanding of racism and its interplay with other social statuses such as ethnicity, class, and sexual orientation.

The Shift in Understanding Cultural and Ethnic Identities

Gosine's (2002) review of conceptions of racial identity construction identified a theoretical shift in education-related scholarship. That is, rather than treating these concepts as fixed, discrete, and easily represented entities (Fordham & Ogbu, 1992), they are now viewed as hybrid and contradictory concepts continually produced and reproduced in relation to shifting constellations of knowledge (e.g., racializing discourses) and power in the larger society (James, 1996; Yon, 2000). However, he warns, the dangers of arguing for such a perspective may cause a fall into a fragmented universe of situated identities and forms of consciousness that make it seemingly impossible to think about group-based identities, issues, mobilization, or interventions (Collins, 2000; Diawara, 1993). Overemphasizing hybridity and the associated blurring of ethnoracial boundaries can also result in playing down the bitter tensions that arise in conflicts between marginalized and dominant groups, thereby misrepresenting the nature of Canadian racism (Loomba, 1998).

Recent dramatic changes in the business world have caused some critical theorists (Grossberg, 1992) to explore the effects of the new economic formations on cultural practice and, consequently, identity. The new work order, or post-capitalism, indicates a shift "from a focus on production to a focus on consumption" (Helfenbein, 2003, p. 14). This in turn creates a "culture based in part on the transfer of information from consumer to producer and vice versa, less meaningful borders, and a well hidden gap between the rich and the poor" (p. 14) in which identity is defined by patterns of consumption.

Helfenbein (2003) argues that schools in general must change in order to prepare young people for the new work order and that multicultural education in particular "needs to address the changing nature of identity in a globalized technologically connected world" (p. 14). Articulating the novel life conditions, subjectivities, and identities of youth; cultivating new multiple literacies as a response to new technologies and the challenges of globalization and multiculturalism; and proposing a radical reconstruction and democratization of education to counter the trend toward the imposition of a neoliberal business model on education are the three major tasks of the new critical pedagogy according to Kellner (2003). He emphasizes, however, that reconstruction of education should not fulfill the agenda of capital and high-tech industries, but should "radically democratize education in order to advance Deweyan and Freirean conceptions of the development of individuality, the promotion of citizenship and community, and the strengthening of democratic participation in all modes of life" (p. 62).

The Shift in Understanding Citizenship and Civic and National Identity

In educational discourse, critical theorists such as Giroux (1991), Dryzek (1996), and Kincheloe (2001) emphasize that "democratic citizenship needs to be 'multidimensional . . . often unconventional' and often should be waged 'against the state, and apart from the state'" (Dryzek, p. 36). Critical reconstructionists, too, tend to advocate "types of civic knowledge that unmask and derail official and state-sponsored 'fairy tales'" (Abowitz & Harnish, 2006, p. 673). They also advocate for a critical civic curriculum that will foster civic identity by embracing the values and skills of questioning, rethinking, and confronting when necessary powerful democratic institutions, including the government and state-sponsored schooling (Giroux, 2003) when they are not working on behalf of all citizens. This process of learning the actual workings of political life instead of mere facts about it would lead to the development of public agency (Boyte, 1994).

Willinsky (1999) connects culture to nation and points out that just as Boas used the "new conception of culture to weaken the racial boundaries that were used to set people apart, the term nation is now being used to fortify national borders" (p. 101). It is expected that teachers become "border crossers" (Giroux, 1992, p. 11) in order to provide diverse students with a sense of history, identity, and the commonplaces of Canada's culture and identity (Diakiw, 1997).

Hébert and Wilkinson (2002) call for the development of a conceptual framework for analyzing citizenship that will "be modified and enriched as necessary to enclose all unforeseen aspects of citizenship," that will allow us to "grasp the overall meaning of citizenship," and whose "full development is achieved when saturation is reached" (p. 233).

Ghosh and Abdi (2004) suggest that a "syncretic national identity" (p. 88) can be achieved in Canada if the notion of critical pedagogy is extended beyond minority groups, and promoting democratic values is combined with school, classroom, and curriculum reorganization, and a revisioning of teacher-student, student-student, and home-school relationships. This in turn can lead to a change in the *we-they* configuration and the construction of an inclusive *us*. They point to the need for the emergence of a new kind of citizenship that allows "the expression of the multiple identities that we possess" (p. 87). Ghosh and Abdi recognize that especially in heterogeneous societies, a unifying political culture is viewed as a force against disintegration. They suggest that political culture and citizenship in postmodern democracies "involve the interconnection between the national and the global, such as the citizen of any one country and citizens of the world, in a transnational interdependency" (p. 88).

SUMMARY, DISCUSSION, AND IMPLICATIONS

I reiterate that the purpose of this review is to examine both the criticisms of multicultural education and some of the suggestions being made in the context of "post-multiculturalism" discourse on how to overcome the unintended negative consequences of multicultural education outlined in the introduction. This concluding section summarizes the key findings of the review and discusses the implications of these findings for multicultural education.

Before discussing any possible implications of the findings of this review for the future of multicultural education, an explanation is needed about the choices made in approaching the task of reviewing the critical discourses in the multicultural education literature. The attempt to identify common points made by the various critical theorists about the main flaws of multicultural theory and practice is not driven by a desire to ignore the differences among these theorists and theoretical perspectives. Nor is it driven by the desire to simplify and reduce to points the complex and multi-layered debates that have emerged over time and in response to particular events in and outside the field of education. Rather, the attempt is aimed at making a connection between the weaknesses of multicultural education theory that most critics have identified and the suggestions made in relation to these weaknesses. Thus, the points presented in the following two sections do not claim to represent all criticisms of multicultural education from all critical perspectives. Rather, what follows is a summary of the main points made collectively by the critics of multicultural education reviewed for this article and how it is suggested that these flaws can be addressed so that multicultural education can become inclusive and better equipped to meet the challenges of the contemporary global social, political, and economic climate.

Summary of the Main Points Made by the Critics of Multicultural Education
Based on the commonly identified issues with multicultural theory and practice, the following main critical points are noted in the reviewed sources.

- Multicultural education is based on the view of culture as a stable, tradition-bound, and timeless entity, the unity of which is given and thus within-culture variations are ignored. By focusing on the preservation of cultural heritage, culture is simplified and reduced to knowable elements such as food, dance, and dress that students can and should learn about. Differences among cultures are emphasized, which leads to strengthening of the boundaries between majority and minority cultures rather than to a genuine dialogue among cultural groups.
- In the multicultural education framework, cultural identities are viewed as already formed, pre-given, and fixed. Thus they are constructed as

essentialized, stereotyped, and normalized in relation to whiteness. By adopting this view of cultural identity, multicultural education forces visible-minority students to choose an identity defined by the common culture of their race, religion, or ethnicity.

- Multiculturalism's definition of culture and its view of a self-culture relationship emphasizes diversity based on essentialized difference in which the role of the dominant (white) culture in the production of "difference" is not problematized. By presenting the relationship between person and culture as one of possession, which reflects property rights, multicultural education makes ethnicity compatible with the dominant capitalist structure of society.

- Renaming difference from racial to cultural is a shift from overt to covert forms of racism that serve the ideology of racelessness consistent with Canadian national mythology. Multicultural education has failed to make clear the relationship between racial and cultural difference or to question the norm of whiteness and the dominance of white culture as making it invisible.

- Multiculturalism has not liquidated systemic racism or served as a substitute for structural change. By depoliticizing the difference, a culturalist ideology of multicultural education not only hinders the achievement of equitable distribution of economic and social benefits, but also reinforces existing inequalities.

- Promoting a homogeneous vision of Canada regardless of its citizens excludes certain individuals and groups from participation in liberal democracy by forcing both non-white and white students to fit into existing structures of society. Such an assimilationist agenda in education leads to self-alienation and consequent problems with citizenship and national identity.

Summary of the Main Points Emerging from the Post-multiculturalism Discourse

Based on the identified shifts in the post-multiculturalism theoretical perspectives, the following main shifts are noted in the reviewed sources.

- There is a shift in defining culture that is now understood as both historical and dynamic and as being able to re-form and transform itself. Adopting a critical, non-essentialist approach to cultural differences that enables students to challenge racist discourses and to develop understanding of complexities of both culture and racism is suggested.

- The creation of a third space as one of negotiation of cultural space that offers opportunities for practices in and between varied modes of meaning, or a fusion of cultures, is seen as a space where multiple, even contradictory, cultural identities can exist. The focus of education is suggested to be on validating students' cultural, social, and gender differences and developing identities.

- There is a shift in defining cultural and racial identities, which are now viewed as hybrid and/or contradictory concepts continually produced and reproduced in relation to shifting configurations of knowledge and power in society.

- The concept of identity is also seen as reflecting the new globalized economy where identity is defined by patterns of consumption. Education is called to address not only the global consumer identity, but also the changing nature of a globalized, technologically connected world. Radical democratization of education, promotion of citizenship and community, and strengthening of democratic participation in all modes of life are suggested.

- Democratic citizenship, defined as multidimensional, is achieved through critical civic curricula that will foster civic identity and public agency. A national identity can then be syncretic, allowing for the expression of the complex multiple identities of individuals.

Discussion and Implications for Multicultural Education

Given the continued heated debate in the English-language academic education literature about which theoretical perspective of multicultural education is best equipped to lead the field in the future, it seems appropriate to heed Ladson-Billings's (2004) suggestion that "current ideas about the term multicultural must give way to new expressions of human and social diversity. . . . [We] must reconceptualize views of difference that are often forced to operate in old social schemes" (p. 50).

As the review presented here shows, when binaries are overemphasized, complex phenomena are simplified, leaving no room for individual variations and nuances of experience and often reproducing the status quo. Current multicultural education practices in Canada based on ethnoracial distinctions (i.e., curricula essentializing knowledge about "other" cultures and celebrating them) have not contributed to the elimination of racism or the unequal treatment of minority, non-white students. Neither have they led to a critical examination of the dominant white, middle-class, Eurocentric culture.

However, the review also shows that the complexity of the issues identified as problematic in multicultural theory makes it difficult to formulate a unified multicultural education mission that speaks to the multiplicity of identities, fluidity of culture, negotiation of power in the cultural space, and the new politics of difference based on universal dignity and equality. It is even more difficult to organize and implement such a mission, especially in the absence of a federal multicultural education policy. Therefore, education ministries across the provinces need to take it upon themselves to re-examine how better to integrate disparate and marginalized voices into the privileged domain and to reinvest in employment equity such that the presence and concerns of minorities are introduced into the classroom by closing the visible-minority gap. In other words, a commitment to ensuring that non-Christian, non-white, non-native English- or French-speaking teachers are well represented in the public school system is critical for providing nodal points of immediate cross-cultural and multi-ethnic identification for students outside the so-called Canadian majority. In this process, opportunity to develop stronger consultative partnerships between communities and educational ministries should not be overlooked as an effective and cost-efficient means of infusing alternative epistemologies into curricula. If essentializing and misrepresentational trends are observed in curricula, the inclusion of minority cultures in the early stages of the deliberative process and maintaining mechanisms of consultation throughout the implementation process will enhance the power of the spirit of multiculturalism by activating it as metaphor and mobilizing it as praxis. This will also serve to counter the intuitive and lived barriers between those within the system and those outside it.

The shifts in post-multicultural education discourse are reflected in the choices of metaphors for describing or labelling multicultural Western societies. Understanding and acknowledging the complexities of the contemporary world is seen in the change in how typical mainstream metaphors like *salad bowl, social fabric, mosaic,* and *family of the nation* that tend to define each individual or group as distinct and somehow fixed or unchangeable in relation to the other ingredients are shifting toward new metaphors such as *jazz* as introduced by Ornette Coleman (in Ladson-Billings, 2004). The new metaphors attempt to capture the complexity of human beings who change in every context and the resulting intergroup variations that constitute the singularity of each [individual's or group's] identification. They also attempt to capture multiculturalism as an evolving relational process rather than as a static policy construct.

In the Canadian context, multiculturalism needs to be conceived of as a global societal project of which institutionalized education is only one component. Heterogeneity of the student body is a fact that education as an institution must address in order to participate in the re-evaluation, rearticulation, and renegotiation of the meaning of national unity in the democratic state.

REFLECTIVE QUESTIONS

1. Would you agree that most schools are not well equipped for the fact that there is increasing diversity in the student body? Explain.
2. What are some of the criticisms of multicultural education that Kirova raises?
3. What have your experiences been with what the author refers to as multicultural practices based on "ethno-racial distractions"?
4. What does she suggest are some possible solutions to current approaches to multiculturalism?
5. What are the differences between multicultural education and anti-racism education as identified in this reading?

ACKNOWLEDGEMENTS

I thank Dr. Joe Garcea of the department of Political Science at the University of Saskatchewan and Dr. Lloyd Wong of the department of Sociology at the University of Calgary for their constructive feedback on this article. I also thank the research assistants, Carolina Cambre and Peter Petrov, who worked with me on this project. The Department of Canadian Heritage, Multiculturalism Branch, and the Prairie Metropolis Centre are also gratefully acknowledged for their financial support of the project.

REFERENCES

Abowitz, K. K., & Harnish, J. (2006). Contemporary discourses of citizenship. *Review of Educational Research, 76*(4), 653–90.

Abu-Laban, Y. (1999). The politics of race, ethnicity, and immigration: The contested area of multiculturalism. In J. Bickerton & A.-G. Ganon (Eds.), *Canadian politics* (pp. 463–483). Peterborough: Broadview.

Abu-Laban, Y., & Gabriel, C. (2002). *Selling diversity: Immigration, multiculturalism, employment equity, and globalization.* Peterborough: Broadview.

Appiah, K. A. (1997). The multiculturalism misunderstanding. *New Review of Books, 44*(15), 30–36.

Backhouse, C. (1999). *Color coded: A legal history of racism in Canada, 1900–1950.* Toronto: University of Toronto Press.

Bhabha, H. (1994). *The location of culture.* London: Routledge.

Bannerji, H. (2000). *The dark side of the nation: Essays on multiculturalism, nationalism, and gender.* Toronto: Canadian Scholars' Press.

Bateson, M. C. (1994). *Peripheral visions.* New York: Harper Collins.

Bennet, C. (2001). Genres of research in multicultural education. *Review of Educational Research, 71*(2), 171–217.

Boyte, H. (1994). Review of Civitas: A framework for civic education. *Teachers College Record, 95*, 414–418.

Brandt, G. L. (1986). *The realization of anti-racist teaching.* Lews, UK: Falmer Press.

Brown, S., & Kysilka, M. (1994). In search of multicultural and global education in real classrooms. *Journal of Curriculum and Supervision, 9*(3), 313–316.

Canada. (2004). *Annual report on the operation of the Canadian Multiculturalism Act, 2003–2004: Canada's diversity: Respecting our differences.* Ottawa: Canadian Heritage.

Carrington, B., & Bonnett, A. (1997). The other Canadian "mosaic": "Race" equality education in Ontario and British Columbia. *Comparative Education, 33*(3), 411–431. Accessed at http://www .edexcellence.net/foundation/publication/publication.cfm?id=65#745

Clifford, J. (1988). *The predicament of culture: Twentieth-century ethnography, literature, and art.* Cambridge: Harvard University Press.

Clifford, J. (1992). Traveling cultures. In C. Nelson, P. A. Treichler, & L. Grossberg (Eds.), *Cultural studies* (pp. 96–117). New York/London: Routledge.

Cole, M. (1986). Teaching and learning about racism: A critique of multicultural education in Britain. In S. H. Modgil, M. Sohan, C. Modgil, & K. Mallick (Eds.), *Multicultural education: The interminable debate* (pp. 123–147). London: Falmer.

Collins, P. H. (2000). What's going on? Black feminist thought and the politics of postmodernism. In E. A. S. Pierre & W. S. Pillow (Eds.), *Working the ruins: Feminist poststructural theory and methods in education* (pp. 41–73). New York: Routledge.

Cornell, D., & Murphy, S. (2002). Anti-racism, multiculturalism, and the ethics of identification. *Philosophy and Social Criticism, 28*(4), 419–449.

Dei, G. J. (1996). *Anti-racism education: Theory and practice.* Halifax, NS: Fernwood.

Dei, G. J. (2005). Resisting the gated community: Responding to diversity and difference en route to excellence in our schools. *Orbit, 35*(3), 34–36.

DePass, C., & Qureshi, S. (2002). Paradoxes, contradictions, and ironies of democratic citizenship education. In Y. Hébert (Ed.), *Citizenship in transformation in Canada* (pp. 112–134). Toronto: University of Toronto Press.

Derwing, T. M., DeCorby, E., Ichikawa, J., & Jamieson, K. (1999). Some factors that affect the success of ESL high school students. *Canadian Modern Language Review, 55*, 103–132.

Diakiw, J. (1997). *The school's role in revealing the commonplaces of our national culture and identity: A multicultural perspective.* Accessed at http://caslt.org/research/multicult.htm

Diawara, M. (1993). Black studies, cultural studies, performative acts. In C. McCarthy & W. Crichlow (Eds.), *Race, identity, and representation in education* (pp. 262–267). New York: Routledge.

Dryzek, J. S. (1996). *Democracy in capitalist times: Ideals, limits, and struggles.* Oxford: Oxford University Press.

Elliston, I. (1997). Reforming education for diversity. In *The state of the art national study. Report #4.* Toronto: University of Toronto.

Flecha, R. (1999). Modern and postmodern racism in Europe: Dialogic approach and anti-racist pedagogies. *Harvard Educational Review, 69*(2), 150–171.

Fordham, S., & Ogbu, J. U. (1992). Black students' school success: Coping with the burden of acting white. In J. J. Macionis & N.V. Benokraitis (Eds.), *Seeing ourselves: Classic, contemporary, and cross-cultural readings in sociology* (pp. 287–303). Englewood Cliffs, NJ: Prentice Hall.

Galabuzi, G.-E. (2005). Factors affecting the social economic status of Canadian immigrants in the new millennium. *Canadian Issues,* Spring, 53–57.

Gee, E., & Prus, S. (2000). Income inequality in Canada: A racial divide. In M. A. Kalbach & W. E. Kalbach (Eds.), *Perspectives in Canada: A reader* (pp. 238–256). Toronto: Harcourt Canada.

Ghosh, R., & Abdi, A. A. (2004). *Education and the politics of difference: Canadian perspectives.* Toronto: Canadian Scholars' Press.

Giroux, H. A. (1983). *Theory and resistance in education: A pedagogy for the opposition.* South Hadley, MA: Bergin and Garvey.

Giroux, H. A. (1991). Beyond the ethics of flag waving: Schooling and citizenship for critical democracy. *Clearing House, 64*(5), 305–309.

Giroux, H. A. (1992). *Border crossing: Cultural workers and the politics of education.* New York: Routledge.

Giroux, H. A. (1993). *Living dangerously: Multiculturalism and the politics of difference*. New York: Peter Lang.

Giroux, H. A. (2001). *Public spaces, private lives: Beyond the culture of cynicism*. Lanham, MD: Rowman and Littlefield.

Giroux, H. A. (2003). *The abandoned generation: Democracy beyond the culture of fear*. New York: Palgrave Macmillan.

Giroux, S. S. (2003). Reconstructing the future: Du Bois, racial pedagogy and the post–civil rights era. *Social Identities, 9*(4), 563–598.

Gosine, K. (2002). Essentialism versus complexity: Conceptions of racial identity construction in educational scholarship. *Canadian Journal of Education, 27*(1), 81–100.

Grant, C., Elsbree, A. R., & Fondrie, S. (2004). A decade of research: The changing terrain of multicultural education research. In J. A. Banks & C. A. McGee Banks (Eds.), *Handbook of research on multicultural education* (pp. 184–207). San Francisco: Jossey-Bass.

Grossberg, L. (1992). *We gotta get out of this place: Popular conservatism and postmodern culture*. London: Routledge.

Hall, S. (1996). Cultural studies: Two paradigms. In J. Storey (Ed.), *What is cultural studies?: A reader* (pp. 31–48). London: Arnold.

Hartman, G. (1997). *The fateful question of culture*. New York: Columbia University Press.

Hébert, Y., & Wilkinson, L. (2002). The citizenship debates: Conceptual, policy, experiential, and educational issues. In Y. Hébert (Ed.), *Citizenship in transformation in Canada* (pp. 112–134). Toronto: University of Toronto Press.

Helfenbein, R. J. (2003). Troubling multiculturalism: The new work order, anti-essentialism, and a cultural studies approach to education. *Multicultural Perspectives, 5*(4), 10–16.

Henry, F., Tator, C., Mattis, W., & Rees, T. (2000). *The colour of democracy and racism in Canadian society*. Toronto: Harcourt Brace.

Hoffman, D. M. (1996). Culture and self in multicultural education: Reflections on discourse, text, and practice. *American Educational Research Journal, 33*(3), 545–569.

James, C. E. (1996). Race, culture, and identity. In C. E. James (Ed.), *Perspectives on racism and the human services sector: A case of change* (pp. 15–55). Toronto: University of Toronto Press.

James, C. E. (2001). Multiculturalism, diversity, and education in the Canadian context: The search for an inclusive pedagogy. In C. Grant and J. Lei (Eds.), *Global constructions of multicultural education: Theories and realities* (pp. 175–204). Mahwah, NJ: Erlbaum.

James, C. E. (2003). *Seeing ourselves: Exploring race, ethnicity, and culture* (3rd ed.). Toronto: Thompson Educational Publishing.

James, C. E., & Shadd, A. (Eds.). (2001). *Talking about identity: Encounters in race, ethnicity, and language*. Toronto: Between the Lines.

Kazimapur, A., & Halli, S. S. (2003). *The new poverty in Canada: Ethnic groups and ghetto neighbourhoods*. Toronto: Thompson Educational Publishing.

Kehoe, J., & Mansfield, E. (1997). The limitations of multicultural education and anti-racist education. Accessed at http://caslt.org?research/multicult.htm

Kellner, D. (2003). Toward a critical theory of education. *Democracy and Nature: The International Journal of Inclusive Democracy, 9*(1), 51–65.

Kincheloe, J. L. (2001). *Getting beyond the facts: Teaching social studies/social sciences in the twenty-first century*. New York: Peter Lang.

Kincheloe, J. L., & Steinberg, S. R. (1997). *Changing multiculturalism*. Philadelphia: Open University Press.

Kymlicka, W. (1995). *Multicultural citizenship*. Oxford: Oxford University Press.

Kymlicka, W. (2001). *Politics in the vernacular: Nationalism, multiculturalism, and citizenship.* Oxford: Oxford University Press.

Labelle, M. (2005). The change of diversity in Canada and Quebec. *Policy Options, 26*(3), 88–93.

Ladson-Billings, G. (1995). Toward a theory of culturally relevant pedagogy. *American Educational Research Journal, 32*(3), 465–491.

Ladson-Billings, G. (1998). Just what is critical race theory and what's it doing in a nice field like education? *International Journal of Qualitative Studies in Education, 11*(1), 7–24.

Ladson-Billings, G. (2004). New directions in multicultural education: Complexities, boundaries, and critical race theory. In J. A. Banks & C. A. McGee Banks (Eds.), *Handbook of research on multicultural education* (pp. 50–65). San Francisco: Jossey-Bass.

Li, P. (1998). The market value and social value of race. In V. Satzewich (Ed.), *Racism and social inequity in Canada* (pp. 115–130). Toronto: Thompson Educational Publishing.

Loomba, A. (1998). *Colonialism/postcolonialism.* London: Routledge.

Lund, D. (2003). Educating for social justice: Making sense of multicultural and antiracist theory and practice with Canadian teacher activists. *Intercultural Education, 14*(1), 3–17.

May, S. (1994). *Making multicultural education work.* Bristol: Longdunn.

McCarthy, C. (1994). Multicultural discourses and curriculum reform: A critical perspective. *Educational Theory, 44*(1), 81–98.

McCreath, P. L. (1997). Multiculturalism: Failed or untried concept. In *State of the art—national study 1997.* Accessed at http://caslt.org?research/multicult.htm

McLaren, P. (1995). *Critical pedagogy and predatory culture: Oppositional politics in a postmodern age.* New York: Routledge.

McLaren, P. (1997). *Revolutionary multiculturalism: Pedagogies of dissent for the new millennium.* Boulder: Westview Press.

McLeod, K. (1997). Introduction: Multicultural education. In *The state of the art—national study 1997.* Accessed at http://caslt.org/research/multicult.htm

Mitchell, K. (2001). Education for democratic citizenship: Transnationalism, multiculturalism, and the limits of liberalism. *Harvard Educational Review, 71*(1), 58–78.

Musgrove, F. (1982). *Education and anthropology: Other cultures and the teacher.* New York: Wiley and Sons.

Nieto, S. (1992). *Affirming diversity: The sociopolitical context of multicultural education.* ED361440. White Plains, NY: Longman.

Nugent, A. (2006). Demography, national myths, and political origins: Perceiving official multiculturalism in Quebec. *Canadian Ethnic Studies, 38*(3), 21–36.

Perry, R. J. (1992). Why do multiculturalists ignore anthropologists? *Chronicle of Higher Education, 38*(26), 52.

Perry, T., & Fraser, J. W. (1993). *Freedom's plow: Teaching in the multicultural classroom.* New York: Routledge.

Pon, G. (2000). Beamers, cells, malls and cantopop: Thinking through the geographies of Chineseness. In C. E. James (Ed.), *Experiencing difference* (pp. 222–234). Halifax, NS: Fernwood.

Pratt, G. (2002). Between homes: Displacement and belonging for second generation Filipino-Canadian youth. Accessed at http://www.riim.metropolis.net/virtual%20Library/2002/wp02-13.pdf

Rosaldo, R. (1989). *Culture and truth: The remaking of social analysis.* Boston: Beacon Press.

Schick, C., & St. Denis, V. (2005). Troubling national discourses in anti-racist curricular planning. *Canadian Journal of Education, 28*(3), 295–319.

Shi-Xu. (2001). Critical pedagogy and intercultural communication: Creating discourses of diversity, equality, common goals, and rational-moral motivation. *Journal of Intercultural Studies, 22*(3), 279–293.

Sleeter, C. E., & Grant, C. A. (1998). *Making choices for multicultural education: Five approaches to race, class, and gender* (3rd ed.). New York: Wiley.

Stables, A. (2005). Multiculturalism and moral education: Individual positioning, dialogue, and cultural practice. *Journal of Moral Education, 34*(2), 185–197.

Strong-Boag, V. (2002). Who counts? Late nineteenth- and early twentieth-century struggles about gender, race, and class in Canada. In Y. Hébert (Ed.), *Citizenship in transformation in Canada* (pp. 112–134). Toronto: University of Toronto Press.

Tator, C., & Henry, F. (1991). *Multicultural education: Translating policy into practice.* Ottawa: Multiculturalism and Citizenship Canada.

Taylor, C. (1994). The politics of recognition. In A. Gutmann (Ed.), *Multiculturalism: Examining the politics of recognition* (pp. 25–73). Princeton, NJ: Princeton University Press.

Tomlinson, S. (1990). *Multicultural education in white schools.* London: B.T. Batsford.

Troyna, B. (1987). Beyond multiculturalism: Towards the enactment of anti-racist education in policy, provision, and pedagogy. *Oxford Review of Education, 13*(3), 302–320.

Turner, T. (1993). Anthropology and multiculturalism: What is anthropology that multiculturalism should be mindful of? *Cultural Anthropology, 8*(4), 411–429.

Vertovec, S. (n.d.). Pre-, high, anti-, and post-multiculturalism. Institute for European Studies. Accessed at http://ies.bs/activities/multicult/vertovec-ies.pdf

Walcott, R. (1997). *Black like who? Writing black Canada.* Toronto: Insomniac.

Watt, D. L. E., & Roessingh, H. (2001). The dynamics of ESL dropout: Plus ça change. . . . *Canadian Modern Language Review, 58*, 203–222.

Watkins, W. H. (1994). Multicultural education: Toward a historical and political inquiry. *Educational Theory, 44*(1), 99–117.

Wax, M. (1993). How culture misdirects multiculturalism. *Anthropology and Education Quarterly, 24*(2), 155–75.

Wideen, M., & Barnard, K. A. (1999). Impacts of immigration on education in British Columbia: An analysis of efforts to implement policies of multiculturalism in schools. Accessed at http://www.riim.metropolis.net/research/working/1998-99.html

Wilhelm, R. W. (1994). Exploring the practice-rhetoric gap: Current curriculum for African-American history month in some Texas elementary schools. *Journal of Curriculum and Supervision, 9*(2), 217–223.

Williams, R. (1976). *Keywords: A vocabulary of culture and society.* London: Fontana.

Willinsky, J. (1999). Curriculum after culture, race, nation. *Studies in the Cultural Politics of Education, 20*(1), 89–103.

Wortley, S. (2003). What are the challenges and where should public policy be directed in order to produce safe, cohesive, and healthy communities? Accessed at http://canada.metroplois.net/events/ottawa/wortley%20paper%201.htm

Yon, D. (2000). *Elusive culture: Schooling, race, and identity in global times.* Albany, NY: SUNY Press.

Zine, J. (2004). Dealing with September 12: Integrative anti-racism and the challenge of anti-Islamophobia education. In G. Dei & N. Wane (Eds.), *Anti-racism education.* Special Issue, *Orbit, 33*(3), 39–41.

17

Equity in Multicultural Student Assessment

LOUIS VOLANTE

Large-scale assessment continues to provoke intense debate across North America and much of the Western world. Advocates argue that only through benchmarking student achievement results, can schools become compelled to improve their instructional approach. Armed with objective assessment data, policy-makers and other educational leaders can make sound decisions for accountability purposes and identify exemplary teaching practices that may be disseminated for system improvement (Covaleskie, 2002; Taylor & Tubianosa, 2001). Critics disagree and argue that overreliance on large-scale assessment produces an oversimplified vision of educational excellence with predictable winners and losers (Kohn, 2000; McNeil, 2000). They note a long history of documented abuses and unintended negative consequences associated with high-stakes testing, particularly in multicultural student populations. Current research on black, Hispanic, First Nations, and English second language students continues to support these criticisms, suggesting large-scale assessment programs are often unfair and require significant rethinking. This paper argues that assessment equity is a multi-faceted construct based on four interrelated issues—technical quality, reporting, utilization, and most importantly, educational opportunity. The proposed framework is meant to inform the direction of future assessment-led reforms and ultimately improve educational outcomes for multicultural students.

NORTH AMERICAN CONTEXT

Large-scale achievement testing has been widely implemented because it is perceived to address a broad array of problems, including low standards, weak student motivation, poor curriculum and instruction, inadequate learning, and educational inequality (Darling-Hammond, 2003). Currently, every state, province, and territory within North America (with the exception of Prince Edward Island) administers large-scale assessment measures. These tests continue to exert the most important influence on curricula and pedagogy within North American schools—particularly since they are often used to make high-stakes decisions for students and teachers. In Canada, these measures often comprise a significant portion (i.e., 30–50%) of a student's final grade or serve as a graduation requirement (e.g., Ontario Secondary School Literacy Test). In the United States, however, these tests also serve high-stakes purposes for teachers and administrators as reflected in the provisions of the federal No Child Left Behind (NCLB) Act. Essentially, schools that fail to meet "Adequate Yearly Progress" (AYP), as reflected in mandated improvements in test scores, are labelled as "failing," and are eventually taken over by the state. Couple this with recent announcements to introduce merit-based pay incentives that are tied directly to test scores, and it is easy to understand why schools inevitably devote excessive amounts of time on test content at the expense of other areas of the curriculum. This tendency to teach closely to the test has been reported in virtually every North American jurisdiction that administers large-scale assessment measures.

INTENDED AND UNINTENDED CONSEQUENCES

The policy intentions and the outcomes of large-scale assessment programs are often incongruent. Although the architects of standards-based reforms sought to correct inequities in the system, the top-heavy testing approach has had virtually the opposite effect and resulted in many unintended negative consequences for multicultural student populations. Research has consistently shown that black, Hispanic, First Nations, and English second language students do not do as well as their white counterparts (Demmert, 2005; Fox, 1999; Froese-Germain, 1999; Gonzalez, 2002; Jones & Ongtooguk, 2002). This achievement gap has not closed and, in many instances, has actually become larger since the introduction of standards-based reforms (McNeil, 2000; Valencia & Villarreal, 2003). The result is that schools serving multicultural students are often compelled to narrow the curriculum even further to boost test scores. When one considers the long-standing criticism that standardized achievement tests do not measure higher-order and critical thinking skills (Ketterlin-Geller, Leanne, McCoy, Twyman, &

Tindal, 2003; Yeh, 2001), it seems logical that multicultural students are more likely to be the recipients of a truncated curriculum.

The pressure to raise test scores also extends beyond mere curriculum concerns. In some contexts, including Texas and Massachusetts, there is a sizable bump in the percentage of students who are retained the year before the states' high-stakes exams are given (Kornhaber, 2004). Unfortunately, the extra year that students are given to "catch up" is associated with increased drop-out rates but not with increased learning (Hauser, 2001). High school completion rates have also fallen in Canadian provinces (i.e., Ontario and Alberta) with high-stakes consequences attached to student performance (Volante, 2007). This negative relationship with student retention suggests external testing may actually push students out of school. Similarly, pressure placed on low performing schools, which typically operate in the most distressed urban areas, often makes it difficult to recruit and retain creative and talented teachers and administrators (Berlak, 2001). Recent statistics suggest that about two-thirds of Latino, African-American, and Native American eighth-grade math students in the United States have teachers who do not have an undergraduate degree in mathematics, compared with half of all white students (Haycock, 1998). Thus, multicultural students' grade promotion status and the pedagogical practices they experience are also compromised by current standards-based reform agendas.

TOWARD A NEW FRAMEWORK

Educators and psychologists have strenuously argued for equity in testing and assessment, for "culture free," "culturally fair," and "culturally relevant" or "culturally salient" testing and assessment (Hilliard & Amankwatia, 2003). Unfortunately, these equity oriented concepts do not encompass a broad understanding of the challenges faced by multicultural student populations since they focus primarily on technical quality issues. Although the latter are worthy of attention, the scope of analysis for equitable assessment is much broader and also includes issues related to utilization, reporting, and most importantly, educational opportunity. Thus, assessment equity is a multi-faceted construct that requires a number of interrelated solutions—some of which extend beyond the control of test developers and educators. Indeed, the most pressing problems facing multicultural students require the active engagement of policy-makers since they have a profound influence on the distribution of resources both within and outside of schools. The next section challenges the current value assumptions underpinning each of the previously noted issues as a way to inform future assessment-led reforms.

Technical Quality

Large-scale achievement measures typically reflect the cognitive styles, contexts, and experiences of white middle-class students (Purnell, 2000). Assessing and evaluating the progress of students from diverse racial and ethnic groups and social classes is therefore complicated by differences in language, learning styles, and culture (Banks, Cookson, Gay, Hawley, Irvine, Nieto, Schofield, & Stephan, 2001). Test developers have responded to this challenge by developing sophisticated statistical techniques such as Differential Item Functioning (DIF) and Differential Test Functioning (DTF) that assess how well two individuals with identical ability but different group membership perform on an item/test (Ellis & Raju, 2003; Gelin & Zumbo, 2003). For example, Banks's (2006) analysis of fifth-grade reading and language arts data from the Terra Nova test indicated that although Hispanic and black students did not differ from matched white students in their cluster scores, black students were differentially drawn to incorrect options that illustrated various aspects of their culture. The latter suggests that even the design of distracters within multiple-choice items, not just the nature of the question stem, must be closely scrutinized to avoid cultural bias.

Although the previously noted statistical procedures are important components of test and scale development, they merely describe anomalies in test performance. The fact that scores on all commercially produced tests show the same 8 to 10 per cent gap suggests that the gap cannot be fully explained by racial or cultural bias lodged in individual test items (Berlak, 2001). Clearly, more profound structural constraints must be acknowledged before one can faithfully validate particular assessment approaches (Kane, 2002). Traditional, on-demand, paper-and-pencil tests seem destined to always favour certain groups since they measure particular skills and types of knowledge. Battiste (1998) refers to this general problem as "cognitive imperialism" and notes the inherent bias of implementing standards from a Western educational frame of reference.

Although research suggests the inclusion of performance-based assessment components in public examinations presents some important challenges (Elwood, 1999), there are compelling reasons to view this approach as a more viable and equitable alternative for the future. Soodak (2000) articulates three key reasons why performance-based assessment should be adopted for accountability purposes. First, performance assessment may accommodate differences in students' ways of knowing by permitting, and even encouraging, multiple presentation and response formats. Second, because performance assessments are curriculum embedded, they may minimize opportunities for biases resulting from a student's lack of familiarity with the language, context, and format of the test. Third, students and parents are more likely to feel that they are involved in the assessment process when performance measures are employed. Educators

can also improve assessment by promoting the inclusion of oratory skills to balance reading skills, by ensuring culturally relevant curriculum, and by factoring
in students' language and experience when judging their abilities (Fox, 1999).

Utilization

It is important to note that changes in the basic form of an assessment, whether
it be traditional or authentic in nature, are unlikely to enhance equity unless we
also change the ways in which assessments are used (Darling-Hammond, 2003).
Large-scale assessment programs that are reliable, valid, and include multiple
measures that tap different learning styles and cultures are still unfair when they
are utilized for high-stakes decisions that outstretch their abilities. For example, denying a student his or her earned diploma based on a single test score is
not fair nor is it an effective method for raising academic achievement within
a school system (Johnson, Boyden, & Pittz, 2001). It is equally unacceptable to
use test results to classify a student as disabled when he or she did not have a
disability or to track a student into an inferior or segregated educational placement (Soodak, 2000). Sadly, multicultural students such as black, Hispanic, First
Nations, and ESL students are less likely to pass exit exams and are more likely to
be placed into special education classes than their white counterparts (Case &
Taylor, 2005; Handy, 1999; Zhang & Katsiyannis, 2002). In addition to limiting
students' life chances, large-scale assessments may also reinforce biases teachers
may have towards particular groups of students. For example, research suggests
that multicultural student populations and those at risk for dropping out report
more bias from their teachers than do white students and those who are more
academically advanced (Wayman, 2002). The cumulative effect is that multicultural students—particularly those who perform poorly on external tests—are
more susceptible to becoming disenchanted and disengaged from school.

Using assessment data to classify a school is equally problematic and also
leads to a host of negative consequences. The customary practice of ranking
schools in local newspapers has precipitated documented cases of inappropriate teacher and administrator behaviour (Simner, 2000). Encouraging low-
performing students to stay home the day of the test, offering subtle cues to correct responses, and even providing correct answers to multiple-choice questions
become more common when relative school performance becomes highly pub-
licized. Ranking also tends to drive highly qualified and competent teachers out
of schools serving vulnerable student populations, such as those within inner
city environments (Delphi, 1998; Hargreaves & Fink, 2006). Thus, it seems clear
that the practice of using assessment results to compare and rank schools creates unhealthy competition and stifles the more desirable objective of fostering
a community of learners (Volante, 2005). The alternative is to utilize assessment

results primarily as vehicles for developing action plans to improve instruction, staff development, school organization, resource and community engagement—as ways of improving students' lives and ensuring that all children receive a high quality education (Earl, 1999).

Reporting

Research across North America has consistently demonstrated that between 40 and 50 per cent of students' scores on a standardized achievement test is attributable to socio-economic status (Crislip & Heck, 2001; Lytton & Pyryt, 1998; Sacks, 2000). Indeed, research from the three major international assessments—Program in International Student Assessment (PISA), Progress in International Reading and Literacy Study (PIRLS), and Third International Mathematics and Science Study (TIMSS)—suggests that the link between socio-economic status and achievement is a pervasive feature around the world (see Marks, Cresswell, & Ainley, 2006; Myrberg & Rosen, 2006; Nash, 2003; Papanastasiou, 2000; Thorpe, 2006; Willms, 2006). Unfortunately, parents and the public are often not provided with information that allows them to clearly understand the differences between groups of students or the limitations that exist with particular measures. This is compounded by the fact that the differences that do exist between groups of students are often exaggerated by analysis and reporting techniques. Berlak (2001) illustrates this point within the California context where the gap between low and high performance on a basic literacy test is 3.2 multiple-choice test items on a 50-item test. Although this is a relatively insignificant difference from an educational point of view, he notes how the norming of the test and the manner in which cut scores are set grossly inflates this difference for persons of colour. For example, African-American test-takers are 3.5 times more likely to fail the test than whites, Latino/Hispanics more than twice as likely, and Asian-Americans more than 1.5 times more likely than whites.

In Canada, differences between schools and districts are also reported in a manner that invites misunderstanding and possible incorrect interpretations. For example, many schools are often compared based on raw score differences with little, if any, attention paid to measurement error. This is despite the fact that when uncertainty is taken into account, many—sometimes most—differences in raw scores between schools and districts disappear (Earl, 1999). Thus, it seems clear that those in the education community need to model effective dissemination of assessment information, whether at the international, national, state, or provincial level (McEwen, 1999). Failure to do so inevitably leads to the perception that multicultural students and the schools that serve them are inferior.

Educational Opportunity

Schools can be thought of as a collection of opportunities to learn with fairness of opportunity determined by comparing the learning opportunities students have within, across, and outside of schools. Opportunities to learn within a school are related to factors such as: a) funding (i.e., small class sizes, quality resources/technology, extracurricular activities); b) teacher quality (i.e., experience, preparation to teach the content, participation in high-quality professional development, verbal ability, and opportunity to receive teacher rewards and incentives); c) rigour of the curriculum (i.e., breadth and depth of content coverage, time engaged in learning); and d) school organization (i.e., safe and orderly learning environment, effective parent involvement strategies, avoidance of rigid grouping practices) (Darling-Hammond, 1997; Gonzalez, 2002). Research suggests that all of these factors are below standard for multicultural student groups (Dreeban & Gamoran, 1986; Lee, 2004). For example, in terms of teacher quality, the least qualified teachers typically end up teaching the least advantaged students—a situation exasperated by inadequate supports for beginning teachers and the poor working conditions within many schools, especially those in urban settings serving multicultural students (Darling-Hammond, 2001).

Similarly, the relationship between funding and curriculum necessitates that schools possess adequate resources to deliver quality programs. As one sixteen-year-old student from Oakland, California, commented:

> We lack resources, we have no money, and other schools when you look at their high [test scores] you wonder why. It's because they have money, they have resources. They have all that which we need over here at the bottom and people don't even bother to think maybe that's the problem. And yet you want to blame it on the youth. (Johnson, Boyden, & Pittz, 2001, p. 9)

This relationship between resources and student achievement can also be extended to broader relationships. For example, Willms (2005) suggests that Alberta and Ontario's high performance relative to other Canadian provinces on PISA is partly attributable to the level of school resources within those educational jurisdictions.

Research is also emerging that should inform future school organization reforms. Consider a recent analysis of student achievement in thirty countries by Marks, Cresswell, and Ainley (2006). These authors found that schools with tracking and other forms of differentiation tended to magnify socio-economic inequalities in education. The latter is a significant finding since tracking fosters a negative self-image and creates reduced expectations for a student's future (Froese-Germain, 1999). Although the previous authors do not suggest completely abandoning such practices, they argue for policies that would delay the allocation of students to different tracks and for greater movement between tracks. Similarly, research suggests that the creation of small schools is vital for improving student achievement (Fine & Powell, 2001). These findings are especially important for multicultural students since they are consistently overrepresented in less rigorous academic programs and are taught within large urban schools. Clearly, schools must be organized to promote contexts of learning in which all students, particularly those from at-risk multicultural groups, are encouraged to form high aspirations for achievement within a supportive learning environment.

Equally important is the recognition that many home-related factors, which are beyond a school's control, have a profound impact on student achievement. For example, student achievement correlates highly with parent education levels and family income. Since ethnic minorities are disproportionately represented in the low-income sector, inequalities in opportunities to learn will invariably contribute to the achievement gap of multicultural students (American Educational Research Association [AERA], 1999; Hilliard & Amankwatia, 2003). Indeed, the presence of material resources such as those classified as *wealth measures* (i.e., room for the student, link to the internet, and number of computers, televisions, mobile phones) along with *educational resource measures* (i.e., quiet place to study, possession of a dictionary, textbooks, calculators) have a significant impact on PISA reading, science, and mathematics achievement scores—particularly in countries with more income inequality such as the United States, Mexico, Brazil, and Portugal (Marks, Cresswell, & Ainley, 2006). Similar findings have arisen from analyses of PIRLS (Myrberg & Rosen, 2006) and TIMSS (Papanastasiou, 2000) data. Thus, making educational opportunities equal within schools is necessary but insufficient for many multicultural students who have socio-economically disadvantaged family backgrounds (Lee, 2004).

By recognizing the importance of both within- and outside-school factors on student achievement, we can avoid the defeatist myth that schools make no difference while avoiding the pitfalls of the other extreme, that they make all the difference (Rothstein, 2002). One way to recognize this balance is to utilize a value-added assessment approach for interpreting large-scale assessment results. Value-added assessment considers family background and emphasizes the degree of progress in students before making judgments about appropriate levels of achievement (Hershberg, Simon, & Lea-Kruger, 2004; Wickstrom, 1999). Essentially, this approach permits an examination of variables schools have control over—instructional approach—with those factors they cannot control—school demographics (Crundwell, 2005). Although there are challenges associated with value-added assessment, it does bring to the forefront one essential truism: not all children begin the achievement race at the same start line. Assessment-led reforms that fail to acknowledge this important fact ensure many children and schools will continually be classified as failures—even when they jump from 10 to 50 per cent achievement in one academic year.

CONCLUSION

Diversity in schools is both an opportunity and a challenge to understand the fundamental differences that influence student learning and achievement. We must find ways to respect multicultural students and help create a collective eth-ic for which all children feel welcomed and appreciated. An important starting point for this discussion is the recognition that overreliance on traditional large-scale assessment measures has often marginalized our most vulnerable student populations. Policy-makers need to begin to examine how various forms of data and multiple representations of student work can be used to present a more accurate and robust picture of student achievement. Essentially, performance-based measures and other forms of curriculum-embedded assessment must be incorporated into existing accountability frameworks. However, no meaningful dialogue is possible if we continue to endorse a market-placed solution to educa-tion that minimizes differences in opportunities to learn.

Fortunately, the preceding discussion suggested some targeted reforms can be utilized to address differences in opportunities to learn and, in doing so, help to close the achievement gap. Some of the suggested changes relate to improv-ing the quality of the teaching/learning process within schools (i.e., high-quality teachers, less tracking, smaller class sizes and schools) while others address more complex home-related factors (i.e., parent education levels, community resources, greater income equity) that require the active engagement of senior policy-makers. In truth, many of these factors indicate that sound educational policies cannot be divorced from the economic and social policies that charac-terize particular governments and countries. To do so treats schools as islands in an ocean, with many multicultural students relegated to contexts that are aca-demically impoverished or essentially barren.

Thus, the ultimate question is not *is this test fair?* but *what is the context for this assessment?* (Cline, 2000). Simply designing large-scale assessment mea-sures with culturally neutral test items will not eliminate persistent problems with the achievement gap. Indeed, characterizing assessment equity within the narrow bounds of technical quality confines the scope of solutions solely to test developers and schools. Concerns with assessment design, administration, analysis, and reporting must also be informed by the inherent inequities that many multicultural students face within and outside of schools. Policy-makers must acknowledge the multi-faceted nature of assessment equity and promote comprehensive reforms that strengthen schools, families, and local communities. The latter would suggest an authentic desire to improve the educational outcomes of multicultural student groups. Clearly, standards-based reforms and the conventional blame-and-shame approach with the public ranking of schools have not delivered on their promises. It's time to explore other options.

REFLECTIVE QUESTIONS

1. This study took place in the mid-2000s. What concerns raised in the reading are still present in the school system?
2. Do your experiences with the integration of technology resonate with those reported here? Give examples to support your answer.
3. Why do these problems with technological integration in teaching and learning persist?
4. What possible solutions can you recommend to the problems identified in this reading and to others you have raised?
5. How is this a curricular issue?

REFERENCES

American Educational Research Association. (1999). *Standards for educational and psychological testing*. Washington, DC: AERA.

Banks. K. (2006). A comprehensive framework for evaluating hypotheses about cultural bias in educational testing. *Applied Measurement in Education, 19*(2), 115–132.

Banks, J. A., Cookson, P., Gay, G., Hawley, W. D., Irvine, J. J., Nieto, S., Schofield, J. W., & Stephan, W. G. (2001). Diversity within unity: Essential principles for teaching and learning in a multicultural society. *Phi Delta Kappan, 83*(3), 196–198.

Battiste, M. (1998). Enabling the autumn seed: Toward a decolonized approach to Aboriginal knowledge, language, and education. *Canadian Journal of Native Education, 22*(1), 16–27.

Berlak, H. (2001). *Academic achievement, race, and reform: Six essays on understanding assessment policy, standardized achievement tests, and anti-racist alternatives*. California: United States Department of Education.

Case, R. E., & Taylor, S. S. (2005). Language difference or learning disability? Answers from a linguistic perspective. *Clearing House, 78*(3), 127–130.

Cline, T. (2000, September). *Principles and practice of fair assessment*. Paper presented at the Minorities in a Pluralistic Society at the Turn of the Millennium, Brno, Czech Republic.

Covaleskie, J. F. (2002, April). Two cheers for standardized testing. *International Electronic Journal for Leadership in Learning, 6*(2). Accessed at http://www.ucalgary.ca/~iejll/volume6/covaleskie.html

Crislip, M. A., & Heck, R. H. (2001). *Accountability, writing assessment, and equity: Testing in a multilevel model*. Paper presented at the Annual Meeting of the American Educational Research Association, Seattle, WA.

Crundwell, R. M. (2005). Alternative strategies for large-scale student assessment in Canada: Is value-added assessment one possible answer? *Canadian Journal of Educational Administration and Policy, 41.* Accessed at http://www.umanitoba.ca/publications/cjeap/articles/crundwell.html

Darling-Hammond, L. (1997). *The right to learn.* San Francisco: Jossey-Bass.

Darling-Hammond, L. (2001). Apartheid in American education: How opportunity is rationed to children of color in the United States. In T. Johnson, J. E. Boyden, & W. J. Pittz (Eds.), *Racial profiling and punishment in U.S. public schools: How zero tolerance policies and high stakes testing subvert academic excellence and racial equity* (pp. 39–44). Oakland, CA: Applied Research Center.

Darling-Hammond, L. (2003). *Standards and assessments: Where we are and what we need.* Accessed at http://www.tcrecord.org

Delphi, K. (1998). Shopping for schools. *Orbit, 29*(1), 29–33.

Demmert, W. G. (2005). The influences of culture on learning and assessment among Native American students. *Learning Disabilities Research and Practice, 20*(1), 16–23.

Dreeban, R., & Gamoran, A. (1986). Race, instruction, and learning. *American Sociological Review, 51,* 660–669.

Earl, L. (1999). Assessment and accountability in education: Improvement or surveillance? *Education Canada, 39*(3), 4–6.

Ellis, B. B., & Raju, N. S. (2003). *Test and item bias: What they are, what they aren't, and how to detect them.* North Carolina: United States Department of Education.

Elwood, J. (1999). Equity issues in performance assessment: The contribution of teacher-assessed coursework to gender-related differences in examination performance. *Educational Research and Evaluation, 5*(4), 321–344.

Fine, M., & Powell, L. (2001). Small schools: An anti-racist intervention in urban America. In T. Johnson, J. E. Boyden, & W. J. Pittz (Eds.), *Racial profiling and punishment in U.S. public schools: How zero tolerance policies and high stakes testing subvert academic excellence and racial equity* (pp. 45–49). Oakland, CA: Applied Research Center.

Fox, S. J. (1999). *Student assessment in Indian education or what is a roach?* Washington, DC: United States Department of Education.

Froese-Germain, B. (1999). *Standardized testing: Undermining equity in education.* Ottawa, ON: Canadian Teachers Federation.

Gelin, M. N., & Zumbo, B. D. (2003, April). *Differential domain functioning on the numeracy component of the Foundation Skills Assessment: Bringing the context into picture by investigating sociological/community moderated test and item bias.* Paper presented at the Annual Meeting of the American Educational Research Association, Chicago, IL.

Gonzalez, R. (2002). *The No Child Left Behind Act: Implications for local educators and advocates for Latino students, families, and communities.* Washington, DC: National Council of La Raza.

Handy, A. J. (1999). *Ethnocentrism and black students with disabilities: Bridging the cultural gap,* Volume I. New York: Vantage Press.

Hargreaves, A., & Fink, D. (2006). The ripple effect. *Educational Leadership, 63*(8), 16–21.

Hauser, R. (2001). Should we end social promotion? Truth and consequences. In G. Orfield & M. L. Kornhaber (Eds.), *Raising standards or raising barriers? Inequality and high-stakes testing in public education* (pp. 151–178). New York: Century Foundation.

Haycock, K. (1998). *Thinking K–16: Good teaching matters a lot.* Washington, DC: The Education Trust.

Hershberg, T., Simon, V. A., & Lea-Kruger, B. (2004). The revelations of Value-Added: An assessment model that measures student growth in ways that NCLB fails to do. *School Administrator, 61*(11), 10–12.

Hilliard, A. G., & Amankwatia, B. (2003, April). *Assessment equity in a multicultural society: Assessment and instructional validity in a culturally plural world.* Paper presented at the National Council on Measurement in Education, Chicago. IL.

Johnson, T., Boyden, J. E., & Pittz, W. J. (2001). *Racial profiling and punishment in U.S. public schools: How zero tolerance policies and high stakes testing subvert academic excellence and racial equity.* Oakland, CA: Applied Research Center.

Jones, K., & Ongtooguk, P. (2002). Equity for Alaska natives: Can high-stakes testing bridge the chasm between ideals and realities? *Phi Delta Kappan, 83*(7), 499–550.

Kane, M. (2002). Validating high-stakes testing programs. *Educational Measurement: Issues and Practice, 21*(1), 31–41.

Ketterlin-Geller, L., Leanne, R., McCoy, J. D., Twyman, T., & Tindal, C. (2003). How do critical thinking measures fit within standards-based reform? *Assessment for Effective Intervention, 28*(3-4), 37–48.

Kohn, A. (2000). *The case against standardized testing: Raising scores, ruining the schools.* Portsmouth, NH: Heineman.

Kornhaber, M. L. (2004). Appropriate and inappropriate forms of testing, assessment, and accountability. *Educational Policy, 18*(1), 45–70.

Lee, J. (2004). Multiple facets of inequity in racial and ethnic achievement gaps. *Peabody Journal of Education, 79*(2), 51–73.

Lytton, H. & Pyryt, M. C. (1998). Predictors of achievement in basic skills: A Canadian effective school study. *Canadian Journal of Education, 23*(3), 281–301.

Marks, G. N., Cresswell, J., & Ainley, J. (2006). Explaining socioeconomic inequalities in student achievement: The role of home and school factors. *Educational Research and Evaluation, 12*(2), 105–128.

McEwen, N. (1999). Using international test results to improve student performance. *Education Canada, 39*(3), 44–46.

McNeil, L. (2000). Creating new inequalities: Contradictions of reform. *Phi Delta Kappan, 81*(10), 729–734.

Myrberg, E., & Rosen, M. (2006). Reading achievement and social selection in independent schools in Sweden: Results from IEA PIRLS 2001. *Scandinavian Journal of Educational Research, 50*(2), 185–205.

Nash, R. (2003). Is the school composition effect real? A discussion with evidence from the UK PISA Data. *School Effectiveness and School Improvement, 14*(4), 441–457.

Papanastasiou, C. (2000). Internal and external factors affecting achievement in mathematics: Some findings from TIMSS. *Studies in Educational Evaluation, 26*, 1–7.

Purnell, R. B. (2000). *Making dry bones live: The rate of testing in equity and access.* Paper presented at the National Council of Teachers of English, Milwaukee, WI.

Rothstein, R. (2002). *Out of balance: Our understanding of how schools affect society and how society affects schools.* Chicago, IL: The Spencer Foundation.

Sacks, P. (2000). *Standardized minds.* Cambridge, MA: Perseus Books.

Simner, M. L. (2000). *A joint position statement by the Canadian Psychological Association and the Canadian Association of School Psychologists on the Canadian press coverage of the province-wide achievement test results.* Accessed at http://www.cpa.ca/documents/joint_position.html

Soodak, L. C. (2000). Performance assessment and students with learning problems: Promising practice or reform rhetoric? *Reading and Writing Quarterly, 16*, 257–280.

Taylor, A. R., & Tubianosa, T. (2001). *Student assessment in Canada: Improving the learning environment through effective evaluation.* Kelowna, BC: Society for the Advancement of Excellence in Education.

Thorpe, G. (2006). Multilevel analysis of PISA 2000 reading results for the United Kingdom using pupil scale variables. *School Effectiveness and School Improvement, 17*(1), 33–62.

Valencia, R. R., & Villarreal, B. J. (2003). Improving students' reading performance via standards-based reform: A critique. *The Reading Teacher, 56*(7), 612–621.

Volante, L. (2005). Accountability, student assessment, and the need for a comprehensive approach. *International Electronic Journal for Leadership in Learning, 9*(6). Accessed at http://www.ucalgary .ca/~iejll/volume9/volante.htm

Volante, L. (2007). Standards-based reform: Can we do better? *Education Canada, 47*(1), 54–56.

Wayman, J. C. (2002). *Student perceptions of teacher ethnic bias: Implications for teacher preparation and staff development.* Paper presented at the Annual Meeting of the American Educational Research Association, New Orleans, LA.

Wickstrom, R. A. (1999). Accountability: Toward an appropriate approach. *Education Canada, 39*(3), 16–19.

Willms, J. O. (2005). Why the difference? *Education Canada, 45*(1), 54–55.

Willms, J. O. (2006). Variations in socioeconomic gradients among cantons in French- and Italian-speaking Switzerland: Findings from the OECO PISA. *Educational Research and Evaluation, 12*(2), 129–154.

Yeh, S. S. (2001). Tests worth teaching to: Constructing state-mandated tests that emphasize critical thinking. *Educational Researcher, 30*(9), 12–17.

Zhang, O., & Katsiyannis, A. (2002). Minority representation in special education: A persistent challenge. *Remedial and Special Education, 23*(3), 180–187.

18

Educating for Global Citizenship:
Conflicting Agendas and Understandings

LYNETTE SHULTZ

INTRODUCTION

For at least the past decade, *educating for global citizenship* has become a main focus of many educators in both the formal school sector and the non-formal and non-governmental organization (NGO) sector. Evaluations of this decade of work reveal that little identifiable or attributable progress has been made (Canadian Council for International Co-operation [CCIC], 2004). In the early 1990s, with help of Canadian International Development Agency (CIDA) funds as well as grand visions of global solidarity, Canadian schools and community organizations joined together in efforts to educate students as members of a global society. Since that time, funding has been cut drastically and coordinated efforts across sectors have decreased as schools face their own local budget cuts and shifting mandates such as producing high scores on standardized tests. In this article I argue that this reduction in effective global education or education for global citizenship is a result of vastly different understandings of what global citizenship entails. Dower (2003) suggests that global citizenship comprises three components, "a normative claim about how humans should act, an existential claim about what is the case in the world and an aspirational claim about the future" (p. 7). I present three programs aimed at global citizenship education, each having a distinct understanding of the role for the global citizen, as well as particular normative, existential, and aspirational claims regarding global citizenship.

Global citizenship education has grown in its extent alongside understand-ings of the process of globalization. McGrew (2000) presents three approaches to globalization that reflect differing positions in the global economic, political, and social system. A neo-liberal approach celebrates the dominance of a single global market and the principles of liberal transnational trade. From this perspective, a global citizen is one who is a successful participant in a liberal economy driven by capitalism and technology. In contrast, a radical approach presents globaliza-tion as an accelerated mode of Western imperialism that uses economic power for domination. A global citizen from this perspective understands how this system creates poverty and oppresses most of the world's population and therefore has a responsibility to challenge state and corporate structures that increase the margin-alization of countries in the global south. McGrew suggests a third understanding of globalization as that of transformationalism. From this position, globalization is understood as cultural, social, environmental, and political as well as econom-ic, resulting in new patterns of inclusion and exclusion, as well as the erosion of North-South hierarchies. Hoogvelt (1997) suggests that an accurate understand-ing of globalization is as a nested arrangement of concentric circles, representing the world's elites, the middle class, and the poor that cut across national bound-aries. "North and South, First World/Third World are no longer 'out there' but nestled together 'right here' in all the world's urban areas" (McGrew, p. 351). From this perspective, a global citizen understands herself or himself as intricately con-nected to people and issues that cross national boundaries. This personal connec-tion with all others reflects an understanding that in order to create communities (local and global) that are just, democratic, and sustainable, citizens must under-stand their connection to all other people through a common humanity, a shared environment, and shared interests and activities. Each of these understandings of globalization suggests a particular role and set of actions for a global citizen.

Understanding the practice of educating for citizenship is equally challeng-ing. Educators, although naming citizenship as key to their overall goals, have had difficulty responding to aspects of citizenship outside its traditional space in the public sector. This is not surprising as even a brief scan of these views presents a tangle of often competing understandings and definitions. As a con-cept often connected primarily with political positioning and participation in the electoral process, citizenship is now being debated in new arenas. No longer connected with just the public sector, the language of citizenship is creeping into both the private sector and civil society. Businesses make claims to good corporate citizenship in response to criticism of their environmental and social effects.[1] Civil society organizations have claimed engaged citizenship as a key descriptor of their activism and social change agendas.[2]

These contested definitions reflect wider discourses and tensions in society. Moller (2002) identifies neo-liberalism as a powerful source of a particularly narrow philosophy about the role of citizens. "For neoliberals, 'consumer choice' is the guarantor of democracy. . . . in this way democracy moves from a political concept to an economic concept . . . Equity is confused with consumer choice" (p. 10). In a modern, neo-liberal society, a citizen's role is primarily an economic one, that of consumer, influencing society through individual acts of consumption. In contrast, a growing movement against neo-liberalism presents active citizenship as the radical force necessary to challenge the hegemony of the market and to protect the environmental and social well-being of society (Apple, 2000; Osler, 2000). Lister (1998) suggests that there are two aspects of citizenship,

> to be a citizen and to act as a citizen. To be a citizen means to enjoy the rights necessary for agency as well as social and political participation. To act as a citizen involves fulfilling the full potential of the status. (pp. 328–329)

Isin and Wood (1999) suggest that an understanding of citizenship needs to be based on the ethos of pluralization as the necessary response to the tensions of multiple identities and loyalties that currently exist in the contemporary globalized world. As transnational and global factors come to affect individuals and communities, new links and networks have been formed to address these factors. The political and social reality has shifted to include the interdependence of relationships as people find ways to address their common needs and concerns locally, nationally, and transnationally as global citizens.

THREE APPROACHES TO GLOBAL CITIZENSHIP
The Neo-liberal Global Citizen
In the neo-liberal perspective, the role of the individual as an entrepreneur in the private sector is a privileged position. With the government role focused on creating space for free market expansion, particularly in areas not traditionally market friendly, the citizenship response is both to access these markets and to "ameliorate the disordered fault of capitalist progress" (Thomas, 2000, p. 43) in the form of interventions at the local level. Thomas describes interventionism as a parallel response alongside neo-liberal development as evidenced by the increase in development agencies or trustees of development such as NGOs and international NGOs (INGOs). There were 6,000 INGOs in 1990 and 26,000 in 1999 (*Economist,* 1999). INGOs, although certainly not homogeneous in approach or mandate, have been instrumental in bringing the discourse of global citizenship to the community level. These organizations employ millions of people who travel throughout the world bringing with them an agenda for "global development."

Interventionism engages people in actions that both remove barriers to modernization and address the problems of neo-liberal development such as social disparity and environmental degradation. This group of people, along with millions of global business entrepreneurs, has taken advantage of advances in technology that make communication and movement across time and space a simple matter of internet access and a jumbo jet. The result is an understanding of the global citizen as traveller. This citizen strives to create a place beyond traditional boundaries and local restrictions where he or she can access the political, social, economic, and environmental rewards of participation in a global society. Social connection through international liberalism is sought by these citizens, and global citizenship from this perspective is enacted through dialogue and participation. Change is created in the interstices of self, other, and the social context, and facilitated by a global economic system. Relationships, both economic and social, are sought freely across time and space without being encumbered by national boundaries. When spending time with people who work in international development agencies, it is always interesting to hear discussions of zigzagging through the world in their work. For example, I was recently in a conversation with two aid workers who said, "I want to get back to the Latin America desk because I only have Indonesia and the Philippines now" and "I have to do project monitoring in Bolivia, Nepal, and Zambia. It will be good to get out of the office" (personal communications, 2004). Iyer (2000) provides another example of this global citizen:

> "One country's not enough," said a sweet, unplaceable soul who approached me one night at a gathering in rural Japan, introducing himself as half-English and half-Japanese, though he thought of himself as Malaysian (he'd spotted me, clearly, as a fellow in-betweener). "When I'm in England, there's a part of me that's not fulfilled; that's why I come here—to find the other part." (p. 19)

Policy Example: International Education

Although there are endless examples of programs that encourage international travel and global experience, I focus on an international education policy that is typical in jurisdictions throughout the developed world. International education programs focus on the recruitment of students from abroad as well as providing opportunities for local students and teachers to participate in international travel. The Alberta government funds and oversees an international education program that is part of its wider international relations policy. The focus on international education as a means to successful participation in global economics is clearly indicated in recent policy that links such participation with the role of global citizenship.

Globalization and our multicultural society have increased the need for know-ledge of other languages and cultures for effective communication, for better human relations in our own diverse Canadian society, and for a competitive edge in the shrinking world of economics. (Alberta Learning, 2003, p. 1)

Alberta will be internationally recognized as a leading provider of education, skill development and industry training, and Albertans will be well prepared for their role in the global market place and as global citizens. (Alberta Learn-ing, 2001, p. 3)

Key components of the program of international education of this juris-diction involve a student exchange, a teacher exchange, and international student recruitment.

International student recruitment in both the basic education and post-sec-ondary sectors and international marketing of Alberta expertise in education and training programs and services, provide net economic benefits to the prov-ince. Subsequent multiplier effects from related business, student and tourism expenditures amplify the benefit to the provincial economy. With expanding worldwide demand for education and training and learners' ability to access leading educational programs wherever they are located, international edu-cation offers important growth opportunities for Alberta's economy. (Alberta Learning, 2003, p. 1)

In the post-secondary sector, Alberta institutions receive funding support to carry out student exchanges in four countries where Alberta has a special re-lationship. These exchanges typically involve language and cultural studies. A number of post-secondary institutions have also developed extensive networks and partnerships with institutions in other countries, which provide Alberta students with study-abroad and exchange opportunities. Exchange partici-pants report that these programs enhance their own learning and international awareness. Home jurisdictions and institutions report that the programs benefit participants' classmates as they study alongside international students. (Alberta Learning, 2003, http://www.learning.gov.ab.ca/IntlEd/Activities.asp)

Approach to Global Citizenship

The key aim of the global citizenship education efforts from this perspective is to increase transnational mobility of knowledge and skills. Global citizenship, then, is primarily linked to global economic participation, either through participa-tion in business or an instrumental interventionism that mediates the uneven effect of such global actions. It is based on a fundamental understanding that as individuals we should be able to move throughout the world freely, enjoying the rewards regardless of national or other boundaries. The role of education, then, is to facilitate this participation through building relationships (e.g., exchange) based on cultural understanding as well as capacities such as language acquisition. This is understood as how to prepare global citizens able to negotiate this liberal global environment. Liberal relationships that result from these exchanges are understood to be the catalyst for successful participation in the global marketplace. However, without attention to issues of power and access, these global citizens will assume that their position of privilege is a natural position and a sign of success. Although they might support intervention efforts, for example, donations to charities, to mitigate the suffering of those who are not successful, the focus disregards any need for structural change and in fact is antithetical to such change. Therefore, promoters of this form of global citizenship will be largely opposed to the social change agendas of the radical global citizenship and transformational global citizenship projects.

THE RADICAL GLOBAL CITIZEN

A radical approach to development and citizenship involves an analysis of the global structures that serve to create deep global inequalities. This analysis identifies a "deepening North-South divide as a consequence of uneven globalization" (McGrew, 2000, p. 350). With governments in the global south having declining power, the role of the global citizen is to challenge the structures that perpetuate these circumstances. Rather than focus on building liberal relationships across the globe, the radical global citizen identifies these relationships and any sense of global or national solidarity as a by-product of the hegemony of economic globalization. The structures that serve to reinforce this hegemony include international institutions such as the International Monetary Fund (IMF), the World Bank, and the World Trade Organization (WTO) also known as the Bretton Wood institutions. These institutions were established at the end of WW II to address postwar reconstruction. Originally just the World Bank and the International Monetary Fund, the World Trade Organization was added in the 1990s. Currently the group of organizations has grown to five, all under the direction of the World Bank. Of great importance is the fact that the World Bank's director is appointed by the United States government (compare www .brettonwoodsproject.org). The Bretton Woods institutions face intense challenges from anti-globalization and anti-poverty organizations for their economic policies, for example, structural adjustment programs.

Since the early 1980s, World Bank and IMF loans have increasingly required that recipient countries agree to Letters of Intent committing themselves to a Structural Adjustment Program (SAP), which typically has the following features:

- massive cuts to government spending, particularly in areas such as health and education;
- mass layoffs of public employees;
- liberalization of trade and removal of restrictions on foreign investment;
- withdrawal of subsidies on basic goods consumed by the poor such as bread, rice, and oil;
- cuts to wages of all public employees;
- devaluation of the local currency—which cheapens exports, but makes imported goods on which the population depends more expensive (and thus represents a further cut in living standards); and
- privatization of state-owned companies such as public telephones, railway, and electricity systems. (McNally, 2002, pp. 163–164, see also, George, 1997; Thomas, 2000)

These policies have been aggressively instrumented in most countries of the world, but not without challenge. As a result, there has been a drive to create the radical global citizen. "Contemporary globalization, in the radical view, is thus implicated in the intensification of global poverty, deprivation, conflict and violence" (McGrew, 2000, p. 351). The radicalized global citizen is challenged to build solidarity through breaking down these global structures of oppression.

Policy Example: Halifax Initiative World Bank Boycott

Policy approaches and programs that promote a radical global citizenship have as their goal a disruption of the structures that hold the dominant global capitalist system in place. Motivated by strong ethical positions of social justice, these global citizens engage in direct actions aimed at forcing radical economic, political, and social change. The World Bank Boycott is an example of a radical approach to global citizenship. It is an international campaign that demands an end to socially and environmentally destructive World Bank policies and projects through grassroots financial and political power. Launched in April 2000 by organizations in thirty-six countries, the campaign links people directly affected by World Bank practices with organizations and investors who can affect the flow of money to the Bank with a goal of halting those practices (Halifax Initiative).

The campaign targets a key source of World Bank finance, international bond sales. The Bank receives most of its resources to finance lending to over 100 developing countries from the sale of World Bank bonds on private capital markets. Bonds are bought by governments, universities, mutual funds, pension funds, trade unions, life insurance companies, churches, and civic groups. Employing the tactics of the anti-apartheid movement, ordinary people are organising locally to boycott these bonds, effectively threatening the Bank's primary source of funding. The boycott campaign has three central demands, which were established by the boycott's international coordinating committee, with representatives from organizations and social movements from 14 countries. The campaign demands an end to the World Bank's harmful structural adjustment policies; 100% debt cancellation and an end to environmentally destructive projects, including oil, gas, mining and dams.

Approach to Global Citizenship

This approach to global citizenship calls people to action against global institutions, particularly financial institutions that are the main architects of global economic liberalism. In order to create the radical change in North-South relations, citizens must understand the link between the economic activities of these institutions of political, economic, and social oppression and economic destruction, for example, SAPS. This project utilizes the power of local citizens to draw attention to the effects of the international institution and to challenge the basic structures that support it. Citizens are engaged as global citizens in linking marginalized people in the south and the investors, mainly in northern countries, and demanding radicalization of these institutions.

The challenge of this approach to global education is seeing global relations as more than one of victors, villains, and victims. The relationships between global institutions and local experiences of oppression are more complex than this approach might suggest, and therefore engagement as global citizens requires finding new ways to be in relationship if change is to be more than just shifting exploitation from one group to another.

> People-centered development for poverty eradication is ultimately about recognizing the rights of the vulnerable and transforming the power relations, and cultural and social interests, that sustain inequality. Development is therefore a political process that engages people, particularly people who are poor and powerless, in negotiating with each other, with their governments, and with the world community for policies and rights that advance their livelihood and secure their future in the world. (Tujan, 2004, p. 7)

Understanding this complexity and finding new ways of being in relationship are needed to fully achieve the justice agenda of the radical global citizen.

THE TRANSFORMATIONALIST GLOBAL CITIZEN

From a transformationalist perspective, globalization is viewed as more than a new form of imperialism or just a path to a single global market economy. Although recognizing that globalization is highly uneven in its effect, it is understood that globalization has resulted in a complex and dynamic set of international, national, and local relationships that has created new patterns of inclusion and exclusion. As a result, new ways of negotiating between local and global actions and agendas, resolving conflict, and acting in solidarity need to be established. There are indications that new models of transnational relations are evolving that link marginalized people throughout the world. There is a shift from a geographic North-South division to a socio-economic division that cuts across nations and regions (Hoogvelt, 1997). The reality is that in both the north and south, there exist concentrations of wealth and power along with increasing poverty and exclusion. This reality has significant implications for the roles of both the state and civil society as new forms of governance are established that include public and private interests, domestic and transnational agencies, as well as an increasing number of North-South coalitions established to influence policy. "A new development consensus is emerging—often referred to as the post-Washington or Geneva consensus—which recognizes development as a shared global challenge and responsibility amongst states and societies, North or South, industrializing as well as post-industrial" (McGrew, 2000, p. 352). The global citizen in this frame understands his or her role as one of building relationships through embracing diversity and finding shared purpose across national boundaries. Understanding that the complexity of citizenship in a global world is created by and creates a vast network of diverse relationships, the global citizen seeks to include and engage others based on their shared common humanity. The overarching theme of the social justice work being done to eradicate poverty and improve the life possibilities of the marginalized is *a better world is possible*. Not content to just challenge the unjust structures that exist, people throughout the world are joining together to create social justice through deep compassion and accompaniment, through creating democratic spaces for building inclusive community, and through action that links the local experience with the shared global experience.

Policy Example: Building Knowledge in Partnership

The transformationalist understanding of the role of the global citizen is illustrated in a recent policy capacity-building initiative that involved Canadian civil society organizations working internationally, their southern partner organizations, as well as other members of southern civil society organizations. The aim of this project was to engage participants in the international voluntary sector in a knowledge-generating process that would build capacity to influence local, national, and international policy. Based on core values of solidarity, equity, and social justice, this participatory process "encouraged collaborative sharing of knowledge and perspective, creativity, innovation and effective engagement" (CCIC, 2003). This project was designed to create a global alliance that allows for engagement on issues of global concern.

> It is important to build strong networks, North-North, North-South, South-South, which take into account strategic access . . . An important part of these relationships is for Northern NGOs to "close the loop" with other Northern based organizations focusing on similar issues . . . The foundation of an alliance must be based on shared values and principles. (CCIC)

The objectives of participation included:

- To explore with members processes of learning and working in North/South partnership to build knowledge for policy influence and the challenges and power dynamics inherent to these processes.
- To begin to collectively examine methodologies for addressing these dynamics and challenges.
- . . . to increase the capacity in the membership for learning for policy influence, and level of involvement in policy development processes. (CCIC)

Central to this approach to global citizenship is the focus on knowledge building, which is the key element of the process and the intended outcome of this project. Participants were engaged in critiquing the processes of sharing knowledge that exist in current relationships. "How can we transform processes of extraction to mutual learning? What knowledge do you need from us? This is the knowledge we need from you" (CCIC). The goal of this process was to transform social and political relationships between people across national boundaries. The fundamental position underpinning this project is that:

> we need to develop political awareness through education and social mobilization at the base, with a critical approach as to how society and political power works. To achieve results civil society must work through coalitions and networks, global, regional and national networks with different commonalities of constituencies. (personal communication, CCIC, 2003)

Approach to Global Citizenship

This project reflects an understanding of the importance of creating democratic spaces for community and coalition building across local, national, and regional boundaries. Through this process citizens are able to link action at the local and global level to build authentic challenges to those forces that perpetuate oppression, poverty, and marginalization. These processes of building relationships and creating space for dialogue and change are meant to engage participants in acting on an understanding of their common humanity and shared concerns. In this the global citizen is a companion, accompanying the *other* on a journey to find just and compassionate responses to injustice. These relations act as fractals, local patterns of embracing diversity that are reproduced to create global stability through creating new forms of inclusion and transnational solidarity. The policy challenge in this approach to citizenship is to ensure that *just* action is achieved in the complexity and complicity of relationships and engagement as a citizen of a global world.

CONCLUSION

As global citizenship takes a more central focus in education policy, it is important that we have a clear understanding of the actual goals of global citizenship being presented. There is a sense that little has been accomplished in the past decade despite significant efforts by formal and non-formal educators to engage students as global citizens. As this study has revealed, approaches to global citizenship are vastly different in their intent and approach. The three approaches presented in this study function in isolation from one another and can be understood as counterproductive in engaging people as global citizens, particularly the neo-liberal approach as compared with the radical and transformationalist positions. The neo-liberal global citizen learns to expect unrestricted access to the rewards of a liberal global economic system. Any challenge to this access is viewed as problematic protectionism. The radical approach to global citizenship that focuses solely on the hegemony of global structures may in fact mask how local and global actors are intertwined to create exploitation and increased marginalization of particular groups, for example, poor women and children, and also how local and global actors can create change in these unjust situations. Global citizens learn that the world is determined by structures that prevent authentic change or relationships from developing. As understandings of how common experiences of poverty and marginalization extend beyond state boundaries have developed, a new approach to global citizenship has developed. Based on understandings of a shared planet and a common humanity, global citizens learn that compassion and care become powerful connections that cross the typical boundaries of state, nationality, race, class, and sex. Power relations become negotiated in localized contexts as spaces of interaction are established for dialogue and deliberation. These become global spaces through the connection of transnational networks and coalitions of solidarity.

Educators include global citizenship goals in recognition that citizens need to be engaged in issues and actions beyond their local context. How this engagement is viewed determines what type of global citizen is created in the process. If citizens of the wealthiest nations learn that their role as global citizens is to compete in the global marketplace, then the structures of inequality that keep members of less wealthy countries marginalized will be perpetuated, if not strengthened. New ways of structuring relations between nations and within nations need to be learned into existence through building spaces of understanding and engagement that extend beyond traditional boundaries and create new ways of negotiating global relations. This must be the role of the global citizen.

REFLECTIVE QUESTIONS

1. Compare and contrast the three approaches to thinking about globalization that Shultz presents.
2. Do these three approaches fit with your experience of global education?
3. From your perspective, is there anything missing in this model? Explain your answer.
4. What approach to global education do you see represented in the curriculum of your province/territory?
5. What might be some of the challenges in implementing these approaches to global education in the classroom?

NOTES

1. For example, one international pharmaceutical company states that "global citizenship is about how a company advances its business objectives, engages its stakeholders, implements its policies, applies its social investment and philanthropy and exercises its influences to make a productive contribution to society" (http://media.pfizer.com/file/corporate_citizenship). A large energy company describes its environmental policies as part of "a philosophy of global citizenship, based on building strong relationships with people, communities and nations" (http://www.shell.com/content/).

2. The CCIC (1996) describes global citizenship from a civil society perspective: "Global citizenship nurtures collective action for the good of the planet and promotes equity. As citizens, each person has equal rights. Global citizenship hinges on Canadians recognizing that they are members of a community of peoples who share a single planet." An international development organization defines global citizenship as "more than the sum of its parts. It goes beyond simply knowing that

we are citizens of the globe to an acknowledgement of our responsibilities both to each other and to the Earth itself . . . it is about the need to tackle injustice and inequality and having the desire and ability to work actively to do so" (http://ccic.ca/002/public.shtml).

REFERENCES

Alberta Learning. (2001). *International education strategy paper.* Edmonton, AB: Author.

Alberta Learning. (2003). *Goals of education.* Edmonton, AB: Author.

Apple, M. (2000). Between neoliberalism and neoconservatism: Education and conservation in a global context. In N. C. Burbules & C. A. Torres (Eds.), *Globalization and education: Critical perspectives* (pp. 57–77). London: Routledge.

Canadian Council for International Co-operation. (1996). *Global citizenship: A new way forward.* Accessed at www.//ccic.ca

Canadian Council for International Co-operation. (2003). *Building policy capacity.* Accessed at www .ccic.ca/e/002/capacity_building.shtml

Canadian Council for International Co-operation (CCIC). (2003). *Capacity-building policy: Capacity for poverty eradication.* Accessed at www.ccic.ca/e/002/capacity_building_policy_capacity_ for_poverty_eradication.sht.

Canadian Council for International Co-operation (CCIC). (2004). *Signs of change.* Accessed at www .ccic.ca/e/002/public.shtml

Dower, N. (2003). *An introduction to global citizenship.* Edinburgh, UK: Edinburgh University Press.

Economist. (1999). *Yearbook of international organizations.* December 11, p. 24.

George, S. (1997). How the poor develop the rich. In M. Rahnema & V. Bawtree (Eds.), *The post-development reader.* London, New Jersey: Zed Books.

Halifax Initiative. Accessed at www.halifax.org/index.php/Issues_WB_BondBoycott

Hoogvelt, A. (1997). *Globalization and the post-colonial world. The new political economy of development.* London: Macmillan.

Isin, E., & Wood, P. (1999). *Citizenship and identity.* London: Sage.

Iyer, P. (2000). *The global soul.* New York: Vintage Press.

Lister, R. (1998). Citizen in action: Citizenship and community development in Northern Ireland context. *Community Development Journal, 33*(3), 326–335.

McGrew, A. (2000). Sustainable globalization? The global politics of development and exclusion in the new world order. In T. Allen & A. Thomas (Eds.), *Poverty and development into the 21st century* (pp. 345–364). Milton Keynes, UK: Open University Press, and Oxford, UK: Oxford University Press.

McNally, D. (2002). *Another world is possible.* Winnipeg, MB: Arbeiter Ring.

Moller, J. (2002, September). *Democratic leadership in an age of managerial accountability.* Paper presented at the 2002 CCEAM Conference: Exploring New Horizons in School Leadership for Democratic Schools, Umeå University, Sweden.

Osler, A. (2000). *Citizenship and democracy in schools: Diversity, identity, equality.* Stoke on Trent, UK: Trentham Books.

Thomas, A. (2000). Poverty and the "end of development." In T. Allen & A. Thomas (Eds.), *Poverty and development into the 21st century.* Milton Keynes, UK: Open University Press, and Oxford, UK: Oxford University Press.

Tujan, A. (2004). Governance: Reclaiming the concept from a human rights perspective. *The reality of Aid 2004: An independent review of poverty reduction and development assistance.* Manila: IBON Books, and London: Zed Books.

19

Curriculum of Imperialism:
Good Girl Citizens and the Making of the
Literary Educated Imagination

KELLY YOUNG

A living story does not pass from the mouth-of-the teller to the ear-of-the listener, but rather it moves—it lives—from mouth-to-mouth, from telling to telling. (Benjamin, 1968, p. 87)

INTRODUCTION

Walter Benjamin's understanding of the ways in which stories "live" through "re-tellings" is helpful to my thinking about how the Girl Guide and Brownie stories participated in my identity-formation because it enables me to conceptualize how "The Brownie Story" was a living story that came to life through dramatization. For example, the story lived in me, through me, and all around me for the majority of my formative years of my childhood. I recall that my aunt was a Brown Owl Leader. My cousins were also involved in Brownies and Guides. My aunt and cousins also read "The Brownie Story." In fact, I remember that the story was often read aloud to the Brownie group. From my childhood memory, "The Brownie Story" went as follows:

An unruly girl wants to become a Brownie when she learns that Brownies are "good girls" who help their mothers by keeping the house tidy and clean. Her mother instructs her to ask the Brown Owl in the forest how to become a Brownie. The little girl enters the forest and finds the Brown Owl. She is told by the Brown Owl to find a pond at the edge of the forest in order to find her answer. Once she is at the pond, she is to repeat aloud . . . "Twist me and turn me and show me the elf, I looked in the water and there saw ____."

The little girl in the story fills in the rhyme with "myself." I recall having to perform the rhyme in front of a mirror surrounded with garland on the floor of the Anglican Church in order to become a "good girl Brownie." I also recall that all of my little Brownie friends had to do the same. My experiences are formative to my inquiry into the ways in which cultural forms, such as "The Brownie Story," play a role in identity formation because the self emerges from one's involvements with signifying systems and practices (Davis, Sumara, & Luce-Kapler, 2000). In a way then, engaging with signifying systems such as "The Brownie Story" involves the work of interpretation, that is, the work of hermeneutic activity by way of engaging the hermeneutic imagination (Smith, 1991).

I recognize that "The Brownie Story" was integral to my participation in the Girl Guide movement. From my Western-educated imagination, the story represents a particular kind of imperial and cultural knowledge and therefore I question how dominant narratives, such as "The Brownie Story" became naturalized and structured, in part, my beliefs about what a good girl image was. After a rediscovery of my Brownie and Girl Guide handbooks in 2000, I began researching seminal texts held in the Girl Guide National Archive of Canada. I became interested in the ways in which the Girl Guide movement is implicated in imperialism and nation building in Canada. Moreover, I became concerned with the ways in which my identity formation was caught up in and mediated through the stories that were part of the Brownie and Girl Guide indoctrination process.[1] For Said, cultural forms, ". . . were immensely important in the formation of imperial attitudes, references, and experiences" (1994, p. xii). For me, "The Brownie Story" represents what was valued in my white Anglo-Saxon culture, and in a very deep sense embodies imperial beliefs and morals espoused by the Girl Guide movement. I turn to Willinsky, who writes,

> At the very least, we need to reconsider how a person coming of age in the West . . . was trained in the aftermath of colonialism among imperial habits of mind that now need to be identified, as they might still contribute to the educational imagination. (1998, p. 19)

If imperial habits of mind are formed through the literary imagination and through citizenship practices that are taught in both public school and the Girl Guides, how might I begin to theorize and practise a disruption of imperial habits of mind?

I situate myself theoretically in the field of curriculum theorizing whereby autobiographical educational experience is used to question how Brownies, as part of the broader Girl Guide movement, played a dual role in my identity formation. In Brownies, I learned to assimilate and be obedient, while at the same time, learning to be independent and capable. My literary imagination was educated, in part, in the image of the British Empire through the Girl Guide movement. I explore the image of the "good girl" in "The Brownie Story" that informed my understanding of the development of my imperial habits of mind. I conceptualize *The Brownie Handbook* as a cultural artifact, a curriculum and a socializing agent and investigate the following question, "How might an understanding of the involvement of 'The Brownie Story' as a social and imperial cultural practice in the construction of self contribute to a twenty-first-century discussion of pedagogy?" For my inquiry, I draw on philosophical hermeneutic inquiry and explore dominant cultural stories, such as "The Brownie Story," in terms of conceptualizing "the whole" and "the parts" of the Girl Guide movement as being important in the development of meaning-making.[2]

What follows is an interpretation, hermeneutically speaking, of the ways in which "The Brownie Story" embodies a particular curriculum of imperialism. In my inquiry, I uncover how the British Empire's Girl Guide movement made use of "focal practices" to perpetuate national and cultural (re)production (Borgmann, 1992; Davis, Sumara, & Luce-Kapler, 2000). I investigate: 1) how extra-curricular activities like guiding and storytelling activities involve a concurrent exploration of culture and identity, and 2) how narratives of nationhood and citizenship practices informed my understanding of an image of a "good girl."

WORKING THE ARCHIVE

In a hermeneutic sense, working the archive means to write about and report on my experiences (Smith, 1991). I explore the reproductive construction of my imperial culture of a good girl identity that involves a particular kind of relation-ship as "good citizen." As I spent time in the archive, there was a familiar sense of knowing and being as I recalled a place of "focal practices" that emphasized an imperial curriculum (Borgmann, 1992; Davis, Sumara, & Luce-Kapler, 2000). Focal practices involve the daily routines and cultural practices that humans par-take in. For example, in the archive, I took notes and often made reflective an-notations and observations in the margins of texts in order to review them later to gain a better comprehension of my experience of tracing the development of my imperial habits of mind.

Smith (1991) outlines several requirements of the hermeneutic imagination to help researchers form a hermeneutic attitude that I use as a framework for this paper. As a hermeneutic researcher, I am to develop attentiveness to language. I am to deepen my sense of the basic interpretability of life and interconnectedness of life because interpreting is viewed as a creative act. I am to be concerned with the hermeneutic imagination and the creation of meaning. Because the first area of concern for a hermeneutic researcher is language, I found the following definition of cultural imperialism helpful to my inquiry,

> Cultural imperialism may be defined as the use of political and economic power to exalt and spread the values and habits of a foreign culture at the expense of a native culture. A familiar example from an earlier period is the export of American films. Although cultural imperialism may be pursued for its own sake it frequently operates as an auxiliary of economic imperialism—as when American films create a demand for American products. (Bullock & Trombley, 1999, p. 419)

With a deeper understanding of cultural imperialism, I begin to peel back the layers of my white Anglo-Saxon identity formation and work toward an awareness of my relationship with imperialism by identifying the ways in which rhymes and stories informed my understanding of the image of a good girl.

A second area of concern for a hermeneutic researcher is the interpretability of life. For this, I turn to Pinar's method of currere. He writes,

> It is regressive-progressive-analytical-synthetical. It is therefore temporal and conceptual in nature, and it aims for the cultivation of a developmental point of view that hints at the transtemporal and transconceptual. From another perspective, the method is the self-conscious conceptualization of the temporal, and from another, it is the viewing of what is conceptualized through time. So it is that we hope to explore the complex relation between the temporal and conceptual. In doing so we might disclose their relation to the Self and its evolution and education. (1994, p. 19)

Currere is in an essential way to recover the dailiness of my life as I probe my experience of guiding. What follows is an autobiographical recounting of an experience of (re)interpreting how ideology operates through the reproduction of dominant ideas via cultural practices that can bring the development of imperial habits of mind into consciousness. I learned vis-à-vis the Girl Guide movement that assimilation towards imperial habits of mind, thriving in "The Brownie Story" and the Brownie promise, was socially desirable.

Brownie Inspection (literary archive journal excerpt August 22, 2002):

> The air at the Anglican Church is particularly stale in the evening. As always, the basement is cold, dreary and void of colour. I enter, hang my coat in the cloakroom, and greet Brown Owl, Tawny Owl and the other Brownies before

jostling for my place along the imaginary circle. Brown Owl stands tall in front of us. She is in her 40s and her pale skin contrasts with her dark brown hair tied into a bun, her blue uniform neatly pressed. Tawny Owl is the younger version of Brown Owl, a twenty year old but just as daunting with her trim figure and her dark hair long over her shoulders. Both have all the knowledge in the world that they are ready to bestow upon us. Brown Owl and Tawny Owl move from Brownie to Brownie as they inspect each one of us from head to toe. They look at our hair to see if it is neatly combed. Then they look at our face to ensure it has been washed and even ask us to turn our heads to see if we have cleaned behind our ears. Next the "all knowing" owls inspect our uniform beginning with our ties and check that it was tied "correctly" (right over left and under, left over right and under).

Our badges and pins have to be neatly sewn on our wrinkle-free uniforms. After that they do the dreaded hand inspection. They make us hold out our hands and they touch each finger to see if our nails have any dirt under them. Brownies always have to have clean white shiny nails. They make fun of Brownies who have nail-biting habits or girls who have not filed or cut their nails properly. Finally, the inspection moves down to our feet. We must have brown socks and shoes on to match our uniforms. I always show up in my blue running shoes (in an early act of rebellion) and never pass inspection with "flying colours." After inspection, we always follow traditional routines: sing O' Canada, repeat the Brownie promise, law, motto and practice our handshakes before storytelling and badge earning activities. (Young, 2002)

My autobiographical description came out of hours of dwelling in readings of seminal texts located in the Girl Guide National Archive, together with continuous anecdotal writings and juxtaposition of theoretical texts with my readings. I used archival texts, such as *The Brownie Handbook* as educational occasions that highlight a research location of cultural imperialism. Archival texts are potential pedagogical sites for learning since they are always an interpretation of relationships with memory (cognition), experience (phenomenology), and text (hermeneutics).

A third area of concern for a hermeneutic researcher is the creation of meaning. I searched for a malleable image to frame my aesthetic response to my reading of the archive. Jameson (1991) writes,

> . . . there was an obvious need for maps in the construction of imperial/colonial relations, and a cognitive map served as a social space of class, nation, local and international realities. [A map is . . .] A representation of subject's imaginary relationship to a real condition of existence. (pp. 585, 586)

Much of how I learned to divide the world, as Jameson (1991) and Willinsky (1998) understand was through my engagement with an imaginary map of the world. In fact, I recall how as a young child, I learned that Canada was an "extension" of Britain vis-à-vis geographic maps. Both real and imaginary maps became part of the development of my imperial habits of mind. Therefore a map became an integral part of my visual response to my reading of the Girl Guide National Archive through a painting titled, *Girls of the Empire* (2003). On three 16 × 20 inch canvases, I represent an aesthetic response to my reading of and engagement with Girl Guide National Archive materials.

Girls of the Empire (© Young, 2003)

My painting became a practice of art and storytelling. Denzin and Lincoln (as cited in Carson & Sumara, 1997; Denzin, 1994; Gallagher, 1992; Jardine, 1998; Madison, 1988) write:

> As with any art form, hermeneutical analysis can be learned only in the Deweyan sense by doing it. Researchers in this context practice the art by grappling with the text to be understood, telling its story in relation to its textual dynamics and other texts first to themselves and then to a public audience. (2000, p. 286)

My attentiveness to the series of identifiable connecting structures of images and stories from long ago helps me to learn from the past through an active reinterpretation of my present historical consciousness. In the archive, I trace the origins of my Brownie and Girl Guide handbooks (Cook, 1975; Dennis, 1975) that I read as part of my participation in the Girl Guide organization. The handbooks were written in accordance with the British Empire's early twentieth-century youth movement of guiding and scouting. The Brownie and Girl Guide handbooks are based on Sir Robert Baden-Powell's (1909) text, *Scouting for Boys: A Handbook for*

Instruction in Good Citizenship Through Woodcraft. Agnes Baden-Powell, sister of Robert Baden-Powell, adapted *Scouting for Boys* into *How Girls Can Help to Build the Empire: The Handbook for Girl Guides* (1918/1936). In my painting, I place scrutiny on Britain and its colonial relationships, while revealing imperial ideological themes of empire and nation building and good girl citizenship that are linked to Brownie cultural practices.

"THE BROWNIE STORY" AND CURRICULUM THEORIZING

"The Brownie Story" was originally written over one hundred years ago, as described by Betty Bradwell, PRA for Sheffield County. She writes,

> . . . originally written over 100 years ago by Juliana Horatia Ewing from Ecclesfield—a village near Sheffield South Yorkshire, (b. Juliana Gatty in 1841), father Dr. Alfred Gatty (Reverend and Vicar of Ecclesfield), writer and local historian. Mother—Margaret—wrote "Parables from Nature" (her father Alexander Scott); Margaret ran a popular periodical—Aunt Judy's Magazine. They provide charity to assist medical profession. Juliana published a story in a magazine, *The Monthly Packet*—titled—*The Brownies*. A story within a story . . . Brownies are a tiny race that teaches qualities of self-denial, consideration, thoughtfulness and kindness. Juliana married Alexander Ewing. Her stories were published in books. Her best known story was called *Jackanapes*—published in Aunt Judy's Magazine, 1879. Others include: *Jan of the Windmill, Mrs. Overtheway's Remembrances, A Flat Iron for a Farthing, Daddy Darwin's Dovecote* and *Amelia and the Dwarfs.* She was a promoter of female emancipation as characters in her stories are usually well educated girls . . . 1910 Girl Guides established by Agnes . . . Robert Baden-Powell wrote a pocket-sized adaptation of Juliana's book—*The Story of the Brownies* in an eleven page booklet. (1995, p. 33)

"The Brownie Story" is an example of what Pinar (1995) terms a "social-efficiency model of curriculum" that was used during the early twentieth century. As a focus on classical curriculum made way for a social-efficiency model of curriculum in the early twentieth century, Pinar (1995) recounts seven principles of education that dominated school curriculum: "1) health, 2) command of fundamental processes (i.e., basic skills), 3) worthy home membership, 4) vocation, 5) citizenship, 6) worthy use of leisure, and 7) ethical character" (p. 99). These same values were taught as part of the Girl Guide movement's rituals and storytelling. For example, "The Brownie Story" participated in the making of my identity by providing a model of a good girl who engages in ethical character, good citizenship, and the worthy use of leisure time. In Brownies, the principles were taught through a curriculum that espoused the engagement of focal practices, which involves an active interpretation of self. For example, I learned to become a Brownie by learning to cook, clean, and sew on the one hand and build a campfire on the other.

ON GENDER AND NATION BUILDING

The institutionalizing and naturalizing culture of nationhood, philanthropy, and homemaking in schools and alternative settings, such as the Brownies and Girl Guides, made it easy for a patriarchal society to embrace liberalism, as Luke argues:

> Liberalism grants women citizenship and a place in the public by replicating the public/private power structure: women's teaching, health care and service labor is seen as a "natural" extension of their domestic abilities. (1992, p. 32)

As a Brownie, my rituals involved what I term citizenship practices. The exchanges of citizenship values through repetitive ritual involved a representational practice of cultural affiliation that mediated my relationship with stories about universal goodness. Walkerdine writes:

> The discourses of natural childhood build upon a model of naturally occurring rationality, itself echoing the idea of childhood as an unsullied and innocent state, free from interference of adults. The very cognitism of most models of childhood as they have been incorporated into educational practices leaves both emotionality and sexuality to one side. (1998, p. 256)

Similarly, McClintock understands nationalism as a gendered discourse and draws on Nira Yuval Davis and Floya Anthias's conceptualization of how women have been implicated in nationalism—biologically, socially, culturally, sexually, and symbolically—as active participants and reproductive transmitters of culture (1997, p. 90). She asserts that nation narratives—from the Latin *natio,* to be born—naturalize the metaphor of the family as "institution" where, paradoxically, McClintock points out, ". . . a woman's *political* relation to the nation was . . . submerged as a *social* relation by the marriage relation within the family" (1997, p. 91). By focusing on the *embodiment* of "The Brownie Story," I pay particular attention to the use of water as a Victorian symbol. *The Brownie Handbook* states, "Twist me and turn me and show me the elf, I looked in the water and there saw ____" (Cook, 1975, p. 7). Of course, the answer to this rhyming riddle is "myself." In my experience of performing the story, water was substituted with a mirror that was surrounded by garland to resemble a pond. Water, as a symbol of purity, can be linked to an early twentieth-century Canadian discourse of moral and social reform. The reform movement involved a campaign to educate the next generation in what Valverde (1991) terms "purity ideals fitting to 'this age of light and water and soap'" (p. 17). In her study of moral reform at the turn of the twentieth century, Valverde (1991) analyzes a discourse of social purity to reveal the ways in which the moral and social reform movement contributed to nation building. She writes:

> The image of reform as illuminating society while purifying or cleansing it was already an integral part of the temperance movement, which developed in the mid-nineteenth century in the US and Britain and was taken up in Canada by such organizations as the Women's Christian Temperance Union and the Dominion Alliance for the Total Suppression of the Liquor Traffic. (pp. 17–18)

Valverde reveals how the purity movement drew upon symbols of purity to advance the moral and social campaign "to raise the moral tone of Canadian society" and describes the reform movement as a "loose network of organizations and individuals, mostly church people, educators, doctors, and those we would now describe as community or social workers" (p. 17). Girl Guides was part of the early twentieth century moral and social reform network through a discourse of character training. Part of the discourse included an image of the good girl that was constructed, in part, through the symbol of water in "The Brownie Story." What follows is an analysis of the image of water that appears in the story. Allegorically and metaphysically, a mirror can have various interpretations. In the case of "The Brownie Story," I turn to McClintock (1997), who writes,

> The mirror/frying pan, like all fetishes, visibly expresses a crisis in value but cannot resolve it. It can only embody the contradiction, frozen as commodity spectacle, luring the spectator deeper and deeper into consumerism . . . Mirrors glint and gleam in soap advertising, as they do in the culture of imperial kitsch at large. In Victorian middle-class households, servants scoured and polished every metal and wooden surface until it shone like a mirror. Doorknobs, lamp stands and banisters, tables and chairs, mirrors and clocks, knives and forks, kettles and pans, shoes and boots were polished until they shimmered, reflecting in their gleaming surfaces other object-mirrors, an infinity of crystalline mirrors within mirrors, until the interior of the house was all shining surfaces, a labyrinth of reflection. The mirror became the epitome of commodity fetishism: erasing both the signs of domestic labor and the industrial origins of domestic commodities. In the domestic world of mirrors, objects multiply without apparent human intervention in a promiscuous economy of self-generation. (p. 313)

There were many parts of the Girl Guide movement that involved economics. For example, we gave weekly dues, purchased uniforms, and worked toward "earning badges." The use of the mirror, however, served as a means to reproduce pretty little girls who wore neat and tidy uniforms as part of the ritual of belonging. A good girl helped to keep everything in the home clean and tidy (including herself and her uniform). The water/mirror symbol served to reinforce an image of a good girl citizen. Another example involves the Brownie promise. *The Brownie Handbook* states,

> I promise to do my best:
> To do my duty to God, the Queen
> And my country.
> To help other people every day,
> Especially those at home.

> (Cook, 1975, p. 1)

In my experience, storytelling and ritual repetition of rhymes and promises became an imperial socio-cultural practice of assimilation in the Girl Guide movement. Kerby (1991) understands this as he states, "As social beings we are already indoctrinated into certain traditional narratives that set up 'standard' expectations and obligations that guide our explicit evaluations; narrative, as Jean-François Lyotard has claimed, is a primary vehicle of ideology" (pp. 12–13). "The Brownie Story," as a dominant narrative, in my white middle-class culture, set up standard expectations that guided, in part, my understanding of what it meant to be a good girl citizen in society. Weekly repetitive Brownie practices contributed to the development of my imperial habits of mind through recurring themes of duty to God, the Queen, my country, and those at home.

IMPERIALISM AND IDEOLOGY

In *Reading and Teaching the Postcolonial*, the authors paint, in Saidian terms, a "contrapuntal" postcolonial aesthetic tableau of the ways in which literature and other art forms are important in the process of interrupting the, ". . . origins claims, the Eurocentric claims, the foundational claims of an essential and indispensable core of knowledge that our children need to know, and so forth—all appeals to ressentiment. These are all tired formulas that have led to the loss of genuine autonomy and creativity in the educational field" (Dimitriadris & McCarthy, 2001, p. 116). With an understanding of Said's (1994), "contrapuntal ensembles," I link imperial ideologies, in the form of repetitive rituals—such as the Brownie promise to do my duty to God, the Queen, and my country—with cultural practices that as a Brownie, I engaged in.

Furthermore, a decade ago, in *Race, Identity and Representation in Education*, McCarthy and Crichlow wrote:

> We call attention to the organization and arrangement of racial relations of domination and subordination in cultural forms and ideological practices of identity formation and representation in schooling—what Louis Althusser (1971) calls the "mise-en-scène of interpellation." We are therefore interested in the ways in which moral leadership and social power are exercised in "the concrete" (Hall, 1981, 1986) and the ways in which regimes of racial domination and subordination are constructed and resisted in education. (1993, p. xix)

Drawing on Italian Marxist Antonio Gramsci, who advances a theory of ideology, whereby the dominant class imposes its view of history and the world upon other classes, McCarthy and Crichlow are interested in the "concrete" practices that embody racial domination and subordination in education. Moreover, anti-humanist-structuralist, Louis Althusser, offers a revised conception of ideology that is useful to my project. Ideology for Althusser (1971) is "lived practice" in the analysis of everyday culture. In her article, "Racism, Sexism and Nation Building in Canada," Roxanna Ng conceptualizes race, class, and gender as "relations" that are constructed and reconstructed in terms of a social production of power—beyond Althusser's context of "the school"—toward Gramsci's formulation of "common sense" that becomes embodied in daily practices (1993, p. 57). I find both of these formulations helpful to my inquiry as I explore the ways in which "The Brownie Story" played a role in the construction my identity formation.

My understanding of Althusser's (1971) interpellation framework involves a concern with a gap between the materialistic and symbolic function of ideology.[3] On one hand, Marxist ideology involves abstract scientific knowledge, with a focus on economics and reductionism, as "social relations of reproduction." On the other hand, the constitution of the symbolic function of ideology, for Lacan, involves subjectivity, psychic identity, drives, and desires. For Althusser, a Lacanian and Marxist understanding of ideology is important in interpreting a "gap in-between" that represents the cultural practices that compel me to become the good girl subject; socially, culturally, psychically.

ON TRANSFORMATION AND PEDAGOGY IN THE TWENTY-FIRST CENTURY

My aesthetic response to the Girl Guide archive in the form of a mixed-media painting involves a relationship between reader, text, historical context, sociocultural influences, and imperial habits of mind that require, in a hermeneutic sense, (re)interpretation. Iser writes:

> Aesthetic response is . . . to be analyzed in terms of a dialectic relationship be-
> tween text, reader, and their interaction. It is called aesthetic response because,
> although it is brought about by the text, it brings into play the imaginative and
> perceptive faculties of the reader. . . . (1978, p. x)

I conceptualize "The Brownie Story" as an aesthetic text. In fact, the text requires young girls to perform parts of the story enabling them to quite literally
become the text. In order to consider the ways in which I can begin to disrupt
my educated imagination, I engage in conversation with others. In particular, I
speak to groups of teacher candidates across Ontario. First, I tell them my story
of reading the archive hermeneutically. For example, I explain that as reader,
archivist, and reporter, I question the implication of imperial cultural nation-
building curriculum in relation to identity formation and consider my participation in the Girl Guide movement. Then, I ask teacher candidates to consider their
role and participation in the movement. I explore gendered traditions embedded
in the handbooks, in terms of the homemaking and philanthropist themes that
are evident in the Brownie promise described earlier in this paper. I use visuals
and describe my archival journey in terms of my aesthetic response vis-à-vis
my *Girls of the Empire* (2003) painting. Dimitriadis (2002) argues that art and
aesthetics provide educators with an opportunity to think differently about the
past. He states that art and aesthetics "is a realm for interrogating new models,
new theories, new intellectual ancestors, new ways of thinking, acting and being
as transformative intellectuals and pedagogues" (p. 4).

Each time I tell my story of reading the archive, I engage people in a larger
conversation about the importance of exploring the educated imagination and
its relationship to the building of a nation that was a part of the British Empire.
I continually build a deeper understanding of the ways in which I learned to
divide the world through geographical and philosophical constructions that
shaped my educated imagination. It is through the retelling of my story that I
question the ways in which dominant stories and cultural practices contribute
not only to questions of identity formation but also to a twenty-first-century
discussion of pedagogy.

REFLECTIVE QUESTIONS

1. Have you had experiences similar to Young's where you felt that you were being "Canadianized"? What happened?
2. What other evidence have you seen of the "imperial socio-cultural practice of assimilation" occurring?
3. What are some of the other ways that gender is both intentionally and unintentionally addressed in Canadian classrooms/schools/society?
4. How did this reading help you to think about the issue of gender in the curriculum?
5. What recommendations would you make regarding gender in the curriculum after reading this article?

NOTES

1. For a critique of the Girl Guide movement as an "indoctrination" scheme, see Buttignol (2000).
2. For an overview of philosophical hermeneutics, see Gadamer (1976), Gallagher (1992), and Palmer, 1969).
3. Interpellation, Latin: *interpellātion-em* n. of action from *interpellāre*. English use became obsolete before 1700, Fr 19C action of interpellating or interrupting by question or appeal. Interpellate— interrupt (a person) in speaking or to break in on or interrupt (a process or action). Source: *The Oxford English Dictionary*, 1989, p. 1466.

REFERENCES

Althusser, L. (1971). *Lenin and philosophy, and other essays*. London: NLB.

Baden-Powell, R. (1909). *Scouting for boys: A handbook for instruction in good citizenship through woodcraft*. Ottawa: National Council of Boy Scouts of Canada.

Baden-Powell, R. (1918/1936). *Girl Guiding: The official handbook*. London: C. Arthur Pearson.

Benjamin, W. (1968). *Illuminations* (Harry Zohn, Trans.). New York: Schocken Books.

Borgmann, A. (1992). *Crossing the postmodern divide*. Chicago: University of Chicago Press.

Bradwell, B. (1995). The Brownie story. *UK Guiding*.

Bullock, A., & Trombley, S. (Eds.). (1999). *The new Fontana dictionary of modern thought*. London: Harper Collins.

Buttignol, M. (2000). Standing on the bank of the tenure-stream and helpful brownies: Two initiation experiences. *Teacher Education Quarterly, 27*(2), 145–161.

Carson, T. R., & Sumara, D. (Eds.). (1997). *Action research as a living practice*. New York: Peter Lang.

Cook, L. (1975). *The Brownie handbook*. Toronto: Girl Guides of Canada-Guides du Canada.

Davis, B., Sumara, D., & Luce-Kapler, R. (2000). *Engaging minds: Learning and teaching in a complex world*. Mahwah, NJ: Lawrence Erlbaum Associates.

Dennis, J. (1975). *The Guide handbook*. Toronto: Girl Guides of Canada-Guides du Canada.

Denzin, N. (1994). The art and politics of interpretation. In N. Denzin and Y. Lincoln (Eds.), *Strategies for qualitative inquiry*. Thousand Oaks, CA: Sage.

Denzin, N., & Lincoln, Y. (Eds.). (2000). *Handbook of qualitative research*. Thousand Oaks, CA: Sage Publications.

Dimitriadris, G., & McCarthy, C. (2001). *Reading and teaching the postcolonial: From Baldwin to Basquiat and beyond*. New York: Teachers College Press.

Dimitriadis, G. (2002). Untitled paper presented at the University of Ohio Education Summit, held in Miami, FL.

Gadamer, H.-G. (1976). *Philosophical hermeneutics* (David E. Linge, Trans.). Los Angeles: University of California Press.

Gallagher, S. (1992). *Hermeneutics and education*. New York: State University of New York Press.

Iser, W. (1980). *The act of reading: A theory of aesthetic response*. Baltimore: John Hopkins University Press.

Jameson, F. (1991). *Postmodernism, or, the cultural logic of late capitalism*. Durham, NC: Duke University Press.

Jardine, D. (1998). *To dwell with a boundless heart: Essays in curriculum theory, hermeneutics and the ecological imagination*. New York: Peter Lang.

Kerby, A. (1991). *Narrative and the self*. Bloomington: Indiana University Press.

Luke, C., & Gore, J. (Eds.). (1992). *Feminisms and critical pedagogy*. New York: Routledge.

Madison, G. (1988). *The hermeneutics of postmodernity: Figures and themes*. Bloomington: Indiana University Press.

McCarthy, C., & Crichlow, W. (Eds.). (1993). *Race, identity, and representation in education*. New York: Routledge.

McClintock, A. (1997). No longer in a future heaven: Gender, race and nationalism. In A. McClintock, A. Mufti. & E. Shohat (Eds.), *Dangerous liaisons: Gender, nation, and postcolonial perspectives* (pp. 89–112). Minnesota: University of Minnesota Press.

Ng, R. (1993). Racism, sexism, and nation building in Canada. In C. McCarthy & W. Crichlow (Eds.), *Race, identity and representation in education* (pp. 50–59). New York: Routledge.

The Oxford English Dictionary. (1989). London: Oxford Press.

Palmer, R. (1969). *Hermeneutics: Interpreting theory in Schleiermacher, Dilthey, Heidegger, and Gadamer*. Evanston, IL: Northwestern University Press.

Pinar, W. (1994). *Autobiography, politics and sexuality: Essays in curriculum theory 1972–1992*. New York: Peter Lang.

Pinar, W. (1995). Understanding curriculum as aesthetic text. In W. Pinar (Ed.), *Understanding curriculum*. New York: Peter Lang.

Said, E. (1994). *Culture and imperialism*. New York: Vintage Books.

Smith, D. (1991). Hermeneutic inquiry: The hermeneutic imagination and the pedagogic text. In E. Short (Ed.), *Forms of curriculum inquiry*. Albany, NY: State University of New York Press.

Valverde, M. (1991). *The age of light, soap and water: Moral reform in English Canada 1885–1925*. Toronto: McClelland & Stewart.

Walkerdine, V. (1998). Popular culture and the eroticization of little girls. In H. Jenkins (Ed.), *The children's cultural reader*. New York: New York University Press.

Willinsky, J. (1998). *Learning to divide the world: Education at empire's end*. Minneapolis, MN: University of Minneapolis Press.

Young, K. (2002). Girls of the empire: A literary archive.

Young, K. (Artist). (2003). *Girls of the empire* [Mixed-media painting].

20

"People who are different from you":

Heterosexism in Quebec High School Textbooks

JULIA R. TEMPLE

For decades education scholars have raised concerns about prejudice in text-books and called for an emphasis on diversity, yet this has generally been in the context of studies of racism and sexism (e.g., Ferree & Hall, 1990, 1996; Gaskell & Willinsky, 1995; McDiarmid & Pratt, 1971). In this article, however, I argue that much more attention is needed on the ways that textbooks exhibit heterosexism: the assumption that heterosexuality is superior to all other types of sexuality. This presumption is pervasive in Canadian society today (Canadian Teachers' Federation, 2002), manifesting itself in subtle expectations and assumptions as well as blatant, even violent, homophobia. But to what extent does heterosexism exist in Canadian textbooks?

This study responds to this question through a content analysis of high school textbooks in Quebec, arguably one of the most liberal regions in the country in regard to sexual diversity. In 1977 Quebec was the first province to add sexual orientation to its Human Rights Code, civil union legislation has included same-sex couples since its inception in 2002, and same-sex marriage is now legal as well. Therefore, I viewed Quebec as an ideal location to analyze the content of twenty francophone secondary school textbooks (Appendix 1) to examine how these texts addressed issues of sexuality and relationships. This analysis enabled me to describe the nature and extent of heterosexism in these texts, examining the often subtle ways that the school system can both reinforce and resist heterosexism.

FEMINIST CRITICAL REALIST PERSPECTIVE

I wish to clarify the perspective from which I approach the topic of heterosexism in education. Following New (1996), I consider my perspective a "feminist critical realist" approach. By this I mean several things. I recognize that each person can know the world only from her or his own perspective, and that claims to objectivity simply serve to disguise the standpoint being taken (Fraser, 1989) and to exclude other perspectives from other experiences (Smith, 1987). I see the world as existing independently from descriptions of it at any particular moment, "though it may, the next moment, be affected by such descriptions" and assert that although people can know things about the world, "our knowledge is always fallible and incomplete" (New, 1996, pp. 6–7). Therefore, although I present my own analysis of these textbooks and argue for its usefulness, I also acknowledge that my reading is one of many possible. Finally, I consider my approach feminist in that I pay particular attention to the power dynamics of sex and gender, and the ways these are intertwined with heterosexism.

THEORETICAL BACKGROUND: EDUCATION AND HETEROSEXISM

Many theorists have expressed concerns about the relationship between education and dominant, oppressive ideologies (Apple, 2000; Bernstein, 1996; Giroux, 1989; Wotherspoon, 1991), arguing that education in Western society can be seen as part of a hegemonic process, one where the world is taught from the point of view of dominant groups while ignoring the knowledge of marginalized groups. In this way, students learn that only certain types of knowledge are legitimate (Apple, 2000; Bernstein, 1996; Giroux, 1989). Through this process of legitimation, "schools reproduce the social organization of inequality at multiple levels" (Smith, 2000, p. 1148). Yet schools are involved in a continuous process of compromise, and therefore "are also places where dominant and subordinate groups define and constrain each other through an ongoing battle and exchange . . ." (Giroux, 1989, p. 141). Texts are an important part of this process, and can play a key role in organizing social relations. Studying texts, then, can reveal these "relations of ruling" (Smith, 1990, p. 5).

I understand heterosexism as the presumption that heterosexuality is superior to all other forms of sexuality, often through claims that it is the only natural or normal sexuality (Buston & Hart, 2001; Shortall, 1998). An understanding of heterosexism, however, depends in large part on how one defines sexuality. Early theorists argued that sexuality cannot simply be divided into heterosexuality and homosexuality, but is instead more of a continuum of sexual behaviour (Kinsey, Pomeroy, & Martin, 1948). Later, others pointed out that it is not so much behaviour itself that is key, but the meanings attached, including sexual and romantic feelings (Weinberg, 1994). Foucault (1978) further complicated sexuality's connection to identity, arguing that the idea of a homosexual as a type of person did not exist until the nineteenth century. Others saw heterosexuality itself as a modern invention, insisting that "the concept of heterosexuality is only one particular way of perceiving, categorizing, and imagining the social relations of the sexes" (Katz, 1990, p. 7; see also Sedgwick, 1990). Today, theorists often use the term queer to denote sexuality that defies sex and gender norms, and the term queer theory "to propose a focus not so much on specific populations as on sexual categorization processes and their deconstruction" (Gamson, 2000, p. 349). The distinctions between heterosexuality, homosexuality, and bisexuality are socially constructed in many ways then, but these concepts can also have important meaning in everyday lives, "shaping the very way in which 'reality' is experienced" (Epstein, 1994, p. 162).

Heeding Fraser's (1989) reminder that "ideology loves dichotomies" (p. 8), I suggest that it is possible to complicate sexuality even further by critiquing the concept of sex itself. Butler (1990), for instance, suggests that "'sex' is as culturally constructed as gender" (p. 7); that in fact, the physical and psychological differences between individuals may be more complex than these two categories represent. Butler goes on to argue that society's conceptualization of sex (and sexuality) reinforces "institutionalized heterosexuality," that "[t]he institution of a compulsory and naturalized heterosexuality requires and regulates gender as a binary relation in which the masculine term is differentiated from a feminine term, and this differentiation is accomplished through the practices of heterosexual desire" (p. 22). Thus "compulsory heterosexuality" and the heterosexist oppression of other sexualities are deeply connected to the oppression of women (Rich, 1980, p. 631) as well as of men who do not fit into the hegemonic masculine norm (Connell, 1995).

Wittig (1996) argues that a patriarchal, heterosexist system creates a "straight mind" that "cannot conceive of a culture, a society where heterosexuality would order not only all human relationships but also its very production of concepts and all the processes which escape consciousness, as well" (p. 146). It is important, then, to look at "heterosexuality as a social and political organizing principle" (Seidman, 1996, p. 9), examining "the ways the very homo/hetero distinction underpinned all aspects of contemporary life" (Gamson, 2000, p. 354). Schools have been called one of the "major heterosexist institutions" (p. 355) pointing to the need to question how they "work to heterosexualize and gender, and with what material effects" (p. 358). Grace, Hill, Johnson, and Lewis (2004) note that heterosexism is intricately bound up with other oppressive systems.

> [H]eteronormativity, as well as Whiteness, have infiltrated educational prac-
> tices and policies, such as desegregation, resulting in (1) the erasure of issues
> of class, gender and sexual orientation and (2) the construction of discursive
> and social practices that have replicated rather than dismantled power and
> privilege. (p. 305)

I see "institutionalized heterosexism," then, as the reinforcement in and by institutions of the belief that heterosexuality is superior to other forms of sexuality
(Butler, 1990; Gamson, 2000).

The curriculum is one aspect of this reinforcement, but the entire school environment "combines official asexuality with an aggressive, indeed punitive, heteronormativity" (Sears, 2003, pp. 185–186). In other words, while heterosexuality
is reduced to social interaction according to specific gender norms, and thus
made acceptable, same-sex sexuality is reduced to sexual activity, and thus pro-
hibited. Yet schools can also be places of resistance to heterosexism. Despite the
risks to teachers (Shortall, 1998) under formal policies of silencing, "some teachers and community advocates continue to struggle for an empowering sex education curriculum both in and out of the high school classroom" (Fine, 1988, p. 34).

In Canada, Wotherspoon (1998) states that "curriculum materials that depict
gay lifestyles are commonly protested if not banned from classrooms" (p. 98).
Shortall (1998) notes that "family life classes rarely discuss gay and lesbian families as viable options, history classes overlook the gay and lesbian civil rights
movement, and Canadian law classes ignore the discrimination against gays and
lesbians" (p. 91). Resistance, though, also exists here: in 2002, British Columbia
teacher James Chamberlain succeeded in having the Supreme Court of Canada
overturn his school board's decision to ban three children's books from kindergarten and grade 1 classrooms because they depicted same-sex parents (Canadian Broadcasting Corporation, 2002). In that same year, the Canadian Teachers'
Federation (2002) published a document called "Seeing the Rainbow," a guide to
help teachers understand "bisexual, gay, lesbian, transgender and two-spirited
realities" (p. 1). This guide specifically addressed curriculum issues, advising
teachers to "add books to the classroom" discussing same-sex relationships and
sexuality, to "integrate the curriculum" by addressing sexual diversity and incorporating mention of sexual minorities into subjects such as literature, history,
art, law, and science, and to "provide appropriate education about sexuality," including sexual diversity (pp. 36–37).

Although a number of general studies of heterosexism and homophobia in
education exist (e.g.: Buston & Hart, 2001; Harrison, 2000; Mac an Ghaill, 1991;
Rengel Phillips, 1991; Shortall, 1998), currently there is an absence of studies that

specifically examine textbooks. This study, therefore, has directly analyzed the content of high school textbooks and how they address (or do not address) the issues of same-sex relationships and sexuality. I focused on high school texts in particular because issues of relationships and sexuality are discussed more extensively at this level. In this article, then, I have addressed the question: Are current French Quebec high school textbooks heterosexist? If so, in what ways and to what extent?

In terms of social significance, this study is perhaps even more important. The issue of extending the right to marry to same-sex couples has been the subject of heated debate across Canada in recent years, with Parliament finally voting to recognize same-sex marriage on June 28, 2005. Thus the issue of whether or not Canadian education systems teach respect or disdain for same-sex relationships becomes a very important issue. Furthermore, the high school curriculum is presently undergoing reform in Quebec, opening up the possibility of directly addressing issues of heterosexism in these texts.

CONTEXT: THE QUEBEC EDUCATION SYSTEM

The Quebec secondary school system covers five years: secondary 1 through 5, for students aged about 12 to 17. Texts for these schools are approved by the Minister of Education, who is advised by a Curriculum Resource Evaluation Committee including representatives from university education faculties, school boards, principals, parents, publishers, and pedagogical experts. This committee recommends texts as well as criteria for their approval, and may hear from concerned individuals or groups on any subject. The law on public instruction governs textbook choices, stating that texts must represent the diversity of Quebec society, be free of discrimination, and respect moral and religious values (Ministère de l'éducation du Québec, 2005).

METHODOLOGY

Analytic Themes

Building on findings of previous studies (Buston & Hart, 2001; Harrison, 2000; Mac an Ghaill, 1991; Rengel Phillips, 1991; Shortall, 1998), I divided the results of my analysis into four themes: ignoring; mentioning; negative contexts; and positive contexts. These four themes collectively structured my content analysis.

Ignoring is the phenomenon where same-sex sexuality and relationships are simply never discussed. Buston and Hart (2001), for instance, found many examples of ways that the topic of same-sex sexuality is avoided. "Examples include defining sexual activity as vaginal intercourse, even when discussing condom use, talking solely in terms of sexual relationships between males and females, and failing to discuss condom use in terms of anal penetrative sex as well as vaginal penetrative sex" (p. 100). Negative contexts indicate discussions of same-sex sexuality or relationships in a context that was discouraged in the text. For example, the subjects of abuse, sexually transmitted diseases, and prostitution were all considered negative contexts in this coding. As Mac an Ghaill (1991) explains, "on the few occasions when [homosexuality] was introduced, it was presented in a negative way; most recently in relation to AIDS" (p. 299). Positive contexts signify discussions of same-sex sexuality or relationships in a context that was either encouraged, or at least discussed without discouragement. Examples include family life, puberty, and sexual pleasure. Mentioning differs from the last two themes in that there is little context at all: instead, these are brief items on same-sex sexuality mentioned separately from the general discussion. Rengel Phillips (1991), for instance, found that discussions of homosexuality were physically separated from the rest of the text and contextually separated from discussions of other aspects of human life.

Definitions

Though sex is often seen as biological and gender as social, a definition of sex as two opposite human biologies has its problems. Understanding of both sex and gender is further complicated by intersexuality (when an individual is born with ambiguous genitals), and transgenderism (identification as born with a wrongly sexed body). To simplify this analysis, however, I have used current standard sex and gender terminology, with the understanding that lived experiences of these terms are much more complex.

The concept of sexuality is perhaps even more difficult to specify. As well, though there is an assumption of a direct link between sexuality and identity, "fixed identity categories are both the basis for oppression and the basis for political power" (Gamson & Moon, 2004, p. 50). Thus I do not assume that all identities are based on sexuality, nor deny the validity of those that are. With this caveat in mind, as well as the arguments of the sexuality theorists discussed above, I understand sexuality as a fluid, complex, and changing ensemble of an individual's sexual feelings, desires, and behaviours. In a practical sense, however, this definition does not translate into a clear method of coding because codes must allow me to reflect the ways that sexuality and relationships are discussed in these texts. To illustrate how these texts dichotomize sexuality as heterosexuality/homosexuality (with the second category very occasionally including bisexuality), I have chosen to use the terms heterosexuality and same-sex sexuality. I define heterosexuality as sexuality oriented exclusively towards members of the opposite sex. This is a much narrower category than the one I created for same-sex sexuality, which includes sexuality that is oriented at some time or in some way towards members of the same sex. I have allowed room in this definition not only for homosexuality and bisexuality, but for sexualities not tied to a particular identity yet which happen to involve sexual feelings for or behaviour with someone of the same sex. I emphasize that I do not wish to conflate homosexuality and bisexuality because I recognize that for many people these are very separate positions and identities. As well, though I support the use of the term queer as empowering, I want to be careful to keep the term complex (Sedgwick, 1990), and not slip into a queer/ heterosexual dichotomy (Gamson & Moon, 2004) by using it in coding.

Following the definition of heterosexism above, I considered texts to be heterosexist if they presented the perspective that heterosexuality is superior to other forms of sexuality, for example, as the only normal or natural sexuality. I also considered texts heterosexist when same-sex sexuality was presented as inferior, for example as abnormal, unnatural, or problematic. In my findings section, I have discussed how I found these criteria to be related to the dichotomizing of sex/gender and sexuality.

Content Analysis

Although content analysis has the advantage of being unobtrusive, it also has the limitation of being restricted to written material. I acknowledge, then, that my analysis excludes the supplementary resources, classroom dynamics, or teacher initiatives that impact upon students' overall learning experience. This said, however, this study provides important insight into the presence of heterosexism in key educational materials.

I have examined only those courses that directly discuss sexuality and/or relationships, basing this choice on a similar decision by Buston and Hart (2001), who in delimiting their study to sex education, argue that "[s]ex education is a site where a heterosexist slant may be most obvious and damaging to those growing up identifying as gay or lesbian" (p. 96). I examined twenty texts currently approved for French Quebec secondary schools in five subjects: personal and social education; moral education; family economics; human biology; and Catholic moral and religious education.

I coded the textbooks by page, a unit of analysis that has the advantage of clear physical separations. I coded only those pages that included themes relevant to this study, for a total of 610 pages. For each page, a main theme and citation were recorded.

I identified eleven sexuality/relationship themes discussed in high school texts, coded in the following manner: (a) personal sexuality (e.g., feelings), (b) reproduction, (c) dating/relationships, (d) marriage, (e) sexually transmitted diseases, (f) abuse/assault, (g) prostitution, (h) laws, (i) contraception, (j) families, (k) effects of drugs on sexual behaviour.

I also recorded the presentation of sexuality for each page, as follows: (a) sexuality defined exclusively as heterosexuality, (b) heterosexuality in a positive context, (c) heterosexuality in a negative context, (d) same-sex sexuality in a positive context, (e) same-sex sexuality in a negative context, or (f) sexuality that does not specify either heterosexuality or same-sex sexuality. Originally, I had planned separate coding of neutral contexts, but did not find this code useful. In addition to this coding, I noted whether pages that mentioned same-sex sexuality included only homosexuality, homosexuality and bisexuality, or a broader definition.

I entered coding data into the Statistical Package for the Social Sciences (SPSS), a program that allows a researcher to examine patterns in the data (such as tendency for negative or positive contexts for heterosexuality or same-sex sexuality) with regard to a large number of variables (such as a particular school subject). In this case, these variables included subject area, school grade, textbook title, publication year, and page number.

FINDINGS AND DISCUSSION

Throughout these books, I found evidence of institutionalized heterosexism in four clear ways: through the maintenance of a rigid dichotomy between heterosexuality and homosexuality; through "heteronormativity" (Grace, Hill, Johnson, & Lewis, 2004), which posits heterosexuality as the only "normal" sexuality; through the problematization of same-sex sexuality as unnatural, abnormal, or otherwise inferior; and, as an integral part of these three processes, through maintaining a strict distinction between male/masculine and female/feminine. This distinction, of course, is necessary to the dichotomization of sexualities (Butler, 1990).

In the basic statistics of this analysis, one analytic theme stands out most clearly: ignoring. In fact, 577, or nearly 95 per cent, of the 610 pages coded made no reference at all to same-sex sexuality. As well, 133 pages, or 22 per cent, explicitly defined sexuality as heterosexuality, and only 33 pages (5.4 per cent) mentioned same-sex sexuality in any way. I see this ignoring of same-sex sexuality as part of the process of institutionalized heterosexism: a way of making clear that heterosexuality is the only normal sexuality and thus the only sexuality relevant to students. As Grace, Hill, Johnson, and Lewis (2004) identified, ignoring same-sex sexuality is part of the way that heteronormativity erases issues of sexual orientation, constructing discourses that further the "power and privilege" of heterosexuality (p. 305).

In addition, the authors of these textbooks rarely discussed same-sex sexuality in terms of everyday life, relationships, families, or life events. In fact, I found same-sex sexuality in negative contexts almost 80 per cent of the time, on twenty-six of thirty-three pages, in topics such as abuse, prostitution, and STDs. As Sears (2003) has described, same-sex sexuality is reduced to sexual activity (and its potential harm) in contrast to desexualized heterosexuality, which is made safe. I understand this as another part of the process of institutionalized heterosexism: problematizing same-sex sexuality and creating it as the unnatural "other" to natural heterosexuality.

I noted that the definition of same-sex sexuality in these texts was nearly always limited to homosexuality, rarely including bisexuality, and that broader discussions of sexuality were not found at all. I view this definition itself as a key part of institutionalized heterosexism. The definitions in these texts dichotomize heterosexuality/homosexuality, setting the stage to see sexuality in terms of opposites of normal and abnormal dichotomies essential to maintaining and reproducing ideologies (Butler, 1990; Fraser, 1989).

I also examined each subject separately. The *personal and social education* course covered sexuality and relationships most thoroughly, making up 45 per cent of all pages analyzed (273 of 610 pages). Although the theme of ignoring was most evident here, mentioning also occurred, and this course contained 58 per cent, or fifteen of twenty-six pages, of negative contexts of same-sex sexuality. The texts for *human biology*, however, exemplify just one theme: ignoring. In fact, not one mention of same-sex sexuality or relationships was found here. These books discussed sexuality only in terms of heterosexuality, assuming the heterosexuality not only of their readers but the rest of the world. In *family economics*, ignoring is once again the most common theme, with 30 per cent of the pages explicitly defining sexuality as heterosexuality. One example of positive context does occur here, though, as discussed below. In *moral education*, textbooks contained examples of ignoring and mentioning, yet also of positive contexts. In fact, of all the texts, these presented perhaps the most ambivalent messages about same-sex sexuality. Though at many points, these texts defined sexuality only in terms of heterosexuality, six of seven positive contexts of same-sex sexuality were also found here. Finally, the textbooks for the *Catholic moral and religious education* course presented the most negative messages towards same-sex sexuality and relationships, exemplifying the themes of ignoring and negative contexts. Although at 137 pages this subject made up 22 per cent of all pages analyzed, it accounted for 42 per cent of examples of negative contexts for same-sex sexuality.

Ignoring

"Inside the classroom what is not said is more significant than what is said" (Shortall, 1998, p. 61). Indeed, in the texts that I studied, the theme of ignoring is distinctly present throughout, regardless of subject, school year, publication year, or publisher. There is a near constant assumption of heterosexuality. For example, in a typical discussion of puberty in a personal and social education text: "All of these transformations are accompanied by an awakening of interest in the opposite sex. Bit by bit, boys become interested in girls and girls in boys"[1] (*Pleins Feux . . .*, p. 67). Discussions of families also assume that parents are of the opposite sex: "You rebelled first against mom and dad . . ." (*Formation personnelle et sociale, 4e secondaire*, p. 12). As well, Catholic moral and religious education texts showed a particularly explicit type of ignoring: "The characteristics of a couple, according to God's plan: a couple that is heterosexual, loyal, stable, united, egalitarian, and fertile" (*Tant qu'il fait jour . . .*, p. 254). Finally, part of this ignoring involves emphasizing differences between men and women, sometimes combining heterosexism with blatant sexism: "Men, no matter what their personal sexual experience, have a marked preference for women with limited sexual experience." (*Formation personnelle et sociale, 4e secondaire*, p. 153). I see such examples as further reinforcing heterosexism through maintaining dichotomies that enforce rigid definitions of what it means to be a man or a woman (Butler, 1990).

Through all subjects, discussions of sexual behaviour tended to focus on vaginal intercourse. Sex, for instance, is defined as "a physical act of introducing the penis into the vagina" (*De la tête aux pieds: Biologie*, p. 334). In particular, these texts emphasized avoiding unwanted pregnancy (preferably by abstinence): "Sexual relations involve certain consequences, the most significant of which is an unwanted pregnancy" (*Formation personnelle et sociale, 4e secondaire*, p. 130). Condom use, then, is discussed only in the context of birth control and vaginal intercourse: "The condom traps the sperm from ejaculation, preventing them from spreading into the vagina" (*Comme un souffle de vie*, p. 344). Such definitions of sexual activity pose heterosexuality as the only natural sexuality, an important way that schools exclude same-sex sexuality (Sears, 2003).

I see all of these examples as a creation of a completely heterosexual world view. This is a silencing of same-sex sexuality that operates by erasing same-sex sexuality from the classroom and making experiences of same-sex relationships or sexuality irrelevant in education (Wotherspoon, 1998). I view this silencing as an integral part of heteronormativity: "the discursive and social practices that legitimize heterosexuality as the norm and make homosexuality and queerness invisible" (Grace, Hill, Johnson, & Lewis, 2004).

Mentioning

Mentioning was also a very common theme in these texts, and the subtlety of these examples further complicated my understanding of the workings of heterosexism. In one personal and social education text, for instance, the only mention of same-sex sexuality occurred in a list of adolescent girls' and boys' reasons for wanting a sexual relationship: "Girl's motives: wanting to prove to her boyfriend that she loves him; Boy's motives: trying to prove that he is not a homosexual" (*Formation personnelle et sociale, 1er cycle*, p. 129). In this short passage, I note two very important elements of heterosexism. For one, though brief, this is yet another erasure of same-sex sexual experience (Grace, Hill, Johnson, & Lewis, 2004), presenting a homosexual identity as unquestionably undesirable and presuming that any sexual activity that an adolescent would engage in would be only with the opposite sex. Secondly, this text maintains a rigid differentiation between girls and boys, again, a key way of reinforcing institutionalized heterosexism (Butler, 1990).

Another example of mentioning occurs in a moral education text, which begins one chapter with a definition of "sexual preference": "This has to do with sexual preference for masculine or feminine partners. Thus we mean heterosexuality or homosexuality" (*Trajectoires*, p. 26). However, although themes of sex and gender are elaborated in great detail, no more is said about sexual preference, and there is no acknowledgement that the term sexual preference itself can be seen in a negative light. As Fine (1988) asks, "How could we speak of 'sexual preference' when sexual involvement outside of heterosexuality may seriously jeopardize one's social and/or economic well-being?" (p. 41).

The most subtle and troubling example of mentioning that I found was one separate, very brief chapter (one and a half pages) entitled "Understanding and Respecting Sexual Orientations." Although this chapter claims to discuss respect, I see it as representing a very powerful form of heterosexism. In fact, this chapter was written with the assumption that you, the student reader, are of course heterosexual, but you will just have to learn to tolerate these other, different homosexuals and bisexuals: "You may find that it is difficult to respect *people who are different from you*, but it is worth it if you want to live in harmony in society" (*Formation personnelle et sociale, 1er cycle*, p. 149, my emphasis). In this way, heterosexuality is normalized (Katz, 1990), and same-sex sexuality is "othered"; there is no room for students to identify with experiences of same-sex sexuality. This chapter also takes pains to assure students that teenagers who like to spend time with members of the same sex are certainly not homosexuals, that they are simply developing according to their own rhythm, and will of course develop interest in the opposite sex eventually. I see this representation of same-sex sexuality as a phase not only as condescending, but as reinforcing "the accep-tance of the corollary that certain expressions of sexuality are 'natural,' while others are therefore 'unnatural'" (Epstein, 1994, p. 189). Again, this is one of the key parts that I identified in the process of institutionalized heterosexism.

Negative Contexts

In many of the texts, discussion of same-sex sexuality tends to be limited to neg-ative contexts such as sexually transmitted diseases, sexual abuse, and prostitu-tion. "But have you wondered who resorts to young female and male prostitutes? They are almost exclusively men aged 25 to 65 and may belong to any social class. As many are homosexuals as are heterosexuals" (*Formation personnelle et sociale, 5e secondaire*, p. 143). Fine (1988) has argued that schools create "dis-courses of sexuality as violence, as victimization, and as individual morality" with a "discourse of desire" almost completely absent (p. 29). In these texts, a similar pattern is found: same-sex sexual desire is erased from the context of everyday life (Grace, Hill, Johnson, & Lewis, 2004), with a focus only on violence and victimization.

I also note this erasure in discussions of morality in Catholic moral and re-ligious education: "A Suspicious Relationship: 'My brother has been living with a buddy for a few months. One of my friends thinks that he is a homosexual. I am worried about him. Can he be happy?'" The reply and discussion go on to say that the Catholic church does not condemn homosexuals, but homosexual-ity is not the way that God wants people to live their lives. The text explains that homosexuals are often marginalized and have difficulty accepting themselves, that homosexual relationships are not complete, and that homosexuals are "in-vited to grow as a person by accepting themselves and directing their life in a constructive way" (*Tant qu'il fait jour*, p. 265). This last line implies that homo-sexuals should avoid all sexual activity, as it is homosexual sex that is a sin. This description of a "love the sinner, hate the sin" perspective is a stark example of the heterosexist reduction of same-sex relationships and identity to sexuality (Sears, 2003). This perspective negates the elements of love and support in a same-sex relationship, maintaining the division between natural, desexed heterosexuality, and unnatural, problematic, sexualized same-sex sexuality.

Another of these Catholic moral and religious education texts also discussed homosexuality with the use of stereotypes: "many homosexual persons live in a closed world, they meet in places that are not very open to heterosexual per-sons"; "there is often a great deal of instability within homosexual relationships"; "for homosexual persons, access to happiness is more difficult because of their marginality, the impossibility of having children, the feeling of guilt that returns to them again and again to the question 'Am I normal?'"; "We might however wonder if the homosexual person, upon entering into such a life as a couple, risks closing themselves in a habit that they would have been able to do without" (*Les enjeux du présent*, pp. 179–183). This image of a same-sex relationship as a troublesome habit is starkly contrasted with discussions of opposite-sex relationships as loving, life fulfilling, and blessed by God. Again, I see these texts as exemplifying the problematization of same-sex sexuality, setting it in rigid opposition to naturalized heterosexuality (Epstein, 1994). Furthermore, I view this as an important example of why the issue of heterosexism is directly relevant for those who identify as straight: with an idealization of heterosexual relationships, this dichotomy leaves little room to acknowledge violence or other problems in relationships between women and men.

Positive Contexts

In total, there were seven codings of same-sex sexuality in a positive context. Some of these, however, involved simple reference to sexual orientation, stretching the limits of my coding definitions. Other examples, however, were a little more thorough, for instance, in a discussion (now outdated) of how families are changing: "Some legal experts believe that the next step in the growing concept of the family will affect same-sex couples. More and more visible, these couples have been demanding their rights for more than 25 years in Canada. It may be that their 'family status' will one day be defined in accordance with Canadian human rights law" (*Économie familiale*, p. 22). Another example occurred in a secondary 3 moral education textbook, which, when talking about changing values, gave an example of a soap opera that depicts two women in a couple, and the process they go through to get their families to accept them. The text says that in this program "the message sounds clearly: lesbianism is not a shameful illness. Such a positive message leaves positive traces in the minds of those who receive it" (*Au delà du miroir*, p. 156).

Overall, I see these positive contexts as revealing potential for change, particularly in their connections to processes outside of the school. After all, textbook selection does not take place in a vacuum, but in a particular context. I view the context in Quebec as involving a tension between the historical power of the conservative Catholic church, and the increasing liberalism that has come with rapid secularization. I theorize, however, that from this tension can come a process of negotiation where same-sex sexuality can begin to be incorporated into the curriculum. Indeed, this is particularly relevant for Quebec, because its education system is presently undergoing reform. This could create important potential for resistance to heterosexism and an opportunity to make the curriculum more inclusive. Unfortunately, personal and social education, the subject where sex education is now most thoroughly discussed, will no longer be included as a regular subject in the Quebec curriculum. Instead, sex education may be incorporated into a number of other subjects, but only at an individual teacher's initiative (Duquet, 2003). Aside from concern for teacher workload, I also have grave concerns about what this will mean for the possibility of consistently inclusive sex education. With no curriculum guide or text to draw on, teachers may be even more hesitant to initiate discussions of same-sex sexuality. As Shortall (1998) points out, no matter how they identify, teachers have reason to fear being labelled homosexual, risking serious social sanctions or even (in some jurisdictions) losing their job.

CONCLUSION: BEYOND HETEROSEXISM

I found Quebec high school textbooks to be fiercely heterosexist. These texts strictly enforce the ideology of heteronormativity (Grace, Hill, Johnson, & Lewis, 2004) by dichotomizing heterosexuality and same-sex sexuality, normalizing heterosexuality, problematizing same-sex sexuality, and emphasizing a rigid distinction between male and female. Perhaps most notable are the silences: nearly 95 per cent of the pages analyzed completely ignored same-sex sexuality and relationships. Over and over, the texts defined a couple as a man and a woman, parents as mother and father, and adolescence as the time to become interested in the opposite sex. In these ways, heterosexuality is continually established as the norm. In contrast, the tiny fraction of mentions of same-sex sexuality (33 of 610 pages) tended to be limited to vague references, warning against the dangers of sex. In the absence of fuller discussions of healthy sexuality and relationships, such isolated statements serve to problematize same-sex sexuality. Indeed, in my view these texts are a key part of schools' reproduction of a larger system of "institutional regulation and management of sexualities" (Gamson & Moon, 2004, p. 51).

The implications of these findings for the curriculum in Quebec, as elsewhere, are that heterosexism in textbooks needs to be addressed by emphasizing diversity in all areas: including same-sex relationships in any discussion of relationships or families, discussing all varieties of sexuality in every lesson on sexual activity or identity, always being careful not to limit sexuality or gender identity to rigid dichotomies, and assuming that students will identify in a variety of different ways. Friend (1997) argues that the goal for schools should be inclusiveness. He says that:

[when] books on the shelves, posters on the walls, and pamphlets in the racks include mention and images of lesbian, gay, and bisexual people, then inclusiveness is promoted. The message, while subtle and powerful, helps to build an inclusive learning community that recognizes multiple voices. (p. 12)

Beyond the curriculum Friend recommends clear anti-discrimination policies, support groups for students identifying outside the heterosexual norm, inclusiveness training for teachers, inclusive events such as school dances, and a "clear strategic approach" to addressing heterosexism and homophobia (pp. 12–14).

Challenging heterosexist schooling is important for many reasons. Sears (2003) argues that:

[t]he sexual repression of official school culture has particularly strong implications for same-sex sexuality, which is obliterated while heterosexuality is magnified through the pressure cooker of its desexed official form and sexually charged outlaw culture. This combination produces a toxic environment for young people who are lesbian, gay, bisexual or transgendered and others who are non-conformists or outcasts. (p. 186)

This heterosexist environment, then, can set the stage for homophobic bullying and harassment, and as Macgillivray (2004) explains, "[t]he deprecation and resulting marginalization of students based on their real or perceived sexual orientation, as well as their identity expression, robs them of the opportunity to participate fully in school and can retard their developmental growth into adults with positive self-identities" (p. 348). However, the issue of heterosexism is directly relevant for all students, regardless of how they identify. Challenging heterosexism not only helps to break down the norms that "confine everybody to rigid gender role stereotypes" (Macgillivray, 2004, p. 366), but also encourages students to develop critical thinking skills to question presumptions and biases they encounter throughout their lives.

I believe that we can challenge and move beyond heterosexism because despite the education system's abilities to silence and shame, it is also a place of great potential for critical thinking and change (hooks, 1994). By describing and analyzing heterosexism in high school texts, I hope that this study has achieved an important step towards that goal.

REFLECTIVE QUESTIONS

1. According to Temple, how has human sexuality been portrayed in textbooks historically?

2. Does your experience resonate with that of the author's in this respect? Give details.

3. Why does the Quebec education system provide a useful case study for examining the issue of heterosexism?

4. What evidence of "institutionalized heterosexism" does the author present?

5. What recommendations can you glean from this reading regarding the issue of human sexuality in the curriculum?

APPENDIX 1: TEXTBOOK LIST

Biologie Humaine

Caron, R., Faublas-Roy, M. J., & Fugère-Godin, M. (1997). *De la tête aux pieds: Biologie*. Laval: Éditions HRW. Groupe Éducalivres.

Économie Familiale

Boisvert-Bellemare, G. (1995). *Aujourd'hui . . . pour demain!* Montréal: Lidec.

Gagné, C. (1995*). Économie familiale. Pour une meilleure gestion de mes ressources* (2e édition). Saint-Laurent: Éditions de renouveau pédagogique.

Janson, J. (1997). *Comme un souffle de vie* (2e édition). Montréal: Lidec.

Enseignement Moral

Bourdages, R.-A. (1989). *Au delà du miroir. . . .* Montréal: Éditions la pensée.

Bourdages, R.-A. (1990). *Singulier pluriel*. Montréal: Éditions la pensée.

Bourdages, R.-A. (1991). *Vers le large*. Montréal: Éditions la pensée.

Debunne, J.-M., & Saint-Pierre, L. (1993). *Un aller simple*. Montréal: Éditions la pensée.

Debunne, J.-M., Saint-Pierre, L., & Bailly, M.-F. (1996). *Trajectoires* (2e édition, revue et corrigée). Montréal: Éditions la pensée.

Enseignement Moral et Religieux Catholique

Bouchard, J.-F., & Lachance, L. (1992). *Tant qu'il fait jour. . . .* Ville Saint-Laurent: Éditions d'enseignement religieux FPR.

Dubuc, M. (1991). *Inventer sa vie*. Ville Saint-Laurent: Éditions d'enseignement religieux FPR.

Durand-Lutzy, N. (1993). *Les enjeux du présent*. Anjou: Les éditions CEC.

Guénette, P., & Toupin, B. (1992*). Faire son chemin*. Ville Saint-Laurent: Éditions d'enseignement religieux FPR.

Formation Personnelle et Sociale

Beauchamp, L., & Pelletier, D. (1988). *À mon tour, 5e secondaire* (1re éd.). Sainte-Foy: Les éditions Septembre.

Beauchamp, L., & Pelletier, D. (1988). *Moi et compagnie, 4e secondaire*. Sainte-Foy: Les éditions Septembre.

Beauchamp, L., & Pelletier, D. (1988). *Pleins feux, 3e secondaire*. Sainte-Foy: Les éditions Septembre.

Beaulac, G., & Dionne, L. (1988). *Formation personnelle et sociale, 1er cycle* (2e édition). Montréal: McGraw Hill.

Beaulac, G., & Côté, C. (1989). *Formation personnelle et sociale, 4e secondaire*. Montréal: McGraw Hill.

Beaulac, G., & Beauregard, H. (1990). *Formation personnelle et sociale, 5e secondaire*. Montréal: McGraw Hill.

Beaulac, G., Côté, C., Côté, J., & Desaulniers, M. P. (1991). *Formation personnelle et sociale, 1er cycle* (2e édition). Montréal: McGraw Hill.

NOTE

1. All translations are my own.

REFERENCES

Apple, M. (2000). *Official knowledge: Democratic education in a conservative age*. New York: Routledge.

Bernstein, B. (1996). *Pedagogy, symbolic control and identity: Theory, research, critique*. London: Taylor & Francis.

Buston, K., & Hart, G. (2001). Heterosexism and homophobia in Scottish school sex education: Exploring the nature of the problem. *Journal of Adolescence, 24*, 95–109.

Butler, J. (1990). *Gender trouble: Feminism and the subversion of identity*. New York: Routledge.

Canadian Broadcasting Corporation. (2002, December 20). Supreme Court overturns Surrey book ban. Accessed at http://vancouver.cbc.ca/regional/servlet/View?filename=bc_ssbooks20021220

Canadian Teachers' Federation. (2002). *Seeing the rainbow: Teachers talk about bisexual, gay, lesbian, transgender and two-spirited realities*. Ottawa: Author.

Connell, R. A. (1995). *Masculinities*. Berkeley: University of California Press.

Duquet, F. (2003). *L'éducation à la sexualité dans le contexte de la réforme de l'éducation*. Québec: Ministère de l'éducation.

Epstein, S. (1994). A queer encounter: Sociology and the study of sexuality. *Sociological Theory, 12*(2), 188–202.

Ferree, M., & Hall, E. (1990). Visual images of American society: Gender and race in introductory sociology textbooks. *Gender and Society, 4*(4), 500–522.

Ferree, M., & Hall, E. (1996). Rethinking stratification from a feminist perspective: Gender, race, and class in mainstream textbooks. *American Sociological Review, 61*(6), 921–950.

Fine, M. (1988). Sexuality, schooling, and adolescent females: The missing discourse of desire. *Harvard Educational Review, 58*(1), 29–53.

Foucault, M. (1978). *The history of sexuality: An introduction. Volume 1*. New York: Random House.

Fraser, N. (1989). *Unruly practices: Power, discourse and gender in contemporary social theory*. Minneapolis: University of Minnesota Press.

Friend, R. (1997, March 25). From surviving to thriving: Lessons from lesbian and gay youth. American Educational Research Association Annual Meeting, Chicago, 1–17.

Gamson, J. (2000). Sexualities, queer theory, and qualitative research. In N. Denzin & Y. Lincoln (Eds.), *The handbook of qualitative research* (2nd ed., pp. 347–365). Thousand Oaks, CA: Sage Publications.

Gamson, J., & Moon, D. (2004). The sociology of sexualities: Queer and beyond. *Annual Review of Sociology, 30*, 47–64.

Gaskell, J., & Willinsky, J. (1995). *Gender in/forms curriculum: From enrichment to transformation*. New York: Teachers College Press; Toronto: Ontario Institute for Studies in Education.

Giroux, H. (1989). Schooling as a form of cultural politics: Toward a pedagogy of and for difference. In H. Giroux & P. McLaren (Eds.), *Critical pedagogy, the state, and cultural struggle* (pp. 125–151). Albany, NY: State University of New York Press.

Grace, A., Hill, R., Johnson, C., & Lewis, J. (2004). In other words: Queer voices/dissident subjectivities impelling social change. *International Journal of Qualitative Studies in Education, 17*(3), 301–324.

Harrison, L. (2000). Gender relations and the production of difference in school-based sexuality and HIV/AIDS education in Australia. *Gender and Education, 12*(1), 1.15.

hooks, b. (1994). *Teaching to transgress: Education as the practice of freedom.* New York: Routledge.

Katz, J. (1990). The invention of heterosexuality. *Socialist Review, 20*(1), 7–34.

Kinsey, A., Pomeroy, W., & Martin, C. (1948). *Sexual behavior in the human male.* Philadelphia: Saunders.

Mac an Ghaill, M. (1991). Schooling, sexuality and male power: Towards an emancipatory curriculum. *Gender and Education, 3*(3), 291–309.

Macgillivray, I. (2004). Gay rights and school policy: A case study in community factors that facilitate or impede educational change. *International Journal of Qualitative Studies in Education, 17*(3), 347–370.

McDiarmid, G., & Pratt, D. (1971). *Teaching prejudice: A content analysis of social studies textbooks authorized for use in Ontario.* Toronto: Ontario Institute for Studies in Education.

Ministère de l'éducation du Québec. (2005). Bureau d'approbation du matériel didactique. Accessed at http://www3.meq.gouv.qc.ca/bamd/info.htm

New, C. (1996). *Agency, health and social survival: The ecopolitics of rival psychologies.* London: Taylor & Francis.

Rengel Phillips, S. (1991). The hegemony of heterosexuality: A study of introductory texts. *Teaching Sociology, 19,* 454–463.

Rich, A. (1980). Compulsory heterosexuality and lesbian existence. *Signs, 54,* 631–660.

Sears, A. (2003). *Retooling the mind factory: Education in lean state.* Aurora, ON: Garamond Press.

Sedgwick, E. K. (1990). *The epistemology of the closet.* Berkeley: University of California Press.

Seidman, S. (1996). Introduction. In S. Seidman (Ed.), *Queer theory/sociology.* Cambridge, MA: Blackwell.

Shortall, A. (1998). *The social construction of homophobia and heterosexism in the Newfoundland education system.* Unpublished Master's dissertation, Memorial University of Newfoundland.

Smith, D. E. (1987). *The everyday world as problematic: A feminist sociology.* Toronto: University of Toronto Press.

Smith, D. E. (1990). *Texts, facts, and femininity: Exploring the relations of ruling.* New York: Routledge.

Smith, D. E. (2000). Schooling for inequality. *Signs, 25*(4), 1147–1151.

Weinberg, M. (1994). *Dual attraction: Understanding bisexuality.* New York: Oxford University Press.

Wittig, M. (1996). The straight mind. In S. Jackson & S. Scott (Eds.), *Feminism and sexuality: A reader* (pp. 144–149). New York: Columbia University Press.

Wotherspoon, T. (1991). *Hitting the books.* Toronto: Garamond Press.

Wotherspoon, T. (1998). *The sociology of education in Canada: Critical perspectives.* Toronto: Oxford University Press.

21

Transformative Environmental Education:

Stepping Outside the Curriculum Box

JULIE JOHNSTON

Picture this: It's the year 2050, and we find ourselves in a rundown courtroom. The teaching profession is standing trial for crimes against humanity and the rest of nature. The prosecutor comes close, looks us in the eyes and asks, "When it became evident, in the late twentieth and early twenty-first centuries, that urgent education and action on global climate change were needed to avert a planetary emergency, what were you teachers thinking? Why didn't you make the changes necessary to transform the education system before it was too late?" To which we meekly reply, "We didn't have time. We had to cover the curriculum."

Of course, this scenario (at least the courtroom scene) won't come true, but our lame defence already has. Covering the curriculum is the leading reason given by Canadian teachers for not teaching our students what they need to know in order to face the twenty-first-century realities of planetary climate collapse and an urgent need to switch to a renewable energy economy (Puk & Makin, 2006).

Remember when environmental education was all about nature? Ecology? The environment? Saving the planet? Now it seems to be more about curriculum alignment. Curriculum links. Curriculum connections. Matching learning outcomes, blending curriculum expectations, melding with curriculum, and investigating curriculum topics. This shift could not have come at a worse time.

Around the world, research is showing that climate change, ecosystem degradation, and biodiversity loss are a threat to the very survival of humanity and most other species on Earth (United Nations Environment Programme [UNEP], 2007).

According to the most recent Global Environment Outlook (GEO-4), "The need couldn't be more urgent and the time couldn't be more opportune, with our enhanced understanding of the challenges we face, to act now to safeguard our own survival and that of future generations" (UNEP, 2007, p. 493).

The world urgently needs transformation—on an emergency basis. The present generation of students is being faced, among other crises, with the daunting task of reversing the current exponential increase in global greenhouse gas emissions by 2015 (Intergovernmental Panel on Climate Change [IPCC], 2007, p. 67). In 2007, the IPCC chair, Rajendra Pachauri, said, "If there's no action [on climate change] before 2012, that's too late. What we do in the next two to three years will determine our future. This is the defining moment" (as cited in Gorrie, 2007). According to NASA physicist and the world's most outspoken climate scientist, James Hansen (2008), we are now beyond dangerous climate change and have to apply drastic and revolutionary measures to secure the future: "[W]e have used up all slack in the schedule for actions needed to defuse the global warming time bomb."

Clearly, our education systems in general, and environmental education in particular, have failed the Earth and the future. According to McKeown and her colleagues, "the most educated nations leave the deepest ecological footprints. . . . [M]ore education increases the threat to sustainability" (McKeown, Hopkins, Rizzi, & Chrystalbride, 2002, p. 10). Stephen Sterling (1996) explains further:

> Education is proclaimed at high levels as the key to a more sustainable society, and yet it daily plays a part in reproducing an unsustainable society. . . . A society faced with a radical imperative to achieve a socially, economically and ecologically sustainable basis within a historically short time needs to reappraise most aspects of its organization; education—as the main means of social reproduction—has to be at the centre of this task, both as subject and as agent. (p. 18)

It is obvious that time is of the essence, that education must revisit its goals, and that the future of humanity is, to a large part, in the hands of educators. If humanity is to mitigate global warming and adapt to a planet with an unstable climate, we will have to ensure that education be rapidly adaptable, making an immediate shift to transformative environmental education and sustainable development learning. But can curriculum-controlled education prepare students quickly enough for a world now facing unprecedented conditions in the biosphere? Unfortunately, curriculum is a slow-moving and slow-changing determinant of what gets taught. Learning for a Sustainable Future (2006) laments that "it is difficult to envision large-scale changes in educational practice and content at the classroom level without first seeing those changes in place in curriculum policy" (p. 5).

How, then, are we to "save the planet" and all future generations (of all species) as long as environmental education and sustainability learning are stuck in the curriculum box? To borrow from Albert Einstein, we cannot stop environmental degradation with the same educational system that allowed environmental degradation to happen in the first place. United Nations Educational, Scientific and Cultural Organization (UNESCO) (1999) outlines a new role for education:

> Education must . . . serve society by providing a critical reflection on the world, especially its failings and injustices, and by promoting greater awareness, exploring new visions and concepts, and inventing new techniques and tools. . . . Education's role in such undertakings is not only to make people wiser, more knowledgeable and better informed, but also more ethical, responsible and critical as well as capable of continuing to learn and respond to new situations. (p. 44)

What role can educators play in safeguarding the future for all life on Earth? We can start by making sure we don't place the integrity of "the curriculum" ahead of the integrity of life. Let's consider, therefore, not waiting for curriculum committees, curriculum mapping, curriculum review, and curriculum revision to allow us to change what we teach. The changing state of the planet, as well as solutions and remedies to deadly climate change, biodiversity loss, pollution, and deforestation, must now guide our curriculum.

Something else we can do is examine why the education system is not mobilizing faster. Puk and Makin (2006) uncovered four other reasons given by teachers for not teaching for ecological literacy. The first, mentioned above, was lack of time in the current curriculum: "The number one response given repeatedly was that as long as ecological literacy was not part of the required, provincial curriculum, there was not enough time to include it as an 'extra' topic" (p. 273).

The second reason given was a lack of resources (Puk & Makin, 2006), despite the fact that we live in the information age and myriad environmental education resources are available online. The third reason was a lack of teacher training; teachers cited their lack of knowledge and comfort in this area (Puk & Makin, 2006). However, if these teachers had learned ecology in school like they learned math knowledge and skills, lack of ecological literacy could not be used as an excuse today. Agne and Nash offered faculties of education a solution to this problem in 1976:

> If our concern is to help future teachers develop a world view which is deeply rooted in a reverence for life . . . teacher educators must begin to be more assertive and less value neutral as they act boldly on behalf of human survival. (pp. 143–144)

Lack of support from colleagues, administration, school board, and parents is the fourth reason teachers gave for not teaching for ecological literacy (Puk & Makin, 2006). This could reflect society's general denial of the global environmental crisis, in part due to the influence of the misinformation campaign by climate change skeptics and deniers (Hansen as cited in Pilkington, 2008), and in part due to the complexity of the issue.

In light of current scientific understanding of the state of the planet, these reasons are no longer valid. If teachers think they don't have the time, resources, training, or support to teach children how to save the future, could it be because they don't understand what's at stake? Or, despite growing evidence that the curriculum box has turned into a death trap, is it because teachers have been conditioned to focus on other aims, conditioned to stay in the curriculum box, indeed to become the box? When the IPCC (2007) reported that if we don't reduce our global greenhouse gas emissions by the year 2100, global average temperatures could increase by 6.4°C (p. 45), how many teachers understood the magnitude of this threat? How many teachers even heard this prediction? It must be the responsibility of every teacher in the world to truly grasp the significance of this projection for the survivability of life on Earth as we know it.

It takes pluck and audacity to buck the system, strength and stamina to swim against the flow, and creativity to figure out how to do it. As a classroom teacher, I looked for occasions to teach about life while "covering the curriculum." For example, I once fought for the right to teach a French language unit on environmental issues instead of the prescribed unit on cars, which was "on the exam." Also, I always stopped my grammar lessons when the pileated woodpecker came to visit a tree outside our classroom window. With good fortune, however, I have had several opportunities during my career to transform what happens in the classroom, both as a curriculum consultant offering demonstration lessons to classroom teachers, and as a teacher with an environmental education non-governmental organization (NGO) providing workshops for students. Admittedly, looking in from the outside makes it easier to view with a critical eye the education system's relationship with the rest of the world. I offer below three examples of times I have been able to take the risks necessary to escape—or at least dance around outside—the curriculum box.

GOOD NEIGHBOURS COME IN ALL SPECIES

Bioregion-based or place-based learning tends to be a missing element in many educational jurisdictions. For example, I now live in the Southern Gulf Islands of British Columbia, Canada, a wonderful place that many consider a natural paradise. Yet I noticed that most of the teachers here only took their students outside for physical education classes, and then only in good weather. North American environmental education guru, David Orr (1992), laments that the importance of place in education has been overlooked, because "to a great extent we are a deplaced people for whom our immediate places are no longer sources of food, water, livelihood, energy, materials, friends, recreation, or sacred inspiration" (p. 126). Unfortunately, our students were learning that the natural community around them offered nothing valuable to learn.

To help create a sense of place for the students in our small communities, and to show teachers that they don't need a background in science to teach environmental education, I developed an arts- and humanities-based program called "Good Neighbours Come in All Species" (an evocative quote from landscape designer, Sally Wasowski), as an offering to schools through my environmental education NGO, GreenHeart Education.

The students (preschool to grade 8) participated in six outdoor sessions designed to help them develop a reverence for all life and kindle their innate connection with the rest of nature:

- *Making Friends with Nature* involved sensory awareness and nature appreciation activities. Each child found a "heart spot" that he or she would visit each week with a different focus, which was a playful way to develop a "sense of place" and an introduction to ecological concepts of energy flows; (re)cycling of air, water, and soil nutrients; interrelationships; and change.
- *Nature's Gifts to Our School* had the students building terraria for their classrooms and bird feeders for their schoolyard.
- *Your Ecological Self* was a time for depicting favourite places and totem elements or animals through masks, banners, and mandalas.
- *Finding Your Song in Nature* included an outdoor poetry trail, music making with natural objects, and listening for one's "song" amongst the natural sounds in the playground.
- *Up Close and Personal*, seeing the rest of nature through new eyes, was accomplished with digital photography, videography, and simple solargraphy.
- *A Festival of Good Neighbours* was a community celebration for sharing the gifts received from our "neighbours" of all species as well as our artwork and poetry.

With indoor education, taking students outside for more than a sports game is already stepping outside the curriculum box. I sensed a fear that other teachers or passersby would question why the students were sitting around outdoors during the school day. But my greatest challenge was keeping the teachers with me! Three out of four teachers took advantage of this "free" time to do other things, rather than participate along with their students. They missed the opportunity to learn strategies for teaching several subjects outdoors—and their colleague who did participate witnessed a wonderful new side of her students as they connected with the natural world.

It must be acknowledged that teachers are extremely busy people with gruelling demands on their time. But saying that we don't have the time to integrate environmental learning into our teaching is like saying we don't have time to light the fire because we're too busy trying to keep warm.

I wish I had done a pre-program survey with the students to gauge their attitudes towards "neighbours of all species" before our work together, but follow-up comments from the children showed a shift in their sense of connectedness:

> Nature is all around us . . . and I learned a lot about it. I liked the Heart Spots.

> Thank you for giving me this gift of knowing so much about nature.

> You helped us find ourselves in nature.

> Thanks for teaching me to be more aware of things around me.

> The best part was learning to be friends with nature.

Good Neighbours was not really about teaching poetry, art, and music; it was about using poetry, art, and music to create connections to the natural environment around their school (a new idea for these teachers) in order to achieve one of the biggest goals of environmental education: giving the rest of nature value in the eyes of our students. I believe that this process of connecting forms the ethical and emotional foundation, for both students and teachers, that allows naturally transformative teaching and learning. Helping our students meet and make friends with other species—literally—will help these children become adults who include concern for all of life in their deliberations and decisions.

SKY AWARENESS

When I served as the Coordinator of Environment and Sustainability Programs at Upper Canada College, an independent school for boys in Toronto, Canada, I looked for every occasion to extend the boundaries of the curriculum and to share with my colleagues how to enlist nature as a teacher. Sometimes what you teach during extracurricular activities makes up for what doesn't get taught during instructional time. I took members of the Solar Club up on a dormitory roof at noon on December 21—a cold but sunny winter solstice and the last day of school before the Christmas break. Our guest was a solar energy expert, a wonderful fellow who had taken this club under his wing, and what we discovered about the students was disconcerting: they had never before looked up!

These students could not tell us how the sun tracked across the sky—where on the horizon it rose and set—and did not understand that the sun was at its highest point in the south on its lowest trajectory of the year in the northern hemisphere. The geometry of solar panel efficiency quickly became a lesson in basic astronomy (which, teachers later told me, is often the first unit to be cut from science courses if time is running out). How will these students become engineers of the renewable energy revolution if they are not even "sky aware"? How can we teach students to be sky aware if we never venture outside the classroom box with them?

Education professor Madeline Hunter is known for saying, "Don't get caught in the trap of 'covering material.' If you do, cover it with dirt and lay it to rest, because without meaning, it's dead anyway" (as cited in Dorn, 2000). As educators with responsibilities inside and outside the classroom, we are going to have to find the time to re-examine the curriculum from the perspective of what our students need to learn for the twenty-first century—versus what we're used to "covering."

SUSTAINABLE DEVELOPMENT MEANS FAIRNESS

Here is my favourite experience outside the box . . . one that gives me hope. In 2006, when I heard that the grade 3 students at Upper Canada College would be studying a unit entitled *What a City Needs*, I saw my chance to try something I had never attempted before: teaching young children about sustainable development. Because fairness is everything to children of that age (eight- and nine-year-olds), I framed the integration principle of sustainable development in terms they could grasp: Is the proposed development fair to all the people involved, present and future (social equity)? Is it fair to the rest of nature (environment)? Is it a fair price for everyone (economy)? And the children understood it immediately!

Before they began designing their own cities, we put the principles of sustainable development into practice by asking what a schoolyard needs (playground equipment in addition to the sports fields, they decided). They posed, in the words of one of their teachers, "phenomenal questions," and kept talking about the concept of fairness throughout their unit. "That was exactly what we were after, so it was perfect," she concluded.

Afterwards, eight-year-old Andrew described his learning this way: "We talked about money, if it's fair to all people, and if it's fair to all the Earth. Then we talked about sustainable, so not taking away from any people, and it would last a long time, and not cutting down so many trees. And then we talked about if the cost was fair." When nine-year-old David was asked what he had learned, he said, "If you put something in, it has to be fair for the environment, fair for all people, and fair for the cost. We talked about sustainable development: if you put something in, it won't affect the future." I asked David how he remembered the term sustainable development. "I like it," he said, "and I like learning about it, and I always think about it."

Imagine all students learning, as they grow up and graduate, that sustainable development (something not usually found in third grade curriculum) is all about fairness. What and how we teach right now perpetuates the unquestioned status quo. What and how we teach perpetrates *unsustainable* development: environmental degradation, economic inequity, and intergenerational unfairness. There is a possibility that Andrew and David's generation, by learning the transformative new paradigm of sustainable development and its principles and processes throughout their education, will create a future that is actually sustainable.

Paulo Freire (1973) liked to point out that "education is an act of love, thus an act of courage" (p. 38). We teachers, if we love our students, our own children and grandchildren, this planet we live on, and the idea of a future for humankind, must summon the courage to break free of "fortress curriculum" if it isn't changing fast enough.

We need to start offering the knowledge, skills, values, attitudes, and habits of mind and heart that students need in order to create the best possible future, *now*. Life, indeed survival itself, must become the curriculum. May this new curriculum be envisioned as a forest, a garden, or a river (curriculum comes from the Latin *currere*, for current), so that it can be organic and live, grow, change, adapt. Or, if we must remain in the curriculum box, may we picture it as a house, a home, with its doors and windows flung open wide to embrace the world outside it.

My hope, for the sake of future generations, is that sharing these stories will help invoke the courage we are all going to need to face down a curriculum-constrained education system in a climate-constrained world. Let this be our transformative gift, our way of showing our love as teachers, to all of the children, of all species, for all time.

REFLECTIVE QUESTIONS

1. What does the term "environmental education" represent to you?
2. What experience have you had with environmental education?
3. What does Johnston mean when she says that environmental education has become trapped in the curriculum box? Do you agree? Why or why not?
4. What does the author cite as some of the reasons for a lack of environmental education in the curriculum? Do you concur?
5. How does Johnston envision environmental education as being transformative?
6. What suggestions does Johnston make for addressing this issue? What others would you add?

REFERENCES

Agne, R., & Nash, R. (1976). The teacher educator as environmental activist. *Journal of Teacher Education, 27*, 141–146.

Dorn, G. (2000). Editor's musings. *Center for teaching and learning email newsletter, 1*(4). Accessed at Minnesota State Colleges and Universities: www.ctl.mnscu.edu/about/newsletter/documents/update4-feb00.pdf

Freire, P. (1973). *Education for critical consciousness.* New York: Continuum.

Gorrie, P. (2007, November 18). Act now or see "unrecognizable" earth: UN. *The Toronto Star.* Accessed at http://www.thestar.com/sciencetech/article/277497

Hansen, J. (2008, June 23). *Global warming twenty years later.* Accessed at the Worldwatch Institute: http://www.worldwatch.org/node/5798

Intergovernmental Panel on Climate Change. (2007, November). *IPCC fourth assessment: Climate change 2007 synthesis report.* Accessed at http://www.ipcc.ch/ipccreports/ar4-syr.htm

Learning for a Sustainable Future (2006, March 15). *Canadian sustainability curriculum review project: Rationale, context, and scope.* Accessed at http://www.lsf-lst.ca/media/CurriculumReview InitiativeMarch_15_2006.pdf

McKeown, R., Hopkins, C., Rizzi, R., & Chrystalbride, M. (2002). *Education for sustainable development toolkit* (Version 2). Accessed at the University of Tennessee: http://www.esdtoolkit.org/esd_toolkit_v2.pdf

Orr, D. W. (1992). *Ecological literacy: Education and the transition to a postmodern world* (SUNY Series in Constructive Postmodern Thought). Albany, NY: State University of New York Press.

Pilkington, E. (2008, June 23). Put oil firm chiefs on trial, says leading climate change scientist. *The Guardian.* Accessed at http://www.guardian.co.uk/environment/2008/jun/23/fossilfuels.climatechange

Puk, T., & Makin, D. (2006). Ecological consciousness in Ontario elementary schools: The truant curriculum and the consequences. *Applied Environmental Education and Communication, 5*(4), 269–276.

Sterling, S. (1996). Education in change. In J. Huckle & S. Sterling (Eds.), *Education for sustainability* (pp. 18–39). London: Earthscan.

United Nations Environment Programme (2007). *Global environment outlook: Environment for development* (English Full Report). Accessed at http://www.unep.org/geo/geo4/media/

United Nations Educational, Scientific and Cultural Organization. (1999, March). *Education and population dynamics: Mobilizing minds for a sustainable future* (EPD.99/WS/1). Accessed at http://unesdoc.unesco.org/images/0011/001163/116355eo.pdf

22

Religion, Public Education, and the Charter:

Where do we go now?

PAUL CLARKE

INTRODUCTION

In a series of three articles examining the interplay between religion and education in the context of Canadian schools, William F. Foster and William J. Smith (2002) conclude in their final article that the time has come "for a policy debate in each jurisdiction about the place which religion ought to play in public education" (p. 260). At the same time, a majority of the Supreme Court of Canada in *Chamberlain v. Surrey School District No. 36* (2002) has recently acknowledged in a landmark decision affecting the rights and interests of gays and lesbians in our public schools that, "Religion is an integral aspect of people's lives, and cannot be left at the boardroom door" (para. 19).

This paper examines what role, if any, religion should have in Canada's public schools. The basic argument is that discussion about religion, as well as the manifestation of religious belief, should be encouraged in our schools because there are good philosophical, pragmatic, and educational reasons to justify this kind of activity. At the same time, it is readily acknowledged that any discussion about, or expression of, religion must respect the values and principles embodied in the Canadian Charter of Rights and Freedoms (1982). As the Supreme Court of Canada reminds us, all freedoms are subject to reasonable limits and both the rights and limits have their origins in these fundamental values and principles, which make up the Canadian polity, and include:

[R]espect for the inherent dignity of the human person, commitment to social justice and equality, accommodation of a wide variety of beliefs, respect for cultural and group identity, and faith in social and political institutions which enhance the participation of individuals and groups in society. (p. 225)[1]

Although this approach is not without risk, it is contended that the risk is worth taking because the potential benefits which true dialogue promotes (tolerance, understanding, and compromise) outweigh the harm to be avoided (indoctrination and fundamentalism) by consigning religious expression to the purely private sphere. Moreover, it is proposed that the Charter, and its underlying values, serves as a reliable bulwark against harmful and unjustifiable manifestations of religion in our public schools.

Part I of the paper explains why some manifestations of religion should be banned from the school gates. Part II explains reasons why legitimate discussion about religion should be promoted in a public educational forum. In the final section, suggestions are offered as to how our schools may support respectful and responsible displays of religious belief. The discussion draws on relevant legal case law and secondary literature pertinent to the subject.

Paul Horwitz's (1996) definition of religion informs the discussion in this paper. He claims that at the heart of religion is "a belief that is spiritual, supernatural or transcendent in nature, whether or not it is shared by anyone else, so long as it is sincerely held" (p. 10). It is acknowledged that religious belief can only be meaningful to the extent that it is protected by religious freedom. The definition of freedom of religion is thus adopted as articulated by the Supreme Court of Canada in *R. v. Big M Drug Mart Ltd.* (1985):

The essence of the concept of freedom of religion is the right to entertain such religious beliefs as a person chooses, the right to declare religious beliefs openly and without fear of hindrance or reprisal, and the right to manifest religious belief by worship and practice or by teaching and dissemination. (pp. 336–337)

At the same time, it is recognized that freedom of religion is a not a licence to do whatever one wants. The court in *Big M* noted the need for restrictions in the following terms:

This freedom is not unlimited, however, and is restricted by the right of others to hold and to manifest beliefs and opinions of their own, and to be free from injury from the exercise of freedom of religion of others. (p. 337)

PART I—REASONS TO EXCLUDE RELIGION

Valid reasons exist to exclude some forms of religious belief and expression from entering our schools. This exclusion is warranted when the state, groups, or individuals use religion, wittingly or unwittingly, to indoctrinate or to undermine the fundamental rights and freedoms of others.

Indoctrination

Indoctrination may take different forms. It may occur in blatant and subtle manifestations. In *Keegstra v. Board of Education of Lacombe No. 14* (1983), a Board of Reference upheld the board of education's decision to terminate James Keegstra's employment contract on the grounds of insubordination.[2] This case is an example of a patent attempt by a public high school teacher to indoctrinate his students into anti-Semitic ways of thinking. In addition, it should be noted that strong and extremist religious beliefs motivated the teacher's actions.

Keegstra taught social studies to students in grades 9 and 12. In class, he presented his view of history founded on the belief in an international Jewish conspiracy. The teacher sincerely believed that Jews were responsible for undermining Christianity and Western civilization. In *R. v. Keegstra* (1990), the Supreme Court of Canada described the teachings in this way:

> Mr. Keegstra's teachings attributed various evil qualities to Jews. He thus described Jews to his pupils as "treacherous," "subversive," "sadistic," "money-loving," "power hungry" and "child killers." He taught his classes that Jewish people seek to destroy Christianity and are responsible for depressions, anarchy, chaos, wars and revolution. According to Mr. Keegstra, Jews "created the Holocaust to gain sympathy" and, in contrast to the open and honest Christians, were said to be deceptive, secretive and inherently evil. (p. 714)

Following parental complaints, the superintendent of schools conducted an investigation of Keegstra's teaching practices. As a result, the teacher received oral and written warnings to change his approach by teaching the prescribed curriculum. When he did not conform to the superintendent's directives, the board of education held a hearing and decided to fire Keegstra. A Board of Reference affirmed the termination. Keegstra's in-class racist opinions amounted to unjustifiable contractual violations. The teacher used methods contrary to the provincial curriculum and refused to remedy his ways after he had received a number of warnings.

In reaching its decision, the Board of Reference noted that Keegstra's approach precluded the teaching of social studies through critical inquiry:

While the appellant may have prefaced his presentation of the material by a general statement that these were only theories, I am satisfied that the students did not have before them any contrary views or any contrary source material which may have led them to conclude that the theories being presented were in error. This lack of opposing views and opposing source materials, combined with the appellant's assertion of his personal belief based upon research of the accuracy or correctness of the information, led to the acceptance by the students of the information as historically accurate and as fact. This is clear from the evidence of Paul Maddox who testified that he and his fellow students believed the appellant and did not question the accuracy or truth of the information and facts presented to them. (pp. 280–281)

Interestingly, the Board of Reference did not use the word *indoctrination* in its judgment. Nonetheless, Keegstra's actions exhibited the hallmarks of the concept. The fanaticism, the closed-mindedness, and the refusal to engage in critical thinking all reflected the badges of indoctrination.[3] Most disturbingly, the teacher's world view was anchored in sincerely held religious beliefs. The case illustrates how one teacher's religious views can be used for nefarious purposes to lure students into a warped and harmful way of thinking.

Indoctrination may manifest itself in more subtle ways. In *Canadian Civil Liberties Assn. v. Ontario (Minister of Education)* (1990), the Canadian Civil Liberties Association and a group of parents challenged the constitutionality of a curriculum requirement, as well as the overarching provincial regulatory framework, forcing public school students to take two periods of religious instruction per week. The relevant legislation also had an exemption from religious instruction for students whose parents opposed their participation.[4] Initially, the curriculum was exclusively Christian. Later, the school board changed it to add sections reflecting other religions. The Ontario Court of Appeal framed the issue in these terms:

The crucial issue in this appeal is whether the purpose and effects of the regulation and the curriculum are to indoctrinate school children in Ontario in the Christian faith. If so, the rights to freedom of conscience and religion under s. 2(a) of the *Canadian Charter of Rights and Freedoms* and the equality rights guaranteed under s. 15 of the Charter may be infringed. On the other hand, it is conceded that education designed to teach about religion and to foster moral values without indoctrination in a particular faith would not be a breach of the Charter. It is indoctrination in a particular religious faith that is alleged to be offensive. (p. 4)[5]

The court ruled that both the regulatory framework and the curriculum provided for religious indoctrination in the Christian faith and that allowing other religions to provide for the same kind of indoctrination did not solve the problem.

In response to this decision, the Ontario Ministry of Education issued a policy memorandum and amended relevant regulations dealing with religion in schools. The Ministry memorandum stated that henceforth Ontario public schools and programs, including programs in education about religion, under the jurisdiction of boards of education (except s. 93 boards) had to meet two conditions: a) they must not be indoctrinational; and b) they must not give primacy to any particular religious faith. In *Bal v. Ontario (Attorney General)* (1994), Judge Winkler highlighted the non-denominational nature of public education: "The public school is secular, it does not present the opportunity for education in any particular denomination or faith. The objective is to promote non-denominational education" (p. 130).

In our public schools, indoctrination along religious lines is wrong because it fails to treat individuals with the respect and the dignity to which they are entitled as self-regulating and autonomous human beings. Hence, it is incumbent upon the state and others (whether communities or individuals) to ensure that individuals have the opportunity and space to make fundamental choices about what constitutes a good life, including whether to embrace or reject beliefs of a religious nature.

Violating the Rights of Others

Any religious expression that undermines the rights of others (most notably, the rights of minorities) also has no place in the nation's public classrooms. As the Supreme Court of Canada stated in *R. v. Big M Drug Mart Ltd.* (1985): "Freedom of religion is subject to such limitations as are necessary to protect public safety, order, health or morals and *the fundamental rights and freedoms of others*" (p. 337, emphasis added). The *Ross v. New Brunswick School District No. 15* (1996) decision illustrates powerfully how the religious expression of an individual teacher may undermine the equality rights and interests of certain minority groups.

Malcolm Ross taught elementary mathematics in Magnetic Hill, New Brunswick. While off duty, he published various writings including: *Web of Deceit, The Real Holocaust: The Attack on Unborn Children and Life Itself, Spectre of Power*, and *Christianity vs. Judeo-Christianity: The Battle for Truth*. He also sent three letters to New Brunswick newspapers and made one public television appearance to defend his controversial views. Like James Keegstra, in Alberta, he argued that Western Christian civilization is being undermined and destroyed by an "international Jewish conspiracy." The following passage from one of Ross's letters captures his thinking: "My whole purpose in writing and publishing is to exult Jesus Christ and to inform Christians about the great Satanic movement which is trying to destroy our Christian faith and civilization" (p. 24).[6]

Public concern about Ross's views prompted the school board to commence disciplinary action. A concerned Jewish parent even filed a complaint with the New Brunswick Human Rights Commission, alleging that the school board's inability to discipline Ross effectively constituted discrimination against the parent's children and other Jewish students because of their religion or ancestry. Ultimately, a Board of Inquiry issued an order removing Ross from the classroom and placing expressive restrictions on his ability to engage in anti-Semitic speech. Ross challenged this order on the grounds that it violated his constitutionally protected fundamental freedoms, namely, freedom of expression and freedom of religion.

Our highest court summed up Ross's freedom of religion argument in these terms:

> In arguing that the order does infringe his freedom of religion, the respondent submits that the Act is being used as a sword to punish individuals for expressing their discriminating religious beliefs. He maintains that "[a]ll of the invective and hyperbole about anti-Semitism is really a smoke screen for imposing an officially sanctioned religious belief on society as a whole which is not the function of courts or Human Rights Tribunals in a free society." In this case, the respondent's freedom of religion is manifested in his writings, statements and publications. These, he argues, constitute "thoroughly honest religious statement[s]," and adds that it is not the role of this Court to decide what any particular religion believes. (para. 70)

A unanimous Supreme Court of Canada rejected the teacher's arguments. The court stated that freedom of religion cannot be used to undermine the dignity and equality of others, values upon which the Charter is grounded:

> In relation to freedom of religion, any religious belief that denigrates and defames the religious beliefs of others erodes the very basis of the guarantee in s. 2(a)—a basis that guarantees that every individual is free to hold and to manifest the beliefs dictated by one's conscience. The respondent's religious views serve to deny Jews respect for dignity and equality said to be among the fundamental guiding values of a court undertaking a s. 1 analysis. (para. 94)

Our highest court also ruled that the purpose of the order removing the teacher from the classroom was to promote equal opportunity that was unhindered by discriminatory practices based on race or religion and that this constituted a *pressing and substantial* objective. In reaching this decision, the court considered a number of factors including: the harmful nature of hate propaganda, the international community's commitment to the elimination of discrimination, and ss. 15 and 27[7] of the Charter which embrace, respectively, the values of equality and multiculturalism. The court then concluded:

> [A]ll the above factors are relevant in assessing the importance of the objective of the impugned Order. In the first place, they assert the fundamental commitment of the international community to the eradication of discrimination in general. Secondly, they acknowledge the pernicious effects associated with hate propaganda, and more specifically, anti-Semitic messages, that undermine basic democratic values and are antithetical to the "core" values of the Charter. The Board's Order asserts a commitment to the eradication of discrimination in the provision of educational services to the public. Based upon the jurisprudence, Canada's international obligations and the values constitutionally entrenched, the objective of the impugned Order is clearly "pressing and substantial." (para. 98)

Similarly, in *Kempling v. British Columbia College of Teachers* (2004), Justice Holmes of the British Columbia Supreme Court has recently ruled that homophobic teacher speech will not be tolerated in the public school context. In this case, Mr. Kempling associated homosexuality with "immorality, abnormality, perversion, and promiscuity" in letters he wrote to the local newspaper and defended these views as a valid expression of his religious beliefs. In these letters, Kempling also identified himself as a teacher and a mental health professional. Justice Holmes described his writings as "discriminatory" and "defamatory." He also upheld the teacher's one-month suspension by the British Columbia College of Teachers who ruled that Kempling's conduct was unprofessional because it undermined the values of respect and inclusion owed to all members of the educational community, including gays and lesbians. Drawing on the Supreme Court of Canada's decision in *Ross* (1996), Justice Holmes rejected Kempling's claims that his constitutionally protected rights to freedom of expression and freedom of religion under the Charter of Rights and Freedoms had been violated.

In sum, hateful and discriminatory religious expression, which is anathema to the Charter values of equality and accommodation, has no legitimate place inside our public schools.

PART II—REASONS TO INCLUDE RELIGION

This section of the paper begins with a consideration of the judicial meaning of the word *secular* in the context of our public schools. The discussion serves as introduction for the primary focus of the section, being an examination of the rationales offered to include religion in our public schools. These rationales are philosophical, pragmatic, and educational.

What does secular mean?

A relatively recent case (2002) in British Columbia forced the courts to consider the meaning of the word *secular* in a landmark decision known as *Chamberlain v. Surrey School District No. 36* (2002). This case arose out of the proper interpretation to be given to the following provisions of the BC School Act (1996), which say:

76 (1) All schools must be conducted on strictly secular and non-sectarian principles.

(2) The highest morality must be inculcated, but no religion, dogma or creed is to be taught in a school or Provincial school.

The Board of Trustees of the Surrey School District passed a resolution in 1997, referred to as the "Three Books Resolution," stating that the Board did not approve the use of three books depicting children with same-sex parents as "recommended learning resources."[8]

The issue arose against a background of considerable public acrimony and religious hostility toward homosexuality in Surrey. The petitioners, led by Mr. Chamberlain, a primary school teacher, applied under the Judicial Review Procedure Act (1996) for an order quashing the "Three Books Resolution" and another on the basis that this resolution infringed the School Act (1996) and the Canadian Charter of Rights and Freedoms. In British Columbia Supreme Court,[9] the Chambers judge quashed the "Three Books Resolution" as being contrary to the above provisions of the School Act. Judge Saunders found as a fact that those who argued in favour of and voted for the resolution were significantly influenced by religious considerations.

Furthermore, she noted that opponents of the books objected to homosexual conduct because of its alleged immoral nature. Judge Saunders ruled that this was contrary to s. 76(1), which forbade the school board from implementing a decision made on religious views.[10] In this regard, she stated: "Section 76 [of the School Act] is an example of legislated protection for freedom of religion, presuming the public school is a place independent of religious considerations" (para. 102). Not surprisingly, the judge interpreted the word *secular* in a very narrow manner: "In the education setting, the term secular excludes religion or religious belief" (para. 78).

In the literature, David M. Brown (2000) criticized Judge Saunders's restrictive interpretation of secular in these words:

Effectively the court is saying: a public body, even an elected public body, cannot listen or take into account concerns raised by citizens which may be motivated by, influenced by, or based upon religious beliefs. Any argument framed in a religious manner or advanced by people who are religiously motivated, cannot be listened to because public bodies must operate on secular principles. With one stroke of the pen, a judge has excluded from the educational political process in British Columbia a significant portion of the electorate and constructed a new constitutional principle that religious persons are disqualified from participating in the debates of public, secular institutions. (p. 604)

The British Columbia Court of Appeal[11] rejected Judge Saunders's interpretation of "strictly secular" on two grounds. First, it was indefensible as a matter of principle. As Justice MacKenzie observed:

Can "strictly secular" in s. 76(1) of the School Act be interpreted as limited to moral positions devoid of religious influence? Are only those with a non-religiously informed conscience to be permitted to participate in decisions involving moral instruction of children in the public schools? . . . Simply to pose the questions in such terms can lead to only one answer in a truly free society. Moral positions must be accorded equal access to the public square without regard to religious influence. A religiously informed conscience should not be accorded any privilege, but neither should it be placed under a disability. (para. 28)

Second, he noted that adopting Judge Saunders's strict construction would lead to "immense practical difficulties":

How would it be determined that a moral position is advanced from a conscience influenced by religion or not? If the restriction were applied only where the religious conviction was publicly declared it would privilege convictions based on a conscience whose influences were concealed over one openly proclaimed. The alternative would be to require inquiry as to the source of a moral conviction, whether religious or otherwise. Both alternatives are offensive and indefensible. (para. 29)

Justice MacKenzie then went on to propose the following definition of "strictly secular":

In my opinion, "strictly secular" in the School Act can only mean pluralist in the sense that moral positions are to be accorded standing in the public square irrespective of whether the position flows out of a conscience that is religiously informed or not. The meaning of strictly secular is thus pluralist or inclusive in its widest sense. (para. 33)

In essence, the Court of Appeal refused to ban religion from the public square.

Weighing in on the proper interpretation of "secular," both the majority and minority judges of the Supreme Court of Canada[12] agreed that Judge Saunders's approach espousing a strict interpretation of the term was not tenable. For the majority, Chief Justice McLachlin stated: "[T]he requirement of secularism laid out in s. 76 does not prevent religious concerns from being among those matters of local and parental concern that influence educational policy" (para. 3). In support of this position, she added:

> The Act's insistence on strict secularism does not mean that religious concerns have no place in the deliberations and decisions of the Board. Board members are entitled, and indeed required, to bring the views of the parents and communities they represent to the deliberation process. Because religion plays an important role in the life of many communities, these views will often be motivated by religious concerns. Religion is an integral aspect of people's lives, and cannot be left at the boardroom door. (para. 19)

Justice Gonthier, writing for the minority, refuted Judge Saunders's reasoning in this way:

> In my view, Saunders J. below erred in her assumption that "secular" effectively meant "non-religious." This is incorrect since nothing in the Charter, political or democratic theory, or a proper understanding of pluralism demands that atheistically based moral positions trump religiously based moral positions on matters of public policy. (para. 137)

It is important to note that the majority of the Supreme Court of Canada, although it rejected Judge Saunders's narrow interpretation of *secular*, agreed with her decision to quash the school board's "Three Books Resolution" banning the use of materials depicting same-sex parented families. Chief Justice McLachlin drew on the principles of administrative law to point out a number of errors underpinning the resolution. Most significantly, she noted that the school board resolution violated the principles of secularism and tolerance in s. 76 of the School Act (1996). Instead of proceeding on the basis of respect for all types of families, the superintendent and the board had proceeded "on an exclusionary philosophy." They had acted on the concern of certain parents about the morality of same-sex relationships. Thus, the school authorities failed to consider the interest of same-sex parented families and the children who belong to them in receiving equal recognition and respect in the school system.

The board could not reject books simply because certain parents, for religious reasons, found the lawful relationships depicted in them controversial or objectionable. In this context, the Chief Justice stated that the demands of secularism placed certain restrictions on religion and its ability to influence school policy:

> What secularism does rule out ... is any attempt to use the religious views of one part of the community to exclude from consideration the values of other members of the community. A requirement of secularism implies that, although the Board is indeed free to address the religious concerns of parents, it must be sure to do so in a manner that gives equal recognition and respect to other members of the community. Religious views that deny equal recognition and respect to the members of a minority group cannot be used to exclude the concerns of the minority group. This is fair to both groups, as it ensures that each group is given as much recognition as it can consistently demand while giving the same recognition to others. (para. 19)

Consequently, the religious views of a few could not be used to justify public policy, which would undermine the equality rights and interests of gays and lesbians in British Columbia's public schools. Furthermore, Chief Justice McLachlin noted:

> The School Act's emphasis on secularism reflects the fact that Canada is a diverse and multicultural society, bound together by the values of accommodation, tolerance and respect for diversity. These values are reflected in our Constitution's commitment to equality and minority rights, and are explicitly incorporated into the British Columbia public school system by the Preamble to the School Act and by the curriculum established by regulation under the Act. (para. 21)

Reasons to Include Religious Discussion and Expression in Our Schools

In *Chamberlain*, the majority of the Supreme Court of Canada noted that, "Religion is an integral aspect of people's lives, and cannot be left at the boardroom door." Although the court does not expand on this, we suggest that there are sound philosophical, pragmatic, and educational reasons to justify the inclusion of religious discussion and expression in our public schools.

From a *philosophical* perspective, it could be plausibly argued that human beings are, in large part, spiritual beings who are stirred or motivated by religious longings and a sense of the transcendent. Our search for meaning(s) is a fundamental part of who we are. It might even be posited that we are hard wired to engage in a quest for significance, which is an integral part of the human condition. As John O'Donohue (1999) notes: "Our quest for meaning, though often unacknowledged, is what secretly sustains our passion and guides our instinct and action. Our need to find meaning is urged upon us by our sense of life" (p. 92). For some of us, this search for truth(s) and meaning(s) plays out in our religious and spiritual practices. These practices include (to mention just a few) prayer, meditation, being part of a faith community, pursuing matters of social justice, and talking to others about what religion and spirituality mean to us. For many people, this day-to-day expression of our religious or spiritual self is an essential part of what it means to be human. Those who take a very narrow or restrictive approach to secularism would suggest that any expression of the religious or spiritual self in the public educational context is inappropriate because it does not respect the lines of demarcation that should exist between church and state, the religious and the non-religious. Assuming, however, that we have a spiritual nature, or alternatively that religion plays an important part in the lives of many Canadians, there is no good or logical reason to preclude the respectful and responsible discussion of religious questions within the school gates.

At the same time, it is important to recognize that there exist a multiplicity of divergent voices and opinions on the subject of religion. This assumption about the transcendent is controversial and not everybody agrees with it. Atheists, materialists, and some postmodernists, for example, would argue strenuously that there is no such thing as transcendent truth or that God is a lie. They would have us believe that their narratives or versions of history and humanity are the right ones and consequently we should abandon our prejudices and superstitions, which must inevitably come from having a faith in the transcendent. Likewise, those opposed to religious belief may be committed to social justice and to a search for meaning that is grounded in the here and now. Nobody would suggest that these voices should be disentitled from engaging in policy discussions about how we run our public schools, including discussions with our students about what gives life meaning or purpose, simply because of their non-religious perspective. It is arguable that the same rules of engagement and inclusiveness be applied to religious perspectives within the context of our public schools. Therefore, it is reasonable to reject the contention that moral views grounded in a religious perspective automatically are disqualified from the public square while those that are not are entitled to be heard. As Justice Gonthier of the Supreme Court of Canada observed:

[E]veryone has "belief" or "faith" in something, be it atheistic, agnostic or religious. To construe the "secular" as the realm of the "unbelief" is therefore erroneous. Given this, why, then, should the religiously informed conscience be placed at a public disadvantage or disqualification? To do so would be to distort liberal principles in an illiberal fashion and would provide only a feeble notion of pluralism. The key is that people will disagree about important issues, and such disagreement, where it does not imperil community living, must be capable of being accommodated at the core of a modern pluralism. (para. 137)

From a *pragmatic* perspective, religion seems to matter in the lives of people. In global terms, a significant proportion of the planet's total population (close to 6.3 billion people) belongs to the world's major faith traditions and the number and percentages of adherents[13] break down accordingly. There are approximately two billion Christians (32.9%), 1.2 billion Muslims (19.9%), 840 million Hindus (13.3%), 370 million Buddhists (5.9%), 24 million Sikhs (0.4%), and 15 million Jews (0.2%).[14] In percentages, the adherents of these major religions represent 72.6 per cent of the world's total population.

In Canada, according to the 2001 Census, the population by religious affiliation of the major religions is approximately as follows: Catholic—12.8 million (43.2%), Protestant—8.6 million (29.2%), Muslim—580 thousand (2%), Jewish—330 thousand (1.1%), Buddhist—300 thousand (1.0%), Hindu—297 thousand (1.0%), and Sikh—278 thousand (0.9%).[15] In percentages, 82.6 per cent of Canadians indicated a religious affiliation in the 2001 Census.[16] In Quebec, Jean-François Gaudreault-Desbiens (2002) reminds us that religious pluralism has become a reality in *la belle province* during the past few decades:

En l'espace de seulement quelques décennies, la société québécoise est passée de la quasi-hégémonie du crucifix, avec quelques *kippas* ici et la, au *hijab* et au *kirpan*. Pendant la même période, de multiples sectes sont apparues, alors que le taux de pratique religieuse chutait radicalement. Autrement dit, la société québécoise s'est pluralisée autant sur le plan religieux que sur d'autres plans. (p. 102)

It is important to acknowledge that the Census also tells us that about 4.8 million Canadians (16.2%) claim no religious affiliation. Furthermore, the numbers cited and the recent growth of religious pluralism in Quebec tell us nothing about the nature of Canadians' religious beliefs and practices, as well as their commitment to things religious. In the early 1990s, Reginald Bibby (1993) painted a grim prognosis of organized religion in Canada. A lack of interest in formal religion, a greying of Canada's religious communities, poor church attendance among young people, and an inability to recruit new members led Bibby to decry: "There's little doubt that organized religion is in very serious shape, with its golden years apparently relegated to history" (p. 115). Yet, Bibby's (2002) more recent work suggests that there are signs of "spiritual restlessness" at play in Canada that reflect a renaissance of religion in our country:

> After a few decades of slumber, there appears to be a stirring among the country's established churches—those same groups that Canadians have been so reluctant to abandon. There is also a stirring among large numbers of people outside the churches, who are pursuing answers about life and death and spiritual needs with more openness than at perhaps any time in our nation's history. Much more private and much less publicized is the fact that three in four people talk to God at least occasionally. Even more startling, two in four Canadians think they have actually experienced God's presence. And then there are those "haunting hints" of a Presence—the cry for wrongs to be made right, the sense that things are ultimately under control, life-giving hope and humour, the need for spiritual fulfillment. (p. 227)

If indeed a religious renaissance is under way in Canadian society and it touches something deep, meaningful, and important in the lives of many Canadians, it strikes us as counterintuitive to relegate religion to the strictly private realm and to suggest, consequently, that it has no place in our public schools. Furthermore, in practical terms, to prevent those whose opinions are religiously based from having their say about educational policy or expressing those views in our schools would silence and arguably disenfranchise a large segment of the school community.

There are also compelling *educational* reasons why discussion about religion and the reasonable manifestations of religious belief should be encouraged in our public schools.

First, in some provinces, Ministries and Departments of Education now recognize that attending to the spiritual is part of educating the child. In Saskatchewan, for instance, the provincial government (2002)[17] has recognized that schools have the following function: "To educate children and youth—nurturing the development of the whole child, intellectually, socially, *spiritually*, emotionally and physically . . . " (p. 1, emphasis added). If the child has a spiritual dimension to his or her being, and we are genuinely interested in developing this part of his or her nature, then we must create the space and conditions under which this development may proceed. To limit arbitrarily discussions about religion to the home or purely private realm is simply inconsistent with the school's underlying mission of educating the whole child.

Second, it is inherently anti-intellectual to suggest that we ban all discussions about religion or manifestations of religion in our schools. This suggests a closed-mindedness or lack of imagination, which is anathema to a curious, inquisitive, caring, and critical mind. Although we must be on guard to insure against indoctrination and other abuses arising from a reckless approach to religion, banning all discussion seems too extreme and fails to recognize the value that religion has in the lives of people. It is right to point out that religion can be misused by extremists who attempt to justify acts of torture, murder, and other forms of horrific treatment such as the beheading of hostages that we have come to witness in recent months in Iraq and the Middle East. Closer to home, religion can also be used to manipulate people by making them feel guilty and worthless, by extracting money from unsuspecting persons through television evangelism while threatening them with eternal damnation should they fail to pledge. Yet, religion can inspire the best in people. The twentieth-century examples of Mother Teresa, Martin Luther King Jr., Mahatma Ghandi, and Thich Nhat Hanh and their relentless and selfless contributions to social justice speak to the most compassionate and generous aspects of our humanity.

In essence, it is acknowledged that religion can bring out the best and the worst in people. Yet, this is true about the study of any discipline. We do not ban the study of science and technology in our schools even though these fields of study fuel the arms race, are used to develop weapons of mass destruction, and can be used for other various and nefarious purposes. Likewise, we do not tell our students to avoid the study of economics and systems such as capitalism even though critics such as Ronald Wright (2004)[18] remind us that at "the end of the twentieth century, the world's three richest individuals (all of whom were Americans) had a combined wealth greater than that of the poorest forty-eight countries" (p. 128). From this perspective, rampant and unregulated capitalism is a highly exploitive and inherently unfair way of conducting our commercial affairs. Yet, we do not keep the study of the subject out of our classrooms. Similarly, we must not be afraid to talk about religion in our schools and we do a disservice to our students when we demonize and marginalize religion by suggesting somehow that the world would be a better, safer, and happier place if religion did not exist.

In a related vein, there is nothing to suggest that the discussion of religion is inconsistent with one of the primary objectives of any liberal education system, namely, the promotion of critical thinking. H. Siegel (1988) offers a number of compelling reasons for accepting critical thinking as a fundamental educational ideal. Morality and respect for persons call for critical thinking:

This first consideration is simply that we are morally obliged to treat students (and everyone else) with respect. If we are to conduct our interpersonal affairs morally, we must recognize and honor the fact that we are dealing with other persons who as such deserve respect—that is, we must show *respect for persons*. This includes the recognition that other persons are of equal moral worth, which entails that we treat other persons in such a way that their moral worth is respected. (p. 56)

Self-sufficiency and preparation for adulthood justify critical thinking:

The second reason for taking critical thinking to be a worthy educational ideal has to do with education's generally recognized task of preparing students to become competent with respect to those abilities necessary for the successful management of adult life. We educate, at least in part, in order to prepare children for adulthood. . . . That is, we seek to render the child *self-sufficient*; to *empower* the student to control her destiny and to *create* her future, not submit to it. (p. 57)

Initiation into the rational traditions provides support for critical thinking:

If we can take education to involve significantly the initiation of students into the rational traditions, and such initiation consists in part in helping the student to appreciate the standards of rationality which govern the assessment of reasons (and so proper judgment) in each tradition, then we have a third reason for regarding critical thinking as an educational ideal. (pp. 59–60)

And, democracy itself requires critical thinking:

The fundamentality of reasoned procedures and critical talents and attitudes to democratic living is undeniable. Insofar as we are committed to democracy, then, that commitment affords yet another reason for regarding critical thinking as a fundamental educational ideal, for an education which takes as its central task the fostering of critical thinking is the education most suited for democratic life. (p. 61)

Siegel's four points reflect "liberal" values of equality, autonomy, self-responsibility, and democracy. Nonetheless, these values are consistent with a contemporary theory of pedagogy and are in large measure both assumed and embraced by our political society. In the school context, the responsible discussion of religion is consistent with the promotion of critical thinking and the accompanying values, which underlie it.

Third, schools are in a unique position to model civil and responsible religious discussion and expression. Kirk Makin (2004), the justice reporter for the *Globe and Mail*, recently outlined a number of priorities for Canada's Minister of Justice, Irwin Cotler. Priority five (of six) reads as follows: "*Combatting hatred, discrimination and intolerance toward identifiable groups.*" Makin then goes on to attribute the following words to our Justice Minister: "We have to create a constituency of consciousness that this is a country where there is no sanctuary for hatred and no refuge for bigotry. Groups have to speak up—Jews when Muslims are attacked; Muslims when Jews are attacked; Jews, Muslims when others are attacked" (p. A5).

How do we create this "constituency of consciousness" of which the Minister speaks? One way is by talking openly and responsibly about the reasons or explanations, which fuel the hatred, discrimination, and intolerance toward identifiable groups, including religious groups. Surely, if we cannot talk about this in our schools, then where can we discuss the matter? Are not educators responsible for challenging the ignorance, stereotypes, prejudices, and fears lurking in the human psyche and imagination? To ban religious expression from the classroom is to relegate it to the private realm where all kinds of misconceptions and distortions are likely to occur. To prohibit religious discussion in our schools eliminates a unique opportunity for our students to be exposed to other, more balanced views, which counter the fanaticism of extremists of all religious faiths whose message is carried in the media and on the web. How will students be able to cope with fanatical messages of hate and violence associated with religion outside the school gates if they have not been exposed to the messages of love, compassion, and caring which the best in our religious traditions have to offer?

In other words, schools have a leadership opportunity to create a dialogic community and to model respectful and responsible discussion in our school communities to promote tolerance, compromise, shared values, and a common humanity. Schools should be the voice of reason and moderation. They should create avenues of interconnectedness and intersections for the expression of religious and non-religious points of view. If our schools and our teachers cannot model these universal principles of respect and consideration, then how can our students be expected to take their place in a multicultural, religiously diverse community upon completion of their studies? If students are not exposed to other ways of being, then how will they confront the difference they encounter outside the school walls? In other words, the schools should act as the forum or crucible where civil discussion occurs. In this sense, schools can be proactive by modelling appropriate behaviour rather than reacting to outbursts of religious intolerance as they occur in school settings or in society in general.

Fourth, discussion about religion is consistent with citizenship education. In Quebec, the Ministry of Education's 1998 policy document entitled *A School for the Future: Policy Statement on Educational Integration and Intercultural Education* states: "Citizenship education concerns both diversity . . . and the shared values and democratic institutions that make it possible for people to live together" (p. 8). In an increasingly complex and pluralistic world, students need to know that their brothers and sisters come from different religious and cultural backgrounds. If they are not confronted, in the best sense of the word, with this difference and an appreciation of the "other" in our schools, our students will have neither the skills nor the attitudinal dispositions to function as tolerant and fair-minded citizens in a rapidly shrinking world whose very survival depends on interdependence, good will, and peace. If we do not understand those who are different from us, we may fear them or fail to take their needs and aspirations seriously. As future citizens, our students must realize that tolerance of religious difference, however, is not a form of ethical relativism, which means that anything goes. As Gaudreault-Desbiens (2002) states:

> [L]a tolérance est . . . à la fois ouverture et fermeture. Elle est fondée sur l'acceptation, par principe, de la diversité des opinions, des valeurs, des croyances, mais elle refuse aussi, par principe encore, que tout puisse être toléré. La tolérance a donc des limites; elle est contrainte par "l'inderogeabilité," si je peux me permettre d'inventer ce mot, de certains principes qui transcendent les particularités et définissent notre commune humanité. "La tolérance entend protéger notre diversité, mais en préservant aussi ce qui nous est commun." (p. 107)

Students must indeed learn that tolerance has its limits. Tolerance is not a synonym for accepting all types of behaviour. As Gaudreault-Desbiens notes, tolerance includes: "[D]isponibilité à la discussion dans une démarche de délibération qui ne pourra éviter l'évaluation des opinions et des choix en fonction de certains principes de vie et de rationalité" (p. 107). Students of different faith communities or of no particular faith allegiance must come to realize that in spite of religious and cultural differences, it is our shared humanity which binds us collectively together. In other words, what counts is how, in concrete terms, one treats one's fellow citizen. Do I treat her with respect and dignity? Do I resolve my differences with her peacefully? Am I capable of compromise and shared responsibility in my relations with my fellow citizens? My intentions and my actions may reflect a particular faith view (e.g., Muslim or Christian world view) or no religious perspective at all. Ultimately, whether my civic behaviour is motivated by a religious or non-religious disposition is beside the point. What matters is whether we can get along, compromise, work out our differences without resorting to violence and intimidation, and celebrate our commonalities as we live out our individual and collective lives.

PART III—HOW TO INCLUDE RELIGION

Including religion in our schools can take one of two forms. First, we can talk about it in our classes with our students. Second, we can allow students and teachers to express their religious beliefs in responsible and respectful ways.

In *Canadian Civil Liberties Assn. v. Ontario (Minister of Education)* (1990), the Ontario Court of Appeal suggested that the following guidelines would help schools distinguish between indoctrination and education about religion:

1. The school may sponsor the study of religion, but may not sponsor the practice of religion.
2. The school may expose students to all religious views, but may not impose any particular view.
3. The school's approach to religion is one of instruction, not one of indoctrination.
4. The function of the school is to educate about all religions, not to convert to any one religion.
5. The school's approach is academic, not devotional.
6. The school should study what all people believe, but should not teach a student what to believe.
7. The school should strive for student awareness of all religions, but should not press for student acceptance of any one religion.
8. The school should seek to inform the student about various beliefs, but should not seek to conform him or her to any one belief. (p. 28)

The court acknowledged that while the test between indoctrination and education may be an "easy test to state," in some instances, the line between the two "can be difficult to draw." We also are aware of the power that comes with teaching. As Mark G. Yudof (1979) states: "The power to teach, inform, and lead is also the power to indoctrinate, distort judgment, and perpetuate the current regime" (p. 865). Public school teachers have a tremendous potential to sway their students' thoughts and actions, by virtue of their position of power, authority, and superior intellectual skills. In *Ross v. New Brunswick School District No. 15* (1996), the Supreme Court of Canada stated: "Teachers occupy positions of trust and confidence, and exert considerable influence over their students as a result of their positions" (p. 857).

Public school students are often intellectually and emotionally immature and unsophisticated. They may swallow uncritically the dishes on the academic menu that the teacher presents to them simply because they lack the life experience and critical faculties of an autonomous and independent-minded adult. For many students, what the teacher says may be the only source of intellectual authority they receive on a controversial topic such as religion and morality. In a match of wits, more often than not, students are likely to be the losers. Recognizing the inherent innocence, naïveté, and vulnerability of young students, the Supreme Court of Canada in *Ross* (1996) declared: "Young children are especially vulnerable to the messages conveyed by their teachers. They are unlikely to distinguish between falsehoods and truth and more likely to accept derogatory views espoused by a teacher" (p. 873). Furthermore, in the classroom, teachers work with a captive audience composed of a majority of students who must attend school on a compulsory basis. Hence, the need for teachers to respect this vulnerability is important because classroom contact with students is direct, immediate, and often inescapable.

Some may argue that even allowing the discussion of religion in the schools runs the risk of having one religion (read Christianity because it is still the dominant religion in Canada) displace, or lord it over, other religions. As Gaudreault-Desbiens (2002) reminds us:

> Car si le sentiment religieux connote l'idée—positive—d'un appel à la transcendance, au dépassement de soi et a l'ouverture a l'Autre, il peut aussi devenir un formidable vecteur d'oppression ou d'exclusion sociale.... Toute religion propose à ses fidèles—ou leur impose—un régime de vérité révélée présenté comme supérieur aux autres. Cette inévitable dimension dogmatique pourra prendre plus ou moins de place selon les époques mais, toujours, elle sera présente. (p. 109)

Furthermore, how can we be sure that teachers are qualified or interested in mediating religious disputes should they arise in the classroom? Or that teachers with their own propensities (anti, pro, or neutral) won't push their own personal agendas vis-à-vis religion? This danger is potentially present in all teaching where issues of substance are raised and divergent viewpoints are held. Nonetheless, it is important not to shy away from these questions simply because they are controversial. To do so, would be the death knell of all serious teaching.

Notwithstanding the potential risks associated with addressing controversial issues, such as religion, teachers are professionals and have the skills and aptitude to canvass such topics in a fair and reasoned manner. I have argued elsewhere[19] that three primary pedagogical considerations require our teachers to cover polemic subjects in an even-handed and appropriate manner. These are: to avoid indoctrination, to promote critical thinking, and to advance equality. First, teachers must avoid indoctrination in teaching by striving for fairness and balance in the presentation of controversial materials or methods. In the literature, P. J. Byrne (1989) reminds us that academic speech attempts to transcend the personal biases[20] of the teachers:

> The unique point is that academic speech can be more free than the speaker; that the speaker may be driven to conclusions by her respect for methodology and evidence that contradict her own preconceptions and cherished assumptions. The scholar cannot argue merely for her political party, religion, class, race, or gender; she must acknowledge the hard resistance of the subject matter, the inadequacies of friends' arguments, and the force of those of her enemies. That is what scholars mean by disinterested argument—not indifference to the outcome, but insistence that commitment not weaken the rigor and honesty by which the argument is pursued. (p. 259)

Second, teachers must exercise self-restraint when employing controversial materials if they wish to instill the virtues of critical thinking in their students. Teachers who demonstrate a disproportionately strong bias in favour of certain views may preclude students from thinking about different or contrary perspectives, which they might have otherwise considered if the teaching had been more balanced. Even older and more mature students who hold opinions that differ from those of their teachers may feel reluctant to speak out in an atmosphere where teachers exert inordinate control and discourage students from expressing dissident beliefs. The refusal to present students with alternative viewpoints and the silencing of minority voices which run counter to teachers' discourse are both inimical to the values of a liberal education which argue in favour of helping learners to think critically and independently.

Third, in *Ross* (1996), the Supreme Court of Canada has endorsed, in strong and unambiguous language, the need for tolerance and fairness in the educational context as a means of promoting equality:

> The school is an arena for the exchange of ideas and must, therefore, be premised upon principles of tolerance and impartiality so that all persons within the school environment feel equally free to participate. (p. 857)

In *Ross*, the teacher's racist attitudes caused fear in Jewish families (or minority groups) that he and the school (or school board) would not treat Jewish children fairly. Thus, controversial expression involving attacks on arbitrary personal characteristics such as religion, language, ethnic background, or sexual orientation may well create a hostile learning environment, which denies equal respect and equal educational opportunity to all students. Teachers who indoctrinate along religious lines may well silence minority students or dissenting viewpoints sympathetic to those students. Hence, the need to foster an open and respectful environment where minority students are valued is certainly a legitimate pedagogical concern. In sum, there exist appropriate checks and balances to ensure that the discussion about religion can take place in healthy, legitimate and rational ways.

Responsible and respectful manifestations of religious belief should also be encouraged in our schools as this has the potential to promote tolerance, diversity, and respect for different ways of living in a democratic and pluralistic society.

In the early 1990s,[21] a secondary school in Montreal informed one of its female students, a convert to Islam, that she was not allowed to wear the hijab, or Islamic veil. Arguably, the wearing of the hijab ran afoul of the school's dress code. The matter did not come before the courts because the student left her school and enrolled in another institution. Nonetheless, public awareness of the issue caused Quebec's human rights commission to publish a discussion paper on the subject in 1995.[22] The Commission noted that the veil is "sometimes an instrumental part of a set of practices aimed at maintaining the subjugation of women and that, in some more extremist societies, women are actually forced to wear the veil." It refused, however, to advocate an outright ban of the hijab suggesting that this would violate the Quebec Charter of Human Rights and Freedoms.[23] In Quebec, the Commission stated that,

> [w]e must assume that this choice is a way of expressing their religious affiliations and convictions. In our view, it would be insulting to the girls and women who wear the veil to suppose that their choice is not an enlightened one, or that they do so to protest against the right to equality. It would also be offensive to classify the veil as something to be banished, like the swastika for example, or to rob it of its originality by comparing it to a hat. (p. 17)

Giving a student the freedom to wear the hijab seems to be a legitimate way of respecting her *religious affiliations and convictions*. It may also educate other students and members of the school community about religious difference and the existence of religious minorities in their school. In addition, it may enable other students and members of the school community to coexist peacefully and respectfully with those who wish to express their religious convictions in appropriate ways. At the same time, the right to wear the hijab or any other article of clothing is not an absolute right. Just as school boards must make reasonable accommodation to respect the religious beliefs of students, students themselves must be prepared to act responsibly in the larger school community. Hence, it is no surprise that the Commission asserted that restricting the use of the hijab could be defended where the wearing of the veil was designed to promote discrimination on the basis of sex. It also stated that safety reasons might justify restrictions on the donning of the veil.[24]

In *Multani (tuteur de) c. Commission scolaire Marguerite-Bourgeoys* (2004),[25] the principal of a French language school in Montreal told a Khalsa Sikh student, Gurbaj Singh Multani, that he could not wear his kirpan, a ceremonial dagger, at school. Yet, Gurbaj's religious beliefs, and his status as a baptized orthodox Sikh, required him to wear the kirpan while attending school. The issue came to the fore when the kirpan accidentally fell from the boy's outer clothing while in the schoolyard. The school board later met with the family and agreed to allow Gurbaj to don the kirpan at school, provided that the flap covering it in its sheath was sewn securely. Moreover, the school authorities were entitled to inspect the flap sealing the kirpan to ensure safety compliance with the wearing of the ceremonial dagger.

The school governing board[26] would not accept the compromise reached between the parties, alleging that the wearing of the kirpan violated the school's rules and regulations regarding dangerous and forbidden objects. The parents appealed this decision unsuccessfully to the school board, which oddly maintained the decision of the school governing board. The family then took the matter before the courts, seeking a declaratory judgment that Gurbaj had the right to wear the kirpan at school in conformity with his religious beliefs and his basic human rights, namely freedom of religion, as set out in the Quebec Charter of Human Rights and Freedoms and the Canadian Charter of Rights and Freedoms.

Given the initial compromise agreement between the parties, the Quebec Superior Court (2002)[27] declared the decision of the school board to be null and void.[28] The court ordered that Gurbaj be permitted to wear the kirpan to school provided:

- that the kirpan be worn underneath his clothes;
- that the scabbard containing the kirpan be made of wood, not metal, thereby eliminating its offensive character;
- that the kirpan be placed in its scabbard, wrapped in a secure manner . . . ;
- that school staff may, in a reasonable manner, verify that the above conditions are respected;
- that the plaintiff may not at any time withdraw the kirpan from its scabbard and that its loss must be reported immediately to school authorities;
- that the failure by the plaintiff to observe any of the conditions of this judgment shall cause him to lose the right to wear the kirpan at school.[29]

Quebec's Court of Appeal (2004) overturned this decision. It had little difficulty holding that the school board's final decision to disallow the wearing of the
kirpan violated Gurbaj's freedom of religion because the decision had the effect
of prohibiting an act that was an important aspect of the practice of the student's
religion. Nonetheless, the court ruled that the restriction on Gurbaj's freedom of
religion could be justified under s. 1 of the Charter as constituting a reasonable
limit on his constitutional rights.[30] Uppermost in the court's mind was a concern
for safety. In addition, Judge of Appeal Lemelin noted that case law upheld a ban
on the kirpan aboard commercial aircraft and in the courtroom:

> The uncontradicted evidence described an upsurge of violent incidents where
> dangerous objects were used. School staff have an important challenge to meet,
> namely, the obligation to provide an environment for learning and to com-
> bat this violence. I can not convince myself that the security requirements of
> schools are less than those required for the courts or airplanes. (para. 84)

Some academics have criticized the decision of the Court of Appeal and the
role of Quebec's Attorney General in this case. I agree with the criticism. First,
William J. Smith (2004) noted that an Ontario court[31] has ruled that the wearing
of the kirpan in school is justifiable, provided the students meet the stringent
security conditions regarding the donning of the kirpan. In the Ontario case, these
safety concerns are strikingly similar to those set out in the original agreement
of compromise between Gurbaj and the school board. Moreover, Smith observes
that there is no evidence anywhere that the kirpan has ever been used in a violent
or threatening way in a Canadian school. He argues that the Court of Appeal's
approach to the legal analysis reflects a fixation with hypotheticals rather than
the best evidence available:

> The failure to accommodate cannot be defended on the basis of possible or
> hypothetical problems, but only on the basis of demonstrable problems placed
> in evidence. This was the position adopted by the trial judge, but rejected by
> the Court of Appeal that accepted the hypothetical problems presented by the
> appellant school board. (p. 125)

Second, Jean-François Gaudreault-Desbiens (2002) underlined the
importance of the Quebec Attorney General's intervention, at the trial level in
Multani (2002), in what seemed to be a consent judgment between the school
board and the student. At this point, counsel for the Attorney General uttered
the following statement:

> I have received a very precise mandate, to put the following position of the Attorney General before the Court: The Attorney General has zero-tolerance for knives in school, and that includes a kirpan. That is the only representation I have to make. (para. 5)[32]

In his commentary of the trial decision, Gaudreault-Desbiens concurs with the compromise reached between the parties. Yet, he laments the regrettable message sent by the Quebec government, through the Attorney General, to the wider community about the state's conception of tolerance in a democratic and pluralist society: "[L]e Procureur général du Québec a envoyé un triste message quant à la conception qu'il se fait de la tolérance au sein d'une société québécoise libre, démocratique, mais aussi plurielle" (pp. 101–102).

For the purposes of this article, the *Multani* case is an important one. The initial compromise reached between the student's family and the school board is a good one, forged on the anvil of compromise and reasonable accommodation. Thus, our highest court should reinstate the decision of the trial court when it hears the appeal of this case.[33] Expression of one's reasonable and legitimate religious beliefs needs to be accommodated in our public schools to promote toleration and respect for diversity. Once again, the accommodation flows both ways. Schools need to bend when it comes to zero tolerance policies when there are good reasons to do so. In this case, respecting the religious freedom of a Sikh student is a compelling reason to treat the kirpan differently from other objects, which can cause harm. At the same time, let us not forget that Gurbaj was subject to very extensive safety restrictions and conditions concerning the wearing of the object. He could not simply do as he wanted and thus had to make a number of concessions concerning the use of the kirpan while on school property. This compromise, between religious freedom of an individual and the security concerns of the collective, should be presented to our students and educators as an example to study and to celebrate in a religiously rich and culturally diverse world.

CONCLUSION

One might argue, like Bibby (2002), that a spirit of restlessness is blowing across our country in the form of a religious renaissance. Assuming this to be true, the cause of this movement is far from certain. As Bibby himself notes:

> How much of this restlessness is strictly human and how much of it reflects the activity of the gods? Is it simply a matter of cultural and social and personal factors leading churches to experience a measure of rejuvenation, or are individuals being more compelled to reach out for something beyond themselves? (p. 227)

Establishing true causes in this regard might better be left to professors of religious studies, theologians, and moral philosophers. What seems undisputed, however, is that many Canadians are keenly interested in addressing foundational questions about human existence, which relate to ultimate concerns of purpose and meaning.

This paper has argued that philosophical, pragmatic, and educational reasons justify the inclusion of religion in our public schools. This inclusion may display itself in classroom discussions about religion or personal manifestations of religious belief through the wearing of objects such as a hijab or kirpan. Yet, one must regulate religious freedom through reason, responsibility, and respect for others. The author is acutely aware that indoctrination and fundamentalism lurk dangerously behind some forms of religious expression. It is important to suggest, however, that the same fundamentalist zeal may animate a certain narrow interpretation of secularism which attempts to demonize and marginalize all religious belief, and consequently, to keep it beyond the school gates. All forms of fundamentalism should be rejected and for obvious reasons.

In the context of our public schools, *secular* should be interpreted widely and generously to accommodate positions that have their origins in both religious and non-religious belief. Most important, the expression of this belief in the educational setting must respect the values and principles set out in the Canadian Charter of Rights and Freedoms. These include: respect for the inherent dignity of the human person, commitment to social justice and equality, accommodation of a wide variety of beliefs, and respect for cultural and group identity. These values may provide the best foundation upon which to build a civil and flourishing society.

Simply articulating these values will not make our problems go away. Real conflict and tension confront us continually. The recent *Multani* case involving the wearing of the kirpan highlights dramatically how Charter values may conflict with one another. On one hand, individual liberty and religious freedom are important. On the other hand, the safety and integrity of the larger school environment must also be guaranteed. Mediating these tensions in responsible, respectful, and creative ways should be of primary concern to today's educators. After all, schools are much more than places where students learn about skills and knowledge. As the majority of the Supreme Court of Canada stated in *Trinity Western University v. British Columbia College of Teachers* (2001): "Schools are meant to develop civic virtue and responsible citizenship, to educate in an environment free of bias, prejudice and intolerance" (p. 801). Promoting *civic virtue* and *responsible citizenship* is a hard slog because it involves the mediation of competing values and claims. It requires our best faith efforts as we seek reasonable compromise, forge consensus, and seek some degree of social cohesion in a complex, turbulent, and fragmented world. The tension between *self* and *other* is always to be negotiated. The tension between the religious and the non-religious is omnipresent. Yet, working through these tensions is necessary if we wish to build a tolerant society for all Canadians, whose religious and non-religious beliefs are diverse, conflicting, and evolving.

Jurgen Habermas (2003) offers a useful distinction between two understandings of the concept of toleration. First, there is toleration of the outsider as a simple expression of the patronizing benevolence of a particular world view that disagrees with another world view but agrees to tolerate it under certain conditions. Second, there is toleration based on mutual recognition and mutual acceptance of divergent world views. Habermas maintains that the first view reflects the covert persistence of old prejudices and is, therefore, inconsistent with the liberal state. He argues that we should adopt the second view because it is premised on the reciprocal toleration of different religious doctrines that the liberal state requires.

In the context of the discussion about the role of religion in our public schools, some basic questions emerge in deciding where to go from here. First, do we want to take an inclusive and reasoned approach to religion that has the potential to offer points of intersection and convergence for radically different world views? Second, if we go this route, and pursue toleration, what form of Habermasian toleration are we prepared to fight for? The first form appears to offer little hope as it may only mask deep-seated prejudices and fears. The second form, however, is more promising. It opens up new possibilities based on a common humanity. Mutual recognition and mutual acceptance suggest that, because of our differences, we can still somehow live together and be enriched, as both individuals and communities, in the living.

REFLECTIVE QUESTIONS

1. What do the terms "religious education" and "secular education" mean to you?
2. What reasons both for and against inclusion of religious education in schools does the author present?
3. How does the Canadian Charter of Rights and Freedoms assist in sorting through these arguments?
4. How prepared do you think teachers feel to address religious issues in the classroom? What does the Jim Keegstra case presented in the article add to this discussion?
5. What do you think of Clarke's suggestions for inclusion of religion in schools? Can you think of others?

ACKNOWLEDGEMENT

I wish to thank Dr. Michael Tymchak for generously engaging in dialogue with the author, during the writing of this article, about the role of religion in Canada's public schools. I also benefited from feedback received on drafts of this paper from Dr. Tymchak, Dr. Peter Bisson, and Dame Rannveig Yeatman.

LIST OF CASES

Canadian

Attis v. Board of Education of District 15 et al. (1993), [1994] 142 N.B.R. (2d) 1 (C.A.)

Bal v. Ontario (Attorney General) (1994), (1994), 121 D.L.R. (4th) 96, 21 O.R. (2d) 681 (Ont. Gen. Div.), affirmed (1997), 151 D.L.R. (4th) 761, 34 O.R. (3d) 484 (Ont. C.A.), leave to appeal refused (1998), 113 O.A.C. 199 (note) (S.C.C.)

Canadian Civil Liberties Assn. v. Ontario (Minister of Education) (1990), 65 D.L.R. (4th) 1, 71 O.R. (2d) 341 (Ont. C.A.), reversing (1988), 50 D.L.R. (4th) 193, 64 O.R. (2d) 577 (Ont. Div. Ct) ("Elgin County")

Chamberlain v. Surrey School District No. 36, [1998] B.C.J. No. 2923 (QL)

Chamberlain v. Surrey School District No. 36, [2000] B.C.J. No. 1875 (QL)

Chamberlain v. Surrey School District No. 36, [2002] S.C.J. No. 87

Keegstra v. Board of Education of Lacombe No. 14 (1983), 25 Alta. L. R. (2d) 270 (Bd. of Ref.)

Kempling v. British Columbia College of Teachers (2004), [2004] B.C.J. No. 173

Multani (tuteur de) c. Commission scolaire Marguerite-Bourgeois, [2002] J.Q. no. 1131 (Que. Sup. Ct.)

Multani (tuteur de) c. Commission scolaire Marguerite-Bourgeoys, [2004] J.Q. no. 1904 (C.A.). Leave to appeal to the S.C.C. granted – see [2004] S.C.C.A. No. 198

Ontario (Human Rights Commission) v. Peel Board of Education (1990), (sub nom. *Pandori v. Peel Board of Education*), 12 C.H.R.R. D/364 (Ont. H.R. Comm.); motion to quash refused (sub nom. *Peel Board of Education v. Ontario Human Rights Commission*) (1990), 72 O.R. (2d) 593 (Div. Ct.), affirmed (1991), 80 D.L.R. (4th) 475, leave to appeal to Ont. C.A. refused (1991), 3 O.R. (3d) 531 (C.A.)

R. v. Big M Drug Mart Ltd., [1985] 1 S.C.R. 295

R. v. Keegstra, [1990] 3 S.C.R. 697, 61 C.C.C. (3d) 1

R. v. Oakes, [1986] 1 S.C. R. 103, 26 D.L.R. (4th) 200 (S.C.C.)

Ross v. New Brunswick School District No. 15, [1996] 1 S.C.R. 825, [1996] S.C.J. No. 40

Trinity Western University v. British Columbia College of Teachers, [2001] 1 S.C.R. 772

Zylberberg v. Sudbury (Board of Education) (1988), 52 D.L.R. (4th) 577, 65 O.R. (2d) 641 (Ont. C.A.)

LIST OF LEGISLATION

Federal Statutes

Canadian Charter of Rights and Freedoms, Part I of the Constitution Act, 1982, being Schedule B of the Canada Act, 1982, (U.K.), 1982, c. 11

Canada Act, c. 11 (U.K.)

Constitution Act, 1867, 30 & 31 Victoria, c. 3

Criminal Code, R.S.C. 1985, c. C-46

Provincial Statutes

Charter of Human Rights and Freedoms, R.S.Q., c. C-12.

Judicial Review Procedure Act, R.S.B.C. 1996, c. 241

Loi de l'Instruction Publique, L.R.Q., c. C-1

School Act, R.S.B.C, 1996, c. 412

International

Universal Declaration of Human Rights, Un-GA Resolution 217/A(III), Dec. 10, 1948.

NOTES

1. See *R. v. Oakes* (1986).

2. In separate proceedings, the state also successfully prosecuted Keegstra under s. 319(2) of the Criminal Code of Canada (1985) for wilfully promoting hatred against an identifiable group. See *R. v. Keegstra* (1990) where the Supreme Court of Canada determined that although s. 319(2) violates the free speech rights of individuals under s. 2(b) of the Charter, the law is still constitutional because it is a "reasonable limitation" under s. 1 of the Charter.

3. From the perspective of critical thinking, teachers who indoctrinate fail to engage in the very qualities and characteristics that they are called on to model. In other words, uncritical thinking demonstrates an unfitness to teach and undermines the very tenets of openness and inquiry upon which good teaching ultimately rests. William Hare (1993) suggests that Keegstra fails to qualify as "an honest heretic" in the classroom because he subverted the critical approach to teaching:

    The decisive point is that Keegstra cut the ground from under the feet of any opposition by making his theory *immune* to counter-evidence. Potential counter-evidence was taken as *further* evidence of the conspiracy portrayed as controlling the *sources* of evidence, namely textbooks, the media and so on. Conspiracies *can* occur, of course, and it is doctrinaire to dismiss such claims a priori. But to accept that one exists we need evidence, and refutation must in principle be possible. By frustrating the falsification challenge, Keegstra revealed the disingenuous character of his teaching. (p. 379)

4. Parents were given one of three choices about their children's participation in the program: (a) take part; (b) opt for an alternate program taught in classes by clergy; or (c) opt out completely. The court rejected this approach and referred to its earlier decision in *Zylberberg v. Sudbury (Board of Education)* (1988). In *Zylberberg*, the Ontario Court of Appeal ruled that exemption provisions during Christian religious exercises such as the recitation of the Lord's Prayer amounted to an unjustifiable infringement of minority students' religious freedom under s. 2(a) of the Canadian Charter of Rights and Freedoms.

5. This discussion did not apply to s. 93 schools (i.e. separate Protestant or Roman Catholic schools) in Ontario whose religious character and nature are protected under s. 93 of the Constitution Act, 1867.

6. See *Attis v. Board of Education of District 15 et al.* (1993).

7. Section 15(1) of the Charter states:

    Every individual is equal before and under the law and has the right to the equal protection and equal benefit of the law without discrimination and, in particular, without discrimination based on race, national or ethnic origin, colour, religion, sex, age or mental or physical disability.

    Section 27 of the Charter states:

    This Charter shall be interpreted in a manner consistent with the preservation and enhancement of the multicultural heritage of Canadians.

8. The Board issued no prohibition on the three books being available as library resources. The difference between a recommended learning resource and a library resource seemed to be that the former "is relevant to the learning outcomes and content of the course or courses" whereas the latter is intended to be merely "appropriate for the curriculum." [See *Chamberlain v. Surrey School District No. 36* (2000) at para. 53.] The three books are: *Asha's Mums* (1990) by R. Elwin & M. Paules, *Belinda's Bouquet* (1991) by L. Newman, and *One Dad, Two Dads, Brown Dad, Blue Dads* (1994) by J. Valentine. In *Asha's Mums*, the young Asha has a problem when she decides to go on a school outing with her classmates. She needs written authorization from her mother and father before she can go on the trip. Asha, however, has two mothers. Her parents visit the school and explain their family situation, which solves the problem. In *Belinda's Bouquet*, the school-bus

driver calls the young Belinda fat. Hurt by this comment, she recovers her self-esteem after being reassured by one of the two mothers of a school friend. And in *One Dad, Two Dads, Brown Dad, Blue Dads*, a young white girl asks a young black boy a series of questions about his two dads who have blue skin. These questions probe whether the dads work, cough, and eat cookies. There is no mention of sex or sexuality in any of the three books.

9. See *Chamberlain v. Surrey School District No. 36* (1998).

10. Furthermore, she concluded that this interpretation was consistent with the guarantee of religious freedom expressed in s. 2(a) of the Charter.

11. See *Chamberlain v. Surrey School District No. 36* (2000).

12. See *Chamberlain v. Surrey School District No. 36* (2002).

13. As defined in the Universal Declaration of Human Rights (1948), a person's religion is what he or she professes, confesses, or states that it is.

14. See *Encyclopaedia Britannica* (2004), p. 280.

15. See *Scott's Canadian Sourcebook* (2004), p. 6-2.

16. In our statistics, we did not include the following groupings: Christian (includes those who report "Christian," "Apostolic," "Born-again Christian," and "Evangelical"—780 thousand (2.6%) and Christian Orthodox—480 thousand (1.6%). See *Scott's Canadian Sourcebook* (2004), p. 6-2.

17. See *Securing Saskatchewan's Future: Ensuring the Wellbeing and Educational Success of Saskatchewan's Children and Youth. Provincial Response—Role of the School Task Force Final Report*.

18. Wright draws on the *United Nations Development Report* (released September 9, 1998) for his statistics.

19. See Paul T. Clarke's article "Canadian Teachers and Free Speech: A Constitutional Law Analysis" (1999), in particular pages 358–361.

20. Bias may take many different expressive forms. The most common and unacceptable forms of bias include sexist, racist, and homophobic speech.

21. See I. Block's newspaper article entitled, "*Behind the Hijab Debate*" (1994).

22. See *Religious Pluralism in Quebec: A Social and Ethical Challenge*.

23. A ban could also violate s. 2(a) of the Canadian Charter of Rights and Freedoms, which guarantees freedom of religion.

24. As the commission noted, "for example, in physical education courses and during laboratory activities where the student may be required to handle dangerous products or materials."

25. For a detailed, careful, and contextual analysis of the case, see William J. Smith's (2004) case comment, "Balancing Security and Human Rights: Quebec Schools Between Past and Future."

26. This body has delegated authority, under Quebec's school legislation (1998), to adopt school rules as proposed by the principal and developed in collaboration with school staff (see ss. 76, 77 of the Loi de l'Instruction Publique).

27. See *Multani (tuteur de) c. Commission scolaire Marguerite-Bourgeois* (2002).

28. The Court offered four brief introductory phrases, which could be construed to justify its position:
    - considering that for the plaintiff, the wearing of the kirpan is based on a genuine religious belief and not a simple caprice;
    - considering that the evidence has not revealed any examples of violent incidents involving kirpans in any Quebec school;
    - considering the state of Canadian and Amercian law on this issue;
    - considering that the school board has proposed measures of accommodation that have been accepted by the parties. (Ibid., para. 6)

    The judgment was written in French and for translation purposes, we are using Smith's (2004, p. 113) English translation of that part of the judgment we have cited.

29. Ibid., pp. 112–113.

30. Section 1 of the Charter states:

    The Canadian Charter of Rights and Freedoms guarantees the rights and freedoms set out in it subject only to such reasonable limits prescribed by law as can be demonstrably justified in a free and democratic society.

31. See *Ontario (Human Rights Commission) v. Peel Board of Education* (1990).

32. Translation borrowed from Smith (2004, p. 112).

33. The Supreme Court of Canada has agreed to hear the appeal of this case (2004).

REFERENCES

Bibby, R. (1993). *Unknown gods: The ongoing story of religion in Canada.* Toronto: Stoddart.

Bibby, R. (2002). *Restless gods: The renaissance of religion in Canada.* Toronto: Stoddart.

Block, I. (1994, December 3). Behind the hijab debate. *The Gazette* (p. B1).

Brown, D. M. (2000). Freedom from or freedom for? Religion as a case study in defining the content of Charter rights. *University of British Columbia Law Review, 33,* 551–602.

Byrne, P. J. (1989). Academic freedom: A special concern of the first amendment. *The Yale Law Journal, 99*(2), 251–283.

Clarke, P. T. (1999). Canadian teachers and free speech: A constitutional law analysis. *Education & Law Journal, 9*(3), 315–382.

Commission des droits de la personne du Québec. (1995). *Religious pluralism in Quebec: A social and ethical challenge.* Montreal: CDPQ.

Encyclopaedia Britannica (2004). Chicago: Encylopaedia Britannica, Inc.

Foster, W. F., & Smith, W. J. (2002). Religion and education in Canada: Part III—an analysis of provincial legislation. *Education & Law Journal, 11,* 203–261.

Gaudreault-Desbiens, J.-F. (2002). Du crucifix au kirpan : Quelques remarques sur l'exercice de la liberté de religion dans les établissements scolaires. Dans P. Chagnon (Dir.), *Développements récents en droit de l'éducation* (pp. 89–110). Québec: Yvon Blais.

Government of Saskatchewan. (2002). Securing Saskatchewan's future: Ensuring the wellbeing and educational success of Saskatchewan's children and youth. Provincial response—Role of the School Task Force Final Report. Regina, SK: Government of Saskatchewan.

Habermas, J. (2003). Intolerance and discrimination. *International Journal of Constitutional Law, 1*(1), 2–12.

Hare, W. (1993). *What makes a good teacher: Reflections on some characteristics central to the educational enterprise.* London, ON: The Althouse Press.

Horwitz, P. (1996). The sources and limits of freedom of religion in a liberal democracy: Section 2(a) and beyond. *University of Toronto Faculty of Law Review, 54*(1) Winter, 1–64.

Makin, K. (2004, October 11). Cotler aims to revamp system for appointing judges. *The Globe and Mail* (pp. A1, A5).

Ministère de l'Éducation du Québec. (1998). A school for the future: Policy statement on educational integration and intercultural education. Québec: MEQ.

O'Donohue, J. (1999) *Eternal echoes: Celtic reflections on our yearning to belong.* New York: Harper Collins.

Scott's Canadian Sourcebook. (2004). Don Mills, ON: HCN Publications.

Siegel, H. (1988). *Educating reason: Rationality, critical thinking, and education.* New York: Routledge.

Smith, W. J. (2004). Balancing security and human rights: Quebec schools between past and future. *Education & Law Journal, 14*(1), 99–136.

Yudof, M. G. (1979). When governments speak: Toward a theory of government expression and the first amendment. *Texas Law Review, 57*(6), 863–912.

Wright, R. (2004). *A short history of progress.* Toronto: Anansi Press.

Further Reading

CONTEMPORARY ISSUES

Aboriginal Education

Chambers, C. (2004). Blurring the ultrascape: A study of First Nations parent and teacher voice in family literacy curriculum design. *Educational Insights, 10*(1). Available at http://www.ccfi.educ .ubc.ca/publication/insights//v10n01/articles/chambers.html

Chambers, C. (2006). "Where do I belong?" Canadian curriculum as passport home. *Journal of the American Association for the Advancement of Curriculum Studies, 2*, 1–18. Available at http:// www2.uwstout.edu/content/jaaacs/vol2/chambers.htm

Cherubini, L., Hodson, J., Manley-Casimir, M., & Muir, C. (2010). "Closing the gap" at the peril of widening the void: Implications of the Ontario Ministry of Education's policy for aboriginal education. *Canadian Journal of Education, 33*(2), 329–355.

Deer, F. (2008). Aboriginal students and Canadian citizenship education. *Journal of Educational Thought, 42*(1), 69–82.

Donald, D. (2009). Forts, curriculum, and indigenous metissage: Imagining decolonization of Aboriginal-Canadian relations in educational contexts. *First Nations Perspectives, 2*(1), 1–24.

Assessment

Kearns, L. (2011). High-stakes standardized testing and marginalized youth: An examination of the impact on those who fail. *Canadian Journal of Education, 34*(2), 112–130.

Lawson, A., & Suurtamm, C. (2006). The challenges and possibilities of aligning large-scale testing with mathematical reform: The case of Ontario. *Assessment in Education: Principles, Policy & Practice, 13*(3), 305–325.

Macmath, S., Wallace, J., & Chi, X. (2009). Curriculum integration: Opportunities to maximize assessment *as, of* and *for* learning. *McGill Journal of Education, 44*(3), 451–465.

Volante, L., & Beckett, D. (2011). Formative assessment and the contemporary classroom: Synergies and tensions between research and practice. *Canadian Journal of Education, 34*(2), 239–255.

Environmental Stewardship

Duvall, J., & Zint, M. (2007). A review of research on the effectiveness of environmental education in promoting intergenerational learning. *Journal of Environmental Education, 38*(4), 14–25.

Puk, T. G., & Making, D. (2006). Ecological consciousness in Ontario elementary schools: The truant curriculum and the consequences. *Applied Environmental Education & Communication, 5*(4), 269–276.

Sharpe, E., & Breunig, M. (2009). Sustaining environmental pedagogy in times of educational conservatism: A case study of integrated curriculum programs. *Environmental Education Research, 15*(3), 299–313.

Suavé, L. (2005). Currents in environmental education: Mapping a complex and evolving pedagogical field. *Canadian Journal of Environmental Education, 10*, 11–37.

Ethnic Diversity

Bickmore, K. (2006). Democratic social cohesion? Assimilation? Representations of social conflict in Canadian public school curricula. *Canadian Journal of Education, 29*(2), 359–386.

Chan, E. (2006). Teacher experiences of culture in the curriculum. *Journal of Curriculum Studies, 38*(2), 161–176.

Chan, E. (2007). Student experiences of a culturally-sensitive curriculum: Ethnic identity development amid conflicting stories to live by. *Journal of Curriculum Studies, 39*(2), 177–194.

Giampapa, F. (2010). Multiliteracies, pedagogy and identities: Teacher and student voices from a Toronto elementary school. *Canadian Journal of Education, 33*(2), 407–431.

Iannacci, L. (2006). Learning to "do" school: Procedural display and culturally and linguistically diverse students in Canadian Early Childhood Education (ECE). *Journal of the Canadian Association for Curriculum Studies, 4*(2), 55–76.

Peck, C., Sears, A., & Donaldson, S. (2008). Unreached and unreasonable: Curriculum standards and children's understanding of ethnic diversity in Canada. *Curriculum Inquiry, 38*(1), 63–92.

Schick, C., & St. Denis, V. (2005). Troubling national discourse in anti-racist curricular planning. *Canadian Journal of Education, 28*(3), 295–317.

Gender

Coulter, R. P., & Greig, C. J. (2008). The man question in teaching: An historical overview. *Alberta Journal of Educational Research, 54*(4), 420–431.

de Freitas, E. (2004). (Dis)locating gender within the universal: Teaching philosophy through narrative. *Journal of the Canadian Association for Curriculum Studies, 2*(2), 61–72.

Gaskell, J. (2004). Educational change and the women's movement: Lessons from British Columbia schools in the 1970s. *Educational Policy, 18*(2), 291–310.

Ghosh, R. (2000). Identity and social integration: Girls from a minority ethno-cultural group in Canada. *McGill Journal of Education, 35*(3), 279–296.

Global Education

Eidoo, S., Ingram, L., MacDonald, A., Nabavi, M., Pashby, K., & Stille, S. (2011). "Through the kaleidoscope": Intersections between theoretical perspectives and classroom implications in critical global citizenship education. *Canadian Journal of Education, 34*(4), 59–85.

Mundy, K., & Manion, C. (2008). Global education in Canadian elementary schools: An exploratory study. *Canadian Journal of Education, 31*(4), 941–974.

Pike, G. (2008). Citizenship education in global context. *Brock Education Journal, 17*(1), 38–49.

Tupper, J. (2007). From care-less to care-full: Education for citizenship in schools and beyond. *The Alberta Journal of Educational Research. 53*(3), 259–272.

Sexuality

Jiménez, K. (2009). Queering classrooms, curricula, and care: Stories from those who dare. *Sex Education*, 9(2), 169–179.

Kehler, M. (2008). Challenging silence, challenging censorship: Inclusive resources, strategies and policy directives for addressing bisexual, gay, lesbian, trans-identified and two-spirited realities in school and public libraries. *Canadian Journal of Education*, 31(1), 268–272.

Loutzenheiser, L. (2005). The ambivalences and circulation of globalization and identities: Sexualities, gender and the curriculum. *Journal of Curriculum Theorizing*, 21(2), 118–140.

Meyer, E., & Stader, D. (2009). Queer youth and the culture wars: From classroom to courtroom in Australia, Canada and the United States. *Journal of Lesbian, Gay, Bisexual and Transgender Youth*, 6(2/3), 135–154.

Spirituality/Religious Education

Bouchard, N. (2009). Living together with differences: Quebec's new ethics and religious culture program. *Education Canada*, 49(1), 60–63.

van Brummelen, H., Koole, R., & Franklin, K. (2004). Transcending the commonplace: Spirituality in the curriculum. *Journal of Educational Thought*, 38(3), 237–253.

Weeren, D. (1993). Collaboration, containment and conflict regarding religious education: Three Canadian cases. *Religious Education*, 88(1), 136–149.

Wiles, J. (2006). Evolution in schools: Where's Canada? *Education Canada*, 46(4), 37–41.

Technology/ Digital Literacy

de Castell, S., & Jenson, J. (2003). Serious play: Curriculum for a post-talk era. *Journal of the Canadian Association for Curriculum Studies*, 1(1), 47–52.

Gibson, S., & Oberg, D. (2004). Visions and realities of internet use in schools: Canadian perspectives. *British Journal of Technology*, 35(5), 569–585.

Haché, G. J. (2005). Developments in technology education in Canada. In M. de Vries & I. Mottier (Eds.), *International handbook of technology education* (pp. 171–177). Rotterdam: Sense Publishers.

Li, Q. (2006). Cyberbullying in schools: A research of gender differences. *School Psychology International*, 27(2), 157–170.

Scardamalia, M. (2001). Big change questions: "Will educational institutions, within their present structures, be able to adapt sufficiently to meet the needs of the information age?" *Journal of Educational Change*, 2(2), 171–176.

Scardamalia, M., & Bereiter, C. (2008). Pedagogical biases in educational technologies. *Educational Technology*, 48(3), 3–11.

HISTORICAL INFLUENCES

Articles

Henchey, N. (1999). The new curriculum reform: What does it really mean? *McGill Journal of Education, 34*(3), 227–242.

Osborne, K. (1982). "The Canadian curriculum": A response to Barrow. *Canadian Journal of Education, 7*(2), 94–109.

von Heyking, A. (1998). Selling progressive education to Albertans, 1935 to 1953. *Historical Studies in Education, 10*(1/2), 67–84.

Werner, W. (1995). Reforming the Canadian curriculum. *The Curriculum Journal, 6*(2), 225–233.

Willinsky, J. (1994). After 1492–1992: A post-colonial supplement for the Canadian curriculum. *Journal of Curriculum Studies, 26*(6), 613–629.

Winter, E., & McEachern, W. (2001). Dealing with educational change: The Ontario experience. *Education, 121*(4), 682–688.

Websites

Curriculum Development (The Canadian Encyclopedia): http://www.thecanadianencyclopedia.com/articles/curriculum-development

History of Education (Ontario Institute for Studies in Education): http://www.oise.utoronto.ca/research/edu20/moments

History of Public Education (The Alberta Teachers' Association): http://www.teachers.ab.ca/Teaching%20in%20Alberta/History%20of%20Public%20Education/Pages/Index.aspx

The Homeroom (Vancouver Island University): http://www.viu.ca/homeroom/content/topics

Contributors

Below are brief biographical notes about the scholars who wrote the articles in this collection.

TED AOKI was professor emeritus at the University of Alberta in Edmonton.

CYNTHIA CHAMBERS is a professor in the Faculty of Education at the University of Lethbridge in Alberta.

PAUL CLARKE is an associate professor in the Faculty of Education at the University of Regina in Saskatchewan.

KURT CLAUSEN is an assistant professor in the Schulich School of Education at Nipissing University in North Bay, Ontario.

KARYN COOPER is an associate professor in the Centre for Teacher Education and Development at the Ontario Institute for Studies in Education, University of Toronto.

REBECCA COULTER is a professor in the Faculty of Education at the University of Western Ontario in London, Ontario.

KIERAN EGAN is a professor in the Faculty of Education at Simon Fraser University in Burnaby, British Columbia.

MICHAEL FIRMIN is a professor of psychology at Cedarville University in Cedarville, Ohio. He is also the editor of the *Journal of Ethnographic & Qualitative Research*.

SUSAN GIBSON, the editor of this book, is a professor in the Faculty of Education at the University of Alberta in Edmonton.

MARK GLOR teaches history and social studies at Linden Christian High School in Winnipeg, Manitoba.

JULIE JOHNSTON is a teacher, teacher trainer, and adult educator who works with learners of all ages through GreenHeart Education (greenhearted.org), an organization dedicated to transformative education for sustainability.

YATTA KANU is a professor in the Faculty of Education's Department of Curriculum, Teaching, and Learning at the University of Manitoba in Winnipeg.

ANNA KIROVA is a professor in the Faculty of Education at the University of Alberta in Edmonton.

LYNN LEMISKO is an assistant dean in the College of Education at the University of Saskatchewan in Saskatoon.

BRENDA MACKAY is an associate professor of early childhood education at Cedarville University in Cedarville, Ohio. She also serves as coordinator for overseas student teaching.

LORNA MCLEAN is an associate professor in the Faculty of Education at the University of Ottawa in Ontario.

ANNE MURRAY ORR is a professor in the Faculty of Education at St. Francis Xavier University in Antigonish, Nova Scotia.

MARGARET OLSON is a professor in the Faculty of Education at St. Francis Xavier University in Antigonish, Nova Scotia.

DAVID PRATT was formerly a professor in the Faculty of Education at Queen's University in Kingston, Ontario.

LYNETTE SHULTZ is an associate professor in the Faculty of Education at the University of Alberta in Edmonton.

JULIA TEMPLE is a researcher with SafetyNet, the Centre for Occupational Health & Safety Research at Memorial University in St. John's, Newfoundland.

LOUIS VOLANTE is an associate professor in the Faculty of Education at Brock University in Hamilton, Ontario.

KELLY YOUNG is an associate professor in the School of Education and Professional Learning at Trent University in Peterborough, Ontario.

JON YOUNG is a professor in the Faculty of Education at the University of Manitoba in Winnipeg.

Permissions

The articles in this book were reproduced with permission from the following sources:

1 Kanu, Y., & Glor, M. (2006). "Currere" to the rescue? Teachers as "amateur intellectuals" in a knowledge society. *Journal of the Canadian Association for Curriculum Studies*, 4(2), 101–122.

2 Egan, K. (2003). What is curriculum? *Journal of the Canadian Association for Curriculum Studies*, 1(1), 9–16.

3 Aoki, T. T. (1986). Teaching as in-dwelling between two curriculum worlds. *The BC Teacher*, April/May, 8–10.

4 Egan, K. (1996). Competing voices for the curriculum. In M. Wideen & M. C. Courtland (Eds.), *The struggle for curriculum: Education, the state, and the corporate sector* (pp. 7–26). Burnaby, BC: Institute for Studies in Teacher Education.

5 Cooper, K. (2003). When curriculum becomes a stranger. *McGill Journal of Education*, 38(1), 135–149.

6 Murray Orr, A., & Olson, M. (2007). Transforming narrative encounters. *Canadian Journal of Education*, 30(3), 819–838.

7 MacKay, B., & Firmin, M. W. (2008). The historical development of private education in Canada. *Education Research and Perspectives*, 35(2), 57–72.

8   Lemisko, L. S., & Clausen, K. W. (2006). Connections, contrarieties, and convolutions: Curriculum and pedagogic reform in Alberta and Ontario, 1930–1955. *Canadian Journal of Education, 29*(4), 1097–1129.

9   Coulter, R. P. (2005). Getting things done: Donalda J. Dickie and leadership through practice. *Canadian Journal of Education, 28*(4), 669–699.

10 McLean, L. (2010). "There is no magic whereby such qualities will be acquired at the voting age": Teachers, curriculum, pedagogy and citizenship. *Historical Studies in Education, 22*(2), 39–56.

11 Pratt, D. (1989). Characteristics of Canadian curricula. *Canadian Journal of Education, 14*(3), 295–310.

12 Chambers, C. (1999). A topography for Canadian curriculum theory. *Canadian Journal of Education, 24*(2), 137–150.

13 Kanu, Y. (2003). Curriculum as cultural practice: Postcolonial imagination. *Journal of the Canadian Association for Curriculum Studies, 1*(1), 67–81.

14 Young, J. (2004). Reflecting today, creating tomorrow: The dual role of public education. *Education Canada, 44*(4), 14–16. First published by the Canadian Education Association in Fall 2004.

15 Kanu, Y. (2002). In their own voices: First Nations students identify some cultural mediators of their learning in the formal school system. *The Alberta Journal of Educational Research, 48*(2), 98–121.

16 Kirova, A. (2008). Critical and emerging discourses in multicultural education literature: A review. *Canadian Ethnic Studies, 40*(1), 101–124.

17 Volante, L. (2008). Equity in multicultural student assessment. *The Journal of Educational Thought, 42*(1), 11–26.

18 Shultz, L. (2006). Educating for global citizenship: Conflicting agendas and understandings. *The Alberta Journal of Educational Research, 53*(3), 248–259.

19 Young, K. (2005). Curriculum of imperialism: Good girl citizens and the making of the literary educated imagination. *Journal of the Canadian Association for Curriculum Studies, 3*(2), 41–53.

20 Temple, J. R. (2005). "People who are different from you": Heterosexism in Quebec high school textbooks. *Canadian Journal of Education, 28*(3), 271–294.

21 Johnston, J. (2009). Transformative environmental education: Stepping outside the curriculum box. *Canadian Journal of Environmental Education, 14*(1), 149–157.

22 Clarke, P. (2005). Religion, public education, and the charter: Where do we go now? *McGill Journal of Education, 40*(3), 351–381.

Index